```
HM      Bach, George Robert,
132       1914-
.B27
        A time for caring
```

Cop. 1

5/82   15.95

		DATE	

CHICAGO PUBLIC LIBRARY
HILD REGIONAL
4544 LINCOLN AVE.
CHICAGO, ILLINOIS 60625

© THE BAKER & TAYLOR CO.

A Time for Caring

A Time for Caring

George R. Bach, Ph.D.
and
Laura Torbet

DELACORTE PRESS/NEW YORK

Published by
Delacorte Press
1 Dag Hammarskjold Plaza
New York, N.Y. 10017

Copyright © 1982 by George R. Bach and Laura Torbet

All rights reserved. No part of this book may be reproduced or transmitted in any form or by any means, electronic or mechanical, including photocopying, recording or by any information storage and retrieval system, without the written permission of the Publisher, except where permitted by law.

Manufactured in the United States of America

First printing

Designed by Judith Neuman

Library of Congress Cataloging in Publication Data

Bach, George Robert, 1914–
   A time for caring.

   Bibliography: p.
   1. Interpersonal relations.   2. Altruism.   3. Helping behavior.   I. Torbet, Laura.   II. Title.
   HM132.B27   158   81-9870
   ISBN 0-440-08925-5   AACR2

To
Peggy Jane Dahlstrom-Bach
and
to the memory of
Dr. C. Rocco Linsaluta
Our models and caring inspiration

Contents

ACKNOWLEDGMENTS / ix

INTRODUCTION / xi

PART I / WHO CARES? / 1
    1 Why Should *I* Care? / 3
    2 Living in Careless Times / 10
    3 The Worship of Autonomy / 16
    4 The Power of the Image / 21
    5 Cleaning Up the Caring Environment / 30

PART II / THE CARING PROCESS / 41
    6 The Ingredients of Quality Caring / 43
    7 Choosing to Care / 49
    8 Intrinsic Care: *The Real Thing* / 56
    9 Balance: *Caring on an Even Keel* / 65
    10 Paying Attention: *Gathering Information for Caring* / 83
    11 Communication: *Keeping in Touch* / 90
    12 Growth and Change: *Bringing Out the Best in People* / 101
    13 Ritual: *Foundation for Caring* / 110

PART III / THE ARENAS OF CARE / 121
    14 Charting the Caring Network / 123
    15 Self-Care: *Foundation for Caring Activism* / 131
    16 The Self-Care Plan / 145
    17 Sexual Intimacy: *Caring In and Out of Bed* / 160
    18 The Caring Content of Sexual Relationships / 177
    19 The Intimate Care Plan / 198
    20 The Family: *Cradle of Caring* / 213
    21 The Family Care Plan / 222
    22 Caring Friends / 235
    23 The Friendship Care Plan / 254

24 Caring in the Community / 265
25 The Community Care Plan / 272
26 The Purchase of Caring: *Some Thoughts on Professional Care* / 279
27 A Professional Care Plan / 288

PART IV / LEARNING TO CARE / 295
28 Learning to Care: *Going into Action* / 297
29 Getting into Shape for Caring: *Exercises for Building Caring Consciousness* / 322
30 Getting into Shape for Caring: *Exercises for Two* / 336
31 Research and Development: *Discovering Your Own Caring Style* / 352
32 Becoming a Caring Activist / 368
33 Future Care / 387

NOTES / 389
BIBLIOGRAPHY / 392

Acknowledgments

We have many people to acknowledge: it's a long, dry list, but the thanks and appreciation it's meant to convey are heartfelt. We would like first to mention the many people who came to the Bach Institute and the couples and families who attended the Caring lectures and workshops at the University of California and at other schools around the country. They were the testing ground, and the inspiration for this book; many of their stories are found herein.

Our families deserve thanks not only for their insights and advice but also for the supportive, caring environment they provided during the writing of this book. We would like to make special mention of Dr. Roger Bach, George Bach's son, colleague, and continuous consultant on this project; George Bach's sister Christel Baumann; his other children, Stephanie, Claudia, and Felicity; finally his grandchildren, Gretchen, Paris, and Stefan.

Many friends and colleagues made valuable contributions, among them Dr. Herb Goldberg, Dr. Lew Yablonsky, Dr. Bruce Parsons, Dr. Steve Harrison, Dr. Vance Kondon, Dr. Seymour Faschbach, Haya and Inge Molter, Dr. Ernst Beier, Dr. Hartmuth Scharfe, Dr. Eräneus Eibl-Eiblsfelt, and Dr. Cedric Emery. We thank Luree Nicholson for her continuous concern and insight and Sandra Burton for her views on the changing role of women and changing mores. We remember Gregory Bateson here for the discussions we had on the place of caring in nature.

Too, we have many friends whose caring ways showed us what caring is all about. To name a few: Connie Holzman and Bill

Searcy, Hap Hatton, Barbara and Don Johnson, Glenn Robbins, Barbara Robbins, Kalia Lulow, Arlie Schardt, Jeffrey Kramer, Morning Pastorok, Monica Pastorok, Millie Klingman, Marty and Harriet Bell, Michel and Caroline Zalesky, John and Linda Cross, Rich and Jean Look, and Craig Nova.

Special thanks are due several people for their part in bringing the book to publication. To Francis Greenburger, our agent, who gave us the idea for this book; to Jeanne Bernkopf, our thoughtful and thorough editor; and to Kalia Lulow and Hap Hatton for their help, friendship, and hard work in writing, editing, and typing this manuscript at various stages of its life.

GEORGE BACH
LAURA TORBET

Introduction

When we set out to write A *Time for Caring*, it seemed like a natural subject for a book, for today people are sincerely concerned about living fruitful lives, even though they are uncertain how to go about it and unsure that such a life is possible in these angry times.

So we were surprised at the reactions that news of our project elicited from friends and colleagues. "No one is interested in caring in this dog-eat-dog world. People today are interested in getting ahead." They intimated that we were overly idealistic, naive about the state of the modern world. And they cautioned us that anything we might say about the wonders and rewards of caring would sound like empty rhetoric in the face of the crime, terrorism, abuse, detachment, and self-involvement that are the stuff of the daily news.

We felt compelled to apologize for our Pollyanna attitude, to continually defend our thesis that caring is the growth- and survival-oriented way to face the future. Yet we ourselves sometimes felt that we were too soft or sentimental. We had to reassure ourselves periodically that we weren't being naive or foolish, that in fact we might even be brave and tough!

But the thing that convinced us about the value and rewards of the kind of caring we have described here was the impact that working on this book over a period of time had on us. As we became aware of the care-denying influences in our lives, we found that we were both clearing the air of people and things we didn't need. We started gravitating toward certain friends and interests. We began going out of our way to do things we'd never been particularly good about—keeping in touch with friends and family, making agendas of caring concerns and plans, becoming aware of the particular caring things that we did—and that others did for us. We felt more relaxed with people, more open and less threatened. The process of writing the book had the effect of reordering our own priorities, and of underlining our conviction that caring concern is a real antidote to the many toxic and virulent influences that undermine our lives.

A Time for Caring is less about tending to the sick or helping the needy than it is about taking an interest, and pleasure, in others. It is more about active support than passive concern, about being involved in others' survival and growth, nurturing strengths rather than supporting weakness and dependency. The new caring is assertive and participatory, concerned with bringing out the best in others.

There are literally thousands of ways to show care, and many of them are not as obvious as sending a birthday card or giving up one's seat on the bus to a senior citizen. *A Time for Caring* is filled with examples and case histories that give an indication of the immense scope and variety of caring ways. The stories and case histories presented are taken from Dr. Bach's private practice, from the files at the Bach Institute, and from anecdotes reported by friends and colleagues. Some are composites of two or more stories.

We wish to demonstrate the power of caring—its potential for growth and for the enhancement of everyday life; the impact of caring—on ourselves and those around us; the liberating effects of caring—in learning to take risks and live more creatively.

GEORGE BACH
LAURA TORBET

Part I
Who Cares?

1
Why Should *I* Care?

In a world marked by crime, terrorism, and exploitation, can we blame a person for his attempts at autonomy, his so-called narcissism, his acquisitiveness? Can we consider neurotic the development of paranoia and loss of trust? Should these things not be understood as self-defense mechanisms, a search for shelter, a harbor in the stormy sea of our less-than-civilized civilization?

It's a dangerous game we're playing these days, a kind of brinksmanship of the soul. But it is a game rooted in a desperate desire to cope with a world moving too fast and incomprehensibly in directions that distort the sense of human scale.

The quest for our peculiar contemporary version of salvation—meaning in life *and* a piece of the action—has left many people confused and anxious. We are drawn by the tantalizing hope that we can have our fair share of what's so glowingly presented to us if we just make the right choices, do the right deal. But our vision is beclouded by the stupefying array of choices. The sense that all the glittering prizes are there for the taking makes people feel all the more pressured to jump on the bandwagon of acquisition and self-actualization. Yet many of the things on which they spend their time, energy, and money actually thwart their chances of fulfillment.

For more than thirty years Dr. George Bach maintained an office in the heart of Hollywood. Half of his patients came to him because they desperately wanted to achieve the kind of success they saw all around them in the glamorous film capital. Yet most of his other patients were celebrities and film tycoons who *had* very much made it. They were just as troubled and unhappy, and they couldn't even offer a reason for their misery.

In pursuit of the life well lived many people have ridden roughshod over their own better nature. They have all but trampled their need to care and be cared for. Yet caring for each other—and for ourselves—is essential to the good life. It's an integral part of what we need to feel at peace with ourselves and the world we live in. By neglecting and trivializing our caring nature, we are betraying our own best interests.

So many aspects of modern life work against learning to care. Caring feelings are denied in the same way it was once correct to deny feelings of hostility or anger. It's not cool to care—it's unfashionable, and it won't win any popularity contests. People today lead busy, demanding, competitive lives. They have to know how to read, write, drive, speak a foreign language, dance, play tennis, negotiate a business deal, balance a checkbook, operate a computer, cook meals, decorate a house, entertain guests, make a presentation at a meeting, plan a vacation, write a term paper, snare a mate, raise children, raise money for charity, organize a car pool, vote responsibly—all to make them strong, fit, rich, attractive, healthy, famous, self-sufficient. Although such skills are necessary and highly rewarded by society, many are skills of competition and survival, and tend to isolate people and pit them against each other rather than to bring them closer.

Many people today are concerned with living lives of credit to themselves and society, want their lives to count for something, want something of value to show for their efforts. Concerned with quality, they are horrified to discover that they've been sold a shoddy bill of goods. They've spent their time, energy, and hard-earned money in pursuit of happiness, yet they remain dissatisfied, anxious, uncomfortable, alone. Their ideas about the good life don't seem to add up to a fulfilling life. The quality of life has become confused with their standard of living. Something is out of whack, but they can't put their finger on it.

Many people feel they're on a treadmill of acquisition and actualization, and they suspect that more of what they've already got isn't the answer. They recognize that a new car, a new lover, a new brand of household cleanser, losing ten pounds, biofeedback, Rolfing, or vitamins won't do the trick. Yet, lacking an alternate course, they put their hope into these very things and try to hide their disappointment. Some give up hope of getting what they want from life and settle for whatever substitutes they can find. Dispirited and cynical, they relinquish their dreams.

Many of these people would like to get back on the trail of the good life, but they've lost the scent. And having once been burned, they are suspicious of new promises, fearful of hoping again, loath to leave the safety of their world of diminished expectations in order to jump on a new bandwagon.

Yet that is just what they must do; or rather, they must jump *off* the old bandwagon. The way to get back on the track of the good life is to give up unrewarding rewards, to reject the dehumanizing aspects of modern life, no matter how alluringly they're presented, no matter how risky it seems, how uncertain the future looks. They must learn to build and enlarge a care-nurturing environment that is compatible with the demands and attractions of modern life. They must learn to minimize and drive out toxic influences.

What is needed is a Caring Network—an interconnected system of family, friends, intimates, and community to restore and sustain those now absent feelings of belonging. With an effective Caring Network we need never be alone while facing the hazards of our times. And the Caring Network is a powerful antidote to excessive narcissism and image fascination, two of the most common and dangerous growth-hindering defenses of today.

THE CARING PARADOX

Most people are not comfortable with ambiguity. They don't like mixed feelings, mixed messages, mixed media, even mixed blessings. They are *paradox phobic*. Yet the truth is that most situations are not clear-cut. Most decisions are not a matter of black and white. Conflicting feelings battle and overlap. A mother is furious with her daughter for staying out late even as she is worried sick that something has gone wrong. She is proud of her ability to send her daughter to college even as she resents the economic burden.

Paradox is everywhere. The person one loves most is the person capable of arousing the greatest anger. The harder one works, the more enjoyable is play. The greater the closeness, the more the longing for freedom. The sense of adventure is tempered by caution. There is wisdom in frivolity and vice versa.

Many people are comfortable only when things fit into place and stay there. They like "nice" people and are confused if a friend shows a mean streak. They think alcohol is evil, so they never enjoy a glass of wine. They find this world too unpredictable to contend with, so they retreat to their manageable posture of autonomous self-sufficiency and minimal involvement.

It's too bad, for there are great benefits to accepting our paradoxical nature. For one thing, when we are able to give credence to mixed feelings without being pressured to make a decision "one way or the other," we automatically reduce our anxiety about our multiple thoughts, ideas, and feelings. As we become more comfortable with paradox we find greater interest and texture in our complex lives.

The Caring Paradox is that self-realization is only possible through caring for others. Caring for and about others *is* caring for ourselves. Caring for others accrues great benefits to us: it increases our self-esteem, attracts the care and concern of others, improves the environment, and enhances the quality of life. All caring is double-edged. We have impact on others by acknowledging their impact on us; we grow by supporting others' growth.

The Caring Paradox is not easy to understand or accept. It is much easier to think of all self-care as selfish or self-indulgent, and all care for others as purely altruistic or self-sacrificing. There is also the attitude that people who care for others are self-*less*: fools or martyrs, oddities in this me-first world. It's hard to comprehend that caring can be beneficial to both parties. (And if that is so, the cynic says, then is caring not selfish and therefore less than honorable? Can it really be caring if it is also self-benefiting?) It is a pointless argument, again an attempt to have an either/or answer.

Most caring feelings are *both* selfish and selfless, self-serving and other-serving. In order to care for ourselves and each other, we must accept the double-edged nature of caring. As we build our tolerance for paradox we learn to enjoy the richness of being human.

CREATIVE AGGRESSION AND CARING

Aggression and caring seem, at first blush, to be strange bedfellows; in fact, they are inseparable. *A Time for Caring* is a direct outgrowth of research and clinical practice at the Bach Institute in Los Angeles as well as of Dr. Bach's more than three decades of private practice.

At the Institute couples, families, and groups learn how to use their anger in a constructive, nonhostile way instead of denying or repressing it in a misguided attempt to be "nice." They learn techniques of Fair Fighting in order to have a way of coping with conflict and of asserting their needs and rights. Dr. Bach's aim is to release the blocked anger constructively and open the way for love and care.

Research has shown that caring and aggression have a classic chicken-and-egg relationship. Dr. Bach had always operated on the premise that people cannot truly care for others if their anger and aggression is stifled or trivialized. He discovered that anger can only be expressed (and accepted) constructively in an atmosphere of goodwill. So establishing a basis of goodwill—of basic caring—between the fight partners became essential to the aggression training. Fighting and caring were two sides of the same coin—more evidence of the Caring Paradox.

The second discovery was that even when the fighting partners loved each other and valued their association, even when they wanted to learn to fight fair and wanted to deal with each other in an atmosphere of goodwill, *they didn't know how.* They found it hard to identify their feelings and hard to express them clearly or to act upon them. They were lacking in the skills they needed to keep their relationships healthy. Their Caring Capacity was in poor working order.

THE CARING CAPACITY

The Caring Capacity is made up of the ability to express caring feelings and of the skills to act upon them. The ability to listen, to observe, to be selective, to share, to speak one's mind, to laugh or entertain, to be patient, to offer advice, to be interested in others, to take risks, to reject carelessness: these are some of the skills of caring.

To be effective, caring should not be at the mercy of whim or expedience, hampered by lack of self-esteem, overly affected by one's mood or the weather. Trustworthiness and a sense of fair play are part of the package. Yet most people, predictably, are highly imperfect carers: they have insufficient skills, unsure judgment, many preoccupations. Caring energies are spent inefficiently or even harmfully. Sometimes they are dissipated in safe places, rather than in areas of vulnerability. Sometimes caring energies are hoarded in a misguided attempt at conservation. Often perfectly good intentions and perfectly good skills are improperly exercised; they're expended on the wrong target, at the wrong time and place. A keen ear is used in the service of business negotiating, a way with a story to impress a date, a risk-taking ability spent on a stock market flier. Caring skills are neglected in favor of skills apparently more useful or expedient for getting ahead in the world. A woman may listen attentively to her customers all day and hand out considered articulate counsel but become restless and inattentive when her son needs advice. A doctor considered a saint by his patients is cold and uncommunicative at home. The role of helper or confidant is uncomfortable for some: many people cannot tend a sickbed, are at a loss for words of comfort or congratulations, don't pay enough attention to others to care for them properly.

The Caring Capacity has been weakened by disuse, lack of reinforcement, and misunderstanding of its potential for growth. Putting it back in working order is a matter of recognizing caring feelings and improving skills. Like unused muscles, these feelings and skills must be limbered up through a process of exercise and reinforcement. Most people need direction in how to use their caring skills appropriately and efficiently. Many people are not sensitive to their own caring needs, much less to the needs of those around them. They don't have a clear sense of their own caring ways, rituals, temperaments. They don't recognize (and would be surprised to acknowledge) the little things they do from day to day that are caring, so they don't develop a sense of themselves as caring people.

Living in a caring context is a tremendous challenge. It involves

A Time for Caring

a commitment to sociability in the broadest sense. It involves exploring our own natures, taking risks, overcoming fears and resistance. It requires giving up old, comfortable ways that inhibit caring. It means bringing a sense of fun, playfulness, and inventiveness to this quest. These days, caring requires daring.

Focusing attention on the caring aspects of our nature is an idea whose time has come. The need for change is readily apparent. The contemporary roads to fulfillment—material acquisitions and self-actualization—seem to have betrayed us. The concern for the self, for *me*, has reached dangerous proportions: the Me Decade and the Age of Anxiety are beginning to look like one and the same. It is vital to individual and collective mental health that we turn the tide, that we turn our attention to building a growth support system of significant others in our lives. The alternative is to live increasingly isolated on a psychological junk-food diet of superficial roles and exploitative, minimally necessary interactions that are hardly more than "connections."

The irony is that most people want to be free to care in a comfortable, meaningful, unthreatening context. Everyone knows the warm feelings of doing a good deed, of feeling needed and loved by others. Yet often we deny ourselves these good feelings out of fear of exploitation or ridicule, or lack of ability or opportunity.

The authors have little nostalgia for the caring of the old days. We feel sympathetic to the contemporary quest for self-respect. The desire for ease, order, and security is all too understandable in this troubled and dangerous world. The world today is rich in possibility for caring concern. This is a crucial time, a golden opportunity we must take advantage of. Cooperation will be more vital than ever in the coming age of diminished resources and scarcity. Given the right tools, the proper circumstances, and a bit of encouragement, the hunger for a life well lived shouldn't be hard to satisfy.

Why should *I* care? Because when we do, we annex others' joys and concerns and expand our horizons. Caring is the leavening agent, or context, in which we can fulfill the promise of the human potential movement and reap the real rewards of our prosperity and technology. With luck and application, perhaps the Me Decade will give way to the We Decade.

2

Living in Careless Times

Arguments about the "true" nature of man have raged for centuries. Are people inherently good or evil? Are they capable of pure altruism? Or are acts of helping, kindness, generosity, always based on necessity, or fear, or expectation of reward?

But if man is by nature hedonistic, why will he help another? Why do something not in his own self-interest? Cynics assign an ulterior motive to all pro-social behavior; some even go so far as to view altruism as a sign of neurosis, a refusal to cope with the realities of life.

Until recently the main thesis about man's evolution was that because he survived by hunting he was therefore an aggressive killer by nature. But more recently it has been felt that it was not the hunting but the cooperation and sharing necessary to survive that led to the enlargement of the brain and accelerated man's evolution. Early man is now described as living "in small groups marked by complex interdependence and much intimate knowledge of each other."[1]

It's impossible to see how we've all survived this far if our better nature hasn't prevailed a good deal of the time. The human infant, unlike the young of many species, literally cannot survive without care. Babies who are not held and properly nurtured often die; of those who survive, many become autistic or turn criminal later in life.

The human infant, in order to survive, requires care after birth far longer than any other animal—about eighteen months. In the long process of civilization and socialization man has even tended to prolong the caretaking period of the young. So complex are the skills and requirements of living in the modern world that the modern child remains for years under the protection of the family in order to acquire them.

Aggression and evil, benevolence and caring, are merely human attributes to be put to use where needed and useful, and are tempered one by the other. Caring surroundings lessen the need for hostility as a means of getting what one needs, while a hostile environment inhibits the expression of caring feelings. Caring is coded into the genetic makeup of the species, reinforced by the very conditions of human life, and is as necessary to survival as aggression and the ability to fight. Lewis Thomas in *The Medusa and the Snail* says,

> Maybe altruism is our most primitive attribute, out of reach, beyond our control. Or perhaps it is immediately at hand, waiting to be released, disguised now, in our kind of civilization, as affection or friendship or attachment. I don't see why it should be unreasonable for all human beings to have strands of DNA coiled up in chromosomes, coding out instincts for usefulness and helpfulness. Usefulness may turn out to be the hardest test of fitness for survival, more important than aggression, more effective, in the long run, than grabbiness.[2]

A CARE-CORRUPTING ENVIRONMENT

When we look at modern life, it sometimes seems that caring disappeared at about the same time as the horse and carriage. It seems that things used to be much different: families stayed together, the young generation cared for their aging parents, nearly everyone went to church, brides were virgins, children didn't talk back—and an ice cream cone was a nickel.

But now most of us know that the good old days were overromanticized; the inequalities and inadequacies of the past are best left behind. Few of us would want to go back to travel by horse and wagon, to do our laundry by hand, to forgo the chance of a college education for our children. In the past, forms and rituals of caring often passed for the real thing. Society kept a stranglehold on the full expression of human feeling: aggression, anger, and lust were emotions to be conquered or denied.

Now, tradition itself is suspect—nothing is venerated just because it is old. The past is no longer considered a reliable guide to the future. Rituals are deplored as meaningless, empty gestures.

In a fervor to establish a totally new order, untainted by the sins of the past, everything has been reduced to ashes, even that which history has proven to be sound and worthwhile. So far, no phoenix of a glorious future has risen from these ashes. We seem to be hanging over an abyss. We don't know what to do, and we've lost much of our faith that there might be some other way. A halfheartedness characterizes our actions and pursuits. The Now Generation has become the No Generation, weaning itself from old values and uncommitted to new ones. It is a generation with diminished expectations, dropouts from public participation, concerned with things they do *not* have or *don't* do.[3]

A look at some of the manifestations of modern life clearly points out how pervasive and persuasive are the noncaring and care-less influences of our present surroundings:

The Sexual Revolution: In no sector has rejection of the past been more complete or more radical than in the area of sexual mores and practice. The one-night stand is the sexual liaison of preference. Sexual pleasure is measured in terms of performance. Pornography and perversion are permissible; intimacy is the real taboo. Getting laid has replaced getting loved.

The Battle of the Sexes: Probably no single factor of modern life will turn out to be more providential for the future of caring than the long overdue battle for women's rights. But it may be a while before the dust settles. Meanwhile, relationships between men and women are strained by violence, extremism, hatred, and most of all, by misunderstanding of sex roles and gender difference.

The Family: There is no longer any such thing as a typical family. Today's couple is less likely to marry than to make an "arrangement" regarding money, possessions, rent, food, chores, sex. Child rearing suffers in a society where self-actualization is seen as a healthy priority and "sacrifice" as sick. Well-meaning parents, poorly trained and lacking confidence, abdicate responsibilities to school and television.

Education: Schools have become child repositories in which education is subordinated to discipline. Students who can't read or write drop out of classes run by once-dedicated teachers who become case-hardened and unconcerned. The egalitarian dream of a college education for all comers has become a nightmare of educational mediocrity, lowered standards, and bankrupt schools turning out undereducated graduates into a glutted job market.

Religion: Organized religions stand accused of everything from repression and hypocrisy to irreverence. Yet the need for faith or transcendence is powerful. Modern society boasts a diverse and bizarre array of fringe religious groups, even hosts the kind of misguided, fanatical faithful who go to their deaths in a mass suicide in Guyana.

Politics and Government: Crushing taxation, inept and strangling bureaucracy, unpopular wars, bogged-down public projects, and the fall from grace of a dishonest administration have called into question all the values of the system. Voters feel their franchise devalued and feel powerless to change the moral and ethical order of things.

Professional Care: The lack of caring in society at large has spawned a huge professional-care industry. People pay dearly to get the care they cannot find at home or within themselves. Yet caring professionals are subject to the same syndrome of exhaustion, cynicism, carelessness and petty corruption that characterizes other sectors in American life.

Work: There is widespread cynicism toward big business, which is seen as making huge profits off the backs of the workers, avoiding regulation and taxation, profiteering from war and adversity.

Attitudes about work have changed dramatically. Few feel loyal to companies they think are insensitive to their plight. Pride in one's work is a joke to many who produce, repetitiously, day after day, the same small anonymous part of a shoddy product. Automation and technology, which on the one hand contribute to the relative luxury and ease of modern life, on the other, take away personal satisfaction in work and even the security of the job.

The inequities of the marketplace have undermined the concept that hard work brings proportionate rewards. In a society where athletes and rock stars make fortunes, in which petty corruption is all but sanctioned, many feel that they are fools for working hard, especially when the work is not in and of itself rewarding. Beauty, cleverness, luck, and connections are what win in the marketplace, not hard work. Menial work is seen as demeaning and a dead end; everyone wants a glamour job with perks and status, something that wins friends and influences people. Even the monetary reward of labor diminishes in the face of inflation and the ever-expanding array of acquisitions required for the good life.

Possessions: The dream of success has succumbed to a nightmare of staying even. People cannot even reject materialism any longer: it has rejected them. They see themselves losing a way of life that represents every promise of their society. Now they are presented with apocalyptic visions of scarcity and conservation, a world of diminution in which even air and water are running out.

The pursuit of material goods as a means to salvation is a disease of modern life. The psychological dependence on money is pervasive, often blinding us to our real desire and goals. We believe in money; it is our faith. In *Wealth Addiction,* Philip Slater says that our individual and collective egos have created a materialistic society that has the effect of helping the very rich—whom he calls the "wealth addicts"—get richer. Our tax structure, he says, is a welfare system for the wealthy. The tremendous influence of the wealthy fosters the tendency to place a dollar value on everything and creates a set of priorities dictated solely by monetary worth.[4] It is a way of thinking that cheapens all human endeavor and completely disturbs all other value scales.

It's a hazardous world for caring, a hostile environment for caring concern. Caring is out of context in a society riddled with violence and hostility.

Frustrated, we lash out at the world: wife beating and child abuse are the bread and butter of the daily news. Perhaps even devastation and violence are a reaction to frustrated hopes and shattered dreams.

Our "nice" society allows little margin for the safe release of anger and aggression, so we turn to sanctioned-hostility rituals for our release: boxing matches, dogfights, football games, disaster movies. We're connoisseurs of bad news; we salivate over fire and famine, watch for the car crash to liven up the auto race, lust for the fighter's blood, hope for the camera to pan to the brawl on the ballfield. In this era of violent professional sports, the ballfield is a battlefield, and we find compensation in watching the battle.

A Time for Caring

It used to be that tough times pulled people together. Families, communities, nations banded together to absorb their mutual problems. Now there are few cohesive families or communities. When people are not connected and can find no common cause, they feel free to exploit and abuse each other.

So it is true that ours is a society riddled with carelessness—with the difficulty of caring. But it is also true that many people *do* care and that many acts of caring go unnoticed. And many more people *would* care if they knew how or if they lived in a world more hospitable to it. They wouldn't need to seek safety in autonomy or security behind an image.

3
The Worship of Autonomy

For more than a decade the pursuit of personal happiness has been both sanctioned and encouraged. After an age of "conformity," of "being nice," of "adjustment," it's not hard to understand the appeal of looking out for number one, or of being your own best friend.

Self-actualization, self-reliance, and self-improvement are buzz words of what has come to be called the human potential movement: that colossal compendium of disciplines, in-groups, belief systems, and religions that has lately pointed the way to personal fulfillment. Under this broad umbrella comes physical fitness and organic foods, cults and conscious-raising, crafts and the back-to-the-land movement, confrontation and group therapy, yoga and fasting, est and Rolfing.

There's much to be said in favor of many of these things; in many areas the human potential movement has fulfilled genuine needs. Also, it was the first concerted and widespread rebellion against what were seen as the false and unrewarding values of a conformist consumer society.

The problem with the worship of autonomy and independence is, as usual, that it has gone too far. As we have noted, many people wonder why it is that with all their new self-improvement skills, their worldly goods and hard-won freedom, they're not more perfect and less tense. One reason is that the goal of self-actualization puts an unnatural burden on the individual to be strong, tough, and self-sustaining enough to go it alone. The very process of self-improvement leads to self-absorption, isolation, and the diminishing of caring social skills. Millions of people have spent millions of hours and dollars learning how to be alone and strong—how to meditate and masturbate—while their skills of intimacy and their ability to function as part of a larger group atrophied.

Even the new life-style groups—communes, religious cults—have become exclusive rather than inclusive, defined by whom they leave out and by their separateness from the larger society. Group members identify with their own kind as distinct from mankind. Ironically, group members are chosen and achieve status not on individual merit but according to how well they fit in with the group. Priding one another on their sameness, group members zealously pick out differences between themselves and outsiders. The kids look down on the older generation; the Eastern Liberal Establishment disparages the Southern Bloc; the Sun Belt laughs at the Eastern Liberal Establishment. Rock music fans think classicists are square; Aricans disparage estians; Hare Krishna followers look down on Moonies. Men and women feel they have mutually exclusive needs and values.

The more the group (or individual) focuses on itself and its uniqueness, the more it narrows the range of people, ideas, and things it can care about.

The psychiatric community has unwittingly colluded in this one-sided quest for self-actualization, convincing people that the answer to their problems lay in "doing their own thing." Psychiatrists' and therapists' offices are filled with men and women seeking sanction for their noncaring, self-actualizing pursuits. They are told they have a right to transcend social needs and norms. "Whatever turns you on" is fine, as long as it doesn't deliberately harm anyone else, of course. People coming to therapy desperately seeking love and closeness are often derided for their "neurotic dependency," told to be self-sufficient. They feel unduly vulnerable and insufficient to the task. The result is thousands of frightened patients pinned to the psychotherapist's couch for extended expensive stays. Hardly an autonomous way to run one's life.

In the past few years the shiny bright star of self-actualization has lost its luster. Its reputation has been tarnished not only by its failure to produce the desired results but by its excesses: its mishmash of mellowbabble and exaggerated claims. Too, it is irrevocably tainted by commercialization, by the very materialism it professes to abhor. Many people and "products" of the human potential movement have fallen prey to the profit motive. Today enlightenment is available to everyone at a price. And, always quick to spot a profit, the corporations are selling health foods, vitamins, jogging shorts, and biofeedback machines—the new lifestyle happiness products—right alongside the fast cars and the Big Macs.

MISLABELED NARCISSISM

After years in which the right to seek self-actualization went unchallenged, the damage done by such a view is now being assessed. The same people who were once lauded for their decision to become more skilled and self-sufficient are now roundly chided for their narcissistic self-involvement.

Narcissism. Lately the word has been applied both loosely and harshly. It's come a long way from Freud. Its clinical definition of autoeroticism has been buried under a blanket that covers any form of self-involvement, self-awareness, selfishness, preoccupation with personal issues, self-improvement, self-interest, single-mindedness, or solo activity.

This is a very unsympathetic view that fails to take into account the quite desperate plight of many people today. They are suffering not from a psychosis, a self-love that excludes all others, but from an inability to find a love that includes them. They are suffering from a deficiency disease, lacking in the skills and sensibilities they need to be intimate with others, to contribute to the community. They are malnourished, raised on diets lacking in care.

Narcissism can be seen as a corrective antidote to the breakdown of orthogenetic caring systems: the family, the school, the church, the community. Many children today are more than adequately fed, clothed, and sheltered, but nevertheless their care lacks depth, resonance, support. They get very little sense of their own nature, of their importance in the larger scheme of things. They feel defenseless, having neither assurance of their own power nor the sense that their family wields any power beyond the front door. Self-love becomes a defense against low-grade love and the indifference of society.

When people view others as competitive rather than comforting, they feel threatened and alone. Self-absorption is self-defense against the dangers of overinvolvement on the one hand and rejection on the other. One-night stands, casual friendships, and feigned indifference are protection against feeling too much. Many people see the choice in terms of either/or: they take the hard line of being strong and invulnerable, as opposed to (they feel) being soft and vulnerable.

To the disenchanted and disillusioned, to those recouping from rejection or disappointment, to those looking for something reliable in the shifting sands of society, self-reliance seems the surest bet. After all, how can they join a group when they don't trust those who would be part of it? Desperate for relief, they see autonomy as a way to reduce anxiety, ideally to become stress-free. They hope that by becoming tough enough and successful enough, they'll no longer be unable to cope.

Some people succeed in being autonomous and free from stress. They don't need anyone, are intolerant of dependency, unaccepting of care. Devoid of performance anxiety, they do not worry about what others think or say and do. They are above it all. Few of these people seek therapy. They feel they have no problems or insecurities. If they do come to therapy, it's to buy help for others: their hysterical or depressed wives, their troubled children. For them it is a modern-day version of noblesse oblige: "I don't know what all the fuss is about. I don't understand what could be the matter. But I am all-powerful and all-together and will take care of you with my money and influence. It is my duty."

But the price of autonomy is very high. Lacking in compassion, unable to share, devoid of understanding, the autonomous person is a threat to society. This is the person who brandishes a gun in gas lines or the person who looks on while a crime is being committed because he doesn't want to get involved. Fortunately, few people have the wherewithal, either emotional or financial, to be completely unneeding of others, totally free of anxiety.

Those who do have major deficiencies, big pieces missing from their personalities. It is far better to reduce unproductive stress or channel it properly than to seek to be free of it. Tension is what makes contact between people (social or sexual) interesting, what makes a good book or movie. Tension is needed for creativity. To be free from tension is to be deadened to feelings. Safe, but rather sorry.

Which leads us to another paradox. The quest for autonomy is an example of poor self-care. Interest in oneself is limiting; the resources of even the most fascinating person become quickly exhausted without the enrichment of others' impact. Even the most diverse person hasn't the skills and resources needed for a full life.

The worship of autonomy is, then, a dead end and a dangerous one, ignoring as it does the basic fact of our interdependence. We are species buddies, cut from the same cloth, more alike than different. That we are so at odds with one another, that we withdraw in fear and disappointment from involvement with others, shows how far wrong we've gone. Our individualism, our uniqueness can only be judged in relation to others. We were never meant to go it alone; as Lewis Thomas points out, we are "coded for usefulness" to each other.[5] It is good to be able to take care of ourselves, but it's even better (and more natural) to care for each other.

Even Jean-Paul Sartre, champion of unbridled individualism, near the end of his life rethought his stand on autonomy: "I left each individual too independent in my theory of others. Today I consider that everything which occurs in one consciousness in a given moment is necessarily tied to, often engendered by . . . the existence of others. . . . What is real is the relationship between thee and me."[6]

4
The Power of the Image

We are bombarded continually with images—on television and in the movies, in magazines and newspapers, books and billboards. Images tell us what we want. We are subjected to a blitz of glittering goods linked to subtle promises. What's interesting is the nature of those promises: we're being sold not just cigarettes or soapsuds, cars or toys; rather, we're also sold the symbolic message behind the image—love and happiness, parental pride, sex appeal, the envy of our friends, peace of mind, the promise of celebrity or stardom—the good life. Most insidious of all, all manner of creature comforts are presented in caring terms: "You're in good hands," "We do it all for you," "We make you feel good inside."

So important is the image to our way of life that in 1980 in New York there was a conference on symbolic consumption, attended by marketing and business professors and retailing executives. The conferees studied products "valued more for the symbolic gratification they provide than for any specific function they perform"; they also studied how to take advantage of the consumer's desire for such gratification.[7]

We end up working for, saving for, and buying an endless stream of goods that fail to satisfy our real needs. Behind the highly criticized image of Americans as gluttonous consumers is the sad picture of a people addicted to symbols of a dream both unfulfilling and impossible to fulfill. For images are addicting: simple and clear, they are presented complete and intact; the consumer doesn't have to do anything but sit back and soak them in. No response or interaction is required. The result is passivity and lack of curiosity. The consumer becomes more and more comfortable with images, less comfortable with real people and things.

The following is Lenny's story of a recent New York-to-California flight:

"I had heard about the battle between air passengers who wanted to watch the scenery and movie watchers who insisted that all shades be kept down. You had to be there to realize how scary it was. The movie was pure junk. When a few people raised their shades to look at the Grand Canyon—the Grand Canyon, for crying out loud—the complaining was unbelievable. The stewardess had to negotiate viewing rights for the scenery. The saddest thing was that there were several children in our vicinity and, as far as I could tell, only one showed the slightest interest in the spectacle outside. My wife said that if a film of the Grand Canyon had been playing as we flew over it, most people would have preferred to watch it on the screen. She was joking, but I'm afraid she was right."

If the real Grand Canyon is more complex and demanding than its image, how much more complicated are real people than their media counterparts. Image addicts find it stressful and exhausting to carry on real relationships; they require so much work, and they don't live up to their image-besotted dreams. Symbols are easy to digest and to switch off and on. After six hours of watching TV, one finds one's spouse or neighbor shocking; they don't fit their symbolized counterparts on *All in the Family*. Symbol shock, like shell shock, is battering and unremittent. It takes a while for the effects to wear off.

People tend to believe the set of values implied in the images they see. And what they see is how important it is to be beautiful, how much respect you get if you're strong and tough, how much fun it is to have a big car and go to fancy restaurants, how much you'll be loved if you wash your husband's shirt.

People believe that achieving the image-inspired goals will make them happy. They put tremendous burdens on themselves to be terrific at everything always. To be "just average" is anathema; the drive to be special is overwhelming. No one wants to be "just a housewife"—there's no more sure conversation-stopper at a cocktail party.

What happens when images have such overwhelming power is that those people who symbolize the right things are *overchosen*. Everyone wants them, wants to be their friend or lover, everyone wants to be like them, to go to them for help, be seen with them, court them, have children by them. The demand for the overchosen is tremendous, far exceeding the supply of acceptable symbols. Many people are summarily ruled out of the running by the narrow profile of acceptability that images present. Those who don't measure up to these imaged standards are shunted aside. They are *underchosen*. If they want to be a contender, they feel their only alternative is to get themselves a marketable image.

English civil servant-cum-eccentric Quentin Crisp puts his finger on the situation in *How to Have a Lifestyle*. With tongue in cheek he asserts that since style is everything these days (actually, *life-style* is everything these days), you should devote yourself to developing a style or image: a manner of speech, an area of expertise, ways of dress and behavior that will distinguish you as an individual and make people want to be with you.[8]

This is exactly what many try to do. They go to great trouble to hone and refine their image, to communicate in the only way they know how—symbolically. They send messages via their furniture, their car, their hairstyle. They dress for success. To be sure the message is clear one has only to read their T-shirts and find out whether they're sexy, cute, friendly, sarcastic, tough, or sophisticated, whether they like classical music or rock, whom they admire, what club they belong to, what their hobby is.

Walking along the beachwalk, or Strand, in Venice, California, near Los Angeles, it is possible to feel that there are no people around—only images. Under the glittering sun on a hot day it seems like a shimmering dream: dozens of Farah Fawcetts on roller skates, Warren Beattys on bikes, Superflys strolling along, sexpots and muscle men, football heroes and cheerleaders, and a dazzling array of bizarrely decked-out, bewigged paraders right out of *Kiss Meets Star Wars*.

All are hoping to be discovered, to create a fantasy of belonging, to get attention, and to have their image read. Not decoded or put to the reality test, but accepted intact.

THE DANGER OF IMAGES

Images *have* their uses. They are shortcuts to communication; they help overcome shyness and inarticulateness; they condense information and convey knowledge simply. It's neither useful nor possible to be image-free. On one level our clothes, car, house, job, memberships *are* expressions of our thoughts and tastes—they convey our *self-*image. We choose the symbols we present to the world. The problem is that the useful function of symbols can easily become perverted. It's when we choose to present symbols that don't fairly represent us but seem marketable that we run into trouble.

People who cultivate images that conflict with their real selves lose touch with those real selves. As they come to assimilate or believe in their own press, they become confused about who they really are. Images are impediments to knowing other people, too. They work in superficial situations: it doesn't matter if we have a false picture of the bank teller or of the maître d'. But it is inhibiting and destructive to friendship, family, and intimacy. Images distance people and keep them strangers from each other. They are hard to maintain in close situations; often they crumble under close examination. Relationships founded on imaged ideas find it hard to survive the intrusion of reality. The energy needed to consume and provide images takes away from the energy needed to consume and provide care.

The dangers of living up to an image are clearly demonstrated in the case of famous celebrities. The same powerful images that make stars can destroy them. Many famous people, unless they have a good helping of self-esteem to begin with, and family and friends with whom they are able to drop their image, run into trouble. The huge gap between the overblown big-screen picture of them in the public eye and their own inside knowledge of their frailty and insecurity is too much to bear. At first the adulation is wonderful and they may take advantage of it: the spoils of victory, so to speak. But few people have the inner resources to enjoy their image without paying a price. If they forget they are only life-size, if they start to think they're as wonderful and superhuman as their image says, if they lack a tongue-in-cheek perspective of themselves, the pressure to live up to the image will result in their conning themselves, forgetting who they are or how to be themselves—and left in a frightening limbo in which only their image remains. Trying to stay alive as a symbol, they lose their real life.

Abbot tells the story of his friend Rich:

"Rich thought he had it made when he hit the big time. Awkward around women, he was self-conscious about his looks and was openly envious of any of our friends who had good relationships or were very successful in pursuing women. Then Rich wrote a couple of books on love relationships that sold very well and that put him on the media circuit—TV talk shows, campus appearances, lecture panels. He was in seventh heaven. Here he was, practically the spokesman, the advocate, on a topic very sympathetic to women. He really made the most of it, changing his clothes, his car, his whole manner of speech. He imagined himself as a man who understood women, and they ate it up. All of a sudden he was pursued constantly by all sorts of beautiful, intelligent women. They'd be waiting for him when he got off the air, they'd write him letters, track him down in his office. His actions with some of these women belied his words in their cause, but he was having a grand time. The only problem is, this new Rich has become totally a product of his image. He can't even talk without pontificating—even to me, his friend. His relationships with women, while plentiful, are basically dishonest, and they all end badly. He keeps wondering why he can't find real love. One of the saddest effects of Rich's image-dependency is that Rich will no longer take long walks on the beach with me as we used to do—talking and looking at the ocean and the women. Why? Because no one recognizes him without his media image—his clothes, his books, his smooth talk. He's trapped with his image and doesn't have a nonimage self anymore. He can't leave home without it."

THE LIMITATION OF THE LABEL

What happens when people turn others into symbols is that they get labeled in return. The movie idol no longer sees individuals; everyone becomes an adoring fan, attached to his or her every word, responsive to his or her every whim.

Image consumers believe the label and expect the merchandise to live up to its advertised claims. The woman who presents herself as a sex kitten should not be surprised when she gets pawed. The man who treats his date as a sex object should not be surprised if she sees him as a meal ticket or stud.

This kind of treatment is called "thinging." It's what happens when we isolate the pertinent or useful part of someone and discard the rest. It's what happens when we pick out one aspect or quality in someone and assume that it represents the whole.

"He's the guy who services my car." "She's my tennis partner." "That's my next-door neighbor." ". . . the delivery boy." ". . . the woman in line in front of me." ". . . my doctor."

Labels are a necessary part of modern life. They're one of the ways we sort out and classify and make sense of the many, many people we come in contact with. Labels are energy savers: they help us define situations, set limits, and focus interaction.

In certain contexts it's foolish and unproductive to go beyond the parameters of the label. It is a mistake to try to entertain your doctor with an overabundance of social talk and questions about his or her family—just as it is to try to ascertain the hobbies and political views of the fireman who is tending to the blaze in your garage.

Nevertheless, labels can become an insidious way not to get to know people and not to have to mess with the complicated whole. As long as we put a label on the man in the service station—"He's the guy who repairs my car"—as long as we don't know anything more about him, what his troubles and concerns might be, we feel justified in demanding good service, paying, and leaving. We want to be friendly enough so that he'll remember our face and give our car prompt attention, but not so chummy that he might waste our time talking about his family or his own car or whatever else he might be interested in. We may have to be nice to the secretary, show her a bit of our private side so she'll feel loyal and important, so she'll stay late and keep the files up to date. But we don't want to become so concerned that she'll start feeling she can stay home to care for her sick daughter or ask us to spend our valuable time to help her find a baby-sitter. At its most dangerous, thinging makes it possible to harm and exploit others.

Compartmentalizing people also drastically cuts down on possible candidates for our Caring Network. We see someone who

A Time for Caring 27

dresses very differently from our image of fashionable dress and we say, "Oh, he's not my type." We casually dismiss people if we don't like the image implied in their accent, or the symbolic impact of their furniture, or if their choice of music doesn't fit our imaged ideas. If they're too loud or too quiet, not witty enough, too talkative, too fashionable, or too dowdy, they're dropped from our consideration without further investigation. In our fervent search for friends and lovers we severely limit our choices by compartmentalizing our contacts, defining them right out of our lives. Labels blunt our perceptions, cut off all curiosity, all inquiry, investigation, reflection. We're too quick to say, "Oh, I know that person." Blinded by the image, we overlook the essence. Potential for interest in others is impoverished by categorization. We become dulled to individual differences and unable to see others clearly enough to know who they really are, or what we might really enjoy about them. Then we wonder why we are bored and why we don't seem to understand what others want or why they behave the way they do.

THE SAFETY OF SYMBOLS

One reason why images are so appealing is that they are safe repositories for intense and sensitive feelings. Though it is fashionable to view the world as cold and careless, there's a good deal of evidence of caring feelings looking for a proper outlet. How else explain the tremendous outpouring of feeling at a rock concert: the swooning, crying, screaming fans? How else explain the devoted following of a football team, the feeling that one's fortunes are tied to the team's success or failure? The search for a hero to worship is at an all-time high. Every possible candidate is made into a celebrity, a star, and passionately worshiped and revered by the very same people who are supposedly so self-involved and alienated and care-less.

Sometimes it seems that everyone who isn't a celebrity is a fan. This atmosphere of adoration and adulation points not to a careless or uncaring society but to a culture with a tremendous untapped store of caring feelings.

It seems that people need to care and want to care, but finding most caring outlets fearsome and threatening, they choose safe targets. When people pour out their hearts to a movie star or put their hopes into a baseball team, there's no risk of rejection—because there's no risk of acceptance. Vicarious caring objects are better than none at all, or better than the risky targets closer to home—friends and family members.

It is ironic that in an age where feelings are meant to be expressed, when the lid is off the repression of once forbidden emotions, there are few safe objects on which to focus those feelings. As a boxing match becomes a safe channel for the expression of anger and aggression, sentimental movies and books give people larger-than-life objects on which to focus intense feelings of love and care. Sometimes the movie expresses their emotions for them. Cool, distant images evoke warm, passionate responses. Fantasies don't disappoint.

Greeting cards are another safe way to express feelings. We might agonize over choosing the right Valentine, get-well card, or sympathy card, hoping that Norcross or Hallmark will have the right words for us. To express our own feelings in our own words is far too risky and liable to misinterpretation; there's no buffer between us and whoever's receiving the message.

Pets and hobbies, even causes, can become safe channels for caring. Most people have at least one acquaintance whose love for his or her dog, whose devotion to his or her begonias or dedication to world peace far exceeds any concern he or she shows for his or her family and friends. Pets, hobbies, and causes are certainly valid receptacles for caring concern, but not if they become a refuge from direct involvements with other humans.

Kirk is a classic example of someone who cares for the world while those close to him are starved for care and attention. A well-known public official, he is a vociferous champion of justice for minorities, an inspired speaker on the subject of saving the environment, a generous contributor to local philanthropic organizations. And his interest is genuine. He spends prodigious amounts of time and energy on causes that interest him and is consequently beloved by his constituents, who see him as a tireless worker for all the right issues. Yet his wife and three children are almost completely neglected. He's rarely home, and when he is, he's holding meetings on the phone or is constantly in demand by scores of people. There's no time to spend with his increasingly troubled kids. Because he doesn't know them, he has little interest in them. He's uncomfortable with their demands. And he's long ago traded in his wife for a series of loyal supporters and office workers who adore him but whom he treats barely better than his family. Kirk is a man with caring feelings who is either afraid or lacking in the skills needed to care on a direct personal level. At the expense of his family's needs, he vents his caring impulses on big causes where his impact is strong, the rewards easy to come by and easily recognized. He feels safe and powerful.

CUTTING DOWN ON IMAGES

The enslavement to images and symbols is ironic in light of the worship of individualism with which it coexists. Nothing could be further from "being yourself" than conforming to images of how that self should be. The more we fulfill an image, the more we fail ourselves; we become not self-actualized, but other-actualized, realized in terms of other's standards: symbolization impoverishes our knowledge of ourselves and our relationships to others.

The providing and consuming of images is an addiction, and addictions are dangerous to emotional health. Like food or alcohol, images in moderation won't kill you; they're enjoyable and have their place. But in heavy doses they make us passive conformists and detract from our involvement in other people and things. It's vital that we all go on an image diet and cut down our image intake while we step up our active involvement with others, build our tolerance for complexity in three dimensions.

Perhaps this passive thrall to images is one of the more dangerous side effects of modern technology; it is only in the last thirty years or so that it's been possible to produce and disseminate images on such an intense immediate scale. Even the most resplendent of French kings had limited means when it came to enhancing their image: jeweled palaces, elevator shoes, painted chariots, all that pomp and circumstance could muster—but nothing to compare with live television or the grand scale of the silver screen.

5

Cleaning Up the Caring Environment

The caring environment is made up of all the things that influence how we learn about and express care: the people we come in contact with, the nature of our work, the movies and television we watch, the books we read, the news we hear, what we see on the street. That environment has tremendous impact, for we tend to imitate the behavior we witness and go along with the tenor of our surroundings.

Safe and encouraging surroundings are vital to caring, yet most people live in a hazardous environment full of distractions and toxic influences—an environment in which it isn't safe to express feelings of concern: they are too easily exploited, rejected, or misunderstood. Caring in a nonsupportive environment is not only difficult and frustrating, it can be foolhardy and self-destructive. We become exhausted—drained by people and situations that are overwhelming, toxic, inhospitable, one-sided, ungiving. This happens to teachers who give their all to unruly classes, to mothers who spend themselves on ungrateful families, to therapists who all day listen to and support troubled (self-involved?) patients, to lovers whose feeling is unrequited. A careworn carer uses up the capacity to care, becoming apathetic or hostile, cynical or burned out.

Cleaning up the environment is a process of detoxification in which care-denying people and things are slowly weeded out in order to make room for caring. In one way or another most people have or create safe areas of operation. One person finds solace from a dehumanizing job in her family. Another escapes a hostile, unloving family in the company of friends or a club or office camaraderie. Others reassure themselves that the world hasn't gone mad by working with other concerned people on community projects. A handicapped person seeks understanding and escape from prying eyes in the company of others like him or her. By broadening the base of the caring environment, adding on new people and things, even new information that reinforces caring, we create a larger and larger arena in which caring works. We move from a narrow context of a lover or family to include more friends, a more supportive neighborhood, a safer community, even a more positively viewed world. We carve out a territory in safe and nourishing soil to which we slowly annex more fertile land.

Caring—like all behavior—is contagious. As a crime-ridden neighborhood begets more crime, a care-ridden environment manufactures care. We go along with the behavior we see, not merely because we're copycats but because we want to contribute to the group and benefit from the rewards, and to belong. If we see everyone doing their part, we'll do our share. If we see others trying to get off lightly, trying to freeload, being awarded special privilege, we're angry and unhappy—and tempted to try the same things ourselves.

CONCERN FOR THE CONTEXT

Within the broad arena in which we live are many mini-environments, each different in its composition and influence. The home environment differs from the climate of the office. The atmosphere in the community is different from the air at a friend's house. Each context has different rules and regulations, varied expectations, different levels of intimacy and importance in our lives. Each supports and enriches a different kind of caring: the contextual details are important to what goes on within each circle.

We don't care for each other in a vacuum; everything is related to and influences that care. Family members are not only concerned for each other, they are concerned with the family entity itself. They want to maintain and preserve the system or context with which they identify. When families are split by divorce, they lose the framework or context that supported them. The carpet is pulled from under their feet.

The need for context is why lovers are concerned with their "relationship." It is why isolated, compartmentalized sexual liaisons don't last. It is why neighborhoods in which people know each other and think of themselves as belonging to a group are likely to be kept clean and crime free.

Sally's story demonstrates the importance of a supportive context:

"I had a very strange experience a couple of weeks ago. Andy and I have been lovers for over two years. We're both still married—I because I want very much to keep my home together until the kids are all in school, Andy because though he and his wife barely have a sexual relationship, he cares for her very much. Andy's wife even knows about me. Our long acquaintance has been very satisfying to both of us. We have a small apartment where we meet that we've fixed up ourselves. We have friends who know us as a couple separate from our families. We have a whole little world—a local neighborhood, certain shops we frequent. We do things together—bike, go to old movies, make huge hero sandwiches—that we never do at home.

Well, two weeks ago Andy had a pulled muscle and was pretty much housebound. His wife was away, and Andy asked me to come over to his house and visit. I was a bit hesitant, but I wanted very much to see him and he was insistent, so I went. It was a disaster. Even though Andy swore it meant nothing to him, I knew he was tense and uncomfortable. We made a feeble attempt at making love, but it was a mess, and we gave it up. We ended up standing in the hall drinking coffee! The problem was there was nothing there that meant anything to our relationship. I felt like I was in limbo—no familiar props, none of 'our' flavor. It was Andy's family's territory, and I felt like I was polluting it."

THE IMPORTANCE OF SHARING

Sharing goes hand in glove with caring. In earlier times, man's ability to live cooperatively in small communities was the most crucial factor in his evolution and survival. Even today, when a certain degree of autonomy is both possible and desirable, the ability to share is still of high personal and evolutionary value. In an age where conservation is becoming crucial to survival, when we must look ahead to a period of scarcity and limited resources, the skills of sharing are more vital than ever.

Most people enjoy their private thoughts, private homes, personal clothing—some even their private clubs and yachts. However, when the acquisition of these things and the desire to protect them or hoard them preoccupies us, our possessions become more of a trap than a liberation. They serve to defend against involvement with others rather than to facilitate caring. A person whose caring is in balance knows what is appropriately private and what is appropriately shared with family, friends, and community.

Every caring action requires some sharing, even if it involves simply sharing one's thoughts. People who care share their time, their energy, their friends, their money, possessions, ideas, knowledge, skills. They allocate their resources in a way that is appropriate and effective. Sharing expands and enriches our lives. When we share an idea with friends, it becomes larger than it was when it was trapped in our heads. Our friends gave it dimension and credibility and value; they add to it and fill it out. When we share our friends, we expand our Caring Network, creating overlaps in certain areas that strengthen the whole. As our friends get to know each other, new combinations and possibilities become part of the structure. Sharing tasks is a way of spending time with others and getting things accomplished more efficiently. When we share rather than hoard, we are surrounded by people who are supportive and whose resources are at our disposal. It is a healthy environment in which to live.

Corrine belongs to a group of women who own small businesses in her town. They originally got together to buy some advertising space jointly and to discuss their business problems.

"It was fascinating how each woman reacted differently to the group. Some wanted help but were so closemouthed about giving information that we couldn't do anything for them. One woman, Shirley, was having severe cash-flow problems. But she wouldn't tell us who her customers were, or her suppliers, and she wouldn't reveal her income. She wouldn't give in order to get. Another woman whose clothes we all admired wouldn't reveal her 'sources.' But the most memorable person in the group was Susan. She listened intently as the 'cases' were presented. She always had scores of suggestions, and she'd come back the next week with new ideas about people to sell to, names of friends who could help, sources for money, legal help, and suppliers. She seemed to have tons of friends and connections, and she'd rack her brain for ideas. As it turned out, Susan had a very small business, but we all thought she was rich as Croesus."

As a footnote to this story Corrine mentioned that Susan lost her lease several months after the group disbanded. "People came out of the woodwork to help Susan. You never saw anyone so rich in resources."

INCLUDING THE STRANGER

Including the stranger—the new family in the neighborhood, the new girl in class, the guy in front of us in the supermarket check-out line—is another surefire way of expanding the caring environment. Yet people sometimes become so phobic and fearful of the stranger, the outsider, that they lose sight of the fact that the stranger is more likely to be friendly than hostile, more likely a potential ally than an enemy. And what they don't realize is that by leaving people out, they weaken the caring climate.

In our day-to-day lives we tend to overlook the strangers in our midst, not to find time for the "woman in the laundry," "the guy who sat next to me on the plane," "the poor." It seems to take a crisis to remind us of our ties to the larger community, to break down our defenses, force us into recognizing our human and communal connections. In crisis we suddenly honor our connectedness. Everyone has heard stories about New Yorkers banding together in time of transit strikes or blackouts. There are tales of shipwrecked sailors sharing their every morsel, of villagers fighting to the death to save their neighbors from a common enemy. Recently it was the hostage crisis in Iran that united the country in an outpouring of outrage and concern, of love and patriotism—a unity that had been sorely lacking for many years.

In *Lest Innocent Blood Be Shed,* Philip Hallie describes what he calls the *mysterious* heroism of the people in a small village in southern France who, during World War II, harbored thousands of Jewish refugees at great peril to themselves and their village. One factor he is able to pinpoint in explanation of this phenomenon is the *belief in caring* fostered by the clergy of their church and the head of the local school.[9]

Caring people don't require such a crisis to bring them in contact with strangers. They are neither unnecessarily wary nor shy. They look upon strangers as potential friends, as fellow humans who might entertain them, enlighten them or liven up their day, or make them feel more secure and comfortable when they're away from home. If they're lost, they ask a stranger for directions; if new neighbors move in, they're curious to get to know them. If they're on an air trip, they talk to their seatmate. This is not to say that they befriend everyone they come across; rather that they are open to others, that they are able to find a balance of autonomy and community that feels right for them.

Just by making contact with outsiders they have evidence that the news of crime, corruption, wars, and hostages doesn't tell the whole story; they affirm their connections with the community, the nation, the world, identify with their fellow man in a trusting and positive way.

Jerome tells the story of his involvement in the Big Brother program in New York. Each participant is assigned to one troubled teen-ager, usually from a broken family, to whom they function as a hypothetical older brother.

"I was dragged kicking and screaming into being a Big Brother," he says. "I was appalled and disgusted by all the teen-age crime I read about in New York and terrified by tales of teen-age gangs, of muggings and knifings and mindless killings. Like many people, I felt there wasn't much help for these kids and didn't see any point in trying. A buddy whom I've always thought of as a bleeding heart—he always sees the good side of everybody—shoved me into giving the program a try, and I was assigned to Samuel. At first it was a disaster. I hadn't the foggiest idea how to talk to this school dropout, hadn't a clue about what to say or do, and I wasn't that interested in finding out. Suffice it to say that Samuel and I have come a long way. I no longer feel like we live on different planets. I'm starting to feel like I can help him, and I think he knows I'm his friend and he feels a bit more positive about his life. Mostly the whole situation has done *me* a lot of good. I feel much closer and more tolerant of people in general, less like I have to defend myself against a world that's out to get me. I was stunned to find out how many people are out there helping kids like these and working in other community programs. It changed my whole outlook on the world."

SIGNS OF THE NEW CARING

It is not always easy to recognize the caring ways that are beginning to reassert themselves in American life. For one thing, the New Caring is quiet and unprepossessing: it has none of the earmarks of martyrdom, of self-sacrifice or self-aggrandizement that characterized the caring of days gone by. The New Caring blends in with modern life rather than separates itself as though it were a distinct behavior manifestation. Today's caring is adaptable and accepting of the world. It is harder to recognize because it is pertinent, specific, personal, and gets little press coverage. It is flexible and diverse.

There is a renewed activism and community involvement that is better informed, better organized, better funded, less elitist and self-righteous than the activism of the 1960s. Contemporary activists are more likely to work within the system by lobbying for legislation, advocating their cause through established channels. Today's activists bring to their task sophisticated skills and a willingness to deal with realities; idealism is combined with knowledge and skill.

In business there is a swing away from ideas of winning through intimidation. The idea of a mutual win and an intent to satisfy the interests of both parties is starting to gain support. A currently popular series of business talks stresses the importance of having others' interests at heart. Many companies are recognizing the importance of community concerns with philanthropic programs and policies that reward employees for their involvement in community affairs.

Surely it is a sign of caring concern when the Nobel prize goes to a nun whose contribution to world peace is simply one of caring. And who in accepting that prize says, "The biggest disease

A Time for Caring

today is not leprosy or tuberculosis, but rather the feeling of being unwanted, uncared for, and deserted by everybody."[10]

The battle for caring is still an uphill battle, but there are signs that more and more individuals are joining what could easily become an army fighting to make the world safe for caring.

BECOMING A CARING ENVIRONMENTALIST

Current environmental activism is a good parallel to the search for caring and demonstrates the potential for change. After years of putting up with a toxic and polluted environment, many are standing up for their right to live in a cleaner world. They are demanding that government give priority to the long-term benefit of the public rather than the short gain of private interest. They have stopped big corporations from polluting rivers, belching foul smoke into the air, and manufacturing products harmful to the environment. They've forced government to halt massive public works projects that would destroy the balance of nature, and they have lobbied for laws to police the killing of endangered animals. In their private lives they try to conserve energy, cut down on their garbage, respect their land.

All this in spite of the fact that they are accused of being naive Pollyannas or fanatical doomsayers. All this in spite of the fact that great numbers of people continue to be wasteful, to overconsume. All this in spite of the fact that corporations continue to produce useless products, try to hedge the pollution laws. All this in spite of the fact that governments try to bulldoze through their public works bills.

These people are actively trying to do something—against tremendous and powerful odds and against the prevailing tenor of society. They are acting at the expense of their own convenience and comfort, rejecting old ideas about what constitutes the good life.

And as the environmental movement has grown—and today it is very powerful—the environmentalists have learned the skills necessary to pursue their cause and have gained confidence in their position. They have also gained in numbers, for their caring and cause is contagious. Other citizens have seen the sense and the reward of their position, felt the impact they've been able to make. Environmentalists have overcome others' cynicism and made their cause attractive and popular. Politicians hoping to attract voters these days must be sympathetic to conservation. Many corporations have taken steps to aid the environment beyond the mandate of law. Converts to the contagious idea of conservation are increasing; seeing is believing.

THE COMPONENTS OF POLLUTION-FREE CARING

In building a care support system each person must assess his own surroundings and decide the best course of action. But there are several ingredients basic to this process:

1. Make a commitment to caring. The first and most important step is simply to decide to do what's necessary to bring about the required changes.

2. Raise your Caring Consciousness. A Caring Activist makes it a point to be more observant and to be more aware of caring in his life.

3. Assess the environment. In order to make changes it's necessary to figure out the strengths and weaknesses of one's surroundings and make judgments about the best course of action to purge the environment of toxic people, careless practices, exploitative ideas.

4. Develop the Caring Network. This is not so much a matter of befriending everyone on the street as it is of maintaining and reinforcing existing caring connections and being open to new associations.

5. Develop caring skills and habits. Caring doesn't come naturally; like most things—learning to ride a bike or to speak a foreign language—it's a matter of learning techniques and then lots of practice.

Marathon group therapy provides a good model for a care-promoting environment. Dr. Bach has conducted hundreds of these nonstop sessions at which groups of six to fifteen people, often strangers to each other, spend at least twenty-four hours, and sometimes as long as ninety hours, together.

The group spends almost the entire time together. Only minimal time is given to sleeping, eating, and so forth. There are no distractions. Their stated purpose is to be a mutual support group: to get to know each other's problems. They are committed to a common goal. All the trappings of their images are left outside: their names, their cars, their jobs and family history. Many of the things that serve to label, define, and protect them are discarded.

Because of the long, exhausting hours and the lack of the usual things to talk about and the usual clues of imaging, defenses and poses are quickly broken down. The group achieves an intense closeness and intimacy very quickly. Group members learn important information about each other: feelings, sensitivities, problems, concerns, hatreds, fears.

The special circumstances or trappings of a group marathon cannot be duplicated in our day-to-day life. The closest that "real life" comes to this situation is in times of crisis—a family illness or traumatic setback, a time of war or economic hardship, or perhaps a situation in which coworkers band together against a pressure deadline. Often in such times we are liberated from normal constraints, outside everyday bounds. We feel connected to others, and useful.

There is a lesson inherent in this realization: If we could learn to bring out these untapped feelings as a matter of course, we would feel better about ourselves, feel more secure in the supportive web of our friends and community, feel less alienated and defensive. We would greatly enhance the intimacy and caring content of our relationships without needing the trigger of a traumatic situation to force these good feelings into the open. The balance of A Time for Caring is about achieving that goal.

Part II
The Caring Process

6

The Ingredients of Quality Caring

The developed Caring Capacity is unique to each individual, bears a particular profile as singular as a fingerprint. It is formed by a combination of genetic tendency, learned responses, cultural reinforcements, and environmental influences, support, and accidents. To put it another way, it's like a stew that tastes different according to the cook, the country of origin, the temperature and climate, available ingredients, the stove, utensils, and so on.

Surprisingly, in this age of intense self-examination, the Caring Capacity of most people remains largely unexplored. In a way it's like a rare stamp that is hidden away in an old album. Sometimes we don't even know that it's there, and rarely do we realize its value, so small and unimposing does it seem.

Sometimes it is in a state of rusty disrepair. All that may be needed to have it humming smoothly again is a change of focus, a shifting of attitude, and a reapplication of skills and feelings. We may sing professionally and never think to serenade our friends. Or we may be using our ability as a good listener not to understand our friends but to find the vulnerability in an adversary.

One of the best ways to tune up the Caring Capacity is to take a fresh look at what kinds of actions can be labeled caring. There are literally thousands of ways to show care, yet many people have a limited concept of what they think of as caring acts. They confine their definition to clear-cut, easy-to-recognize behavior: sending a birthday card, saying "I love you," helping an old lady across the street (or giving up a seat on the bus), tending to someone who's ill, giving money to a worthy cause, volunteering one's time at the hospital, comforting a grieving friend.

But these are only the obvious ways of caring, and not everyone is good at all of these things. A person uncomfortable with other's grief or careless about birthday greetings may all too easily chastise himself for being a poor carer.

Caring behavior ranges from small gestures that go unnoticed to the much-heralded magnanimous act, from the fulfilling of predicted duties to uncalled-for acts of heroism, from the rituals of everyday life to the most personal of behavior. It isn't possible to count the many ways of caring, but here are a few examples that hint at the range of possibilities:

"My kids all do their chores, but Kenny is the only one who does his without procrastinating or complaining or trying to get out of it or making me feel guilty."

"My pal Joan thought of a name for our new baby."

"Alison stayed on my case all through my diet, alternately congratulating and haranguing me about losing weight."

"When I have to bring work home, Al keeps me company by reading a book instead of going out or going to bed."

"I'm very good at putting newly acquainted groups of people at ease. I make introductions, initiate conversations, find the connections between people."

"I'm often suspicious about compliments because in my position many people try and gain favor with me. Arnold's compliments always show that he knows and cares about me. They're specific and often are about something not at all obvious."

"My wife, Elaine, is a constant source of new information—clippings, books, news reports, rumor—about whatever subject I'm researching at the moment."

"I've learned to enjoy Adam's Little League games now that I taught myself more about baseball. It used to be a motherly chore. Now we can discuss the game; I practice with him sometimes—and I like it."

"Fran is attuned to my need for privacy or company. She has a sixth sense about when I like to be alone and doesn't get upset or feel neglected if I'm silent for hours at a stretch."

"Andy understands that I go berserk from all the baby talk around here. He always has stories to tell about his day—he saves them for me. And he's one of the few men I know who has some understanding of what goes into taking care of three small kids all day. He wants to know about it."

"A coworker whom I hardly know pointed out to me, directly but tactfully, that I was alienating my boss by certain behavior. He probably saved my job."

"Giving gifts is one of my strong points. A little bell goes off in the back of my head when I see something one of my children or friends would like. I'm always ready for Christmas or birthdays."

"My brother is the family archivist. He keeps records, takes pictures, initiates family get-togethers."

"One reason my friend Jane is so caring is that she's very much aware of the things she does for others. She's not embarrassed to bask in her own good deeds or give herself a pat on the back."

"The way I keep going with all these kids is to treat myself well. I set aside a certain amount of time to myself and budget a bit of money just for me."

"My grown daughter Marie is one of the least jaded people I know. When I'm out with her for a few hours, she notices everything—people's clothes, changes I hadn't noticed, funny incidents. She makes everything seem interesting. I always feel like I've had an adventure."

"Hank has a gift for bringing people together. He introduced two friends who enjoy biking, three people who own local retail stores, a whole group that likes an occasional poker game. Being everyone's mutual connection, he has *many* friends."

"Everything I know about photography I learned from my wife Doris."

"Barbara tags along with me when I go scouring the countryside for rustic furniture and tramp art. I enjoy having someone to talk to about my interests; she's full of questions and ideas."

"Evelyn always seems to have a few jokes and tidbits of good news when I'm feeling down."

"What I like about David is that he's so patient about listening to all my troubles and complaints, yet he doesn't try to ram advice down my throat."

"After living for six years with a husband who never let me know what was on his mind, Dan is a pleasure. He simply says, 'I'm not in the mood for a movie' or 'It pisses me off when you don't call when you're going to be late' or 'I like you in red.' It's so simple."

"It's nice to have a friend who really wants the best for you. Lois is always thrilled when I get a new client or make a successful presentation or get written up in the trade papers. She could easily be jealous; instead she's my biggest fan and supporter."

"It was my husband's encouragements that convinced me I could go back to school again."

"Carl's example inspired me to leave my job and paint."

"I know I can call my parents at any time for any thing."

"Evin always tells me things he notices about me. He helps me see myself."

QUALITY CARING

Quality Caring is the kind of care that is the natural product of a fine-tuned Caring Capacity. While Quality Caring has partly to do with the quantity and scope of our caring acts, it is more concerned with *how well they are performed*.

It is nice to have caring feelings—to feel bad about our friend who lost a job, to sympathize with the victims of an earthquake, to be concerned about our child's struggle with the kids in the new neighborhood. But all the good, kind thoughts and loving feelings in the world count for very little unless they are communicated to others and are acted upon. Quality Caring requires involvement and a commitment to a caring way of life. But it carries with it incredible rewards.

Certainly we enjoy those things that are pleasurable in themselves, more than those things that we do in order to achieve something else. We work to earn money to buy things we want and need. But when we actually enjoy our work, the pleasure is far greater. We jog to keep fit, but how much nicer it is if we can take pleasure in the running. We call Grandma to do our duty on Mother's Day, but how much better it is if we really enjoy talking to Grandma.

Though much of our day-to-day caring arises out of necessity or duty, out of the desire for reciprocity or the hope of winning favor with others, as our caring skills improve we take more pleasure in what we do for its own sake. Confidence in our skills makes us more comfortable with others, more interested in them. We get more out of our lives. The good feeling and self-esteem that accompany Intrinsic Caring are their own very generous rewards. Anything more—and it seems to be the nature of caring that other rewards follow—is a bonus.

People who practice Quality Caring achieve a balance among providing care, consuming care, and self-care. Again the paradox: There is no caring for others without self-care, and one must get care in order to be able to provide it. Unless a balance is achieved, caring doesn't last. People who provide care and never consume it—whether by choice or not—eventually become burned out and exhausted. Those who consume it without providing their share eventually exhaust and alienate their benefactors and end up helpless to take care of themselves.

Self-care is the third part of the caring triangle. Self-indulgence and self-neglect are both detrimental to Quality Caring, both signs that our caring is out of balance. Treating ourselves to a gourmet dinner each night may seem like excessive self-care, when in fact it's self-neglect: not at all in the best interest of our health or finances. Yet denying ourselves an occasional gourmet meal because we feel we don't deserve it or can't afford it is also contrary to our own best interest. Identifying and doing those things that are truly self-caring is part of maintaining that crucial balance.

Part of the balance required is attention to the various caring arenas of one's life. This is a matter of allocating one's time properly to family, friends, lovers, the community, work, and so on, so that no area is overattended or neglected.

In addition to balance, it takes trained powers of observation, a keen ear, patience, and attention to be able to care properly. For every situation the caring most appropriate to it differs. As caring skills are improved and honed we become more sensitive to each situation and learn to allocate caring energies properly and our skills efficiently. We learn to do or say the right thing at the right time. We become tuned in to the dynamics of the situation, to what is needed. Confidence in our perceptions and skills help us to be specific and effective.

Communication is an essential connector to others. It's how we let others know about ourselves, how we ask for what we need from them and express our feelings toward them. Silence, especially withdrawn, punitive silence, is far from golden. Caring communication ranges from simply being there—standing by, passing the time of day—to idle chitchat, sharing our inner dialogue and inviting the confidence of others. Communication needn't be verbal—touching and gestures of affection are powerful communicators. Caring communications are direct and as free of mixed messages and double binds as possible.

By acknowledging that we recognize others' characteristics, needs, and accomplishments, we let them know that we see them as individuals and are involved in their life. We contribute to their psychological growth by acting as a sounding board to their ideas and feelings, by feeding back our responses to them, offering support and advice, introducing them to new things, expanding their life by sharing parts of ours. Growth-producing caring makes the ordinary special and enhances day-to-day life.

In recent times, as we have noted, adherence to tradition or ritual has been practically taboo. Traditions are considered meaningless relics of the past; rituals are considered uptight and lacking in spontaneity. Quality Caring recognizes that rituals support interaction and can ease the way for mutual understanding. We need to keep the proven traditions of the past, find new rituals that are pertinent to contemporary life, and develop personal rituals that reflect our own caring ways.

Caring is an art. The person who has made the decision to care, and who has acquired the skills and awareness to do so, finds that there is a tremendous aesthetic to caring, an art that involves form, composition, innovation, and wholeness. With the tools and talents at his disposal the caring person becomes creative in his approach to others, is not afraid of humor and playfulness. He is adventurous and develops elegance in his approach to caring concerns. Any aspect of life—jogging, playing the saxophone, chess, gourmet cooking—assiduously pursued and intelligently practiced elevates itself to an art. So it is with caring.

7
Choosing to Care

The first and most important step in practicing Quality Caring is to make the choice to care. That is neither as easy nor as foolish as it sounds, for we live in a society in which it is perfectly possible to get by with a minimum amount of caring, except where duty or expediency dictates. Certainly many people have had the experience of having their attempts to care rejected, derided, misunderstood, or exploited. Certainly there are many seemingly attractive life-rewards and -goals that don't require much caring. But once you accept the premise that caring is the most direct and appropriate way to true self-actualization, then you must make the decision to care.

The choice involves acknowledging oneself, both privately and publicly, as a caring person. It signifies a decision to act in caring ways, to be aware of and exploit opportunities for caring action, and in general to take on the challenge and responsibility of behaving in a caring manner—to take the time and make the effort to learn how to take action.

The caring stance is an open one, accepting of many viewpoints, of variety, of the complexity of the world we live in, of the gray areas in which decisions must often be made, accepting of personal idiosyncrasy and nonconformity. The caring person must be flexible in action and thought, must not rigidly hold on to concepts of right and wrong. The ability to share oneself—physically, emotionally, socially, mentally, materially, in proper proportions and without unnecessary defenses—is also part of the caring posture, as is a receptiveness to others' gestures of care.

Trustworthiness and an integrity in dealing with others are also required, for people put their faith in those who care. The secrets, foibles, and sensitivities and joys entrusted to the carer are never willfully violated.

Perhaps this seems very complicated, more work and effort than we can find time for. Yet it is in fact quite simple, for much of the "work" is in our heads: it's a matter of shifting our priorities. Taking a caring stance is not meant to interfere with the choices we make or the course of our lives. It's not a new hobby to replace our interest in disco dancing. It is a core from which we operate, a core that tempers and informs our action and choices, actually enhancing and making more satisfying the things we already do.

WHAT KEEPS US FROM MAKING THE COMMITMENT TO CARE?

Caring is not for the faint of heart. The decision to care requires assertiveness and a sense of self-worth that many people just don't have. Many feel that much that goes on in their lives is out of their control. Their lives are influenced more by sources outside themselves and their immediate family than from within. Once upon a time people grew their own food, raised their livestock, built their homes, educated their children. Today they have neither the power nor the ability to do these things themselves. Schools educate children, as do TV and movies, and scores of experts tell people the proper way to raise them. Committees, governments, and bureaucracies make decisions. Farmers raise food and livestock; contractors build houses. People work at jobs in which they perform a small part of a bigger operation that they never grasp the whole of. They're constantly being fed expert opinions, facts, guidelines.

In this almost overwhelmingly complex world, it's not surprising that we often feel powerless to make a mark, to choose the right path, to know the proper things to do. It seems almost presumptuous to try to figure things out ourselves in the face of the psychologists, sociologists, doctors, lawyers, accountants, educators, philosophers, physicists, and politicians who know so much more and can tell us so much better. It's no wonder people feel so passive and unsure of themselves.

We are in the midst of a crisis of confidence about ourselves—always seeking to know who we are, what we should do, what will make us and those we care about happy. This lack of confidence is one of the major inhibitors of caring concern. We're not even sure that our caring counts. We are afraid to care because we think we don't know how and are afraid to ask for caring because we feel we're not lovable enough to deserve it.

Fear is another effective care-dampener, another offshoot of low self-esteem. When we're not confident of ourselves or our caring abilities, we play the "What if?" game:

"What if I start a conversation with this man sitting next to me and he snubs me?"

"What if I give Marcia a birthday gift and she thinks I'm being pushy, or that I'm trying to buy her friendship?"

"What if I help Steve and he thinks I'm trying to steal his job? Or angling for a promotion? Or that I'm a sap for working more than I have to?"

"What if everyone says that I'm wearing my heart on my sleeve for Andrew?"

"What if I ask Gina out to dinner and she thinks all I'm interested in is sleeping with her?"

"What if I call Howard to wish him a speedy recovery and he thinks I want something from him? Or he laughs at my softheartedness? Or he thinks I don't have any other close friends?"

On the other hand, when caring concern is shown us, we're suspicious: "She's probably angling for a raise." "He's only calling because he couldn't find another date." "I don't need any help from them." No one is more suspect than the caring person who seems to have something up his sleeve. "Is there something wrong with him?" "What does he want from me?"

Fear, then—of rejection, of being misunderstood, of being laughed at or thought foolish, of being taken advantage of—inhibits caring actions. People refrain from doing anything rash or spontaneous, and their chances pass them by. The risks seem formidable. So they play it cool and keep up their aristocratic, above-it-all façade. They are admired for their smoothness, their savoir faire, their devil-may-care manner. They operate in the "comfort zone," eliminating as many risks to their vulnerability as possible, resigned to what is acceptable and what is not, sensitive to overstepping boundaries of propriety. They care in ways that are safe, permissible, accepted. They stifle any impulses that might get them into trouble, might shatter their carefully constructed image. The trouble is that if they stifle their impulses long enough, they literally lose the knack of caring.

Courage is what is required to overcome our fears and inhibitions. It is not a label usually applied to caring, but it has a very real application when a commitment to care is made. It refers to grace under fire, doing what is required in spite of one's fears and lack of confidence and incomplete skills. It refers to getting involved rather than passing by, doing the tough things when necessary.

But what is needed is not recklessness, not a throwing-caution-to-the-winds abandon. On the contrary, we need the courage of small steps, of testing the water as we go, reaching a little farther each time, building our caring strength.

At the very heart of caring is the *doing* of caring things. It is easy to deny caring needs, to retreat from caring action, to leave caring to others. The caring person may feel awkward or overwhelmed or unhopeful about the outcome, but the secret of real courage is that the caring person *keeps on doing* what is meaningful and what he believes in no matter how difficult, no matter how much it contradicts what others do or believe. Caring requires the courage of confrontation, of conviction, of going against the grain of acceptability and expedience at the risk of rejection and misinterpretation.

In developing a Caring Capacity, everyone goes through levels or stages—perhaps from a neutral or even negative position to this most important decision to care, through stages of discomfort, fear, awkwardness, or tentativeness to a growing sense of confidence and reward, fulfillment and growth. The rewards tend to parallel the level of effort, commitment and skill. The person who makes a decision to care slowly stretches himself to fit his new commitment, to explore and test this new world. He feels that he is back in control of his life.

To whatever degree one takes up the challenge of caring will the results show. Every little bit helps. Every time the smallest caring actions or gesture is used, every time we stand up and face a situation rather than retreat, another particle builds up around a core, like a pearl, adding to our sense of confidence and worth, validating our courage and the rewards that go with it.

The old saw that virtue is its own reward is not empty rhetoric. The proof is in the caring.

THE REWARDS OF CARING

Even to talk about the rewards of caring is suspect; it raises the hackles of the self-righteous and the cynical alike. Aha! you say, if there's a payoff, doesn't that devalue the caring, doesn't that put it on the level of all other exchanges? Am I supposed to show a profit on my caring? Remember the Caring Paradox: What we do for others is by definition self-actualizing.

Relax. Sit back and enjoy the fruits of your caring. The fact is that caring pays off handsomely—with gratification of a high and lasting order.

CARING ENHANCES SELF-ESTEEM

Studies of what is called prosocial behavior or altruism have repeatedly shown that people who believe in themselves and who are self-assured are more likely to act in a caring manner than those whose self-esteem and faith in their abilities is at a low ebb. Again we are confronted with the Caring Paradox: Those who are cared for and loved and who feel good about themselves are more likely to take the time and energy, and, more important, have the confidence, to care and to do unto others. People who feel unlovable, unworthy, unsure of their abilities are not likely to feel capable of helping others and are preoccupied with their own insecurities and problems.

Fortunately, it is part of the Caring Paradox that acts of caring themselves build self-esteem and courage, and that self-esteem and confidence grow with the repetition of caring actions and the practice of caring skills. Caring actions reinforce our confidence in our ability to function maturely, to take charge of situations.

Caring has impact. We feel powerful and in control when we care. We feel productive and worthy of others' care and attention. We see ourselves in a positive light. We all know that very real "inner glow" that results from a good deed or a contribution to a worthy cause. We want to feel good about ourselves and do so when we are conscious of our caring nature.

CARING BRINGS RELIEF FROM STRESS

Hostility and rudeness tax our psychological well-being. Caring is an effective tool for disarming apparently unfriendly, rude, arrogant, closed, and hostile attitudes. As we expand our caring actions we become less needy of defensive behavior or power games, less likely to withdraw from involvement with others. Caring begets caring, and as the base of our caring expands, life becomes easier, more interesting, and less stressful. When we care, we feel less isolated and wrapped up in ourselves; we are relieved to be able to focus our attentions on something outside our own navel-gazing. We are more relaxed.

This is not to say that caring is stress-free. Some caring situations can be very taxing or confusing; often there is great temptation to withdraw. But when we act, the stress is discharged rather than turned in on itself. Caring is a boon to mental health.

CARING IMPROVES THE ENVIRONMENT

Caring solidifies the community and improves the world in which we live. Strangers become part of the group instead of threatening outsiders. (A friend won't mug you!) We increase the number and variety of people we can call friends. We strengthen our sense of belonging: we welcome new people instead of viewing them as an added burden. We have the assurance of help in crisis, of feedback and aid from people who really know us. We have a good chance of being properly advised and administered to, of being sympathetically understood. We are the objects of concern not of professionals who are strangers but of people with some depth or resonance about us and the care we need.

The people we come in contact with in care-promoting situations also benefit, for caring brings out the best in people. They get the message that they are worthy of care, that they are observed and valued and entitled to attention. And they tend to live up to our expectations. They feel less insecure, less stressful. They are less lonely. They become less defensive and more disposed in turn to care about you. The arena in which it is safe and rewarding to care expands. The quantity of caring becomes large enough to offset the effects of carelessness and petty criminality. Examples of caring offset the dangerous models of autonomy and self-involvement. Caring creates a cushion of warm comfort in an often cold world.

CARING ENHANCES THE QUALITY OF LIFE

Caring is expansive. As the Caring Network grows and caring skills improve, the world becomes more interesting and appealing. More relaxed with others, more at ease in new situations, we become fascinated by people, curious about their lives, observant of their individuality. We annex the interests and joys of others to our own. We take more pleasure in everyday occurrences: day-to-day life seems less boring and mundane. Caring has the gift of making the ordinary special. As we get more of what we need from contact with others, as we find more interest in the world at large, we feel less need for marginally useful material things or constant diversions that isolate us from others.

Number Our Days is a book about a group of elderly people affiliated with a senior citizens' center in Venice, California. Though they are poor, old, infirm, often neglected by their families (if they have families), their lives are testimony to the power and rewards of caring. Instead of existing in misery as their circumstances might seem to indicate, they add dignity and interest to their lives through their concern for each other and their involvement in the community. While it might be expected that others help them, they turn the tables and help others, and themselves.[11] What might easily be closed, constricted lives are filled with meaning and add to the community's store of caring.

The result of being free to function in a care-conducive environment is that we find ourselves in a situation that supports growth and change. We're possessed of new confidence, new skills, supportive friends. We feel confident and competent, stimulated by a world that we've learned to observe in an open, non-threatened way. The impediments to expanding our horizons are removed. And we have at our disposal other resources, advice, help, support, even inspiration.

8

Intrinsic Care:
THE REAL THING

The ideal kind of caring has no strings attached. It is not care motivated by a sense of obligation or duty. Nor is it tainted by a desire for reciprocity, or by any other ulterior motive: power, status, popularity. Genuine care is motivated by the desire to care; the rewards are in the enjoyment of the caring process and the self-esteem and sense of closeness that ensue. Intrinsic care is the kind that feels terrific, the kind that infuses us with a warm glow and the sense that the world is an okay place.

The most clear-cut situation in which we see genuine what-you-see-is-what-you-get care is in the case of parents' caring for an infant. Caring feelings come through uncomplicated by other motives. There is no thought of a fair exchange. It is a good, clear, unmixed emotion.

Intrinsically rewarding caring (or other behavior) can be difficult to identify: the feelings are diffuse, the effects often inconcrete. Following is a list of clues to help recognize the nature of our behavior.

INTRINSIC	EXTRINSIC
The action is in itself pleasurable and rewarding.	The action is the means to a desired end.
I am interested in the action.	I am uninterested.
I am involved.	I feel detached.
I feel good, elated, confident.	I feel bad, depressed, bad taste in mouth.

A Time for Caring

It feels spontaneous and varied, creative.	It feels routine, programmed.
The effects of my actions are more vague, less noticeable, unpredictable.	The effects are clearly known, predictable.
The action seems loose, unstructured, unritualized, searching.	It seems direct, systematic, ritualized.

Of course, it isn't possible for all caring to be simon-pure. There are many things about everyday life that obstruct genuine care. When we're plagued by illness, financial worries, an overbusy social schedule, too heavy a workload, our ability and time to care must suffer. When we have to be careful about our care—afraid of offending our boss, of scaring away a potential lover, of insulting a guest, losing a client, of being rejected or exploited or misunderstood—the quality of that care is impaired. Jealousy of another's attainments or possessions can also blight care.

"Doing one's job" can interfere. Sal remembers an assistant hotel manager in Vienna who was so worried about overstepping boundaries that it interfered with his perception of need. Sal went to him for help: she urgently needed a doctor or a specific medication. Afraid to make a decision outside his normal job, the assistant avoided the issue of Sal's need. "I'll have to check with my boss," he told her, though he knew the boss wasn't available. Both his desire to do his job right and his insecurity about his ability to care inhibited that care.

Lack of skills can interfere. Once a week Ted takes his grandchildren to visit his very ill mother-in-law. Every week when he goes, he starts out full of anxiety and trepidation. He doesn't know what he'll say or do. The kids, of course, have no anxiety about their proper performance. They have a fine time, while he's fulfilling a duty. Lately he's begun to realize that when he leaves, he feels good. He's learned something—from the kids or from his infirm mother-in-law. Now he can see both sides of the situation. By selectively focusing on the benefits, he minimizes the duty aspect.

Everyone has duties and obligations. Negotiated trades of goods, services, and favors are part of life. But in a free-market system the rules of the marketplace often influence caring behavior, and acts of caring tend to resemble deals, with similar payoffs. In a society that emphasizes reward it is easy to lose sight of the inherent values of caring. Often the anticipation of reward or the striving for a goal blunts the potential pleasures in the process of achieving them.

Tom works fourteen hours a day, not because he loves his job but for the generous salary it pays.

Samantha detests her daily regimen of jogging and calisthenics but does them to keep fit. Her real goal is even more removed: she keeps fit in order to be attractive to others.

Yvonne changed her painting style a couple of years ago so she would be accepted by a more prestigious gallery.

The reward system pervades our lives. We're bombarded by behavioral models made exciting by the offer of a reward, rarely reminded of the possible pleasures along the way to the reward. If you do a good job, you'll get a raise. If you're a good boy, Mommy will take you to the movies. If you buy this perfume, love will follow.

The reward system carries over into our caring actions. People care so that caring will be reciprocated, so they can get specific things they want and need. It's the old story about the woman snuggling up to her husband so he'll spring for a new dress, or the husband bringing flowers so his wife will forgive his poker playing. It's the employee suddenly staying late to butter up the boss for a raise, or the candidate making promises of caring concern to constituents in exchange for votes.

Greg's story illustrates well how ulterior motives can sabotage the effectiveness of caring, as well as the rewards.

"My friend Martin stopped by after dinner last week, preoccupied with some business problems, wanting my advice. I'm proud that Martin seeks out my opinion, and I enjoy going over his problems and trying to help him out—in the past I know my advice has been valuable to him. But this time as he was explaining his problem to me, I found that I was distracted by a scheme that kept building in my head about how I could do some specialized consulting work on this problem for his firm and make a lot of money.

A Time for Caring

I lost my objectivity. Suddenly I wasn't paying close attention. I was suddenly more self-interested than Martin-interested. My remarks became slanted toward my own ends—getting him to get his company to hire me."

Caring neutrality is violated by the expectation of reward or exchange. Often the more specific the expectation, the greater the deterioration of bona fide care.

Focusing single-mindedly on goals can blot out any possible enjoyment in the process of reaching them. The man fixated on collecting his paycheck at the end of the week finds it hard to glean satisfaction in the day-to-day details of his job. The woman obsessed about achieving fitness is not likely to be attuned to the pleasures of running, stretching, breathing. The man who brings his wife flowers as a sop to his poker playing is not likely to enjoy picking them out or smelling them on the way home, nor will he likely enjoy his wife's surprise and pleasure or the warm feeling of having done a good deed. With the promise of a movie foremost on his mind, Johnny will not likely see other benefits and pleasures of being a good boy. She who buys a perfume for the love it promises may not notice the bottle it came in, the cool feeling of it on her skin, the delicious smell.

Even sexual pleasure can be sabotaged by ignoring the process in favor of the goals. Today many people have hidden agendas or goals for their sexual activities. Their goal is to attract a partner, to enslave that partner, to impress the sexual partner with one's proficiency, to substitute for passion missing in other things—or to get even with one's partner, to express hostility. Sometimes just being fixated on the orgasm at the end of lovemaking inhibits pleasure along the way. In other words, many people bypass the sensual, affectionate, genital, loving pleasures of sex on the way to other goals. Then they wonder why they don't enjoy their sexual encounters, why they become jaded or even dysfunctional. Sidetracked by the end game, the pot at the end of the rainbow, they undermine their enjoyment and diminish the pleasure-giving possibilities of their lives.

It's as though we're not supposed to enjoy the day-to-day actions of our lives on the way to our goals; it's expected that the path to the payoff may be difficult or dull, but that with luck the payoff itself will be worth it. In some cases, people who find enjoyment along the way are suspect. This is evident in the public's attitude toward artists: actors, musicians, dancers, writers. It is generally understood that these folks love their work. Because they have so much ongoing enjoyment from their work, the public attitude is that they don't need or want the kind of monetary rewards that accrue to those who work at less beloved jobs. Punishment for the intrinsic enjoyment of one's work is a kind of backlash of the reward ethic.

THE TRAP OF RECIPROCITY

Seeking an even exchange for caring actions is another sure way to undermine the pleasure of caring. When we expect or demand a tit-for-tat exchange for our caring energies, we are likely to be disappointed and to spoil the innate pleasures of our actions.

Yet it's almost too easy to get caught up in a battle of reciprocity: If I care for you, will you care for me? I'll do your laundry if you buy me a dress. I'll sleep with you if you take me out to dinner and dancing. Making deals instead of commitments endangers caring. The let's-make-a-deal syndrome is especially insidious when it creeps into intimate relationships: the successful and powerful male trades his income for the care and services of the female. This commercialized caring is exemplified by what Dr. Roger Bach translates as "I'll love you for one-half of the gross."

At any given time the quality and quantity of caring interaction between two people is out of balance, as are their abilities and caring needs. Two people never care for each other equally *and* simultaneously. Whether a caring balance is achieved is only discernible over a period of time, and everyone's standards for judging are different. Everyone has a different expectation of rewards for their caring actions, and a different formula for having their caring needs met.

This is not to say that caring should be indiscriminate or unmindful of the response it evokes. Careworthiness is an important criterion for caring. It makes no sense to care for those who are uncaring or unappreciative, to lavish attention on things of little value or merit. It is both unproductive and self-destructive to expend caring energies that don't merit the expenditure. But it is also

A Time for Caring

unproductive to be so afraid of doing too much or of being taken advantage of that care is withheld or tempered by suspicion.

Achieving a fair exchange in caring is mostly common sense. The rewards aren't always apparent; they often come from unlikely sources at odd times.

THE PRETENSE OF CARE

One of the most insidious ways to sabotage caring pleasures is to use a pretense of caring concern to manipulate others. On some level, at some time, most everyone is guilty of this kind of "caring." They use flattery to ingratiate themselves with someone they want to like them. They feign concern for another's problems so they will appear to be likeable people. In subtle ways they present themselves as involved, concerned about doing the right thing, supporting the right causes. They pay insincere compliments in order to be liked. They feign interest or enjoyment where none exists, hiding true feelings in the interest of expediency, not wanting to rock the boat. Most of it is well-meaning, a way of getting the care and attention they need, or a misguided way of being nice.

In the business world, showing concern for the needs and objectives of the customer or adversary is an important ingredient of salesmanship. It is part of the ability to negotiate, to maneuver, to "play your fish." Often the semblance of caring—the presentation of oneself as nonmanipulative, as concerned, as desirous of closer relationships, as involved in the other's interests—helps close the deal. The salesman's show of concern for the customer makes that customer feel more comfortable and self-confident, inclines him or her to buy the product offered. Caring salesmanship is acceptable in business. It's a mutually understood aspect of the game, tied in to honesty and fair play, and it's seen in its context of abetting a successful negotiation. In many areas of life fairly negotiated exchanges of goods and services are both acceptable and desirable.

The problem occurs when fair-market, goal-directed caring becomes so intertwined with intimate, professedly goal-free caring that the two can no longer be separated or distinguished from each other. When the attitudes of the marketplace filter down to the personal level, the potential for manipulation multiplies because the rules of the marketplace are understood to be suspended: the defenses against exploitation are down. It is the pretense of goal-free caring that is particularly insidious. It exploits the hunger for caring and undermines the potential for genuine care on the part of the pretender.

People are naturally attracted to those who seem to care—for them, for others, for ideas, and for animals or flowers. They have an alluring energy and radiance. So it is particularly onerous and dishonest when people ingratiate themselves by pretending to care. Herbert Gold refers to these caring con men as the "people people." These are the ones who image themselves as full of concern for others, desirous of intimacy, openly sharing their feelings, understanding, kind, involved. Often these people are so in love with their image that they fail to see the exploitativeness and seduction of their own ways. They would be hurt to be called insincere.[12]

A much publicized incident shows how pervasive is the con man and how vulnerable we are to both image and the promise of caring (and celebrity). An unattractive and boorish man was arrested for having impersonated Richard Avedon, the famous fashion photographer. During his reign as Avedon he had raped, robbed, and bilked dozens of women. He was caught only when one woman overcame *great embarrassment* and reported him. He had approached his victims by flattery, singling them out as special, promising them careers as models and celebrities. So anxious were these women for a piece of the action, so happy were they for the attention, that they went along, despite the fact that the press reported him as singularly repulsive—fat, with bad breath, and poorly dressed.[13]

Even bona fide caring is suspect in the midst of con men and impostors. Leery of the persuasiveness of flattery and seduction, we steel ourselves against the real thing as well.

MAXIMIZING INTRINSIC CARING

The real rewards of caring come from the satisfactions we derive from the *process* of caring. And the way to get more benefits is to learn to recognize and enjoy the doing of caring things. For this it is necessary to set aside the preoccupation with extrinsic goals, the need for reciprocity, and the manipulative imaging of oneself as a caring person. It also helps if we can find some pleasure in those things regarded as duties or obligations, for much of our caring is defined by the roles we play in our families, on the job, and in the community. Recognizing and respecting our roles and duties in their proper perspective is part of Quality Caring.

It is not possible to achieve 100 percent intrinsic caring. It is not always possible to be spontaneous, to care when and how we would like to. There are bound to be times when we cannot muster any caring feelings to go with our caring obligations. There are times when no amount of acceptance and goodwill makes the drudgework less than drudgery. There are detested and detestable relatives who must be cared for. There is a job or a coworker we cannot abide. At times it is not even possible to muster sympathy, much less take action.

But by focusing on the caring process, through a change of attitude, a loosening of goals, a new perspective, much of the rote and duty caring can become meaningful and rewarding.

Sometimes it can be a struggle to maintain one's enjoyment in the caring process, as Hal's story shows.

"When I attended the law conference in Chicago last year, I found myself with a free afternoon and decided to visit Luke, who was my son's best friend all through school and who practically lived at our house during that time. I knew Luke lived outside Chicago and had recently had his first child. I was all excited about seeing Luke, and of course I felt great when I called and he made it clear he was thrilled that I was coming to see him.

"I bought a present for the baby and some wine and borrowed a car, feeling like a wonderful fellow. Then I realized how far it was—over a two-hour drive. And then it started to rain. Suddenly my spontaneous good deed was turning into a burden. The whole situation seemed out of my control, a duty. I began to feel resentful of Luke for living so far away, for not warning me of the distance, for not offering to come to Chicago himself instead of expecting an old man like me to drive out there in the middle of a busy convention.

"Then I decided that by visiting Luke I was fulfilling an obligation, doing what was expected of me. I adopted an attitude of stalwart altruism, a good Samaritan pose. But I felt none of the lightness and joy I had at the outset, when my motive was spontaneous. I was merely persevering at this stage.

"Finally, though, I decided to make the best of it—to enjoy the drive and the scenery and the time alone for a change. The bad feelings subsided, and I did enjoy it. And once I got there, Luke and Carol made a big fuss over me. They were delighted to see me, impressed by the effort I'd made. All my doubts and resentments disappeared. The drive back was a breeze."

The more satisfaction we can derive from our caring actions, the more we expand the base of intrinsic caring rewards, the less dependent we are on other goals. As we learn to take pleasure in the process, our life becomes more interesting and varied and stimulating.

We may start out observing others with the goal of improving our ability to pinpoint others' caring needs. Soon we derive satisfaction from the observing itself. Suddenly we're entertained by what people wear, what they say, how they move.

We begin by writing letters to old friends in order to strengthen and reinforce our Caring Network—we end up enjoying the letter-writing process. We find that we're learning to express ourselves in new ways, taking pleasure in reliving recent events, in being forced to describe our feelings.

It's surprising how much of the humdrum quality of our lives fades away, how rich our lives can seem when we care. A long drive is made interesting when we can derive pleasure from the passing scenery. The smell of clean clothes and the feel of hot soapy water can take the hard edge off doing the laundry. An appreciation of the beauty of food and the tools of cooking can give enjoyment to preparing a meal. An awareness of one's competence and comfort-giving skills can ease the burden of nursing a sick child.

Consciously seeking to derive benefits from our day-to-day activities is the surest way to maximize the amount of intrinsic caring and its rewards. It's simply a matter of focusing on the pleasure rather than the pain, the process rather than the goal.

9

Balance:
CARING ON AN EVEN KEEL

As we have noted, balance as applied to caring is about finding the right proportion among providing care, consuming care, and self-care.

Out-of-balance caring doesn't work. A 50-pound child and a 180-pound adult on a teeter-totter can pretend they're both making it seesaw back and forth, but neither the illusion nor the enjoyment can be sustained for very long. Neither the adult doing all the work nor the child getting the free ride gets as much benefit from the experience as does a more balanced team. So it is with caring.

The struggle for balance in caring is an ongoing one, for there are many things to throw it off kilter. It is easy to fixate on one caring channel or on one caring object. Devoted to her child, a woman neglects herself, her friends, forgets her passion for gardening. A man dedicated to the cause of world hunger never has time to share a meal with his family. This kind of tunnel vision, a kind of caring specialization, leaves many people and things out in the caring cold.

On the other hand, indiscriminate carers have no criteria by which to allocate their energies. They'll devote themselves to an uncareworthy cause or person and wonder why they feel exhausted and abused. They'll care for anyone and everything that crosses their path except themselves. Then they wonder why their concern becomes indifference.

It is possible to have unrealistic expectations of care. One person, for some reason or another, feels entitled to be cared for without assuming any responsibility for providing care. Another's perceptions of his duties, or his low self-esteem, leads him to expect to provide care; he is resistant to accepting care or asking for help. Still others have a vision of care that isn't fulfilled.

A psychologist friend reports that some of the most troubled kids he sees are the children of psychologists and ministers. He theorizes that the reason these kids are so intensely upset and angry is that they see their parents devoted to helping others, see them lauded and respected for their caring while they, in a more private arena, are neglected. The children of businessmen or laborers haven't the *expectation* of care: the gap isn't as great between what is anticipated and what is received.

A major ingredient of the caring balance is nothing more than fairness, doing a fair share of both the giving and the getting of care. But as we have seen, the scales of caring are never in perfect balance. In each relationship, in each arena of life, the scales teeter back and forth as the balance shifts from providing to consuming care, from giving too much to taking too little. Rarely do two people care for each other equally and simultaneously. Only over time can the balance be measured or judged. But prolonged and chronic excesses on either side of the scale are perilous and render any stability in the relationship impossible: eventually the relationship keels over on one side and can't be righted. The caring cargo must be constantly balanced and shifted around the overlapping corners within the triangle of providing care, consuming care, and self-care.

The importance of that triangle of balanced caring is well-illustrated by Andrea's story.

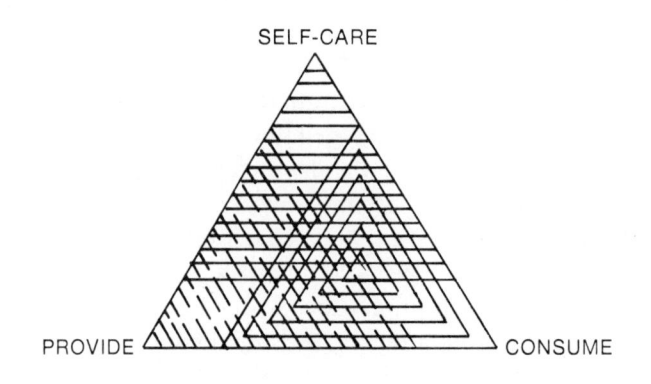

"My daughter Nan has gone from one extreme to the other this year. She's always been pretty stable. Then about a year ago—after several years of not too serious dating but increasingly serious looking around, she met Stephen, her dream man. His devotion to her made her very open and giving; she was very happy and was suddenly more helpful around the house, more attentive. Then they had a big fight and all but split up—they saw each other rarely. Nan was miserable. She became very concerned with her health, her clothes, finding an apartment. She no longer had any energy or interest in anyone else. Licking her wounds became her major preoccupation; she became very demanding of me and her dad. It was a kind of defensive self-involvement, but it made her incapable of caring for anyone else. Also, she started over-indulging herself. She ate too much, spent too much money on clothes, ended up getting her dad and me angry with her.

"Then last month Stephen and Nan made up and they're getting married this fall. Nan's a different person again. She's been very loving and concerned toward us and her friends."

SELF-CARE

We will deal with the importance of and the ingredients of self-care later. For now, all we need note is the part it plays in the constant struggle to maintain the caring balance. Attention to one's own well-being is necessary in order to have the self-esteem and energy necessary to provide care for others. Care for oneself is also necessary if one is to attract care from others or to feel worthy to ask for care. And self-care is needed to fill in the gaps when the care that normally comes from others is not available.

While too little self-care results in self-neglect and dependence on others, too much results in self-indulgence and isolation. People wrapped up in their own soap opera find little time for others or, determined to be self-reliant, resist what care is offered. So finding the right balance of self-care makes it possible to provide and consume care in proper measure.

CONSUMING CARE

Consuming care is every bit as important as providing it. The intake of care provides the nourishment in terms of energy, self-esteem and general well-being that fuels the impetus and ability to provide care. Infants and children are major care consumers. The care they receive when young powerfully influences the care they're later able to provide. The transition to care providing is slow; the balance shifts over time. But all through life a certain level of care consumption is vital.

Unfortunately, many people have a hard time balancing their caring diets. They tend to over- or underconsume, often with serious side effects.

OVERCONSUMPTION

The overconsumer of care might seem to be an enviable fellow. Somehow he's lucked out; he manages to get waited on hand and foot, is catered to by others, and never seems to have to return the favors.

Usually he falls into one of two categories. One is that of the helpless consumer. This is the person who is too weak or infirm or unskilled to provide care. While this is acceptable from children or sick people, it is particularly manipulative in able-bodied adults. It's one thing for a child to say, "But I don't know how to tie my shoe" or "I'm afraid to walk to school alone." It's quite another when a teen-age girl protests that she doesn't know how to use the washer and dryer or when a grown man insists he's too ignorant to fix his own dinner. Helpless overconsumers wield their weakness like a powerful club.

The second type of overconsumer is the person who feels entitled to be cared for. As one such person said, "I feel I grace the joint. I'm not afraid to ask for anything." Often such people feel that something they possess—money, status, power, beauty—entitles them to the privilege of being cared for without having to provide care in exchange. The caring they get is contractual in nature. "I am a famous rock star. You may follow me around and handle my correspondence and prepare my meals and in general adore me in exchange for being able to be around me."

Overconsumption of care has its limits. Many times the overconsumer of care hooks up with what would seem to be his natural counterpart: the overprovider. But this liaison has only a limited time before it wears very thin. Eventually the overprovider becomes exhausted and burned out, unable to provide the called-for care. The provider may become indifferent to the consumer, even angry or resentful at receiving so little in return. At some point the provider must get care from somewhere in order to give it. Eventually the freeloader wears out his welcome and must ante up his share. Often it is exactly this pushed-to-the-wall situation that is necessary to get the exploitative care consumer to capitulate.

While care consumers often seem powerful and independent, the effect of having all their care provided is that they become unable to care for themselves. They are less in control than the competent people who care for them. If their care-support system—their spouse, their plumber, their secretary—suddenly short circuits or is taken away, they're helpless. They are not only unable to provide care for others, they haven't the skills to help themselves. They are incapacitated in the caring department. It has also been shown that people who take caring for granted, or have their caring contracted for, lose their ability to express appreciation or to feel empathy for their caretakers. They lose their ability to see spontaneous rewards for caring because they are blinded by the reward system.

The issue of fairness needs further discussion before we leave the subject of overconsumption. A good deal of overconsumption is a matter of trying to get away with doing less than one's share in a given situation or relationship. It's an all-too-human testing of one's power or of the other's devotion. But the fairness doctrine as pertains to caring balance involves accepting responsibility at every level, recognizing the just-as-important-as-I value of those one cares about. *It means doing one's share of the caring.* That includes doing one's share of the day-to-day chores, of the drudgework, shouldering willingly one's responsibilities in the life one shares with each cared-for other. Expectations of privilege, of holding the position of caree without some equitable exchange, is a low and insidious form of carelessness, often ill-covered by showy acts of concern. The gap between the pretense of care and action is often the source of alienation, anger, and eventual carelessness and burnout that sabotage the Caring Network.

Fair caring doesn't happen automatically. It's all too easy to take advantage of one's power or privilege, or even money, and let others shoulder the burden of caring. It's easy to take up the slack for one you care about, to make excuses for why they shouldn't have to do their part.

There are lots of insidious ways to get out of doing one's share of the caring. Some people scream and get so angry that it's unpleasant to make demands on them. Some people sulk and act sullen and unhappy. Others make false accusations or claim to be too busy, or incapable. "I don't know how to make the bed."

Getting rid of such crazymaking behavior[14] is a prerequisite to equitable caring. In a way, it boils down to common courtesy: if we treat others as our equals and deserving of the same respect and the same treatment we want, we're bound to take our fair share of the responsibility of caring.

"I used every ploy in the world to avoid doing the things I didn't want to do at our house. But Mom stuck to her guns." Ken is sixteen, and he and his fourteen-year-old sister Beth have lived in an apartment in Los Angeles since his parents' divorce last year.

"When Dad was around, I never had to do anything. All of a sudden Mom was after me to help with the laundry and set the table and pick Beth up from guitar lessons. I tried ignoring her when she'd ask for something. Or I'd pretend to forget. Or I'd make fun of her clothes, even accuse her of being a ball breaker, which I knew made her feel bad. Even doing a terrible job on the laundry didn't get me out of it. What happened is that Mom and Beth just 'cut off services,' as they put it. No meals. No wake up call. No ride to school. No smiles. It was a very simple lesson. Of course I was furious at first, but the truth is that even though I often hate doing the chores, I feel relieved in a way. I knew I was getting away with murder, and I knew that they were doing more than I—though I didn't see how much. Beth is much less resentful of me, and Mom and I are getting along better than ever. I think she actually loves me more than she used to."

A Time for Caring

UNDERCONSUMPTION

While for some people caring goes down smooth as honey, others find it hard to swallow. It sticks in the throat. For some people it is precisely because it is supposed to feel good, because care is given as a sign of love and esteem, that it is hard to digest. Feeling unworthy of care, they are suspicious of what's offered. Fearful of rejection, they hesitate to ask for what they need. They experience care consuming as hazardous.

Others are unable to accept care because their role prohibits it. Locked into a strict code of behavior, they persist in thinking that allowing others to care for them is a sign of weakness. And in so doing they deprive not only themselves of good feelings and valuable support, they deprive others of the pleasures of caring for them.

Liz's story illustrates the frustration and the ultimate unworkability of a relationship with someone who can't accept care:

"It sounds looney to say that I split up with my husband because he was too good to me, but that's what happened. On the face of it Carl seems too good to be true—good-looking, funny, intelligent, and always willing to help out. When I met him, I was just moving to a new apartment/office, just starting my own business. From the beginning he helped me in every way he could. And I mean every way—painting, moving furniture, finding great buys in secondhand stores and lugging them up three flights of stairs, wiring, plumbing. He'd make phone calls, help me update my portfolio, tout me for new business; he even learned to do layouts and paste-ups. He was wonderful, and I was happy to be married to him.

"What I soon realized, however, was that it was nearly impossible for me to help him. He was very closemouthed about his own business and his own problems. He'd help out with my new venture while he neglected his own work. He'd buy me a new blouse or some drawing pens and find something for himself at a thrift shop or literally pick it from the garbage. If I bought him something, he'd seem to like it, but he'd never wear it. He'd find every excuse for not letting me help him out with his work or turn aside my questions and offers. He was unable to show care for himself, for he had a low opinion of himself in spite of his many good qualities, in spite of the fact that he was extremely well-liked. It drove me crazy, because of course there are all too many people willing to take advantage of someone like Carl. He was always doing outrageous favors for people, working for nothing. Nothing could dissuade him, and I hated watching him be exploited. People don't believe it when I say that our marriage broke up because he wouldn't let me do anything for him, but it's true. While I loved all the care and attentions, it eventually was very frustrating to me that there was nothing I could offer Carl. The give-and-take in our relationship was too lopsided and ironically it was I who was upset because I couldn't give. It was very hard to split up over such a seemingly unreasonable complaint. Carl wouldn't quite believe it. He didn't say so, but I'm sure he felt he'd done everything for me. And he had. That was the whole point."

Still others are poor care consumers because they fear loss of control or helplessness and combat this fear with a posture of self-reliance.

Earl had always considered himself a pretty healthy consumer of care until he had his heart attack.

"I never had a bit of trouble about being taken care of," he says. "I was a pretty typical example of a man well attended to by his wife and family, catered to at work by secretaries and underlings, deferred to in the community. I lapped it up with never a qualm. Then when I had my heart attack I really was helpless and really needed care. I was terrified of being cared for, horrified to be in a helpless role. My reaction was to fight the helplessness in every way I knew how—to argue with the doctors, question my medication, try to do things I was too weak to do, insist that I didn't need my family's attentions (for once!). I think there were two reasons for my behavior. First, I realize that in all other situations I was very much in control of the caring provided for me. I called the shots, asking for what I wanted, establishing a certain level of expected care. I prided myself on the powerful devotion I inspired. Second, I think unconsciously there was something very seductive about being helpless—I could retire early, collect disability; I wouldn't have to make decisions, everything would be done for me. I found it frightening to consider this; it made me worse. I felt left out of life, a nonparticipant. Yet I can see how in our passive, medically dominated culture, it's easy to fall into this trap. It's a chance to get something for nothing."

Many people, of course, are underconsumers of care not by choice but because they can't get the care they need. They are usually poor in self-care. They choose friends and lovers incapable of providing care. They lack the self-esteem necessary to attract care or to ask for it. Perhaps they're unskilled at communicating their need. Whatever the reason, the underconsumption of care is as unhealthy as overindulging. Undernourished people eventually run out of energy to care for others.

PROVIDING CARE

It is, of course, the providing of care that ultimately proves the most rewarding. Providing care is where the action is. Here lie the excitement, the dynamism, the real power. Along this route lies the potential for growth and self-realization. Providing care is a magnet for attracting care.

Unfortunately, care providing is prey to as many excesses and misdirections as care consuming, and many people tend to lose their balance and go overboard in this area as well.

OVERCARING

Voracious care consumers are not the only villains. People who overdo their caring do just as much damage to themselves and to those they profess to care for. Sometimes overcaring results from a misguided sense of duty or lack of perspective on the overall caring balance. Many well-intentioned people want to do everything for those they love. They minister uncomplainingly to every need, anticipate every wish, jump to every command. Those they care for end up dependent on the care provider, unable to provide for themselves, and without the skills and inclination to care for others. The overcarer steals their initiative, removes all need for action.

Insecurity may be behind overcaring. People who feel they have little to offer to others, offer themselves as slaves or doormats. They try to make themselves acceptable or indispensable; they buy love and favor with caring services. But while the overzealous care provider is often motivated by a desire for love and devotion and appreciation from his beneficiaries, what he often gets instead is guilt and resentment. The receiver of such care feels overwhelmed and at a loss to reciprocate; he's angry that he should feel grateful, guilty that he doesn't.

Power is another motive for overzealous care. Many such seemingly self-sacrificing carers want to dominate and direct those around them, and do so by seducing them with lavish care and attention, by being the provider of everything. In being all-giving, they are all-controlling. Often the power-driven overcarer is uncomfortable and threatened when others try to help themselves or reject their care. They collect indebtedness and like to see the coffers full. These people use caring the way others use wealth or celebrity.

Overcarers, not surprisingly, are often underconsumers of care as well. It's hard to do anything for them, it undermines their control and evens up the score too much. Their strength, though it rests on a shaky foundation, lies in their lopsided control.

"Everyone refers to my wife Emma as an earth mother," says Nick.

"She takes everyone under her wing—me and the kids, their friends, sundry relatives, a succession of cleaning ladies, lost souls, stray dogs. She provides food, shelter, comfort, and advice round the clock. In some ways it's wonderful. If she takes on your case, you're home free for life—you never have to lift a finger, everything you say or do is wonderful.

"Up to a point there's a great benefit to this kind of concern and approval. But I've also seen the downside of it. While it's okay of course for me to be spoiled rotten, it drives me nuts that the kids are so lazy; they take this care for granted. As they get older it's having a very bad influence on them. They're very lazy about school and try and get by with the least possible effort. And they wonder why everyone doesn't think they're as wonderful as Mom does. My son's been living on his own for two years, but you'd never know it. He comes home for meals whenever he feels like it, just plops down, as usual, to be waited on, and he brings his laundry along for Mom, who incidentally painted his apartment for him a couple months ago. When Emma says nothing's too much for her family, she means it.

"But she's very sensitive about having her caring appreciated. She expects thanks and gratefulness for her efforts—which as I say are considerable and well-meaning and meant as a show of love. The one way to alienate Emma is to reject her ministrations or fail to show proper appreciation. She'll dump you like a hot potato. In fact, that's how Emma keeps from completely exhausting herself, I think. She chooses exactly who she'll care for and how; she has no qualms about excluding those she finds wanting. She doesn't give them a thought."

Overcaring creates false assumptions and expectations about caring. The beneficiaries of such caring come to think that they must be pretty special to be able to inspire such care without having to provide care in return. Unprepared for balanced, healthy caring, they rebel against losing their special position. And once this false self-image is established, it's hard to change.

"My ex-husband Chad turned into a spoiled, insufferable, overconfident jerk, and I'm afraid I made a major contribution to the transformation," says Nancy.

"Not that there wasn't plenty of raw material to work with or that his mother didn't get him off to a good start. I have a tendency to overindulge people anyway, to always find their good points. I'm almost incapable of criticizing. I'd tell a white lie rather than say something bad. Anyway, I was mad about Chad, and he seemed to need a good bit of reassurance about everything—his looks, his intelligence, his clothes, his job, his opinions. I was only too glad to give it to him, full of praise at everything he did, laughing at every joke, going out of my way to find special things about him. I showed my love by doing everything for him, even shopping for his clothes and entertaining his family. And I never made any demands on him, always insisting that I could take care of everything.

"Well, I created a monster. It was bad enough that he would

ask me to do anything at any time without any thought or concern about the effort involved or my own time. And slowly he forgot even to say thank you, taking it all for granted. What was really awful was that he got such a swelled head that he really did think he was Mr. Wonderful. His every opinion became gospel, every word out of his mouth a pearl to be savored and commented on, his tastes unassailable. Naturally I eventually rebelled and found his posturing and his demands impossible, though I realize that I was as responsible as he for what happened."

Overcarers are as dangerous to themselves as they are to others. Eventually they become exhausted by their own efforts. They haven't adequate caring income to offset their caring expenditures.

Overcarers are easy prey for those who would exploit them. They attract those who would gladly consume as much care as is offered; the more the better. Overcarers go hand in glove with overconsumers. They are drawn to the helpless people who are bottomless wells of needs and demands. It's a fatal match.

Overcarers become burned out, apathetic, unable to provide the high level of care they're accustomed to providing. This is not because they're unhappy with what they're doing. Burnout is most common among mothers, teachers, nurses, psychotherapists, and medical professionals—often the most dedicated of them. Sometimes it is exactly their devotion and concern that leads them to overextend themselves. Mothers who expend their energies on young children while getting little in return, teachers who lead unresponsive classes and haven't a supportive family at home, doctors with unappreciative, complaining patients, have no way of balancing their caring output. Sometimes it is a matter of skills. They are undertrained for the intense and sophisticated level of care they are called upon to provide. Eventually they fizzle out or become hardened and less concerned as a measure of self-defense. Overcarers who don't learn to balance out their caring eventually cross over a boundary beyond which they either leave or are abandoned by their beneficiaries, for it is an intolerable situation. The overcarer either tunes out emotionally or falls apart physically or suddenly rebels. Meanwhile the beneficiary, overwhelmed by such stifling care, may decide to leave.

Will's story is a stunning parable of the perils of unbalanced caring relationships. Will met Irene twenty years ago when he was an enthusiastic and idealistic young counselor and advisor at a pioneering drug rehabilitation center in Michigan. He was thirty, Irene was beautiful and twenty-one. She had been a heroin addict for six years. Will was completely taken with Irene—she was spunky and fresh and irreverent and seemed to have a great drive to rise above an unspeakable childhood. Will was fascinated by this woman so different from the conventional women he grew up with. Devoted and helpful by nature, he welcomed the opportunity to help Irene change her life. He was sure he could do it. Irene fell hard for the White Knight who came to rescue her. So they married.

They have been married about twenty years and have an eighteen-year-old daughter. It has been an often troubled marriage. Now all of a sudden Irene has taken to staying out all night, drinking and dancing, neglecting her daughter. Will suspects she is on drugs again. It doesn't look like their marriage will survive this latest upheaval.

"Several people tried to dissuade me from marrying Irene, and I thought they were all jealous meddlers. Now they're pressing me to get out of this awful marriage. Yet I keep resisting and hoping that things will straighten up again. I keep trying to make excuses, but I've begun to see how impossible our situation is. When Irene and I were first married, she couldn't have been more loving and attentive. She was practically a geisha, fondling me and fixing special meals, telling me how much she loved me and how happy she was that I'd rescued her from the drug center. I was thrilled about having a child, ecstatic when our daughter was born. But the moment she was born my wife transferred her affection to our child and seemed to cut off all feelings for me. Our sexual relationship practically came to an end, except for a kind of grudging service. I think now that Irene knew I would stick by her because she took care of our daughter, and she knew that our child meant everything to me. Also I think she had me figured by then for a sucker; she knew I would go on caring for her and trying to help her, for of course that's exactly what I did.

"Irene has no education and in ways was very ignorant about how the world worked, though she's clever and learned fast. Over the years I've spent a good deal of time trying to help her launch an acting career, or to study a new profession, or get a job . . . none of which has worked. And she's always put pressure on me about these things and made me feel responsible, as if only I can help. And I do like to help. It's been a constant job to keep her feeling healthy and good about herself, not to let her feel worthless or despondent. Irene has always needed lots of presents and clothes and fancy furniture to keep her happy and secure—though none of these things appeal to me, and I have a hard time earning enough money to pay for them.

"This whole thing sounds crazy, doesn't it? All these years I've been taking care of her and she's been taking everything, making demands and giving little in return. I'm so used to giving that it's even hard for me to get angry about it when others point it out. But I'm coming to realize that our marriage is really a no-win situation. There is no possibility of equality, no likelihood of an equitable give and take, because Irene has nothing to give. She has no history of caring in her family; she hardly knows how to strike a fair balance.

"The truth is that she doesn't have much to offer a relationship, and this insecurity is probably what makes her the way she is. She knew I'd stay with her if she took good care of our daughter, and she did. I think now that our girl is grown and will be leaving soon, she feels I have no reason for putting up with her anymore, so she's acting out and running around so that that can be my excuse for leaving rather than her inability to hold up her half of an equal relationship. Now that I look back, I can't believe that it's gone on this long, that I never made demands, never had expectations. In my way, I had all the power and control; she's angry now because I had to always help her, always came to the rescue."

Many people have the impulse to provide the kind of Pygmalion caring that characterizes Will's marriage. Every lover, every mother, every therapist—in fact, all people of good will—have in some measure a Pygmalion complex. They want to guide those they love, to help them realize their potential, to avoid pitfalls. The problem arises when people try to fulfill their own images and dreams rather than to bring out their protégé's intrinsic nature or stated goals. No matter what success or improvement results from the mentor's efforts, the protégé is resentful or grateful according to whether or not the mentor is pursuing a course in accordance with his own dream or the mentor's wishes and abilities. In cases like Will's the situation is complicated by the fact that he chose to expend his energies on someone incapable of living up to his expectations.

UNDERCARING

An undercarer, as we have seen, is often the flip side of an overconsumer of care. This is the person who offers very little in the way of care. For any number of reasons undercarers somehow feel it isn't necessary to do their share. And they may try any number of things to avoid doing this share. They don't acquire caring skills and use their ignorance or helplessness as an excuse. They latch on to others who are only too happy to do their share or who have no expectations of caring for themselves. Undercarers usually leave many people out in the caring cold. They are a weak link in the Caring Network.

ESTABLISHING AND MAINTAINING A CARING BALANCE

It is possible to monitor our caring to be sure it doesn't get too lopsided. By being watchful we can right the situation before we shift too far in either direction. Alert to imbalances in each relationship and in each arena of our lives, we can fill in the gaps as they arise, before the holes get too large and require major repairs. Most people are weighted to one side of the scale or the other and need to shift their energies and attentions to where there is a deficiency.

Overcarers find it hard to comprehend that getting care is just as important as giving it. Those who overdo it in the care-providing department need to learn to consume care. What they must do is train themselves to ease up, to give up some of their control, to allow themselves to be helped and attended to. They need to learn to ask for care and, if necessary, to fight for it. They perhaps need to be choosier about those they care for and avoid those who would take advantage of their all too willing nature. They must learn to set limits on what they will do for others and be careful about how much time and energy they devote to difficult and toxic people. They have to be more discriminating about catering to others and becoming their victims. They must take responsibility for letting others know when they've overstepped their limits, must retrain others to moderate their demands and to provide care themselves. And the poor care consumer often needs to pay more attention to self-care.

"I have a friend who visits me about twice a year for a week at a stretch," says Helene.

"He is wonderful company—lively and interesting—and he is the only person I know who likes to explore New York with me, so we really do the town when he's here. The only problem is that he's rather spoiled and demanding, and I tend to go along with his demands without thinking. Then toward the end of his visit I find myself resentful and tired. I feel like I've been had. I like to be a helpful hostess, but I also like to feel that what I do isn't just expected service. This time when Art visited I had worked out a whole retraining program. When he would ask for something, I didn't just knuckle under, I enlisted his help and participation, often designed to make his demands easier to fulfill and to help him recognize what was involved in fulfilling his request. For example, rather than just washing and ironing his laundry and having him find it neatly returned to the closet—as he was inclined to expect!—I had him sort it out and put it in the washer. Later I asked him to transfer it to the dryer, then take it out and set up the ironing board, still later return the clothes to the closet. I still did most of the work, but since he helped and was appreciative, I didn't mind. What he doesn't know is that next time *he's* going to do the laundry. And maybe the time after that I'll have him doing *my* laundry. Also, incidentally, I asked several small favors of Art during this visit—to bring me a cup of tea, to make a phone call about a movie, to pick up a quart of milk. Just small things, but a guy like Art gives the impression—carefully cultivated, I'm sure—that he isn't available, or will be difficult, if he's asked to do something. And in fact, when a request is made, he's miffed. But he's learning, especially since he knows I'm on to his tricks."

A Time for Caring

Overconsumers of care need to learn to provide it. They need to understand the power and reward of being helpful and compassionate, and to see the false sense of power and the hidden helplessness of always being the consumer. It is often incumbent upon those who have been provided their care to take an active part in their retraining.

Here is John's story of his caring reeducation.

"I was dragged kicking and screaming into showing more care for others, as well as being more self-sufficient and appreciative of others' care. I resisted fiercely. After all, I know I had it good. I was practically a sultan in the midst of my adoring family, and even among my colleagues. Who'd want to give up such privilege? It wasn't so much that my family forced me to change, although I must admit I could sometimes sense their resentment—and knew on some level that their adoration was very much mixed with fear of upsetting or angering me. I used that fear to encourage the high level of care I got. What made me change, in addition to my growing sensitivity to the undercurrents of resentment, was the fact that it became harder and harder to deny that what I was doing was selfish and wrong. There came a point when I could no longer deny to myself that I was getting away with murder. It was a big change for me. I was brought up in a wealthy aristocratic European family in which being cared for was a sign of status. The extent and quality of one's care indicated importance. Complaining about the servants was a topic of everyday conversation, like the weather. Times of course have changed, but I for a long time saw no reason to give up a good thing.

"Well, even though a part of me wanted to change, I was not (am still not) an easy convert. I still try to get away with things, still am tempted to extract care as a sign of my power or others' devotion. And of course I'm not very good at doing some of these new things. I feel clumsy and then I get frustrated and angry. I'm sure it's all my wife can do sometimes to keep from laughing. The scary thing is that I realized how helpless I was. In the last couple years I've learned a lot—mostly the kind of thing that any fifteen-year-old can do. Mostly things like fixing my own breakfast, making plane and hotel reservations, planning a dinner party, balancing a checkbook, buying a suit, operating the dishwasher. Alice has been training me to understand and appreciate what's involved in having the house running smoothly. She'll point out the flower arrangement or the repaired wallpaper or the six loads of laundry. She makes it impossible for me to take these things for granted or to ignore the fact that someone has to do them.

"The most interesting aspect of my reformation is that I get tremendous pleasure out of doing things for myself and for others, in spite of my resistance. I really enjoy fixing breakfast myself, actually find pleasure in preparing food and cleaning up. Now I shop for my own clothes and go to the dry cleaners and the stationers. I choose gifts for my family instead of having Alice take care of it. I still feel like a pasha, but now it's because I feel big about giving gifts instead of receiving them."

It is important to view caring excesses sympathetically if change is to be effected. It is important to allow the overconsumer time, and to have patience while he learns new skills and grasps the pleasures of providing care. Too, the smothering ministrations of the overprovider are often well meant and are especially needing of patience and understanding during transition.

But it is only when crazymaking behavior is minimized that a caring balance can be achieved.

10

Paying Attention:
GATHERING INFORMATION FOR CARING

Probably the most important requisite of Quality Caring is being tuned in to the world around us. Many people walk the streets with their heads down, their eyes averted, lost in their own thoughts. They sit mesmerized in front of the television, their sensory systems all but shut down. Lacking time for, or interest in, their surroundings, they make snap judgments about what they see at first glance, form opinions about what they hear after just a few words. Lacking sensitive powers of observation, their judgments are often wrong. Uninterested in further investigation, their misjudgments stick.

Yet careful observation and attentiveness have broad application to caring. Paying attention gives us information to help us deal with the world, allows us to have a considered and consistent approach to our caring actions. With adequate information at hand, we're in a position to be selective, to make judgments and allocate our caring energies properly.

Caring people pay attention to what goes on around them. They want to know what people are like. They want to understand how they think and act and feel. They care to see how people behave, what they do, their way of being in the world.

Contrary to the old cliché, familiarity does not breed contempt, unless a particular relationship was based to begin with on images that must eventually fail under closer scrutiny. On the contrary, the person who with attention and practice becomes a student of human nature usually develops an enlarged capacity for concern and tolerance, a better view of his fellow man. It is isolation and lack of social and observational skills that breed fear, and thus hatred, suspicion, and contempt.

Every experience the authors have had with group therapy bears this out. As group members become closer and learn to trust each other, they are able to observe and be reassured that their secrets and sensitivities are safe with others. As they see that their vulnerability is not violated the fear and hostility that they often start out with dissipates, and they are freed to feel love and caring for their fellow group members (and, by extension, for those outside the group).

Sensitivity to people and situations helps us to be selective about whom we care for and what we do. We're able to pick and choose among the many candidates for our attention. We develop criteria for *careworthiness* and are less likely to waste our energy in the wrong places. As our newfound awareness involves us deeper with others, it also protects us from falling prey to exploiters or hopeless causes.

Finally, one of the best arguments for sharpening one's powers of observations is the pure pleasure of people-watching. Watching how others behave, seeing the diversity of people's looks, styles of dress, ways of reaction, is an endless source of entertainment. People-watching is diverting, heartening, surprising, uplifting, frightening, thrilling. It can make you laugh (or cry) out loud.

THE STAGES OF AWARENESS

There are three levels to building one's powers of observation:

PAYING ATTENTION TO PAYING ATTENTION

Many people pay attention as a matter of course. They may not even realize that this shows inherent caring for their fellow beings. But people who aren't used to being observers find it hard to do at first. They are easily distracted, feel clumsy, or lose interest quickly. They don't know what to look for or how to listen; they are not amused. As with learning a language or playing tennis, it's confusing and not even entertaining until a certain level of basic competence has been reached.

Becoming a good observer requires taking in lots of new information, concentrating, focusing in on people. It means being alert and watchful, and it is time-consuming. At first we have to force ourselves to study. We must keep reminding ourselves to pay attention and purposely set aside time to do so. A good way to do this is to give ourselves little tasks and follow them up with feedback about what we observed. "I'm going to watch that man in the black bowler walking in front of me." "When Fred shows me his new carpentry project, I'm going to try to learn something." "I'm going to look out the window all the way downtown on the bus." "I'm going to try to remember what my third-grade teacher was like."

Ask yourself questions as you go. If you've set yourself the task of tuning in to the train ride on the way to work, ask: How many stops does the train make? Where do most people get on? What does the station look like? Is there a parking lot next door? Which is the busiest station? What kind of ads are up around the station? What color is the seat upholstery in the train? Do most of the people seem to be going to work? Are most of the men in suits? Or work clothes? Reading newspapers? Or books? What books? Are there as many women on the train? What are some of the sights the train passes? The number of possible questions is endless.

Report to yourself on the results of your observations. For example, after a coworker has spent five minutes in your office, take a minute to see what you've learned: "Ken was wearing his usual chino pants and crew neck and loafers, but the sweater was red—unusual color for him. He was tan, probably was running this weekend. He didn't laugh much at the joke I told him, but roared at the story of my lost laundry ticket. I noticed his habit of crossing and uncrossing his legs—he's otherwise so cool. He's left-handed, hardly ever blinks, moves slowly and deliberately, doesn't gesture much when he talks." Again, the number of things to notice is endless.

IMPROVING THE QUALITY OF OUR OBSERVATIONS

We soon learn that watching other people and the world around us is much less boring than we thought it might be. We begin to appreciate the variety of human nature, to differentiate, and to feel more confident about our knowledge of others, less afraid and defensive. Passivity gives way to participation and involvement. And the more we pay attention, the better we get at it, the more natural it becomes.

As our perceptions sharpen, one inevitable result is that we become very sensitive not only to appearances but also to the thoughts and feelings behind them. We pick up nonverbal messages, hidden signals, body language. We become more acutely aware of the diversity of people and things around us. We suddenly have a great deal of information at our disposal with which to respond more specifically to whatever is fed in. We become not only confident but fascinated by what once seemed a dull existence. Everyday life takes on new interest.

Nothing more effectively overcomes imaging and compartmentalizing people than really paying attention to them. Labeling is only possible under conditions of ignorance or when we're incapable of making distinctions. When we're tuned in to nuances of feelings, small gestures, a tone of voice, a manner of dress or style or response, we can no longer generalize about people. We see them as a whole, we can no longer dismiss big chunks that we don't want to deal with.

At the highest level, skills of observation are manifested in a kind of resonance. Like a finely tuned instrument, we become capable of receiving and reproducing a broad spectrum of feeling and tone. We pick up everything that radiates from others, look for the essence of the people we're in contact with.

USING OBSERVATIONS TO INFORM ACTIONS

Eventually this finely honed awareness becomes a way to deepen caring actions. We become aware of the ways of those in our Caring Circle. We know what pleases or hurts them. We know their insecurities and strengths. We know where we fit in—what we must provide and consume from each other. Aware of the broad possibilities for caring behavior, we are supremely capable of chosing the right thing at the right time, that which makes sense.

A *Time for Caring*

ACCURATE CARING

As we become attuned to the needs and temperaments of those we care for, it becomes easier to know what kind of care is most useful and effective. And as we become attuned to our own caring ways, we learn what kind of caring we're comfortable providing, what kind we're comfortable consuming. We have the information we need to allocate our caring energies and skills efficiently. We're able to care appropriately and choose a specific action or gesture for each situation. As the song goes, we "know when to hold 'em and know when to fold 'em." Active carers are adept at picking up the signals and information needed to home in on a problem and properly provide the care that's called for. Their caring is on target.

"I used to get furious when my wife Lola would get into one of her 'moods,' " Jerry recalls.

"I never knew what she wanted or what would help, and she always insisted that there was nothing I could do. The way I finally figured out what to do was I started watching Lola more closely when she was feeling down, tried to listen more carefully to what she was saying. What I learned was that when Lola's upset she doesn't want me to leave her alone—which I thought she wanted. She doesn't want me to make jokes or try to cheer her up particularly. She just likes me to be there—to sit in the kitchen and help her fold the laundry or keep her company while she's taking a bath or watch TV with her. She likes me to talk with her a bit about what's going on with me, nothing serious. It's gotten so I am very aware of her moods and can see just how I can help her. It's so simple, and I have a sense of contributing something important. My antennae are very sensitive these days.

"I'm also more aware of what the kids need. With my youngest son, Johnny, I always felt I was doing the wrong thing, and I was—always trying to get him to talk to me about his problems, getting angry when he wouldn't respond. Well, it doesn't work with Johnny. What he wants is for me to go for a walk with him, or a drive, or play catch—by himself, without his older brother. And I've learned that if *I* do the talking, tell him what's worrying me, he eventually opens up in return.

"One thing about myself I've learned is that I get very upset if I don't understand what to do or if demands are made on me that I'm not prepared to meet—or don't know how to meet. As time passes I become more and more aware of what kind of caring makes me feel good, and what I still need to learn. For example, Johnny can bring his friends home every day of the week and they can hang around and I'll join them if they want to play basketball. But I hate school meetings and all these activities they try to get me involved in. Johnny's always trying to get me to chaperon school trips or coach at school. I've told him it's one of those things I just hate to do."

Herman has a story that illustrates the impact of a simple but very specific caring act that resulted from careful observation.

"The other day I was having dinner with a buddy in a local restaurant, a place where I go frequently. As usual I dumped out my pile of about a dozen vitamin pills on the tablecloth to take with my meal. The waitress took our order, poured water in our glasses; about two minutes later she came back with a straw—'to make it easier for you to take your vitamins,' she said. Well, it was no big deal, but I've taken my vitamins there dozens of times with ice water, filtering it through my teeth so I wouldn't swallow the cubes. She'd not only noticed, but she knew what to do about it. It may sound sappy, but I was impressed, and I felt like she went out of her way to provide special care."

Pam's story shows another aspect of how consciousness of other's quirks and habits help inform caring acts.

"Gene and I lead a very unregulated life. We both freelance and both of us are temperamentally unsuited to rigid schedules or overplanning. But last spring when my brother and sister-in-law visited from Belgium, I knew I'd have to make some changes while they were here. I love my brother Paul, but we're very different. He's very orderly. He likes to know exactly what's planned and where we're going and who will be there and what's to eat. And as he get older he gets more locked into his habits. Last time they visited I wasn't cued in to this, and in a fervor of being a good hostess, enthusiastic about introducing him to our fair city, I just about drove him crazy with a round of little restaurants we like and art galleries and shopping—all extemporaneous. About halfway through his visit I realized he was nervous and on edge, though he was trying to enjoy himself. I felt upset and unappreciated and teased him for his lack of spontaneity. This time when he visited I adapted myself to his behavior. We did things on a schedule and got up at the same time each day. I was very careful to keep him up-to-date on all plans. They had a wonderful time, and I felt like I'd been a great hostess. It was kind of interesting to change my tempo and be *like* him."

11

Communication:
KEEPING IN TOUCH

We can learn a great deal from what someone is wearing or how they live, from their job or their nervous habit or manner of speech. We can make assumptions about what people are like or how they think or what they want or why they do what they do. But it is not in fact possible to read their minds. Sooner or later direct contact must be made. We have to check out what we've observed to see if it's accurate. We must, in other words, communicate.

Like paying attention, communication itself is a way of caring. When people talk to each other, they include rather than exclude. They imply by the act of making contact that they are interested in what the other has to say, interested in telling the other what's on their mind.

Strangely, in this era of mass communication the personal communication skills of many people are not very highly developed. The art of good conversation or of letter writing today has practically the status of a bygone folk art, near extinction. Today many people are better receptors than transmitters. The media convey the messages, and so pervasive are those messages that everyday conversation tends to seek the level of television dialogue, pop culture clichés, and ad copy.

In many people the ability to communicate is so atrophied or the fear of misunderstanding so great that their communications are sparse and indirect. The result is the " 'Where did you go?' 'Out.' 'What did you do?' 'Nothing.' " style of communication. Many communicate more with silence and shrugs and innuendo

A Time for Caring 91

than with words. Or their words are loaded with hidden meanings and dangerous traps. Caring gets lost in the communication gap.

Caring communication is nothing more than a direct and continual exchange of relevant information. It doesn't require facility with words or the ability to tell an amusing story. Caring people just make it a point to stay in touch with those in their Caring Network, near and far. They keep each other up-to-date; they exchange ideas; they discharge what's on their mind. They disseminate information that helps others to know and understand them and that enriches their association. They air their joys and hurts; they make demands and answer questions. They maintain their connections in good working order. And they do these things as directly as possible, trying as well as they can to avoid the loaded silences and mixed messages and unproductive hostile outbursts that miscommunicate.

There are many ways of communicating a sense of caring:

STANDING BY

At its basic level, this means literally being physically present for those one cares for: in the same room, around the house, in the next office, cuddled up in bed. Simple as it seems, if often requires considerable effort and readjustment for many people. They prefer to be alone, not to have to contend with others—with their presence, their problems, their conversation, demands, feelings. They are uncomfortable with small talk (or don't know how to make it), uncomfortable just "hanging around."

Edwin is a good, if extreme, example of someone whose ability to be with others is very limited. Edwin is a "hacker," a member of a growing subculture of people whose greatest pleasure is playing around with computers. His story sounds like an apocryphal one about the dangers of an alienated, highly technological society; unfortunately, it is true. The problem of Edwin and others like him is that they get more and more hooked on computers, using the terminals to set up problems and play games during the wee hours when they're not in use. So involved did Edwin become that he became very uninterested in anything but the keyboard and screen. He barely spoke to anyone outside his circle of fellow hackers. He was finally pushed into therapy by his brother. "I was probably a prime candidate for computer addiction," Edwin says.

"I'd always been shy and took refuge from people in fairly esoteric hobbies and books. The computer thing involved me and took me away from thinking about anything else—these games can literally fill up your mind. Also, I'm quite a whiz, so I had a bit of status among my fellow hackers. Until I was in therapy I had no perspective on how detached I'd become; whenever I'd start to question my life, I'd stamp out the doubt immediately. When I first started trying to change, it was very difficult. I had to set a schedule, continually cutting down on my computer time. It seemed ridiculous. I still need 'props' to help me deal with others. Now I'm involved with a chess and checker club near me—it sounds pretty cerebral, I know, but compared to the midnight hacking it's very social. I'm slowly learning how to be with people—I like it."

Others have a hard time standing by, because they're bored, self-conscious, or wrapped up in their own thoughts. Mom doesn't want to listen to Jimmy's boring story about the geography test. Dad doesn't want to have to play with the kids after a day at the office. Jack doesn't want to sit around the house all evening while Anne studies for her exams. Brad would rather just send a card than visit Jim in the hospital. Anne wants to go to bed early and read; she hasn't the patience to keep Tom company while he finishes repairing the dining room table.

Don't underestimate the importance of such simple acts. Being there is one of the simplest and most effective of caring ways. It is one of the most powerful ways of affirming attachment to others. A Caring Activist knows when it's important to take the time to be with those he cares about, even if he must overcome feelings of discomfort or forgo time from private pursuits or expect to be bored.

When Carl was in the hospital recovering from multiple broken bones, he received ample cards and flowers, even telegrams. But they did little to pass the time, and he was lonely. Even phone calls didn't fill the bill. Then a friend whom he hadn't thought of

A Time for Caring

as particularly close up until that time took to dropping by after work every day or so.

"At first we didn't have too much to talk about. We'd have coffee, he'd report on the outside world, I'd complain about the doctors. Sometimes we'd run out of things to say and we'd pass the time just watching TV. As time went by, of course, we loosened up and became more at home with each other. Now we're pretty good friends. But it wouldn't have mattered. Just his dropping by was a lifesaver to me. His stock went up 1000 percent in my eyes. I'd do anything for him now."

An interesting sidelight to Carl's story is that his visitor had been in the hospital himself a couple of years earlier. Chances are he knew the importance of visitors; he knew the best and most effective way to care was to visit.

Spending time together is an important part of maintaining relationships in good working order. Friends, families, even communities, define themselves partially by the simple fact that they spend time in the same place.

Elly has a friend, another busy mother like herself with small children. They solve their problem of never having time to see each other by doing their laundry together once a week. Elly takes her small son over to Roberta's house and does most of her week's washing and ironing while Roberta does hers. "Sometimes we talk the whole time," Elena reports, "but sometimes we're very rushed or the kids keep us busy, or we're very tired, so we don't get a chance to say much. But I don't care, it's just nice to see Roberta, to *look* at her and know we're still in touch, still there for each other."

KEEPING CURRENT

Maintenance is a big part of caring relationships. Most people today lead very busy lives just trying to eat, sleep, work, clean house, go to the movies, read the paper, watch the news, shop for groceries, practice the guitar, do the laundry, go to the PTA meeting, the dentist, fill up the car, and so forth. The hectic pace and the endless possibilities for filling up one's time make it hard to find time to keep up-to-date with friends, family, mates, lovers, community; so many things intervene and vie for attention.

Commitment and application are necessary to keeping current. It means finding time to talk and exchange information about each other's doings and feelings. It requires not letting time pass or being too busy to keep the lines of communication open. It means letting those we care about know what is on our minds as things come up, not letting things fester. The danger of noncommunication, even about seemingly nonessential things, is that people quickly become strangers to each other. They don't have information on how the others spend their time, what they think, what their current worries or joys are. They tend to keep hurts and joys stored in a gunnysack rather than to confront problems as they arise; eventually their stored resentments explode without warning.

Keeping current involves thinking of oneself as a local newspaper reporting the events and feelings in one's life, a limited-circulation newspaper to be read by those one cares about and those who want to keep informed about the "local" state of affairs.

It does not need to be a very serious newspaper. Most people enjoy simple chitchat, not for the information conveyed but for the fact that it creates a sense of closeness, reinforces contact. The content is an incidental reporting of observations and feelings: what happened today, what was in the news, who telephoned or visited, an idea for a vacation, a joke heard in the office. Chitchat develops the habit of communication.

Some people have great difficulty making small talk; they feel their thoughts and observations are unimportant. Others claim to be above it. But our lives are made up of small details, less-than-earthshaking acts and observations. The way we learn about others and let others know us is by sharing without editing too much. When we filter our words to say only the important things, or what we think others will be interested in, or what will impress them, we're building walls rather than bridges. To call it idle chatter is to underestimate the power of small talk to make caring contact.

When Marianne first moved to Santa Monica she knew no one and was both wary and shy of her new neighborhood. She and her family had transferred from a much simpler town in Idaho. Sus-

A Time for Caring

picious and uncomfortable with strangers, she wasn't making friends and didn't know where to start. But she learned from Nora, an Ohioan who had moved into the neighborhood about two months after Marianne.

"If Nora would see me outside my house, she'd stop and chat—about anything. She'd go on about where she'd just come from, and who she saw at the store, and about her son's soccer league, and the way to plant a rock garden, the painter who was working at her house, the book she was reading. She seemed curious about what I did to save time, and which route I traveled to go in to L.A.

"I, on the other hand, was practically tongue-tied. And at first I was intimidated by the ease with which she made conversation, wondered why she seemed so interested in me. Well, the truth is that Nora was interested in just about everything. She was confident that I would find her observations interesting, and that she would be interested in what I had to say. Thanks to her I loosened up. I found that with encouragement and practice I actually had many things to say and that I wasn't too shy to say them. I'll never match Nora for either self-confidence or interests, but it's becoming natural to me to pay attention to others and to share what's on my mind."

In the natural progression of caring concern, confidence grows as we learn to spend time with others, as does our sensitivity to the presence of others. What starts as a mere passing the time of day becomes a sharing of thoughts and desires, then a planning of activities that both enjoy or that one will enjoy supporting the other in. With time and practice we learn to find a comfortable and appropriate place in different situations.

In some situations and relationships you may be the leader, introducing a friend or family member or group to new people, a new activity or idea, showing them the ropes. In another situation you are the follower or tagalong, content to be the learner or the subordinate, being shown and introduced. One day others are going along with your preferences, and the next you are keeping your friend company on her itinerary.

SHARING THE INNER DIALOGUE

There's almost always a lot going on in our heads. We're thinking about what we're going to wear, what to say next, where to put our pen down, why is that picture crooked, should I call Sally, do elephants eat meat, how far is it to Denver, what's my favorite color, there's a spot on the rug, John McPhee has a story in *The New Yorker*, what time is it, low ceilings are bad for the spirit, remember when we ate the whole gallon of ice cream . . . The inner dialogue goes on and on and inexorably on. Unless we learn to share at least some parts of it with others, it remains trapped in our head, an interminable soap opera that at times amuses, confuses, bores, or scares us. Keeping silent, not sharing one's thoughts and observations, is a bad habit, one that interferes with our caring potential. If we keep silent, we maintain our distance from those around us.

Sharing the inner dialogue is a matter of saying what's on our mind to people we care about and trust. "I was just wondering whether elephants eat meat." "I realize I'm more worried about Tom than I thought." "This meeting is dragging on too long." "I'm upset that you didn't call me." "All the way home I was watching the sunset out the window of the train. It goes through quite a few changes as we progress through the city. First you just see it reflected off windows and cars. Then it reddens up the brick of all the buildings and the shadows look very black. Then the sky itself becomes the most interesting part. Yet this is the first time I've noticed it. I ride that train every day with my head in the paper." "There are two stories on laser research in the newspaper." "I seem to keep daydreaming about playing softball."

Letting others in on what we're thinking helps us break out of the loneliness and unremitting monologue of introspection. It opens us to others, letting them know in the most direct way who we are, what we're like, what's on our minds. It's a way for others to understand us and to feel that we're important to them. It lets others know we like and trust them and find them valuable and useful to us. It airs grievances and aborts stored resentments. When we as a matter of course share our inner thoughts without fear of misinterpretation, without censoring or editing them unnecessarily, we're in a very real way reaching out to others.

INVITING INTIMACY AND CONFIDENCE

The flip side of sharing one's inner dialogue is to invite others to confide in you. Most people are not so much secretive as they are afraid to confide, fearful of rejection, of being thought foolish or dull by their confidants. Caring people invite others' intimacy and welcome the confidences that others share with them. They *want* to be "bothered" by what those around them observe and feel. They are interested in what others think and feel: they want to know what's going on.

By inviting and encouraging intimacy, one shows one's willingness to share part of another's life, to become involved, to give up privacy and introspection for participation.

One of the surest ways to inspire others' confidence is to be open oneself. Parents who keep their "adult" concerns to themselves shouldn't be surprised if their children are closemouthed about what they do after school or reluctant to answer questions about their social lives. Couples who withhold the minutiae of their day from each other deprive each other of a sense of what a part of their lives is really about.

Claude and Barbara are a good example of such a couple. They both had ostensibly good reasons for not troubling each other with the details of their daily routines. Barbara felt that her usual day was boring: by the time Claude came home she'd forgotten most of the details and was too tired to tell her story. Claude didn't feel Barbara would be interested in the making of TV commercials; he didn't want to trouble her with stories of his job pressure, nor to confide in her that he spent an hour a day playing squash. Consequently they recapped their day to each other in two minutes flat, mostly in predictable platitudes; neither had more than a vague idea of how the other spent the largest and most important chunk of their time. Realizing how unfamiliar they were becoming with each other's world, seeing the breakdown of common connections and concerns, they made a pact just to try to say what was going through their heads. "At first it was hard," Claude said. "I'd find myself literally at a loss for something to say.

"Then I realized that my brain was churning along as usual, but I was acting as a censor. 'Barbara wouldn't be interested in that; that will upset her; or she'll think I'm crazy if I say that.' Learning just to report what was going through my mind was incredibly difficult. It took awhile before we were able to do this without second-guessing and embarrassment or fear of reprisals. But I must say the results have been fantastic. Just being able to say out loud what's in my head is like having a valve through which piles of stored-up trivia can escape. I'm amazed at how much I've learned about Barbara. I have so much more to admire her for and talk with her about. She seems much more complicated and interesting. And I feel delighted that she likes being involved with my job. Keeping my thoughts to myself was a hard pattern to break, but I feel Barbara and I have found a whole new way of being together."

KEEPING IN TOUCH

It is the nature of modern life that we often literally "lose" our friends: they scatter across the country and around the world with an ease heretofore unimaginable. They divorce or marry and move out of our "social circle," or change professions and move out of the economic arena in which we operate. They, like ourselves, get so busy that it's hard to keep up. So they are traded in for new friends, ones easier to be in contact with by dint of their proximity and similar professional and social circle—low-maintenance friendships. This disinclination to make the effort (and it *is* an effort) to keep in touch is a devastating commentary on the way in which we trivialize friendships and thus minimize the caring aspects of those friendships.

One way in which care is demonstrated is by making the effort to maintain a line of communication to those we value. It can be a letter every few months, a long-distance phone call, a card at birthdays and at Christmas; it may involve taking time out from sight-seeing to drop a line while on vacation.

Separation, especially for intimates, can be very stressful. Taking the time to make phone calls to the family during a business trip, to keep one's child at college posted on the news at home, is in itself a welcome demonstration of care, a relief to the one "out of touch."

"Like many people, I love to get postcards and letters, but I hate to write them," reports Jim.

"I can't find the time to do it and I feel clumsy at it. It's hard to think of interesting things to say. But I've always sent Christmas cards, ever since I got out of school. I'm a designer so I've always had sources who would print them inexpensively. As years went by I found it harder and harder to come up with an original idea, harder and harder to find time in my busy life to send out all those cards. But my friends expected a card (and a clever one), so I made the time. It's been well worth it, because I've ended up twenty years out of school with an extensive network of friends from my past who correspond occasionally and send postcards on their travels or call me when they're passing through town.

"Nowadays when I'm on vacation, I buy a stack of postcards and stamps the first day I'm away and address them at the first possible chance. Then as I find time—and I force myself to find it—I send them off. At first it seemed a chore. But now I've learned to notice certain things for other people and to pass along information I feel would be interesting. I'm getting to feel much more at ease with writing the cards and much more original. Also, I sometimes get the feeling that I'm able to see things through others' eyes as well as my own."

TOUCHING

Simple physical contact is another part of active care. But whether to touch, and how, and when, have become loaded questions. In this age of sexual liberation, people paradoxically are starved for physical affection and afraid to ask for it. Parents are afraid of smothering their children with love. Sexual acts lacking in affection are commonplace. Reaching out to touch others can be misconstrued these days as asking for too much, as being a come-on, as spoiling the child, as a demand for unwanted intimacy, as sexual license, as phony feeling. Too, some gestures of affection have become so highly ritualized that they lose their meaning. Ladies meeting for lunch kiss the air in the vicinity of their friend so as not to smear their lipstick. Distanced husbands and wives exchange good-bye-in-the-morning, hello-in-the-evening kisses devoid of feeling. For some, the social kiss is the equivalent to the handshake, magnanimously bestowed on every passing cheek.

People who are comfortable with their caring actions are not afraid of being misunderstood, not afraid of physical contact with those they care for, not afraid of showing affection, for they are appropriate to the kind of attention they show.

Caring activists understand that gestures of affection, though nonverbal, are powerful communicators. They understand the comforting effects of a touch, the healing power of a kiss, the appropriate use of the hug.

When Grace first met Bill, he was very wary of physical overtures; at the same time he felt very alone. She, on the other hand, was very affectionate and outgoing, given to hugs and backrubs. But she was also both sensitive to the fear of affection behind Bill's glib, self-possessed manner and sympathetic to it. She knew that affection was what he craved, even as she knew he would withdraw from it.

"I feel good about how I helped Bill overcome his fear of affection. In the past I've had the tendency to overwhelm or embarrass people. Now I've learned that the bulldozer approach doesn't work. What I did was ask Bill to give *me* affection. I let him be the initiator and set the pace. Instead of smothering him with solicitation and kisses, I would tell him how frazzled I felt from my day and how much I looked forward to a big hug. Pretty soon he was offering the support and affection. And recently he's felt confident enough to say, 'Tonight *I* need the hug.' Bill feels much more confident with my demonstrativeness, and I feel I've learned something about how to love someone."

Again, caring action contributes to the growth of all concerned.

12

Growth and Change:
BRINGING OUT THE BEST IN PEOPLE

All care is nourishing and growth supporting. Just the presence of care contributes to a healthy environment. But as caring concern grows there is a progression in the level and quality of care. At first the Caring Activist becomes sensitive to others, aware of how people are, respectful of their diversity and uniqueness. The next level of concern is with making caring connections, building a network of satisfying relationships, strengthening communications. At the highest level, caring manifests itself in the desire to be actively involved in the growth and well-being of others, to enhance the lives of those one cares about. The best kind of caring helps others to see themselves clearly, to realize their potential and their dreams. It brings out the best in others.

ACKNOWLEDGING OTHERS

The observant carer notices the unique qualities of those he comes in contact with. The *active* carer reports his observations to others. By letting others know specifically what he notices about them and specifically how he reacts to them, he reinforces their sense of their own qualities and of their impact. The more thorough and detailed the reportings, the better. By letting others know what we see in them, we help them to know themselves and to understand their place in our lives and in the world.

Paying a compliment, for example, in a specific way, has effects far beyond the surface result of making the recipient feel good. In the specificity of the compliment is the message that you really see and appreciate a certain quality or aspect of the other that he may not recognize in himself or that he may feel is unappreciated or undervalued by others.

A specific and sincerely meant compliment can have long-lasting impact. Sean vividly remembers a junior high school teacher who, during a period in Sean's life when he was feeling lost and troublesome, picked out a quality he hadn't seen in himself before or, more specifically, hadn't seen as an asset. "You have a remarkable ability to make people talk about themselves and do things they wouldn't otherwise try," the teacher told him. Sean remembers clearly that this remark gave him a sense of personal value and importance in the group, where before he had felt out of place and without anything to contribute. Reinforced further by examples of specific instances provided by the teacher, Sean began to be aware of his skill and the effect it had on others. He began to use his power to motivate and inspire and draw people out. He was the one who would approach the newcomer to class, find out where he lived, what he liked to do, what kind of toys he had. He would encourage the kid who never got picked for the team to practice with him.

He felt special because he realized that the other kids couldn't make friends as easily as he could.

"I began to feel like I had a 'gift.' Before, I used to speak up just to make trouble or get attention. I didn't want to be left out, so I'd cajole and wheedle and fast-talk the other kids into doing crazy things. This teacher changed my whole focus. He made me feel that my way with people was a special talent, a way of making friends rather than trouble. He made me feel big about what he assured me was a rare asset. I ended up putting *myself* at ease by using my ability to show others what they could do."

Ambiguous acknowledgments aren't very educational. A remark that could apply to any number of people denies the individuality of the person on the receiving end. "It's good to see you," is mushy and conveys little information. Far better: "When I see you, I immediately relax" or "You make me laugh after a long day's work" or "You always wear something colorful." These are all specific comments, germane to the person spoken to. They also say something about the speaker. The person being addressed is likely to feel stronger and more secure in knowing that he or she is being seen clearly seen by someone who's taken the time and interest to pay attention. This reinforcement of personal image goes as well for negative comments. "I don't always look forward to your stories because you always pick out the horrifying aspects" or "Your habit of jangling the change in your pocket drives me up the wall" are also valid and specific recognitions. This kind of comment lets others know that you recognize them far more effectively than generalizations like "That's boring" or "You're acting stupid" and provides constructive roots for change.

Sally's story illustrates the impact that people who are observant and direct communicators can have.

"There's a new young research director in our office who knocks me out with the things she comes up with," she says. "Sometimes I think she has X-ray vision or something. She's an incredibly keen observer, gets right to the heart of things, always has something informative to say about herself, about me, about others in the office, even about the weather. The other day she remarked, 'You certainly have a consistent approach to things. When you're down, you wear slacks and flat shoes and pull your hair back in a knot. You have one folder open on your desk. You don't have coffee. You write slowly and neatly. You hardly make any phone calls. I know, for example, that you're not likely to return my call. When you're feeling good, your hair is flying around, you wear high heels, usually a dress. Your desk is a clutter of papers and unfinished cups of coffee. You're very communicative.' It was an amazing report. Though I'm usually aware of my moods, I had never stopped to think how they show. Last week she pointed out to me that my assistant would probably get twice as much work done if I shifted her duties a bit so that she could spend more time writing the synopses of my projects—'because that's the kind of mind she has, and she needs the stimulus,' she said. She also told me that she's noticed that I pace and 'choreograph' (as she put it) my reports so that I build the reader toward my conclusion. I thought no one noticed these things. I felt terrific. She is quite devastating. In a way she's kept a kind of childlike innocence. You know how kids can cut right through the bull, they can be deadly accurate.

I find that I experience almost a thrill of anticipation when I'm working with her. I always learn something about myself or others I know—there's a real jolt or buzz that goes along with her comments. I feel watched, noticed in a positive way."

A caring supporter acts as a forum for the ideas, aspirations, dreams, struggles, joys, hurts, and interests of the other. He performs the function of a sensitive litmus paper for the other's thoughts, a testing ground, an extra brain through which the other can process his thoughts.

SUPPORTING THE ACTIONS OF OTHERS

In addition to giving safe harbor to another's private thoughts, the caring person will help weed out the clutter of thought, add ideas and suggestions to his own, veto what he considers unproductive or harmful ideas, and help overcome fears and inhibitions. He contributes his knowledge, wisdom, perspective, experience.

And once a course of action is decided upon, the caring intimate on some level involves himself in the quest. It may be through continued moral or emotional support, by his availability for counsel, by advice, or it may be active participation in the execution of the task itself. It is interesting to note that studies of personal involvement in others' goals have shown that when we see others approaching a goal with which we are sympathetic, we are more likely to offer our help and support. The support also seems to grow stronger as the goal is neared. We take on responsibility for the successful outcome of the other's quest.

SHARING INTERESTS

Sharing one's interests, skills, and enthusiasms with others is one of the most pleasurable of growth-enhancing ways of caring. It provides an outlet for venting our enthusiasms, a hedge against the dampened feelings with which we are more likely to react if we're alone. Most people recognize the feeling that says, "I only wish Mike were here to see this" or "It would be so much more fun if Lorraine liked to play tennis." The Caring Activist says,

"This is a movie that I can take Mike to see" or "If I could teach Lorraine to play tennis, she might get over her feeling that she's uncoordinated and clumsy" or "If Lorraine could meet Mike, she could probably get involved with that artist's co-op."

"I used to tag along with Vince when he'd go gallery hopping," says his wife, Muriel. "At first I did it just to keep him company when we were traveling. He seemed to like to have someone to exclaim to and 'ooh' and 'aah' with as he looked at his beloved drawings. At first I wasn't very interested, but Vince was very articulate and knowledgeable about the drawings and the artists; he'd answer questions and point things out to me. Without realizing what was happening, I found myself noticing certain things about the drawings and picking out certain qualities that interested me. Vince and I turn out to have quite different tastes in drawings, but his enthusiasm and patience have made me as enthusiastic a gallery-goer as he, and we have much more to talk, and argue, about. And I think Vince feels closer to me and proud of my artistic accomplishments."

"What I like to do is walk and look around," says Andy. "Over the years I've certainly walked every possible path within twenty miles of here, and I walk the territory whenever I travel. It's my form of relaxation. I've become a great observer of birds, bees, rocks, wildlife, flowers, streams, clouds, weather patterns, even people. I'm like a detective, I just watch and sniff around and let myself forget all my cares. Over the years I've walked alone, with my wife, Fran, and with friends, but nothing can beat the joy of walking with my daughter, Jess. I really didn't try to push her or instruct her along our walks, but she seemed so interested and full of questions. Mostly she seemed interested in being a detective like her dad. She's been sniffing along with me for three years now, and between us we don't miss a trick. She sees things I never even looked for, and I can still surprise her. She's enriched my walks tenfold, but best of all, I feel like I've given her a valuable gift that only I could bestow."

MAKING THE ORDINARY SPECIAL

One fringe benefit of caring, a result of growing observation and involvement, is that it adds spice to what can otherwise seem to be a humdrum, day-to-day life. Boredom with everyday activities is a result of not paying attention, of not taking an interest in the process of accomplishing things. Caring concern adds interest to the boring and routine aspects of life, making ordinary events and activities seem more special. Caring people are able to share and communicate this feeling to those around them. The very nature of their caring concern makes the ordinary seem special; caring people recognize the potential for elevating the humdrum to the sublime.

When Sandra waits in the check-out line of the supermarket, as she does every week, she has half a dozen possible ways to while away the time. She plays guessing games; she invents life histories of the people around her. If the people in line with her seem like they might be interesting (which she judges by her keen powers of observation), she'll start a conversation. She picks a topic that's bound to be fun and a bit different for people to talk about. She'll ask, "Where would you go if you could plan a dream vacation?" or "Do you think it would be fun to be a movie actress?" or "Here's a story that says food prices will double again in ten years" or "I wonder what life will be like in the year 2000." Sally says she's made her waiting time much more enjoyable and learned a good deal about people, to boot.

"Waiting around in check-out lines can be pretty dreary if all you can think about is how long it's taking," she says. "Sometimes people get grumpy and irritable. When I get people talking, time passes quickly. Sometimes the checker joins in, and I've had it happen that people stand around after their groceries are all ready to go. My guess is that a lot of people don't think about these things, or if they do, they don't talk about them to everyone. People seem to have fun talking about these things; often we end up on a completely different subject."

Caring people are inventive about their day-to-day lives. They make sure that they don't fall into dull routines. They'll drive

A Time for Caring

home by a different route, try a different radio station. They'll have family members switch places at dinner, trade chores with their mates. They point out things they observe to others and make it a point to remember interesting stories they've heard. They practice *raconteuring*—recounting stories, news, gossip, jokes, bits of information that liven the day. They're not afraid to entertain, for they're comfortable with their families and friends. They'll do an imitation of the boss for their spouse, or tell the kids a ghost story. They open others' eyes to the possibilities for making life interesting.

DOING THE TOUGH THINGS

This is the area where the "nice guy" and the phony carers are often caught out—not to mention the faint of heart. Here is where nerves, courage, and the overcoming of fear and of the desire to keep one's nose clean are put to the test. The demands of a caring commitment sometimes exceed their foreseeable limits, for caring may mean spending day after day after day at the bedside of a sick child. It may mean watching a loved one die, being his confidant and link to the world. It may mean ending a destructive relationship. Perhaps it requires telling a friend or loved one things he doesn't want to hear or withdrawing support from one whose actions you feel are destructive. Often there is risk of offending or alienating those you care for. It may mean giving up a lucrative promotion to spare one's family a disruptive move, or working for years to put a child through school. Sometimes it's just a matter of facing up to one's own mistakes or stupidity and bad behavior. It may mean apologizing for one's rudeness or owning up to the fact that it was you who let the bathtub overflow. It may also be a matter of putting in extra time and energy at crucial, though positive, points in one's life. There are passages in life where caring becomes very important—marriage, the birth of a child, getting a new house, starting a business. Each has its own qualities and requirements.

There are the times in the course of caring commitment when such difficult and demanding actions are appropriate and necessary, when they have a rightness untinged by a tendency toward martyrdom or a false sense of duty or indirect hostility. And it is these tough jobs that often bring the greatest rewards, show us and those we care about our true colors, and plumb the depths of our caring capacities.

"My friend Frank was the only person who had the nerve to confront me about my drinking," reports Jonas, a respected doctor and community leader.

"I guess most people are afraid of me, afraid of alienating me or losing my so-called favors. And I guess I counted on that to keep people off my back about the drinking. Frank didn't put up with it for long. He told me that he knew I was drinking, that he was wise to my tactic of sneaking off in the corner for drinks at odd hours—he painted a pretty sordid picture. He didn't go on about how bad it was for me. He probably figured I knew that. He just told me that aside from the fact that I was doing great harm to myself and my family at great risk to my career, I was obnoxious when I was drunk, and that although he valued my friendship, it wasn't worth it because I became so offensive when I drank. He said he wasn't going to hang around if I kept it up. I was roaring mad at first—who the hell did he think he was anyway? But after I cooled down I was shocked and impressed. Shocked that I was drinking so much and that it was obvious—I'd lost all perspective. Impressed that he cared enough and was gutsy enough to confront me. The next day we took a walk together and talked about my drinking. We made a plan for how I could cut down, and we made a wager about my drinking that he took the trouble to monitor for months."

"Sometimes you have to fight for the right to care," says Priscilla, "especially in New York. I've lived here almost fifteen years now, and I admit I have it good. I live in Greenwich Village in a quiet, friendly neighborhood where I know the shopkeepers and some of the people on the street. My building is pretty safe, though over the years there have been robberies. I've had a couple of scares, but nothing serious has ever happened to me. I'm reasonably careful and try to avoid being in the wrong places at the wrong time.

"But I still tend to smile at people on the street or talk to people in shops or on a bus, or to cabdrivers. Not always, of course.

A Time for Caring

Often, I'm preoccupied or grouchy or too busy to pay much attention. And of course I am careful about whom I smile at or talk to. Several times I've stopped on the street if someone was hurt, or if a derelict seemed to be in real bad shape. I've even tried to break up a couple of fights or tried to stop kids who were harassing people on the subway. Many times people have said to me, 'What's the matter with you? What are you doing that for?' 'Mind your own business, lady, you're looking for trouble.'

"The one time I got in trouble was when I went to the rescue of a young kid who was being teased and intimidated by some tougher classmates on the subway. The boy was wearing very thick glasses, and in the midst of their hassling one of the kids knocked the glasses off onto the floor about six feet from me. Without thinking, I dove for the glasses. Immediately the kids started for me, taunting me, calling me names, threatening me for having interfered. I was crouched down on the floor of the subway; one of the kids had his hand on my neck and his knee against my back. I was deciding whether or not to be apologetic and meek or to make a run for it, when a very big and imposing black man quietly ambled down from the other end of the subway car. He took the kids one by one and shoved them into seats. He helped me up and sat me down. He took the glasses from my hand and returned them to the boy. Then he stood in the middle of our little group with a menacing look on his face. I got off at my stop, and five seconds later my knees were trembling and I had to sit down, and I started crying. But I was okay. And I think that man came to the rescue *because he saw me trying to help and was prodded to do the same.*

"Sometimes people I start to talk to act frightened or intruded upon. They react like I'm crazy. In this town you have to fight to show care—many people don't respect anything but a tough, uninvolved attitude. I'm not as outgoing as I used to be, but I persist. Otherwise I'd become very discouraged and cynical about this town, which I love. Besides, by being open I've met many other people who are willing to get involved. By getting involved I have a real sense of personal power in this big town; *I build a better New York.*"

13

Ritual:
FOUNDATION FOR CARING

As we have said, the very ideas of ritual and tradition have gotten a bad name in our do-your-own-thing age. Rituals contradict popular notions about spontaneity and hanging loose. People rebel against acting in preordained ways they now consider phony or empty, uptight or old-fashioned. Long-standing traditions—valuable pieces of our history, important connections to our childhood, our heritage, our memories—have been discredited and abandoned without a backward look. We are a ritual-poor culture.

Yet many of our activities can be labeled ritualistic. Watching TV is a ritualized way of tuning out: often people don't even pay much attention to what they're watching. Rock concerts are tribal rituals of the young. Disco dancing is a ritualized way of regressing to childlike antics without feeling foolish. Office parties are festivals of office camaraderie. Sports contests are ritualized hostility releases for "nice" folk.

Widely accepted and mutually understood rituals are vehicles for much of our communication and actions. After all, if we were to have to invent from whole cloth our words and behavior for every situation—to do it our way—we would soon become exhausted from the effort of all the "creativity," and we would certainly in many cases be misunderstood, as though we were speaking a new language. If every time we met someone we felt compelled to invent an original and appropriate greeting, we'd soon feel so overwhelmed that we'd stay home and not even answer the phone.

Our daily lives follow a pattern—a combination of our own and of society's making—habits of eating, working, sleeping, grooming, socializing. Even the hermit—"free" to do as he pleases—devises for himself a life of routine, however eccentric it may be. Very few people have the luxury or the desire to do everything as the spirit moves them. People follow patterns by choice, even if they do not choose all the patterns they follow. We don't invent a new way of cleaning our teeth each morning. However personal and idiosyncratic our method may be, in all likelihood we follow it the same way each time.

It is true that rituals are often empty shells devoid of feeling. Rituals repeated over and over thoughtlessly can lose their significance: when we perform them unthinkingly, we forget their content and meaning. Certainly there have been periods in history when propriety or form was "everything" and to step outside the bounds of convention was taboo. Spontaneity was the great sin. Going through the motions of caring was all that was necessary. Often we plod through the predictable course of a wedding or funeral without experiencing real feeling.

But without the framework of these supports, many of us would not know where to begin in the observance of our mournings and marryings. Rituals are useful common reference points. They grease the skids of interaction, smoothing the way for showing our love and concern. They allay our fears about what to say and do, and allow us to enter frightening territory safely. The question should center not on the merit of ritual but on which kinds of ritual and in which situation and how much.

If the rituals of the past have become outdated, then they must be supplanted by timely new ones. But before we throw away everything that smacks of the past, we should recognize that the solution might best be a coalition of new and old.

We need rituals. They are the facilitators of communication. Instead of inhibiting spontaneity the supportive framework of ritual provides a taking-off point for the original, the imaginative, the spontaneous. It cushions our caring.

FORMS OF RITUAL

There are rituals to cover just about every occasion for human interaction, from forms of greeting to those of leave-taking and everything in between. Handshakes, common to many cultures, have evolved from their ancient purpose of demonstrating or confirming that one was unarmed to their current, more symbolic function in greeting. Even the simple handshake has its subtleties of meaning. One shakes hands when formally introduced to a stranger or in a business meeting. But handshaking is usually inappropriate with a shopkeeper or an intimate. With certain people one shakes hands at every meeting. Yet as the relationship becomes more familiar, the handshake may be dropped, or it may evolve into a backslap or a hug, or a "social" kiss—factors determined by role, recipient, personal style and preference. Such gestures are meant to communicate, not to avoid communication. We personalize them with our own inflections and interpretations but depend on other's understanding of the "big picture." The spontaneity and subtlety of meaning occurs within the understood strictures of the ritual.

There is no interpersonal situation that doesn't have rituals to help it along. When people part, there are ways of easing the separation: a casual wave to someone we'll see again soon. Formal thanks to people whose hospitality we've enjoyed. A hug, a pat, a kiss for an intimate friend. Talk about future plans to reassure someone who's leaving for a period of time.

Even sexual approaches are eased by a code of behavior. In bygone times this code was completely and intricately detailed by the church, and then by a code of chivalry. The Art of Courtly Love left nothing to whim. Even in today's age of sexual freedom there are passages on the road to intimacy that must be observed if we are not to be misunderstood. In some cases the very denial of a desire for real intimacy is a ritualistic prelude to sexual union—the mutual acknowledgment that no strings are attached, that the intent is to bed, not to wed.

Rituals also serve to reinforce bonds between people—be they intimates or strangers. They stress points of community and common interest. They remind us that we belong to each other. When an audience applauds a concert, an entertainer, or a ballet, it signifies by the length and intensity of that applause the degree of its satisfaction. It is not hollow applause. The members of that audience put their sincere feelings into this commonly accepted gesture. If, instead, they turn around in their seats three times or wave a blue flag as a sign of approval, they would not be understood. There would be no communication—just a message sent and none received.

Members of an audience feel good to be part of a group of people who feel the same—they identify with others like them who appreciate fine music, brilliant dancing, or high comedy.

THE DEVALUATION OF HOLIDAYS

It is during holidays and on special occasions that we are most aware of ritual and tradition. It is fashionable nowadays not to care about holidays—to leave town for Christmas, to disparage the ceremonial aspect of weddings, to let one's birthday pass unnoticed, to overlook the religious or patriotic meanings of a day off from work. The argument goes that holidays have become empty occasions, excuses for commercial excesses, gross parodies of their original intent. There's certainly a valid argument here, for who would deny that we are often at the mercy of our warped consumer ethic or that rituals at times become an excuse to avoid feeling. But the excuses too become a way of avoiding the opportunity to be close to family and friends, to warm ourselves in the company of others, to indulge our sentimentality.

Those who send a bottle of liquor to their clients and run out on Christmas Eve to buy something, anything, for those they profess to care about are the very ones who make holidays commercial, cheap, and empty. Spending weeks making Christmas decorations and shopping for the perfect gift, hanging Christmas stockings, inviting friends over, kissing under the mistletoe, or throwing the special birthday party or having a barbecue on the Fourth of July—actively observing special occasions—are the caring ways.

"When you're single and living far from your family in New York," says Shirley, "it's not easy to celebrate Christmas—and I really like Christmas. For one thing it's hard to find people who don't just write the whole thing off as an overcommercialized rip-off. And there's no question that if you want evidence that Christmas has been commercialized, you can find it. I think all these things are excuses, however. I do my Christmas shopping throughout the year as I see things in store windows or during my travels. That way I never have to venture into the crowded department stores during the peak of the season. And I don't spend extra money on last-minute purchases. Once a year I make a nighttime, off-hours walking tour of Rockefeller Center and the store windows with a few friends.

"Up until a few years ago, before I got so busy, I even made many gifts. During my years in New York I've managed to evolve a few Christmas traditions that friends have come to expect. I keep a batch of baker's dough (a combination of baking soda, salt, and flour) moist in the refrigerator, and as friends drop into my office during the weeks before Christmas, I have everyone I can convince to try it make a dough ornament for a small tree in the office. Over the years I've accumulated quite a collection. I also have a party where everyone brings something to eat or drink. This is known as Shirley's Drawing-board Smorgasbord. It's worked out that certain people bring the same thing year after year. With persistence, and probably with something of a Pollyanna attitude, I manage to continue to enjoy Christmas and not feel overwhelmed by the commercialism and the cynicism of others. What I like is that several of my friends now join in wholeheartedly."

NEW RITUALS

What is needed, then, is not fewer empty rituals but more full ones: better, more appropriate, more carefully applied rituals. Along with reinstating those time-tested reminders of what is good about the past, we need new rituals that meet the needs of modern life, and personalized rituals that reflect our own needs and style.

One dismal ritual that has popped up in recent times is a perverted form of testimonial known as a "roast." In bygone days a testimonial was a serious affair, a chance to praise the person being honored. The roast takes a different tack. The guest of honor is ridiculed and lambasted by his friends and fellows, raked over the coals with wit and wisdom. Amusing on a superficial level, it is fundamentally a sad commentary on our inability to show softness or sentiment without embarrassment. We feel more comfortable taking refuge in cynicism and black, attacking humor.

A more serious contemporary ritual, yet one that is often

A Time for Caring

laughed at, is the divorce party or "unwedding." It is a get-together of the friends and family of at least one—but preferably both—parties to a divorce for the purpose of ritually observing or marking the occasion.[15] This new ritual is often the butt of jokes and is often carried out—or miscarried out—with overtones of bitterness or cynicism. Yet it is a perfect example of how ritual evolves to fit particular times and needs, and of the importance of observing publicly, with those who care around us, the important events of our times.

Even in these days when divorce is so common, the stigma of failure is still attached to it, along with pain and confusion. It is far from amiss to observe the occasion with a ritual that makes the parting easier by gathering friends around and thereby easing the tension and the sense of loss of the divorcing parties and their children.

Barbara and George had been married eleven years and had two young daughters when they divorced. Barbara tells about their divorce party.

"Probably a divorce party isn't right or possible for everyone, but George and I, despite all our fights and hard feelings, are still on speaking terms, and we're concerned about Anne and Sarah, our daughters. For us it was definitely the right thing to do. When people divorce, friends often feel they have to be loyal to one or the other parties—the couple ends up losing valued friends. The party brought everyone back together. It was a gesture of solidarity, a boost for the continuation of friendship on both sides. We preserved, rather than divided, our friends; they were relieved not to have to choose sides. It was a simple party—an informal get-together with the same people who'd partied together before, plus a few more family members (my parents came; George's didn't), a few of the girls' friends, and even the minister who married us. We had hamburgers, corn on the cob, and drinks. The 'ceremonial part' was very, very brief. Our good friend John made a formal announcement of our divorce and then another friend, Joan, made a short speech about the importance of marking the occasion, about how all our friends hoped to continue to support us, about their best wishes for us and for our daughters' happiness. There were a few more toasts and some jokes. All in all it was a very 'up' occasion. I think the girls felt relieved and reassured. George and I discovered that we still have a basis for possible friendship. And I think it's going to help us get off to a good start on our custody arrangement."

Janet and Bart's story of their wedding illustrates their way of dealing with our ritual-impoverished society.

"Bart and I wanted to get married very much, but we almost didn't do it. So many of our friends pooh-poohed the idea of getting married as being archaic and meaningless. And whenever I thought about mouthing all those platitudes about love and obey, I'd get cold feet. It seemed too tacky for words. Bart and I wanted to make a commitment to each other, but we also wanted it to be true to our own feelings and needs. In the end we wrote our own wedding ceremony—not one of your 1960s you-do-your-thing-and-I'll-do-mine rites but one that we felt expressed our feelings about our marriage. We were married in church. It was a great wedding. Many people said that they were very moved by it and had a renewed sense about the meaning of marriage. And the minister plans to adapt our 'ceremony' for her parishioners."

Here are excerpts from their wedding ceremony.

Minister:

We have all come here today to celebrate the marriage of Janet and Bart. The fact that we are here *today* is of some importance. Today, when society no longer demands marriage of those who live and love under one roof, marriage is not really necessary. Today, with the complexity, personal freedom, and instability of the time, marriage is far from secure. And today, when our laws favor a single status, marriage is not even practical.

So for Janet and Bart, marriage must be the only means to a relationship so rare and valuable that the ritual itself takes on a new meaning; the risks shrink beside their belief in one another; and the sacrifices become small payment for the rewards. Each has come here today with certainty and eagerness in his desire to give something exceptional to the other—a part of himself. They have come with conviction and pride in their choice; eyes, hearts, and minds open and full with triumph and satisfaction in difficulties overcome, and with strength and willingness for those that lie ahead.

In bringing mutual respect, understanding, and shared values to their marriage, Janet and Bart bring a great fortune. It is a fortune inherited from you, their families and friends, passed on through the love, friendship, and support you have given them. Not, then, merely as witnesses but as contributors and participants in this happy event, I welcome you.

Janet and Bart have esteemed and loved each other, both when it has been easy and when it has been hard, and so it is fitting that they should now express to us what has been expressed already between them.

Janet, do you want Bart to be your husband?
Janet:
I do.
Minister:
Bart, do you want Janet to be your wife?
Bart:
I do.
Minister:
Together you have selected rings with which to mark the beginning of your life together. As you speak your vows, let these rings testify to their faith and give them weight.
Janet:
This ring represents my spirit and my love. I give it to you as a reminder that they are always with you, in all things [puts ring on].

And with it I give my commitment to work hard at making our marriage enduring and happy. I promise to give freely of my time and energy, to listen and help, whenever you need them, and to be sensitive to your unique feelings, however different from mine and difficult for me to understand. I promise to honor your independence and to be worthy of your trust and friendship, so that your life with me will be contented and calm. I love you so much, and I am so happy.
Bart:
I love you too, and I am very happy. I give you this ring as a symbol of my love and of the promises I make to you now: I promise to be worthy of your love, trust, and respect; to be un-

derstanding of your needs and hopes; and to sympathize with you in times of difficulty and disappointment. I promise to be supportive of your efforts to be a good person and to improve your own life as well as the lives of those you wish to help. I promise to be responsive in times of disagreement, and to strive for resolution so that we can continue to build our marriage. And I promise to be as good a companion to you as I can, so that we can always have fun and be happy together.

Minister:

You are now husband and wife, partners for all time. The wine in this cup signifies the flow of life. Drink to your marriage, and let the essence of your lives flow one into the other, leaving the warmth of commitment deep inside you, and the sweetness of love under your tongues.

Now you will feel no rain, for each of you will be shelter to the other. Now you will feel no cold, for each of you will be warmth to the other. Now there is no more loneliness, for each of you will be companion to the other.

Now you are two bodies, but there is only one life before you. Go now to your dwelling place, to enter into the days of your togetherness, and may your days be good, and long upon the earth.

PERSONALIZED RITUALS

Rituals cannot be invented out of thin air; there's no such thing as a one-shot ritual. But chances are that just about everyone already has some established private rituals. They just have to be ferreted out and given a bit more encouragement and perhaps substance. They need to be labeled, shared, witnessed, and publicized as such.

What might some of these things be? Perhaps a habit of getting to the office early to read the papers. It might be a special song or nickname between lovers. Dining at a particular table in a favorite restaurant with one's spouse. Taking the kids on a picnic on the first day of spring each year. Walking to work with a friend. Or they can be self-care rituals: taking a hot bath after the kids leave for school. Or doing a crossword puzzle while waiting at the Laundromat.

A Time for Caring

These are the things that give form to day-to-day life, that shore up relationships and give them a special flavor. Each ritual we reinforce—for ourselves, our families, among friends in the community—strengthens the Caring Network, expands the caring environment. Active carers look for opportunities to add new rituals to their repertoires.

"Breakfast is Julie's and my special time together," says Andrew, speaking of his fifteen-year-old daughter. "Everyone else in our household likes to sleep late; Julie and I are the early birds. We have our set routine. I prepare the coffee maker at night and set the table. Julie turns it on in the morning and puts out the milk and cereal and jams and makes toast. I'm in charge of going outside for the paper and slicing fruit onto the cereal. It's a very simple routine, but the patterns are set. We don't usually talk until after we've looked at the paper for ten minutes. Julie always gets the news section first. I look at the sports. Then we'll talk. Unless there's some pressing issue, we'll chat about what's in the news, and usually we actually give a little report or a rundown on what we've been up to. We clear the table and she walks me to the door or to the car and we kiss good-bye. That's it, but it's a real ritual between us. Every once in a while, when Sally or one of the other kids gets up early and joins us, we both feel intruded on, because our breakfasts are a private affair."

Part III
The Arenas of Care

14
Charting the Caring Network

The Caring Network is the interwoven mix of family, friends, lovers, organizations, community groups, issues, and ideas that make up the fabric of our caring environment. Many factors go into the weave of that fabric: the number of people and things within our sphere, their variety and function, their closeness or distance from us, the amount of time we devote to them and they to us. The Caring Network defines the context in which our caring takes place.

Every caring act has its own rules, roles, and rituals, depending upon the arena in which we're operating and the particular mix of people and circumstances. We behave differently with the family than we do among our coworkers, differently with our lover than with a stranger at the Laundromat. Our health, our moods, and our sense of duty are all part of the context and produce in each situation a different response.

A strong, varied, active Caring Network is of primary importance for our growth and well-being. It is a powerful antidote to stress, isolation, and the casual carelessness found in so much human interaction. But developing and maintaining a strong supportive Caring Network demands energy, attention, and skill.

We need to get to know our individual Caring Circles, to pinpoint the ways in which caring manifests itself in the many arenas in which we operate. Defining the limits of our caring helps us to use our caring energies appropriately and efficiently. Obviously, we do not do for a stranger what we do for our closest friend. And we do not do for our closest friend what we do for our child.

Within each caring arena are additional limits defined by specific situations: We do not do for one child what we do for another, or we do not do today what we might do tomorrow. Motivation is another factor of context. We do some of our caring out of love, some because of a sense of duty or obligation. There are caring acts that our conscience dictates, and some that come seemingly at whim.

A man leaves for work in the morning. He kisses his young son and daughter on the cheek, ruffles the hair of his older boy, gives his wife an affectionate hug and kiss, waves to his neighbor, shakes hands with an acquaintance he runs into, gives a coworker a small pat on the back as he enters his office, nods to his secretary, says hello to his boss. He doesn't think about these things; they are natural yet they are appropriate and conform to expectations defined by their context. If they were randomly shuffled around, they'd be hopelessly out of place and would cause shock and misunderstanding. (Try kissing the boss hello sometime.)

The next thirteen chapters will examine the major arenas of care: self-care, sexual caring (caring in intimate relationships), family caring, caring among friends and peers, professional care, and caring for the larger community—for the world, for ideas and causes. Each of these caring arenas has a different set of guidelines: different dynamics, rules, roles, and rituals common and appropriate to the situation. And for each arena there is a subnetwork within the large Caring Circle. The more you know about your Caring Network, the better you can manage your caring energies.

CHARTING THE CARING NETWORK

At caring workshops and lectures we have discovered that the best way to learn about the Caring Network is to draw a picture of one's Caring Circle and place within it, in approximately accurate positions, all the people and things it encompasses.

Many people take it for granted that they have a pretty good picture of their Caring Network. However, when they do the exercise we are about to describe, they are surprised at the friends they have "lost track of" or "hadn't thought about in months." They've neglected their interest in gardening, or forgotten about the local recycling campaign. They've never thought about the balance of give and take in their relationships. They're horrified that they spend so much time with a negative, thoughtless person or that they don't know a single person who shares their interest in flowers or foreign languages. They realize they're not finding enough leisure time for their kids.

Participants in this exercise have been surprised by the diversity of their charts and delighted by how much they have discovered from them.

So here is how to make your own Caring Circle.

---

1. Set aside a couple of hours for this exercise. Have on hand a couple of large sheets of paper or cardboard, the bigger the better. Also, paper to cut up, scissors, glue, colored markers or pens. You can make it easier by buying some small self-adhesive stickers, in colors, from the stationery store. Incidentally, you might want to persuade a friend or family member to do a chart at the same time—it's interesting to see how networks overlap.

2. Draw a circle on a small sheet of paper and divide it up according to the time spent in the various arenas of your life: your family, intimate sexual relationship(s), your work life, friendships, the community, the time you spend alone. The size of each segment will vary according to where you concentrate your attention. Do you seem to spend a good deal of time alone? Just with your mate or lover? With your children? At large family gatherings? With a few close friends? At a club? In big social groups? At work? In committee meetings? At civic functions? In political meetings? On hobbies? The circle might look like one of those shown on page 126.

3. Enumerate the people and things that constitute your Caring Network. This is not easy, for we all come in contact with a great many people and are constantly making choices, whether conscious or not, about whom to spend our caring energies on, and whom we'd like to care for us. The best way to be sure you've looked in all corners is to make a list of the people you know, the things you are involved in. It is helpful to do this by category or context: separate lists of family members, lovers, friends, hobbies, issues. For now, list as many things and people as come to mind. Don't make any judgments about their importance of function. That comes later.

Use whatever devices you can think of to help you make your list: an address book, a directory of people who work for your company or belong to an organization you're a member of, old school friends. Think of who

126   *A Time for Caring*

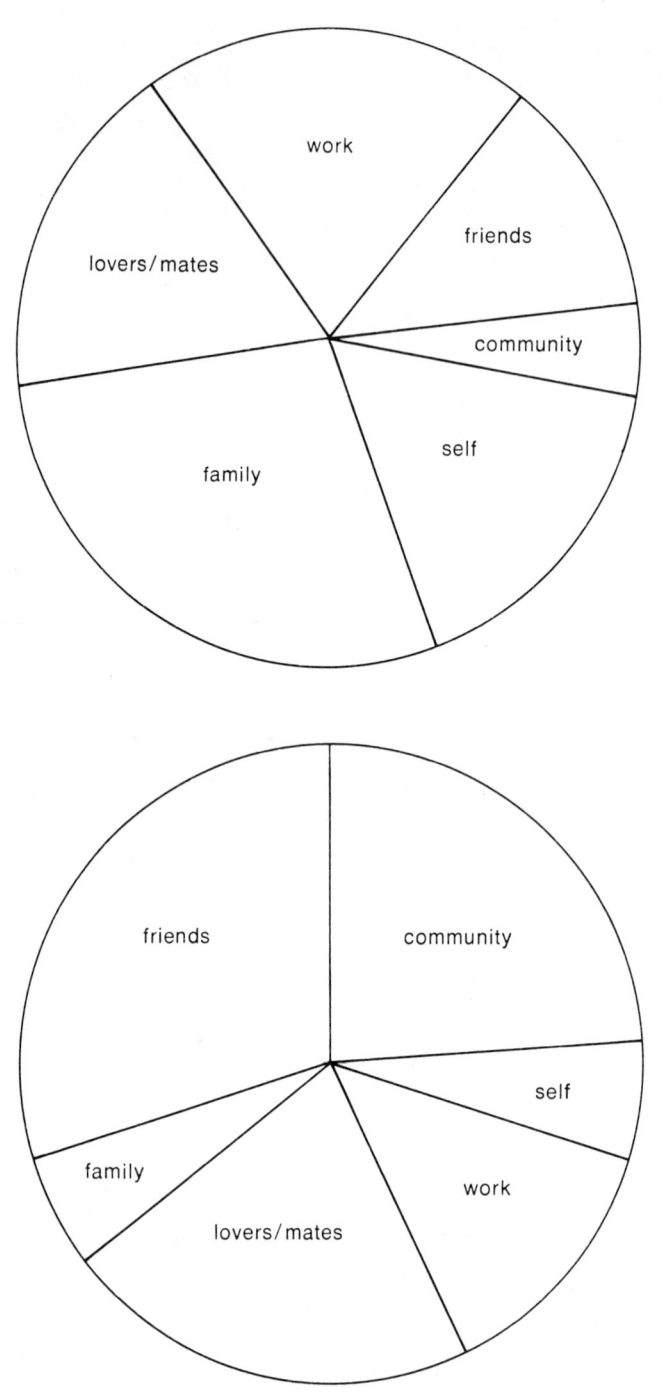

A Time for Caring

came to your last party, whose parties you've gone to in the last year. Who's visited from out of town? Who have you phoned in the last month? Written to in the past year? Who called on your birthday? Who are your enemies? Who bores you? What special-interest magazines do you subscribe to? How do you spend your spare time?

These categories will prod your imagination:

Family
  mate
  parents
  children
  grandparents
  aunts and uncles
  cousins
Friends
  lovers
  confidants/close friends
  family friends
  old school friends
  special interest friends: tennis playing friends? book club friends? fishing buddies? drinking buddies? organization or club friends: flower club friends? YMCA friends?
Coworkers
  employers
  employees
  professional association contacts
  clients
  customers
Community
  neighbors
  church groups
  school groups
  shopkeepers or service people
  civic groups
  political groups
Hobbies and Interests

4. Take a large piece of paper, the bigger the better, and at the very center of the paper draw a small circle with the word "Me" inside.

Now go back over the lists you just made and place each person, group, or interest at the proper distance from the center of the circle. In deciding how close or far from the center of your network each person should be, think of concentric circles of influence radiating out from "you" at the center. Consider each person on the list separately. How much time do you spend with the person? How much of your energy is spent doing things with or for that person? Thinking about that person? How influential is that person in your life? How strong are your feelings, positive or negative, for that person?

You may be surprised to find that a number of people or things fall at the very edge or even outside of your circle, or that someone you hardly see actually ends up very close to your center—perhaps even someone with a negative influence, or someone who's very demanding of you. You may be surprised by the scope of your network. Perhaps there are too many people—or too few.

Place each person on your Caring Network chart as close or as far from the center as seems right to you. You can draw circles at the appropriate distances and place the names inside, or use those self-adhesive stickers.

The best way is to cut up some paper into one-inch squares and write the names on them. This way you can shuffle all the elements around on the chart and keep changing them until it feels right. Then glue the names in place. You may find that some people on your list don't fall inside your Caring Circle at all and can be eliminated.

5. Just knowing who and what makes up your Caring Network and their influence on your life provides you with a great deal of valuable information.

But now you need to probe the nature of the caring in your life, find out the circumstances under which you care, those under which you're cared for. And what kind of care is provided and consumed.

So go over again the lists of people and things that make up your Caring Network. Cross off the lists any people you may have eliminated in step 4. This time through, try to figure out when and why you care: i.e., what role or function does that person or interest have in your life?

For each person or thing on your list, answer the following questions:

What kind of caring is involved: Is the time and energy spent a duty? responsibility? business? Do you do it for love? for fun? for laughs? to pass the time? as a matter of guilt or fear, as a matter of reciprocity? as a way to be liked or to get cared for?

When does this caring take place: Is it important in your day-to-day life? in connection with work? in times of crisis or emergency? at holidays or times of celebration? Are certain times or circumstances conducive to caring with that person?

6. Now it is time for a final run-through of the people and things in your Caring Network to determine what role or function each plays in your life and how you go about caring for each other. What do you do with or for the other? What don't you do? What role do you fulfill for the other and vice versa? What is the direction of the caring: do you provide the caring in the relationship? or consume it? or is it balanced?

Every Caring Network has certain requirements—certain roles or tasks that need to be fulfilled or that we need to fulfill for others. Figuring out the kinds of caring relationships in your life will help you see if all the needs are fulfilled, or if there are gaps. You'll see whether or not you're overloaded or underloaded in certain areas: too few caretakers and too many advisors, or too few role models and too many good-time buddies. Everyone does not need the same mix. You may favor the role of advisor and caretaker, not have much need of shoulders to lean on. You may be happy with one or two good friends, not feel deprived for not having dozens of pals.

In trying to determine the nature of each relationship, think about

A Time for Caring 129

what you do with or for the other person. Sometimes, as in the case of a parent, or child, or teacher, or spouse, the role is quite clear. In other cases you have to ask yourself questions that will give you clues: Do I confide my troubles to that person? my dreams? Does that person come to me for advice? Do we share a special interest? Do we only get together because of a mutual interest? because of a mutual friend? Who leads in the relationship and who follows?

Who makes me laugh? Who inspires me? Who injects the common sense when I get carried away with wild schemes? Who encourages me to pursue my wild schemes? Who talks back to me when I get out of line? Who helps me make sense of my life, or gives me a sense of place? Who has a bad influence on me?

Remember that roles or functions overlap. Your spouse may also be your caretaker (and vice versa), your advisor, and fishing buddy. You may be a role model to one friend in the area of business and that friend a role model to you in the area of entertaining or courage.

7. Using the information gathered in steps 5 and 6, write down in a few words the role each person plays in your life. Use simple categories, such as: caretaker (parent, spouse), ward (child, spouse, other family member), advisor (on what?), advisee (on what?), coworker (in what role?), role model (to you? Who you are a model for?), confidant (in what area?), community member (in what area?), special-interest buddy (what?).

Also note the balance of that care with the letters *P* (if the person gives you care, i.e., is a care-provider), *C* (if the person consumes your care), or *B* (if there is, over time or in various areas, a balance of care).

Write these brief remarks on the small slips of paper or within the little circles you've made for each item in your network.

8. As a postscript to all this, it is fun and instructive to compare your network with those of your close family members and friends to see where they overlap. What friends and interests do you share? Do they have the same importance or play the same role? Is your mate's best friend important to you too, or does he or she fall on the periphery of your network? Does your best friend's relationship to a third person enhance the relationship between the two of you? dilute it? cause problems or jealousies? Overlapping networks should expand and strengthen your own, not threaten it. Crossovers should be initiated and encouraged.

That's it. You now have a master chart of your caring environment. You've got the "big picture" of who and what are important to you, and in what ways. At least for the moment. Your Caring

Network chart should be reexamined periodically to reflect changes and shifts in the scheme. This information will help you be a focused and specific Caring Activist and give you a blueprint for making changes. And it is the basis for further exploration of the caring arenas of your life.

15

Self-Care:
FOUNDATION FOR CARING ACTIVISM

We have already noted the essential paradox of caring: self-care is a prerequisite for caring for others, and care for others is a vital component of self-care. It is a matter of balance, of finding a comfortable spot on the vast plain between self-indulgence and self-neglect. In the span of a quite brief period of recent human history, both extremes of self-management have been held up as correct and desirable. In the not-so-old days the impetus for caring was tied to ideas of duty, moral obligation, being nice, being good. Selflessness, conformity, adjustment, sacrifice, and good works were extolled; personal needs were consequently minimized and neglected. Today these ideas have been quite thoroughly discredited, swept aside by a formidable tide of belief in the inalienable rights of the individual and the pursuit of self-actualization. Today's virtues are yesterday's sins: autonomy, personal power, self-help, hedonism, self-realization.

Yet in spite of the big self-interest movement, many people don't seem to care for themselves very much. Or very well. Self-loathing, self-deprecation, and lack of self-confidence are common. People who care for themselves don't become addicted to alcohol, drugs, cigarettes, coffee, or junk food, or sportsex. Scratch the surface of what seems like hedonistic self-involvement and what's revealed is often a desperate attempt to escape inner voices of fear and self-loathing, to tune out a world gone sour.

Hedonism and denial—the extremes of self-care—are dangerous to both the individual and the community. The self-neglectful person eventually becomes weak and debilitated from lack of care—his own or that which he refuses from others. He becomes aversive to himself, unable to deal with a complex world using only his either/or standards. The self-absorbed person eventually discovers how limiting, and frightening, self-reliance is. He is a threat to the community in his nonparticipation and to the degree that the priority of his personal needs might sabotage group action.

There is a distinction between self-care and self-indulgence. It's still important to look out for number one, but it literally can't be done properly without also looking out for others. Every study of altruism or prosocial behavior points out that a sense of self-worth is necessary to caring behavior. And that conversely a sense of self-worth is a by-product of others' positive regard.

Caring requires confidence in one's ability and acceptability as a carer. This confidence comes about through raising one's consciousness of oneself as needed, loving, helpful, growth-oriented, capable of caring. Part of self-care is a belief in caring for others. It assumes interaction with others as a proper way to life.

Self-care is a matter of maintaining oneself in good working order: physically, mentally, and emotionally. This maintenance requires, aside from an understanding of the role of others, self-knowledge, fairness to oneself, and the building of self-benefiting skills and habits.

THE LIMITS OF SELF-CARE

There's only so much we can do for ourselves before we have to rely on someone else: family, friend, community, government. That seems a simple enough point, yet many people pursue self-reliance as though it were a cardinal virtue.

This is not to say that a goodly portion of self-reliance isn't desirable. It is. The ability to care for ourselves in essential, appropriate ways relieves those around us of the burden of obligation in relation to our care. As a result, a greater proportion of the care we receive is voluntary and intrinsic. We are likely to get more care from others when we demonstrate that we can care for ourselves. As one mother remarked, "Nothing moves me quite so much to care for my children as seeing them do things for themselves, especially if those things were once *my* responsibility."

Self-care increases our sense of self-esteem and confidence in our ability to cope. The wherewithal to care for ourselves is necessary in times of need: when our Caring Network has broken down, when friends and family are far away, in times of personal stress or crisis, when we are called on to provide the caring for others.

Each of us must find the place between autonomy and dependence that seems right for us. Each of us must find the areas of care where personal strengths are strong and where independence is desirable, and those areas where we are willing to relinquish care to others, where we feel glad of others' contributions.

The current trend of going it alone—by making oneself strong and self-sufficient, free of need for others—is a desperate and unhealthy trend. In a society that worships autonomy, that praises the hero who can fend for himself, the dangers of such a stance aren't readily apparent. But most people aren't equipped with the character and skills of true self-reliance; frightened when they don't live up to the standard of autonomy, they become self-involved and defensive. These troubled people increasingly turn up in therapy. And they have a difficult time, especially in group situations, for they are not able to accept the advice, criticism, or even the emotional support of a group. Too, their self-involvement prohibits them from taking an interest in their fellow group members and making a contribution; eventually the group, normally supportive and understanding, turns away. It is this autonomy worshiper, unable either to take care of everything himself or to allow others to help, who is a prime candidate for suicide.

To adopt a loner style is hazardous. It perhaps seems easy and unstressful to have to answer only to oneself, to shut down one's social systems, to not have to deal with the world. It seems a manageable posture; it can become addictive. But self-interest is limiting. There are boundaries to fascination with oneself—clever and endearing as that self may be! And there are boundaries to personal resources and capabilities, which lead to frustration and anxiety.

The burden of total self-management is exhausting. Connected people, though stressed by the complexity and unpredictability of involvement with others, nevertheless are more stimulated and more confident of their ability to cope.

Even communes fail with false goals of autonomy. Many a

well-intentioned group, bound together as a mutual-support community by shared goals of self-sufficiency, has failed because of a needless insistence on being totally independent of the larger society. Wasting time and energy on producing goods and providing services easily available on the outside, isolated by choice, they aspired to a near impossible ideal of self-reliance when with a modicum of involvement in the larger community, they could still have maintained positive aspects of self-reliance—and established around them a supportive, extended network.

ALONE VERSUS LONELY

Everyone needs to spend time alone: to recharge batteries, to think and rest, to do things that are a pleasure to the self, to get a sense of oneself, to be free of the influences of and the concern for others. To be care-free in the best sense.

More people today live by themselves, or spend a great portion of their time alone, than ever before. For some people this is a choice, one made possible (especially for women) by some financial independence and by the increased acceptability of such a lifestyle. For others it may be a circumstantial necessity, albeit temporary—a recent divorce, a relocation in a new town, an inability to find a mate or to establish a network of family or friends.

Yet the sad fact is that increasing numbers of these people, whether alone by choice or circumstance, report that they are lonely.

There's a big difference, or there should be, between being alone and being lonely. Loneliness is a widespread problem in our society. In big cities where many people live in circumstances of proximity like those of the proverbial sardines, loneliness is even more acute. For what more poignant reminder of loneliness can there be than the constant presence of others who totally ignore us? While it is human nature to feel lonely at times—even in a crowd or among loved friends and family—this kind of existential aloneness differs from the chronic loneliness so rampant in modern life. This latter-day loneliness can be seen as a failure of caring, a failure of both ourselves and others to provide care. People who live without a support system of family, friends, and community to turn to cannot expect to feel comfortable surrounded by strangers. Their inner resources are often limited: what can be the source of self-confidence of those without memories of care, without interests and involvements? Loneliness is what people feel when they have neither the supportive network nor the personal resources to be by themselves.

People who live alone are no more likely to be lonely than those who live with others. Yet many are conditioned to fear solitude. These people try desperately to avoid being caught alone, run a race with loneliness by being constantly with others, by saturating themselves with friends and work and parties and a busy social schedule. They obliterate their inner terrors by escaping to whatever contacts with others they can find—in the same way another might escape with alcohol.

But there is no substitute for the ability to spend time alone—serenely, productively, enjoyably. It is an essential balance to the roar of the crowd—and of the thruway, for that matter.

Everyone's need for solitude is different. For one person, five minutes alone with the newspaper each morning and an occasional Sunday walk are sufficient. Another, though he has a few close friends and a family he sees occasionally, can't imagine living with someone else; he needs time for reading and reflecting and stamp-collecting and a very idiosyncratic schedule. For one, time alone means doing nothing; for another, it's writing or exercise. But everyone needs it—the people-saturated partygoer who fears his solitude, as well as the overworked mother of three who has no privacy, or the busy corporate executive. And as the family decentralizes, as divorce rates rise, as the number of elderly increase, as being alone becomes more and more a fact of modern life, the ability to be alone and to cultivate the resources and strength to do so becomes a more crucial aspect of self-care.

NO ONE KNOWS YOU BETTER

Self-care begins with self-knowledge. After all, knowing one's wants and needs, being sensitive to one's own feelings, being tuned in to dreams and fantasies, would seem necessary for being able to do right by oneself. Surprisingly, however, many people don't have a good idea of what's best for themselves; they don't know what they want for breakfast, much less what they want from their lives. They don't know what they dreamed last night, or what stresses them or what makes them laugh out loud. They'd be hard put to articulate what turns them on, or what turns them off. They don't know when they've eaten too much, or worked too hard, until they see the results—overweight or tension that seems to come out of nowhere. They are more likely to try to find out from television and books and magazine articles what will make them happy than by listening to their own hearts and minds. They assume a doctor knows better than they where it hurts. They are strangers to themselves.

Even people who are good observers of others are often unable to see themselves. People often come to therapy and talk at great length and offer considerable insight about the others in their lives. Rarely do these people see their own part in the drama they're reporting on.

Self-knowledge begins with the decision to pay attention to oneself, to ferret out the information necessary to care for oneself. It involves giving credence to one's wishes and feelings, putting in perspective what one reads in the papers, what others—even loved ones—advise.

It would be hard to find a better example of the process and benefits of proper self-care than Norman Cousins' recounting of his own illness and treatment. It is a story of self-care, the story of a man dying of a sickness neither he nor his doctors understood. Because he knew himself and knew what, if anything, would make him feel better, he took his treatment into his own hands. With the support of his doctor, with tremendous care for his own well-being, working with what he knew about himself, monitoring his mental, physical, and emotional status all the way, paying attention to his needs, Cousins healed himself by means and methods totally geared to his personal needs.[16]

SOME WAYS TO KNOW YOURSELF

Probably 80 percent of all we do is unconscious; most of the time we're on automatic pilot. Clever as we are we cannot will ourselves to digest our food, or fall asleep, or have an orgasm. We cannot choreograph our dreams. If we are to know ourselves, it's

A Time for Caring

necessary to get closer to our unconscious, to befriend it, for it holds many of the secrets.

Many people today are too reality-bound. They don't believe in the messages of the unconscious. They can't learn anything from a slip of the tongue, a forgotten appointment. They believe what they see, and miss out on the 80 percent that's invisible.

The opposite of this superrealist is the person who treats every message of the unconscious as though it were literal gospel, or as a fact in a large puzzle. They're always looking for meaning in the internal soap opera or trying to translate their fantasies into reality—a dangerous undertaking. Neither extreme is conducive either to self-knowledge or to self-care.

The best solution is to take a tip from Freud: learn to be intrigued by your unconscious, use it both for fun and the profit of self-knowledge. These are ways to get to know yourself, both inside and out:

Take note of how you *are*. This seems simple enough, but many people are reluctant to attach any meaning to their everyday behavior. But if there's some truth to the adage that "you are what you eat," then you can learn about yourself from what you had for lunch. You can also learn something from where you had lunch and with whom. In other words, you can learn a great deal merely by noting what you do, where you work, who your friends are, what you read, when you laugh or cry, where you vacation, what you wear, how long you sleep, and every other observable fact.

Tune in to the signals your body sends out. Become familiar with your coughs and wheezes, itches and headaches, tension spots and tingles. Know which are important and why they show up and what to do about them. Know as well your body's signals of well-being and how they come about. Figure out whether or not what brings on a headache is overwork, hot weather, or cool friends. Know whether the cure is two aspirin, a hot bath, a movie, or a phone call to a friend.

Pay attention to that endless monologue in your head. Your mind is always working, churning out thoughts, ideas, and observations faster than you can process them. Your thoughts are a hotbed of information about who and how you are. Just taking note of the passing parade of thoughts will tell you a great deal about what's important to you, what makes you laugh, what kinds of things you notice, how you process things you see and hear, what you use and discard. You'll come to understand and appreciate your imagination and the variety and scope of your mental activities. Your mind is not a dull place. Let it entertain you and make your life more interesting.

Consider your dreams over morning coffee. It is not necessary to get heavy-handed about interpreting dreams in order to benefit from them. Much of our dreams is just undigested matter, leftovers from the day, not all of it insightful or momentous. Psychologists have overburdened us with unrealistic standards about the deeper meaning of dreams; it's not necessary to buy the whole bill of goods. But there are lots of nuggets to be mined from dreams without refining the ore. Dreams tell us a lot about our mood; they reveal tension or tedium, wishes and fears. If we can be open to what we dream, enough to try to remember them before they fade and flee, to think about them over morning coffee or while we shower, we can gain an expanded sense of the boundaries of the self, a vision of greater personal potential, of untapped boundaries, unexplored areas.

Having assembled the information, don't hesitate to draw conclusions. Make judgments about what makes you feel good, what hurts, what's stress-provoking. Make judgments about what it means when you break out in a sweat, or whether a backrub or a footrub feels better. Figure out whether your friends upset you because they're negative or because you don't want to hear what they're saying, whether what you like about your work is the pleasant office or the fascinating reports you get to see. Take note of the fact that you seem to make many observations about your physical surroundings, or that you worry a great deal about getting sick. Or that being late doesn't bother you. Or that you're prejudiced against people in loud suits. Or respond well to people who laugh. Or that you're good at remembering names and terrible at faces. That you feel better when you walk home from work. Or feel worried if you owe even a little money. Or that you hate to make beds but don't mind doing the dishes. Hate bees but aren't afraid of spiders. That your desk is neat but your closet's a mess.

That you only like to write with ballpoint pens. That you spend too much time looking for your keys.

The more informed you are about yourself, the more efficiently you can care for yourself.

PLAY FAIR WITH YOURSELF

For all their apparent self-involvement many people don't seem to care for themselves very much. No one is a perfect self-carer, and most people have ways of tripping themselves up on the path to self-care. Most people are hard on themselves. Anxious about bringing out the best in themselves, about not wasting their time or their lives, they become victims of their own near impossible expectations. They try to meet impossible standards—of love, success, popularity, efficiency. They are susceptible to media-popularized ideas about everything from being your own best friend, to multiple orgasms, to living without anger. They overtax their minds with an endless round robin of decision and doubt. People who don't like themselves find it hard to allow themselves the care and kindness they need. Their Inner Enemy taunts them, saying, "Who do you think you are, you little twerp?" every time they try to do the right thing by themselves. Sometimes those who seem most self-indulgent are actually sabotaging themselves every step of the way with *self*-destructive habits. Self-punitiveness manifests itself in someone who parties every night and is miserable and inefficient all day at work. Or in someone who overspends on clothes and personal gifts, using funds needed for other things. Or in work, procrastination that leaves one anxious and even further behind.

Jerry always thought of himself as erring on the side of self-indulgence. When he tried to assess his fairness to himself in the area of self-care, he was astonished.

"I've actually felt guilty about what most people would consider a pretty cushy life-style. And I would have been the first to say that I treat myself pretty well. But just in the course of today I came up with a few pretty good examples of poor self-care—examples that are especially telling because at first blush they seem okay. Like this morning after breakfast I talked to my partner, Julie, in New York and was feeling on top of the world because a project we've worked on seems to be going very well and will probably be done soon. As a celebration of our success to come, I took a very long, hot whirlpool bath, daydreaming about how fantastic our project is and how jealous everyone will be of our success and what a lucky guy I am—and by the time I remembered to get out of the tub I was so weak I could hardly walk and had trouble breathing and broke out into a sweat and had to lie down for an hour and cancel a lunch with a client to whom I'd been looking forward to bragging about my new conquest.

"Then in the afternoon I was sitting looking out the window at some flowers I'd planted earlier this spring. One of the things I truly love to do is work in the garden—it's calming and rewarding and smells good and feels good, and it's one of the few things I do that doesn't get measured in the same terms as the rest of my life. But as I looked at the garden and started to plan what I would plant next, I realized that though I love gardening more than just about anything, I repeatedly sabotage myself whenever I plan to garden—I get distracted by something else, or I don't have the right supplies, or I convince myself that I haven't enough time to start. I also realized that I have not one single friend interested in gardening and that my girl friend actually makes fun of it. When it comes to gardening I'm easily seduced away from it by other things—distractions I convince myself are more fun or more productive or more profitable. In other words, I don't let myself do something I really enjoy.

"This is getting to be a long story, but I know of a couple of other self-sabotages I've pulled in the last twenty-four hours.

"I ate a whole bag of cookies this afternoon with the rationalization that I'd be working out at the gym tomorrow. I felt I 'deserved' it, but meanwhile I'm upset about not losing weight.

"This morning I read through a whole stack of magazines instead of writing a report I should be working on. I told myself that I'd probably turn up some interesting tidbits for the report. Now, of course, I'm in a sweat about being late with the damned report.

"I spent twenty minutes today worrying about whether I worry too much, another ten minutes worrying about whether my dreams are 'seriously' weird.

"A pretty dismal report for a guy who supposedly likes himself, no?"

Our own Inner Enemy often gives us a harder time than any outside influence. When the voices of doom, gloom, and self-defeat get the upper hand in our inner parliament, we're in trouble. Learning to play fair with ourselves, to keep a perspective on the interminable soap opera of our overworked imaginations, to avoid the addiction (a pill, a candy bar) the antiself is so quick to suggest, to say no to the alluring distraction (the movies, a quick roll in the hay) that sabotage our own best interests, is the best way to show we care for ourselves.

THE WAYS AND MEANS OF SELF-CARE

We all want to live a life of credit to ourselves and the community. We are anxious about wasting our time on unfruitful pursuits, upset about the unfulfilling relationships that threaten to dampen our lives. We're tired of being careless with our lives but don't know how to get back on the track.

A care-full life starts with a Self-Care Plan. The skills of self-care range from knowing how to boil an egg or repair a flat tire to knowing how to make a friend or a plane reservation.

Habits of self-care include such things as yearly dental check-ups, daily periods of reflection, remembering to take your vitamins, keeping in touch with friends, planning your leisure time, budgeting your money, seeing a movie once a week, evaluating your life goals periodically.

Knowing how to make things easier on yourself is also part of self-care. This includes such self-care behavior as having a place to put your keys so you won't lock yourself out of the house; avoiding overscheduling yourself into exhaustion and frustration; knowing what you *don't* need and *don't* have to do.

Knowing how to placate the Inner Enemy when it threatens to sabotage your self-care is also important. One way to do this is to have your own self-punishment ritual. Instead of letting your psyche do you in when things are going too well, *choose* your form of self-flagellation and use it when it is called for. A self-punishing ritual might be scrubbing floors or an hour of strenuous and boring calisthenics—any difficult or particularly odious task.

A personal stress-relief ritual is also part of self-care. As we should know what causes us stress, we should know what relieves it. And because we cannot always count on others to bring that relief, each person should have a personal stress release. This might mean pounding a pillow, taking a walk or a drive, screaming in the privacy of our room, muttering to ourselves, eating a double-dip ice cream cone.

An escape hatch is another useful self-care tool. Everyone should have some idea what to do if . . . a child becomes ill, a spouse leaves, money or a job is lost. It's important to go over one's options to have a lifeline, a nest egg of ideas or resources or money or friends to be available in emergencies.

Planning for Pleasure is yet another way to be self-supporting. Set aside time to do the things you want to do, to see the people who interest you. Recognize that you're entitled to enjoy yourself. Keep a list of things that interest you, things you'd like to find time for, treats you'd like, things you want to buy when you can afford them. Planning for Pleasure is especially important if you tend to be hard on yourself.

Watch out for image addiction. Being yourself is one of the most vital and difficult aspects of self-care. Images are limiting, especially if you get locked into ideas of correct behavior, afraid to do what appears unsophisticated or unseemly. A woman who loves to go dancing reports that she feels out of place in the discos she loves because she's too old and not dressed right. She is conscious of the younger people looking at her oddly, perhaps laughing at her. A man who spends his days wearing three-piece suits and presiding over important meetings must overcome his sense of embarrassment and lost dignity in order to play on the floor and make funny noises with his own child. An elderly couple are afraid to show their passion lest they expose their love to ridicule and cries of impropriety.

The way to make a fair Self-Care Plan is not to set up a long list of impossible goals or a regimen of self-improvement that would stagger Pollyanna. Instead, make an evenhanded, nonhysterical assessment of areas of your good and poor self-care, based on your needs, resources, personal style, and wishes. Then set goals for change and make a plan for bringing about that change.

Gary had very fastidious habits of health and grooming and housekeeping and budgetry. His area of poor self-care is a common one today:

"I can honestly say that the greatest accomplishment of my Self-Care Plan is that I've learned to get through and even enjoy periods when I don't have a steady girl friend without driving myself crazy with activity or going out with every lady I meet.

"I have wasted so much time and so much energy and so much money going out on empty dates with women I didn't care about, just because I felt that's what I should do. Or that's what guys were supposed to do. I've been with women I didn't care about, women who didn't care about me. I've had fun and good times, but I've also been absolutely miserable and had terrible times. I've asked women out whom I wasn't the least bit interested in. I've gone out on dates and sulked the whole night because I was bored. I've slept with women I wasn't turned on to. I've even had VD. Yet most of the time I convinced myself that this was what I was supposed to do. It was what my two best buddies were doing, and besides, I didn't know what I'd do with myself if I didn't have a date.

"It took me a while just to figure out why I was so unhappy, why I never met anyone I cared about, why I was losing interest in sex. I realized that I had never been without a steady girl friend before I moved to this city. As a matter of fact, where I come from, the kind of casual sex that's so common here is practically unheard of. And while it has its appeal, it's not really my style. I also realized a couple of other things: I haven't any friends here that like to do two of the things I like—play basketball in the park, play cards. And since I moved to this city I haven't done sports photography—a longtime hobby.

"In the last six months I have literally learned how to be celibate when the situation calls for it. This seems almost a joke today, considering how easy it is to get laid and how popular it is to brag about it. I should know. But I am truthfully saying—having examined both sides—that sex-free periods beat the hell out of poor sex-filled periods. Not to put too fine a point on it, it's almost like purification. I feel stronger about myself and more sure of my sexuality. Now that I don't feel compelled to go out with every woman I run across, I'm more likely to find out what I like about them. And I'm learning about lots of other things I like to do in all my newly acquired spare time."

16
The Self-Care Plan

The Self-Care Plan that follows is the first of six covering the various arenas of care. Because the other plans take off from this one, this is the most important. The amount of time and energy you spend in making and implementing these plans is up to you. It's important that you do what feels comfortable for you. But the rewards will tend to parallel your efforts.

STEP ONE: DRAW A SELF-CARE CIRCLE

Using the same principles given in Chapter 15, draw a picture of your self-care circle, placing the ingredients of your self-care at their approximate position from the center depending on their importance.

First, try to get an overall picture of how your self-care is apportioned in terms of physical, mental (intellectual), social, economic, and emotional sectors.

Your chart might look like one of those shown on page 146.

Once you've made these rough divisions, cut out labels listing the specific things you do for yourself and place them within the appropriate areas according to their priority or importance in your life. The self-care circle is meant to give only the most general picture of your current self-care, so don't worry about getting everything in exactly the right place.

A self-care circle might look like the one shown on page 147.

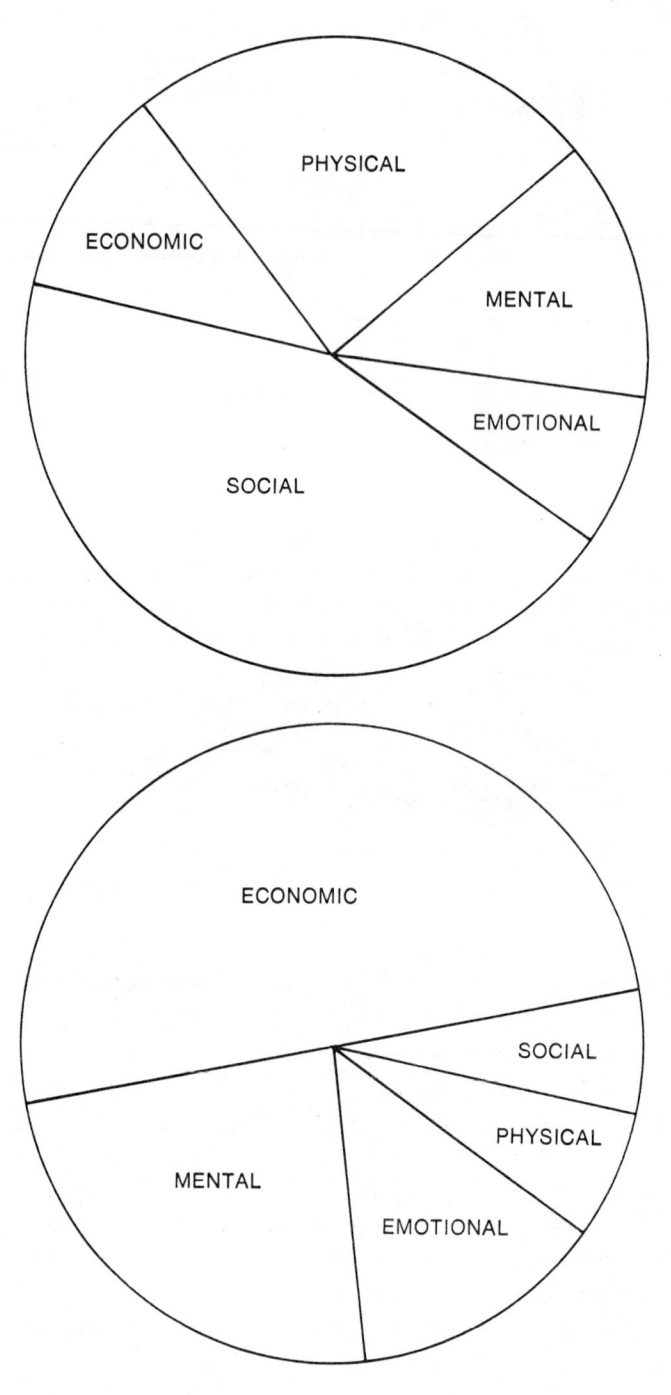

A Time for Caring

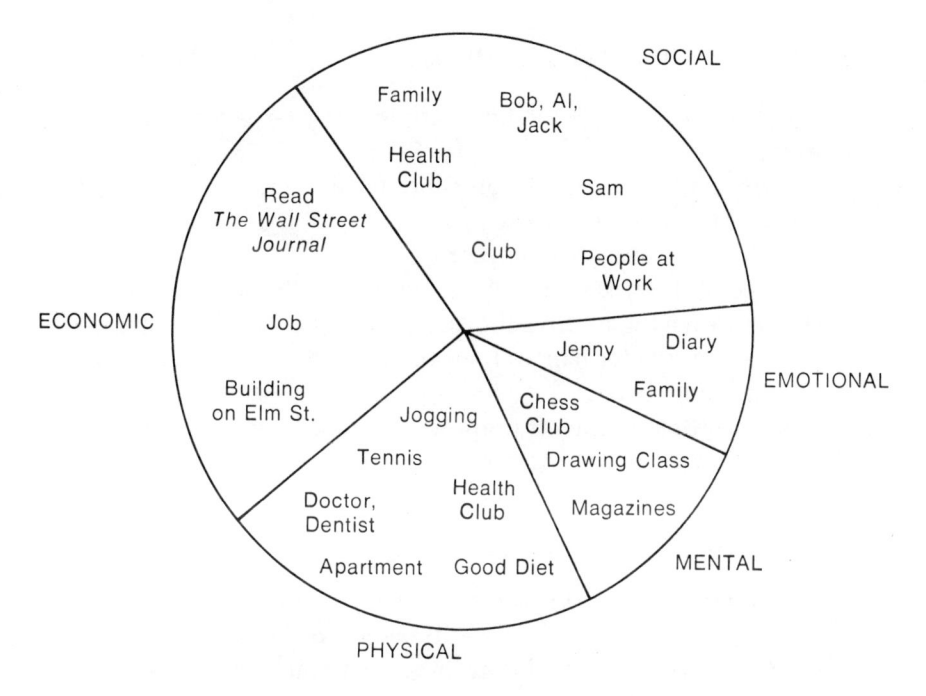

                          SOCIAL
              Family   Bob, Al,
                         Jack
             Health
             Club   Sam
      Read
   The Wall Street
      Journal   Club   People at
                              Work
ECONOMIC   Job
                         Jenny   Diary
     Building   Family   EMOTIONAL
    on Elm St.   Jogging Chess
                          Club
             Tennis   Drawing Class
      Doctor,   Health
      Dentist   Club   Magazines
             Apartment Good Diet
                                  MENTAL
                PHYSICAL

STEP TWO: MONITOR YOUR SELF-CARE PATTERNS _____

Before you actually draw up your own Self-Care Plan, give yourself a couple of weeks to check out your present self-care habits. Remind yourself several times a day to watch what you're doing, to notice where your self-care is strong and where it slips. Watch where neglect creeps in, or overindulgence. Most especially, note the things that bother you most and that you would like to do something about.

Two exercises can help you in this investigation.

THE SELF-CARE JOURNAL

Try noting on your calendar or on a special memo pad each day anything that has happened relating to your self-care. Note both the good and the bad, the major and the minor. The purpose is not to judge but to become better tuned in to how you operate. The information you gather will help you form your Self-Care goals. Do this for a week or so until you feel you've gotten some insight into your ways and needs.

Here are some sample entries:

Sat with my feet up for five minutes when I got home from work.
Got my son to pick up the groceries for dinner.
Forgot to take my medicine.
Didn't do my exercises this A.M.
Stopped at the bakery for a fresh muffin on the way to work.
Got stuck having to drive the kids to and from the ball game.
Listened to Ada for half an hour on the phone again. She didn't even ask how I was.
Made a list of arguments to use when I ask Franklin for a raise.
Locked myself out of my car.

THE ME/NOT ME EXERCISE

It is important that you get a fair trade-off in life, a sense that your life is made up of components somewhat of your own composing. A good way to find out how much you're in control is to give your actions the Me/Not Me test.

At various times in the day, at whatever is keeping you occupied, stop yourself and ask, "Is this me? Or is it not me?" "Is this something that I want to do, or want to say?" "Does this represent me fairly?" "Or is this something I dislike?" "Are these words I don't mean?" "Is this something someone else wants me to do?"

Too many "not me" answers are a sure sign that you're failing in self-care, letting others influence and overrun your life. And too much "me" probably indicates overindulgence; you may be ignoring or trampling over others, having your own way at others' expense. If you *always* say what comes to mind, *always* do exactly what you want to do, take note. Always doing your own thing is a pretty sure sign that you're rarely doing *others'* things—which indicates a lack of caring.

STEP THREE: EXAMINE YOUR SELF-CARE PATTERNS _____

Take a look at your current self-care attitudes and actions. You may be surprised to find that many of the things you do for yourself, though they seem indulgent, are actually neglectful of your

A Time for Caring

real needs. Your self-absorption and the time you spend indulging your whims may be actually detrimental to your happiness. A pattern of what seems to be self-neglect can turn out to be a way for getting others' care and attention, or a way of wielding power, of seeming superior.

The following questionnaire is meant to help you identify the bits and pieces of your self-care. The questions are meant as a stimulus to an examination of your personal ways and habits.

As you answer them, try to tune into your inner self. Put words to your anxieties and hopes, try to grab those signals inherent in wishes and dreams. Don't overlook the trivial. At this point, just put down the facts. Don't judge or evaluate; that comes later.

PHYSICAL ASPECTS OF SELF-CARE

Health:
  Do you get enough rest? Sleep well?
  What exercise do you do? What do you do to relax?
  Do you smoke? Drink? Take drugs or medications? How much?
  Do you eat regular meals? When?
  How much do you eat? Take vitamins? Do you know anything about nutrition?
  Do you have a doctor? A dentist? Have regular checkups?
  How often are you sick? In what way—colds, headaches, rashes, stomach trouble, muscle aches? What do you do for yourself when you're ill? Do you know anything about medicine? Or first aid? What's in your medicine cabinet?

Appearance:
  How much time do you spend on your appearance and grooming? Are you fastidious? Sloppy? Do you have many grooming aids and supplies?
  What are your daily grooming habits? List them: brush your teeth, shower, shave, wash your hair, curl your hair, brush and comb your hair, manicure, pedicure, makeup?
  Do you have many clothes? Are clothes important to you?
  Do you shop often? How much money do you spend? What do you buy? How would you define your "style"? Do you take good care of clothes and possessions?

Surroundings:
Where do you live? Describe the place to yourself. Do you like it? Do you spend much time there? Is it furnished and equipped the way you want it? What do you need? Is a comfortable, or beautiful, or efficient place to live important to you?

MENTAL ASPECTS OF SELF-CARE

Work:
Where do you work? How much time do you spend working? Is the work interesting and involving? Would you prefer to be doing something else? What would you do for a living ideally? Are you challenged by your work? Is it easy? Does it use your capabilities well?

Outside Interests:
What do you do with your leisure time? Do you have enough? Do you read? Keep up with the news? What do you do for intellectual or mental stimulation? Do you have friends or family with whom you can have a serious discussion, whom you can challenge at games, whose wit you admire?

ECONOMIC SELF-CARE

How much money do you earn? Is it enough for what you need? How much money would you like to earn? Do you aspire to be rich? Comfortable? How do you spend your money? What do you buy? Are you on a budget? Do you stick to it? Are you frugal? Extravagant? In debt? Do you have any savings or investments?

SOCIAL SELF-CARE

How much time do you spend alone? By choice? What do you do? Do you enjoy your time alone?

Do you have a spouse or lover whom you feel good with and who cares for you?

Is there a family group that you feel a part of and care for?

Do you have close friends that you can confide in and call on for advice or solace?

Do you have friends who share your interests and ideas? Do you know what kind of people you enjoy?

Are you comfortable with your coworkers? When you meet new people? Do you know your neighbors? Belong to any community groups? Clubs? Ever talk to strangers on the street or in a shop?

EMOTIONAL SELF-CARE

Are you usually aware of what you're thinking and feeling? Do you daydream a good deal? Remember your dreams? Do you take time to review your thoughts and goals, to reflect on your feelings and wishes? Are you able to relax? How? Do you worry much? About what? Does your mind run on too much? What do you do for yourself when you're feeling down? Do you know what cheers you up? What makes you happy? What makes you tense or upset? Do you feel confident? Afraid? Overburdened with worry? Lonely? Do you feel able to cope with most situations? Do you feel you know and understand yourself most of the time? Are you good to yourself? A harsh judge of yourself? Is yours a positive outlook? Do you know what makes you laugh? Do you feel loved? Rejected? Are you moody? Even-tempered? Angry? Dependent? Stoical?

STEP FOUR: EVALUATE YOUR SELF-CARE

Look at the information you have just gathered with an analytical eye: What's good? What's bad? What's missing? What are the indications of lapsed self-care, the signs that something is amiss? Don't be fooled by surface appearances; it will take a bit of digging to get at the truth. And don't be hard on yourself. No one is a perfect caretaker, even of oneself. To expect to be is a manifestation of punitive self-care. It's a matter of how often and how much one does this or that that determines whether it's a sign of poor self-care. Many people take their health for granted and put off medical and dental checkups. But they take care to take vitamins, eat healthy food, and jog. All to the good. But when fitness turns to fanaticism, when it takes up time and attention needed for other people or things, when it keeps us from participating, it becomes poor self-care.

Everyone needs some level of mental stimulation. It's all too easy these days to become a TV zombie or to spend all one's time keeping fit or socializing. If your job isn't very challenging, you should seriously ask why you are still with it. Perhaps the money or the prestige is worth it. Perhaps other opportunities are limited, or perhaps you are afraid of a more difficult challenge.

If you have no particularly intellectual interests, ask yourself why. Do you really have no time? Is your composite of activity in balance? Are you depriving yourself of reading because you are afraid of being alone?

Look at your social life with a critical eye. Why don't you have any friends whose conversation challenges you? Do you really like all those good-time Charlies, all those backslappers?

Very few people are so clever that they are able to find the proper mix of private and social lives. They squander time at work and neglect the families who care for them. They withdraw to their rooms when their friends would happily cheer them. They have many hail-fellow friends and not one they can count on. They go to big parties and hang out at singles bars and discos, wondering why they don't meet anyone they like or why no one seems interested in them. They view the world with detachment and then wonder why everyone seems an adversary. They feel smothered by their families but have no interests outside. They take their lovers for granted and then wonder why they seem cold.

As you go over everything you've learned about your self-care habits, divide your findings into two columns labeled "Good Self-Care/Strengths" and "Poor Self-Care/Weaknesses." This will give you an idea of how things balance out. Come up with as many observations as possible.

A list might look like this:

GOOD SELF-CARE/STRENGTHS	POOR SELF-CARE/WEAKNESSES
Physical:	
I eat regular meals, little junk food.	I haven't gone to the dentist in three years.
I play hard tennis twice a week.	My job requires me to sit at a desk all day.
I gave up smoking two years ago.	

A Time for Caring

I treat myself to a beauty-parlor shampoo and set once a week.
I'm careful about driving.

Mental:
I belong to several book clubs.
I follow the chess column avidly.
My girl friend and I share an interest in folk art.

Economic:
I earn a good salary.

Social:
I have many friends I do things with.
I have a loving family.
I date a lot.
I can talk easily to strangers.

Emotional:
I like having my own apartment, my own things.
I feel confident at work, and know I do a good job.
I can usually take care of myself.
My attitude is usually positive.

About twice a week I stay out too late on work nights and end up feeling awful in the mornings.
I'm always misplacing things and running out of stuff like soap and toilet paper.

My job offers little mental stimulation.
I'm so busy I hardly keep up with the news.
None of my friends reads or plays chess, except Jim, and I never see him.
I watch too much late-night television.

I never keep track of the money I spend.
I buy too much junk that I never use, especially clothes and makeup.
I don't have a cent saved.

I don't have a close friend I can talk to at this time.
My friends are spread all over the country, and we never find time to get together.
I never seem to go out with the same person more than twice.

I feel lonely if I spend the evening by myself.
I'm good at small talk, but I am afraid to confide in people.
I would be embarrassed to call somebody if I felt sad.
I rarely stop long enough to check out my feelings.

STEP FIVE: SET SELF-CARE GOALS

Now you have the information you need to formulate your plan and set your goals—to eliminate or change those things that cause bad feelings, that are care-less and self-neglectful. Be sure to make your goals realistic. Incorporate plans for changing those things that *can* be changed with a reasonable effort. Don't tackle the impossible—and—don't try to change everything. Think of the smallest and most easily accomplished changes that will make a difference and start with those. That way you'll get a feeling for the process of change and improvement and you'll be encouraged by the potential for improvement. For example, if you oversleep because you forget to set the alarm, start with that—a simple, manageable goal. After you gain confidence with a few simple improvements, *then* tackle your career change.

Probably many of the things on your "poor self-care" list don't bother you much. Pick those things that are most self-defeating or care-less. Don't be hard on yourself (*that's* poor self-care) and be flexible in your approach. Make changes gently: no radical upheavals are necessary.

Set goals that reflect your personal values. If your poor dietary habits don't trouble you, let them go for now. Don't tackle your lack of a stimulating job if it bothers your mate but not you. Decide what you need and what you feel it's possible to do. Start with two to five goals. You may find it helpful to redraw the self-care circle as *you would like it to be*.

Say you come up with this sample list of goals:

1. Come in by one o'clock on work nights.
2. Fix up the apartment so it's comfortable to spend time in.
3. Develop a close friendship with someone I can confide in.
4. Get involved somehow in the community.
5. Spend less time shopping.

Let's look at goal 2: *Fix up the apartment so it's comfortable to spend time in*. Just what does that mean? There are many things that could come under the heading of making an apartment more comfortable. Is new furniture needed—maybe there's not a comfortable chair, or maybe heavier curtains would cut down the noise and light from the street? Maybe it needs a paint job and

A Time for Caring

cheerier lights? Or little conveniences—a place to hang coats, an extra closet, a place near the door to hang the keys, a place where Scotch tape, scissors, extra light bulbs, and stamps are kept? An extra telephone? A work area where you can type or sew or work on your stamp collection? Fresh flowers and a bowl of fruit? The refrigerator stocked with enough food to make dinner at home appetizing?

STEP SIX: EXPLORE ALL POSSIBILITIES FOR IMPLEMENTING YOUR GOALS

Once you've determined the exact nature of your goals, the next step is to figure out how to implement them. There are many ways to tackle any given problem. Your job is to think of as many options or techniques or resources as possible for reaching your goals. Take advantage of your own strengths and abilities. Think about what resources are available at work or in the community. Develop a plan of attack that is comfortable and workable for you and that will capitalize on the assets you can bring to bear on the problem.

Let's go back to goal 2. You might decide that there are various things you can do:

(a) Create a workspace for typing, letter writing, and sewing. Include storage and organization space.

(b) Invite people over once a week—even if just for a drink, or to play cards, or to watch TV or talk.

(c) Keep basic food supplies in the house.

(d) Have flowers on the coffee table and on the bedroom dresser.

It's up to you to figure out which of these things would do the trick: which would make the difference, and which are "do-able" with the time, money, and effort you wish to devote to this goal.

You must figure out the arrangement and construction of the workspace and decide what will make it convenient. You must figure out what you can do yourself, what help you can get from friends, what you must buy or what can be rearranged from what's already available in the apartment. Then you have to figure out the best way to schedule food and flower shopping and make a list of what you need and can afford. And you must begin inviting friends or family to visit.

The more specific your plan, the better. It might go something like this:

- "I'll bring in that old chest of drawers from the bedroom and have Jim pick me up a load of plywood from the lumberyard. I can put up extra shelves on the far wall, and get a lamp from the store near the office. I'll put all my sewing supplies and stationery stuff in the chest of drawers, bring up that old cabinet from the basement to store fabric, give it a coat of paint. I can put my books in the new shelves."

- "I'll budget $8 a week for flowers. I'll pick them up on Thursdays after work from the vendor on the corner of Twelfth Street because I always come straight home to change for my class. I'll buy enough for the table in the living room and for my dressing table."

- "I'll start by stocking up on basic staples this week—spices, grains, soups, canned tuna fish, rice, cereal, sugar, etc. Then I'll try to save each Saturday morning for going to the market for fresh fruit and vegetables, meat and cottage cheese, etc."

- "It's Art's birthday next Friday. I'll invite him and Ellen for dinner. Then I'll try to have people over once a week, even if just for a drink."

STEP SEVEN: PAY ATTENTION

Once you decide on your plan, be attentive to it and remind yourself of your goals. Try not to slip from your schedule. (But remember not to set yourself impossible, easy-to-foil, goals.) See if it works and whether or not you should modify it. Does it feel good? Is it an efficient plan? Be attuned and flexible to modification of your plan.

STEP EIGHT: BE SELF-SUPPORTING AND REWARDING

Give yourself a pat on the back whenever you do something that brings you a little closer to your goal. Let yourself feel good about the progress you're making. *Care* for your own progress. If you make a phone call that is difficult, or take another step in a long-range task, or try something new, take notice of it. It's these little

A Time for Caring

milestones that build up confidence and self-esteem and provide reassurance.

It also follows, of course, that you must not chastise yourself too harshly for every little slip or infringement of your goals. Remind yourself that you're only human and that what you're trying to do is not in fact so easy. You're changing long-ingrained patterns, giving up comfortable props. Be flexible and understanding.

It is also a good idea to set yourself a real reward for the completion of your goal. Sweetening the pot will give you an additional focus and extra impetus and support during the hard times. The reward should be unrelated to the goal. Weight lost on a diet should not be rewarded with food. Waking up to an alarm should not be rewarded with extra sleep. But treating yourself to something special as a reward for *caring* for yourself is good self-care. It's helpful to keep a list of possible rewards, small and large, from which to choose. You can then refer to the list when needed and use it to encourage yourself to achieve your goals. Rewards can range from a movie to a massage to an ice cream cone to an evening away from the kids.

STEP NINE: ENLIST THE HELP AND SUPPORT OF OTHERS

Let others in on your plans. Be careful to pick people who are sympathetic and helpful—don't sabotage your self-caring plan with toxic influences. Be specific. Tell people what you are doing and let them know what kind of help you would like.

"I'm so nervous about giving this party. Could you come early and help introduce everyone? You always seem so comfortable in these situations."

"I'm trying to set up a workroom in my bedroom and I can't seem to figure out the best way to do it. I'd like your advice. Could you come over and take a look at the space some day this week?"

"Does my dress look right for a job interview?"

"Can I call you if I get together a poker game?"

"When I spend an evening at home alone, I end up wasting time watching TV or going to bed early. Now I'm trying to fix the place up a little so that it's more welcoming."

"Do you know of a good place to buy cut flowers?"

Don't be afraid to ask. It is possible that some people will say no. But most people are glad to help in these situations. They like to help others reach goals they are sympathetic to. They feel needed and are glad for your appreciation. And don't forget to support yourself.

Also, be sure to listen to others' reactions and advice. Their feedback is important. While in many ways you probably know best what you need, the advice and suggestions of others—especially where there is special knowledge or training—can often be invaluable.

STEP TEN: WRITE OUT YOUR SELF-CARE CONTRACT AND PLAN TO REVISE IT PERIODICALLY

A form for a self-care contract follows. Keep yours where you can refer to it regularly.

Review it periodically to see if your strategy is working, your goals are being attained. Be sure to "cement" the gains you've made, making them a part of your life, adding to the pile of strengths, the accumulation of positive self-care habits. Try to build. Use newfound skills and strengths to implement new goals and plans for self-caring.

SELF-CARE CONTRACT

Name:_____

My Self-Care goals are:

1. _____
_____

2. _____
_____

3. _____
_____
_____

My strategy is:

_____
_____
_____
_____
_____

My resources are:

_____
_____
_____
_____
_____

My support system is:

_____
_____
_____
_____
_____

I'll reward myself with:

_____
_____
_____
_____
_____

I will review this agreement on _____

Date: _____

Signature: _____

17

Sexual Intimacy:
CARING IN AND OUT OF BED

THE PROBLEM WITH INTIMACY

Simply put, the formula for sexual caring is this: Care about those you are intimate with, and don't be intimate with people who don't care about you. Simple, but by no means easy. It is puzzling and frustrating that, given today's open-ended social and sexual freedoms, with innumerable options to choose from and a dazzling range of possible types and permutations of acceptable relations between the sexes, so few people find their way to happiness and satisfaction. Psychotherapists' offices—and singles bars—are filled with men and women sincerely seeking closeness and sexual satisfaction, and failing to find it. Not getting love, they often settle for getting laid.

People today not only have legitimate reservations about love but a downright conviction that love won't and cannot work. They feel that autonomy and sportsex connections are their only choice, so they make the best of it. Their credo is "once burned, twice smart." Some withdraw from the fray, frustrated and disappointed in their search for a meaningful relationship. As a defense against further hurt they cultivate a cynical detachment, for intimacy itself is seen as a threat to their hard-won well-being. The trouble is that with practice, with repeated denial of feelings, their pose becomes a habit. They avoid romance, purge the "unhealthy" emotions of possessiveness and jealousy from their repertoire. They cultivate coolness. At the extreme, they become part of the problem: seducers and exploiters of the hunger for intimacy.

A Time for Caring

There is no question that achieving intimacy on a one-to-one basis, especially where sexual content is involved, is not easy. Sex is as fragile as it is powerful. It brings people together—with their sensitivities and needs, their secrets and their nakedness—at the closest range, in the most vulnerable setting, no matter how seemingly casual the liaison. This is as true of the one-night stand as of the thirty-year marriage. This is as true in relationships in which love is not an issue as in those in which love predominates. Yet despite the pitfalls, most people persist in their search for intimacy, for the hunger is intense and the rewards for success immense.

The search is complicated by the fact that there's little to guide today's would-be lovers and little to reassure them. Although they are free to follow their own preferences and inclinations, they flounder while trying to find the vital link between sex and intimacy: the link of caring.

There are long-enduring marriages riddled with carelessness, and there are one-night stands that are orgies of care. Without caring content, sexual intimacy is just seduction, exploitation, manipulation, depersonalization, a cushion against loneliness, a thrill, a duty, a diversion, a habit, a way to burn up calories. It becomes an arena in which to act out everything from aggression and anxiety to power and punishment—everything but love and sexual pleasure.

Perhaps no human quality has suffered so much at the hands of sexual revolution as has genuine intimacy. Another paradox, for the sexual revolution certainly broke down many seeming inhibitors to intimacy: false taboos, puritanical thinking, hypocritical rules and regulations, the ostracism of those who deviated from the norm. It opened up new areas of sexual exploration, new varieties of experience, offered more freedom of choice, new configurations and forms. It legitimized pleasure. All changes that should have encouraged greater intimacy yet all too often manifested themselves in alienation, exploitation of others, obsessiveness, perversion, and a denial of the connection between caring and sex.

Sexual freedom is too often viewed not as an opportunity for developing truly intimate and unique sexual relationships but as a license to be profligate and promiscuous. The "with it" person is supposed to view perversion and pornography, sadomasochism and segmentalized sex, with blasé acceptance. Proving oneself alluring, adept, available, irresistible, and unshockable is the surest way not to be alone on a Saturday night. Manipulators are admired, as is the ability to attract and seduce: the object is to arouse the emotions of others while holding oneself apart and unscathed.

Today's sexual animal can be sexually free, can manipulate the emotions of others and yet not get personally involved—indeed, may not be capable of emotional involvement. It's a ludicrous situation. Sexual one-nighters are accepted as a matter of course, but having breakfast the morning after or exchanging personal information may overstep the "proper" bounds of the situation. Promiscuity has become an escape from emotional involvement, a way of shielding oneself from caring about the sexual partner. What it amounts to is a new kind of sexual Victorianism, just as oppressive as what came before. It says, "I want to be intimate with you, but not *intimate*." It has its own taboos: love, commitment, vulnerability, concern.

SPORTSEX

One of the beneficial effects of the sexual revolution is the idea that sex is good, and pleasurable, and that it needn't necessarily be intertwined with love, much less marriage. Also, incidentally, that women may enjoy sex too, and not just loose women. So far, so good. But, as often happens, when humans pick up and run with an idea, they don't know when to stop.

Somehow the idea that sex-without-love-is-okay got turned around into the dogma that *only*-sex-without-love-is-okay. Perhaps this idea is the wishful thinking of people who are ignorant, unskilled, or disappointed in the quest for intimacy. In any event, segmentalized sex-as-sport is very much the order of the day. Sexual variety, number of experiences and expertise are major concerns. Anything that smacks of involvement, concern, commitment, is out. The dogged pursuit of gourmet sex becomes a way to fend off love.

Sportsex has its place in the sexual arena. Sex for its own sake can be very pleasurable. At times one's attraction to another is almost purely sexual. At times plain old sex is just what the doctor ordered: a way to still the incessant inner babble, to gain confidence, to forget everyday problems, to overcome hurt, to feel connected to another, to have a good time. People rebounding from a divorce or the breakup of a love affair often use sportsex as a mechanism to reassure themselves of their appeal, to forget their trauma momentarily, or as a bridge between involvements. But every episode of sportsex needs at least a soupçon of care and concern if it is not to leave the participants feeling empty or vaguely dissatisfied.

A continual diet of the empty calories of junk-food sex eventually fails to satisfy. Most people outgrow their sportsex phase or become very disillusioned with it: they then search for a deeper commitment or withdraw to an autonomous, even celibate, lifestyle.

Those who don't get past the sportsex stage eventually run into serious problems. Continuous consumption of sex out of context becomes a habit; pleasure and joy become harder to find and harder to sustain. Feelings become blunted. Sex becomes trivial and meaningless, like shaking hands; any hint of involvement feels threatening. The habitual sportsex practitioner becomes incapable of a sustained relationship, terrified of engulfment by another. To this person there's "safety in numbers."

At the Bach Institute we've seen many sportsex addicts. Judging by our clientele, the happy-hooker-as-happy-hedonist is a myth. Many of these people can't put their fingers on what's wrong. They're dazed and puzzled, passive and cut off from their feelings even as they pursue a sexual itinerary that would make Don Juan blush. Some cope by becoming supercompetent but mechanical lovers, totally free of any performance anxiety or concern about the other's pleasure or opinion. Many are victims of what the Institute calls the Marina Syndrome, named after the life-style of the singles who inhabit the chic apartments of Los Angeles's waterfront marinas. Healthy, educated, liberated, outfitted with every status symbol and instrument of pleasure, they jump from amusement to amusement and from bed to bed in a frenzy they may or may not be able to sustain.

A continual diet of junk-food sex eventually causes malnutrition. In practice, sexual freedom becomes irrelevant at best and dumb at worst—like stopping off for a snack at McDonald's on the way to a gourmet dinner. The legitimization of the pursuit of sexual pleasure has turned into a great snark hunt—a single-minded, all-directions pursuit of something that doesn't exist: pure, context-free sex.

The heights of sexual fulfillment cannot be reached in segmentalized sex. The components of sexual satisfaction are inextricably interwoven with the totality of our lives, our values, our undeniable human needs . . . and those of our lovers.

THE PROBLEM WITH SEX

It's hard to say whether or not the sex war and the sexual revolution have caused the high incidence of sexual dysfunction and impotence or have just brought it out in the open. But we do know that problems of sexual performance have spawned a big sex-therapy industry complete with hospitals, clinics, retreats, books and articles, sexologists and sex therapies. The Masters and Johnsoning of America has been swift and thorough. Sex therapy has proved beneficial for some, especially those whose problem was either ignorance of or inhibition about sexual function. But for those whose problems have to do more with sexual context and destructive societal ideas about sex, most contemporary sex therapy has the devastating effect of encouraging segmentalized sex and the idea that performance is what counts.

Much of what is termed dysfunction or impotency is better treated as a functional disorder that affects the whole organism. Rarely is genital retraining at the hands of a sex surrogate the answer; in fact, it reinforces the idea that good sex is a matter of mechanics. What's needed is the reestablishment of the connection between caring and sex, the minimizing of mixed messages between lovers, as well as techniques for understanding and managing the role of aggression in sex, for role reversal and flexibility, for assertiveness, and for broadening (or desegmentalizing) the context of sexuality.

The fallout from the sexual revolution has been devastating and disorienting, judging by some of the symptoms: in addition to the high incidence of sexual dysfunction and impotence, there are the jaded sexual appetites demanding bigger and better kicks to attain pleasure. A dearth of romantic gesture. High divorce rates. An atrophied capacity for devotion. An easy abandonment of relationships that don't immediately click or that become troublesome. Obsession with sexual competence. A rise in prostitution. Loss of sexual confidence. The trivialization of sex. The mechanization of sex. Loss of hope in finding love. All in all, a high price to pay for pleasure.

Yet the sexual revolution has its up side. Freedom of sexual choice, the softening of the double standard, lessened guilt, expanded knowledge of sexual function, are all an improvement over ignorance and taboo. Perhaps in time people will settle down to more intelligent application of their new knowledge and freedoms. One of the reasons people feel so stressed about achieving intimacy and become so disenchanted with segmentalized sex is that they do know that intimacy is important. After all, if they didn't care, they wouldn't be unhappy. Many who prowl the singles bars night after night are looking for love and care: sexual gratification is often a substitute to tide them over until they find the real thing. People who feel condemned to the dehumanizing process of meet, mate, and separate become discouraged or cynical, but would be willing to try again if they saw a more promising way. Very few people really want to live in a world without love. They just wish they knew how to find that love-filled world.

THE GENDER WAR

Suspicion, name-calling, and acrimonious fighting have eroded the foundation of trust and goodwill essential to caring intimacy between men and women. The territory on which men and women try to get together these days has more the character of the battlefield than the boudoir. Sexual relationships are tainted by hostility, mistrust, and guardedness.

Women regard men as usurpers of power, as denying their rights and status. Men resent women encroaching on their territory and feel threatened by the upheaval of the old order. So polarized are the sexes that rational dialogue and interaction are sometimes impossible.

Much of the problem boils down to confusion and disagreement over sex roles and sex differences. Traditional role expectations—established divisions of labor, and even of acceptable feelings, according to sex—have created havoc. They have defined the providing and consuming of care as much as they defined who earns the money and who raises the children. It is true enough that women have, as a result of training, habit, and heredity, more practiced caring skills and feelings close to hand. But because the caring is both expected on the one hand and held in such low esteem on the other, today's woman sees the caring role as a way to keep her from growing, a way to insure her continued subservience to the male. She wants to be able to *choose* to care, not to have to pretend to want to care because it is her only choice. So women are rebelling against or denying the existence of the caring nature that they view as sabotaging the fight for equality, as aiding and abetting the enemy.

The male is angry with this woman who all of a sudden won't comfort him, won't uncomplainingly take care of the home and raise the children, won't be understanding when he strays. He's angry at the undermining of authority, at the loss of service, the outrageous demands. He is terrified of her toughness and intractability, her insistence on reapportionment of life's spoils.

Even more threatening, women now want the sexual prerogatives of the male: the right to choose and reject sexual partners, the opportunity for sexual variety and pleasure. Actually, women want it all: sexual satisfaction along with the giving *and* getting of care.

Both much and little are made of the innate differences between the sexes. On the one hand there is adherence to the idea of an unbreachable chasm between the sexes, the cult of masculinity and feminity. "He's a typical man; he'll never understand." "It's just like a woman to deny it." Sex differences are not seen as complementary but as alienating factors, excusing and explaining the ability to get along.

In the next breath the same people will deny that there *are* any real differences between the sexes, other than those culturally induced by a sexist society. They will insist, using ridiculous tautological arguments, that men and women have, underneath all the conditioning, the same emotional makeup, skills, physical strength, needs, and that this is desirable. In the face of all the evidence of gender differences, they will insist that androgyny is the natural and desirable sexual disposition.

In a fever of liberation and reform, anything that even remotely smacks of sex-role playing or sexual differences comes under attack. Today, any self-respecting feminist who dared even whisper *"Vive la différence"* would be shot on sight, her body paraded through the streets as an example of treachery.

The thorough discrediting of all notions of sex roles or sex differences is just as inhibiting to an understanding between men and women as were the tradition-bound ideas that have rightfully been discarded. It is unquestionably a relief to be able to shed traditional role expectations that hobble rather than enhance, to expand rather than contract sexual potentials, to leave behind Don Juan and the femme fatale. But to deny all difference makes no sense in the face of strong evidence that there certainly is *la différence*. To deny it impoverishes the potential richness of feeling and sensibility that men and women have to trade and share with each other.

The cause of caring intimacy has been both savaged and saved by the pitched battle now being waged. But the battle is a worthy one, for intimacy is blunted by inequities. Bleak as the present situation looks—with the old order in a shambles and but a shaky foundation for a satisfactory new order—there is cause to hope for a brighter future. Behind all the vitriol and name-calling is the recognition that men and women need each other (desire each other!), that each needs the qualities and sensibilities of the opposite gender. There have already been big strides made toward a basis of equity between the sexes, steps necessary to eventual peace and intimacy between the sexes. The effect of the women's movement has been to present a case that will benefit both sexes. In championing the right of women to a broader base for fulfillment and growth, it clears a path for men to discover what they are missing and to take title to their own needs for their feelings: their desire for nurture, their right to be passive. It has shown that both sexes may function better without unnecessary labels or expectations.

Having established a base of equity between the sexes, the women's movement seems to be lobbying, this time from a position of strength, to balance the desire for family and care with needs for other achievement and fulfillment. They've put aside distracting and unwinnable causes—like rewriting "herstory" in an attempt to eradicate by fiat the male-dominated past.

The concern for both men and women will be to fulfill the requirements of their human nature: the desire to nurture and the desire to achieve. There are still many battles to be fought; there is still a gap of understanding and lack of concern that will not be resolved while men and women act out their hostilities and fears in their sexual liaisons. Already the price has been high: alienation of affection between the sexes, a kind of secondary or defensive homosexuality, and especially lesbianism—a withdrawal from consorting with the opposite sex.

Women who regard men as exploitative beasts cannot open themselves to intimacy, cannot let their defenses down. Men who see women as castrators act angry and remain aloof. What is needed is a basis of trust and goodwill, if people are to be victors and not victims of the war between the sheets.

IMAGES OF INTIMACY AND INTIMATES

Images hamper the possibilities for care and love. When people are shown what lovers *should* look like, how they *should* feel, what they *should* say and do, they develop a narrow and unrealistic profile of their own acceptability as lovers and of their own choice of love objects. After all, most people are automatically ruled out of contention in a society where the profile of the ideal love object is a lithe, jeans-wearing blonde under thirty eating yoghurt and reeking of Charlie! while at the wheel of a Camaro. The only guy who has a chance with her is a tall, strapping fellow who isn't afraid to put his Ralph Lauren boots up on the sweeping desk of his art-studded executive suite. People today tend to be either over- or underchosen as love objects, depending on how well they conform to the symbolization.

It is natural for people to want to present themselves at their best, to put their best foot forward. It is natural for them to try to improve their chances in the love sweepstakes. Unfortunately, there are no laws that govern truth in imaging. That's why there's disappointment and anger when a man dates a sex bomb who doesn't "put out." That's why she's upset and puzzled when all her suitor seems interested in is getting her to bed. The problem with imaging is that it's hard to stop, it's hard to be temperate.

A Time for Caring

People link themselves with their image and then wonder why they aren't loved "for themselves."

Here is a conversation between a couple who have just met at a camera club gathering. Look at how seemingly innocent—and how rife with potential for future problems—is their imaging:

THEY SAY	THEY THINK
He: Well, you're certainly a welcome addition to our group.	Can't I ever say something clever?
She: Thank you. It certainly is friendly and interesting.	He's cute.
He: My friends call me Stretch. It's left over from my basketball days. Silly, but I'm used to it.	It's safer than saying my name is David Stein.
She: My name is Candy.	At least my nickname is. He doesn't have to hear Hortense O'Brien.
Stretch: What kind of camera is that?	Why couldn't a girl named Candy be Jewish? It's only a nickname, isn't it?
Candy: Just this old German one of my uncle's. I borrowed it from the office.	He could be Irish. And that camera looks expensive.
Stretch: May I? [He takes her camera, brushing her hand and then tingling with the touch.] Fine lens. You work for your uncle?	Now I've done it. Brought up work.
Candy: Ever since college.	So okay, what if I only went for a year?
It's more than being just a secretary. I get into sales, too.	If he asks what I sell, I'll tell him anything except underwear.
Stretch: Sales? That's funny. I'm in sales too, but mainly as an executive. I run our department.	Is there a nice way to say used cars? I'd better change the subject.

THEY SAY	THEY THINK
I started using cameras on trips. Last time it was in the Bahamas. I took—	Great legs! And the way her hips move—
Candy: Oh! Do you go to the Bahamas, too: I love those islands.	So I went just once, and it was for the brassiere manufacturers' convention. At least we're off the subject of jobs.
Stretch:	She's probably really been around. Well, at least we're off the subject of jobs.
I did a little underwater work there last summer. Fantastic colors. So rich in life.	And lonelier than hell.
Candy:	Look at that build. He must swim like a fish. I should learn.
I wish I'd had time when I was there. I love the water.	Well, I do. At the beach, anyway, where I can wade in and not go too deep.

This couple's imaging has erected barriers rather than broken them down and has created false impressions and expectations that will have to be corrected if they decide to stay together. And it may not work. It seemed risky to tell the truth at the onset, although in fact it's dangerous not to.

Symbols deny the idiosyncrasies of matchmaking, the unique and unpredictable qualities of individual couplings. A lack of spontaneity infuses the relationships of many men and women already injured in the love wars. Skittish about further hurt or rejection, they guard against loss of control and work to stay cool. Jealousy or possessiveness are felt as dangerous and threatening. Romantic gestures are disparaged as trivial and potentially embarrassing, even as they are longed for. Lacking confidence and skills, drenched by images, and misinformed about the nature of intimacy, they are their own worst enemies in the search for love.

A Time for Caring

CRAZY LOVE [17]

Lack of knowledge about intimacy and image saturation combine to create outlandish expectations for blissful, perfect, untroubled, continually exciting relationships. Besotted by images of perfect love, unprepared for dealing with problems or conflict or with the mundane details of day-to-day living, people find relationships hard to sustain and easy to abandon. Problemphobic, fearful of real intimacy, they are puzzled as they set off in search of a new love about why the old love didn't last, why it didn't work out. The realities of adult love, the conditional nature of relationships, don't mesh with their vivid images.

One contemporary way of handling the problems of intimacy, of day-to-day routine, and the need for constant bliss, is with what might be called "love spurts." These are liaisons in which the couple gets together intermittently, perhaps for a few days at a stretch, three or four times a year. Each time it's like a fresh relationship. It's a love bug that strikes periodically, like a recurring virus. The couple has lots to talk about: new clothes, new jobs, new stories, new successes. They make love endlessly and imaginatively. It seems the ideal situation: it has all of the fun and none of the problems of a day-to-day relationship. There is no fighting, no need to sustain interest through tedium or hard times, no need to broaden their context. They can allow themselves to enjoy their feelings, yet not be trapped by them. They can temporarily be open and abandoned in a relatively stress-free context. Love spurts are a defensive ploy used by decent people fearful of genuine intimacy, a way of being crazy in love without going crazy.

There are love-crazy components to almost all love relationships. It is the ability to make the transition from the love-crazy stage and to establish the basis for a continuing relationship that is crucial.

There are three phases of the love-crazy state:

1. *The Fantasy of Love:* This is the phase of the formation of a fantasy of an ideal relationship. It is here that images and expectations mix, that a magical partner is dreamed of. The fantasy may have much or little probability of fulfillment, may or may not move to stage 2.

2. *The All-Electric Trip:* This is the crucial stage in which the fantasy fixes on an object. The ideal partner. The heady, dazzling All-Electric Trip is under way—exciting, miraculous, joyous, thrilling. Cupid has shot his arrows and they've found their mark. The lovers are giddy; they laugh and confess foolish thoughts. They are open and intimate. Their pulses race; every touch excites. Enraptured with each other, they tune out the rest of the world.

This overmobilization of emotion seems to be human nature. People need to discharge these feelings that perhaps are an attempt to replicate infant perceptions of unconditional parental love.

It's a wonderful feeling to be drunk with love. It makes for poetry and charming movies, but it is a shaky foundation for lasting intimacy. It's a form of romantic roulette; the odds are against it.

A one-sided, love-crazy trip is bound to end in disaster. Although at first it may be flattering and ego-building to the beloved and an exciting fantasy come true to the pursuer, the great imbalance will not permit the situation to go on very long.

Because the All-Electric Trip is based a great deal on fantasy, it can only hold out against the encroachment of reality for so long. Couples who can enjoy the excitement while being prepared for its eventual tempering and transition stand a good chance for a continuing relationship. Unfortunately many couples are loath to spoil the dream. They become overcautious about their behavior, careful of everything they say and do, denying or burying potential problems. They rationalize this by saying it is only natural in the throes of courtship to try to please. They repress the need for change, using delaying tactics.

This conversation between Carol and Will takes place after they've been going out for a few weeks. Carol has just agreed to spend the night at Will's apartment. Driving home late from a long, wine-filled day at the beach, both realize how tired they are and begin to regret their plan to spend the night together, but neither speaks up. They are trapped. Now, tired, making love for the first time, they are trying to show concern and passion for each other.

A Time for Caring

THEY SAY	THEY THINK
Will: Carol, darling—	I hope she can come soon. My back is ready to break, and I don't know how much longer I can wait. Maybe if I show more passion, she'll get more excited.
Carol: Oh, Will, darling!	Oh, my sunburn!
Will: I love you, Carol!	My left leg is cramping.
Carol: Yes, yes!	I can't come. I know it. I'm too tired.
Will: I could go on all night!	Please come. You said you could. I don't want to lose control. I remember what you said about men who were selfish and immature in bed.
Carol: Yes! Yes! Harder!	Well, I can't go on all night. I'm losing all sensation. I wish you'd just go ahead and come. Please.
Will [complying]: Like this?	As if it wasn't tough enough to hold back before. Two plus two are four; four plus four are eight. Eight and eight—
Carol: Yes! More!	I think he's weakening. If he'll only come, he won't think I'm frigid. I know I'll come with him another time. Maybe I could even fake it. I bet he couldn't tell.
Will: Oh! Carol, I—Can—can you—make—it?	Please say yes. I'm at the end of my rope.
Carol: Yes! Yes I can! The minute you—do!	Damn, I'm closing up or something. It's starting to hurt. I'll just have to fake and hope for the best.
Will: I hate to have it end.	I'll hang on another minute. Sixty-four and—

THEY SAY	THEY THINK
Carol: Now, darling! Oh, Will!	For pity's sake, get it over with. Is he? I'm almost sure. Well, I'll try to be convincing.
Will: AH!!	At last!
Carol: OH!!	Hallelujah. I thought he never would.

[There is a moment of silent relief.]

Will: Did you?	
Carol: Did I ever! Was it nice for you, Will?	I really hope he liked me.
Will: Did I like it? Silly girl! Was it really all right for you?	I wonder if she'd be awfully hurt if I just went to sleep. Burke is coming in for that meeting very early tomorrow.
Carol: Oh, Will. [She sighs.] I knew you'd be a real man. Are you always so strong?	I hope he doesn't want to talk long. I have to do something with my hair before I can go to work.
Will: I think I would be for you. I didn't get too rough for you at the end, I hope?	She wants to talk awhile. Well, I don't really mind.
Carol: No, you'd never hurt me. But you are quite a man.	He wants to talk. Oh, well. He would. He's really a fine lover, but it's so late.
Will [beams]: Am I? Of course, what else could I be with that wonderful body of yours? [He strokes it.]	I'm glad she feels that way. I can see how important sex is for her.
Carol: And I love *your* body. [She caresses him.] Most men just want to go to sleep.	I'll need at least an hour for my hair. It's so salty.
Will: I'm not most men. Besides, I've waited so long to touch you.	She really is special. If only Burke weren't coming so early.
Carol: Oh, Will! [She reproves.]	I know I'm supposed to want this, and it's sweet. But the time is—Hey! I really like for him to touch me there, but—hey!

A Time for Caring

THEY SAY	THEY THINK
Will: I'm not hurting you?	
Carol: No, I like that.	Except at three in the morning. I really should return the gesture.
Will: Oh, Carol. You'll turn me on. Oh, Carol—	It is now three A.M. Burke is due at eight thirty. Maybe she's trying to tell me she needs more. I wonder if I could—
Carol: Do you want to again, dear?	I may as well hear the news.
Will: I want to, but you must be so tired—	What can I say?
Carol: I'm not too tired if you need me—	What am I saying? But after all he's said about cool, unsexed women—
Will: Really?	Does that mean she expects more?
Carol: Really.	I knew once wouldn't be enough for him.
Will: Darling. Do you like this?	It's a flat offer. I can't refuse.
Carol: Oh, yes. And do *you* like this?	I do, but why *now*?
Will: Oh . . .	If she keeps that up, I just might make it.
Carol: Darling, now!	Let's get it over with.
Will: You're wonderful, the way you can say things right out so frankly. Is this what you have in mind?	Let's get it over.
Carol: Oh . . .	And he'll expect me to come.
Will: Oh . . .	And she'll expect me to come.
Carol: Aaah . . .	There's no choice. I'll just have to fake it again.
Will: Aaah . . .	I'm sure I can't come. It's a miracle that I can do anything at all. I wonder if she could tell if I faked coming?

Thus accommodation begins, seemingly innocently and with the best of intentions. But Carol and Will are setting themselves up for perpetuating the dozens of seeds of misinformation sown this night. Knowing that this occasion of mutual sexual acceptance was important, both parties chose to set aside their real feelings in favor of presenting the best face and of making their partner feel good. Now they have given each other ideas about their sexuality that are untrue but that they will nevertheless try to live up to so that their partner doesn't feel deceived. Coming down to earth from the All-Electric Trip is bound to be a hard landing for Carol and Will.

3. *Crazy Exits:* When reality threatens, many people would rather split than have to be real. They are unwilling to give up the fantasy of crazy love. When reality threatens, they'd rather split than have to be real. For them, exit is the only answer, even though the tendency to deny the wish to exit, to try to prolong the fantasy, is enormous. The end to fantasy doesn't come easily and can have dangerous side-effects, ranging from double-bind messages, such as "I don't want to leave, you do," to literally killing the love partner either as a means of escape or as a way of punishment for destroying the fantasy.[18]

18

The Caring Content of Sexual Relationships

One of the pluses of the sexual revolution is the acceptability and accessibility of diverse styles of sexual relationships. There are marriages and long-term love-ins of twenty years' standing, monogamous or "open" in construction. There are short-term relationships that go on as long as the fun, or the summer, lasts. There are one-night stands. And all of these relationships apply to homosexual couples as well as heterosexual ones. There are no rules about age, race, or sex. Regardless of the statistics or details that describe a couple, the same caring content should apply to all.

But everyone handles intimate relationships differently; the amount, tenor, and logistics of the intimacy differs from person to person. Each couple is pair-specific, governed by their own rules and needs, their own idiosyncrasies. And that is as it should be. Preconceived ideas about coupledom are perilous to the fulfillment of each couple's personal needs. Then, too, what works during one period of a couple's life may be totally unsatisfactory at another. There are few guidelines in the search for the most satisfying intimate life-style. Except for one fact: Whatever the nature or intended duration of the liaison, it is the caring content that makes it work, that makes it intimate and not exploitative:

> Neither duration nor proclamation of commitment is necessarily the measure—there are ephemeral explosions of passion between strangers that make more erotic sense than many lengthy marriages, there are one-night stands in Jersey City more glorious than six-months affairs

in Paris—but finally there is a commitment, however brief; a purity, however threatened; a vulnerability, however concealed; a generosity of spirit, however marbled with need; an honest *caring*, however singed by lust, that must be present if couplings are to be salubrious and not slow poison.[19]

THE CARE AND MAINTENANCE OF LOVE

Meeting and mating is just the beginning. The problems of sustaining a relationship are very different from those of starting one, one of the first problems being that of making the transition from the trouble-free romantic rapture stage to the realities of everyday life. People are often hurt and puzzled by relationships that suddenly break up or that die a slow, lingering death. They ask the most poignant and important question of all: "What makes love stay?"[20]

The answer can be found by looking at some of the characteristics and components of healthy sexual liaisons:

REALISTIC EXPECTATIONS

Caring intimates know how much concern, work, and attention a good relationship takes, and they are willing to put in the required time and effort. They are *not* love crazy, living on dreams or images of love. They are aware of the intricacies of intimacy and don't expect everything to fall effortlessly into place. They don't expect great sex every time, or *any* time unless they make the time and effort to love. They anticipate crises, emergencies, routine, hard times. They are willing to cultivate and nurture their love.

MUTUALLY UNDERSTOOD GOALS

Caring intimates do not deceive each other about their desires, be they long- or short-range plans. It is understood between them that this is a one-night stand, a summer romance, or a hoped-for long-term relationship. A man who wants a roll in the hay should not profess undying love to the woman who wants a ring on her

A Time for Caring

finger. The caring con man—full of phony words of love and manipulative promises—is the most insidious of pretenders.

Caring couples have an understanding that their dream is to work for ten years and then move to the country, or to save their money to buy a sofa and not splurge on a vacation. If the goals differ, that too is mutually understood, and disparities are discussed openly. One wants to get married; the other is not ready. They both want marriage, only one wants children. One aspires to wealth, the other to social prominence. Ideally there is room for negotiation, for compromise or change.

CONCERN FOR THE RELATIONSHIP

Caring intimates are concerned about the entity they have created through their union. They feel committed to their coupledom and its preservation and growth. They look for ways to deepen its roots and are involved with the development of its own rituals and the nurture of its particular environment.

BALANCE

Relationships that last have a foundation of fairness in which both partners are of equal importance, and the concerns of each have equal value. Though they may start out of whack or teeter from one side to the other periodically, over time an equity of give-and-take is achieved.

This is not to deny the complementary nature of many successful relationships in which one partner is more intelligent, or more playful, or stronger, or earns more money. In these relationships the balance is achieved by trade-offs of strengths and weaknesses, each partner compensating for and augmenting the weak areas of the other.

But very rarely does a one-sided relationship survive, even when both parties want it to last. It is too lopsided and eventually will topple. At first it seems right that the forceful, domineering man finds a dependent, submissive woman who wants to be looked after. At first it seems logical that a shy, retiring fellow has a wife who helps him find a job, manages his social life, is happy to be the sexual aggressor. But resentments build; these relationships become static and intolerant of any upset or change in the lopsided balance of power.

Intimates need to see each other as having equal (though different) contributions to and responsibility for the maintenance of the relationship. Respect must be mutual if there is to be a balance of self- and other-interest, if one party is not to feel entitled to a larger share in accordance with his or her larger contribution.

Imbalanced relationships are breeding grounds for manipulation and exploitation. The party who has the upper hand is tempted to use his or her position to get what is wanted, to get more than a fair share, to shirk duties and drudgework. The powerless party manipulates indirectly, using weaknesses as an excuse for avoiding responsibility or getting attention.

The balance in a caring relationship is always shifting. The idea that both parties should simultaneously feel or get the same is a false goal. The balance of give-and-get goes back and forth. Roles reverse. The partners alternate between active and passive, lover and beloved, submissive and dominant, from man-on-top to woman-on-top. Ideally, both players get to play both parts.

CONCERN FOR THE OTHER

People who like and respect each other recognize the importance of the other's concerns. They feel that their partner's feelings and sensibilities, their ways of doing things—no matter how different—are of equal value. They are sympathetic to the other's wishes, dreams, hurts, needs.

Yet it's so easy for lovers to get into destructive patterns of poor communication. Afraid of the repercussions of what they think, they hold back, or distort the truth. Afraid of hurting their partner, they keep quiet. Unskilled in the art of direct communication, they give out mixed messages or expect their partner to read their mind.

Each of us has areas of inarticulateness or shyness. Each of us has secrets to keep and hard-to-break miscommunication habits. Each of us has hidden agendas for our conversations. But caring intimates work to develop a system of communication that satisfies their own way of functioning. They are able to voice the concerns, reservations, wants, and needs of their mate. And they are willing to speak up for what's important to them, what hurts or irritates them. They do not shy away from confrontation for fear of damaging the relationship, of bursting the bubble of romance. They evolve a system of physical or verbal clues to shortcut their communications and help them over the rough spots. They have rules and regulations of communication, a system for negotiating the negatives of their day-to-day life. They're careful not to store up resentments in a gunnysack that can spill over at the wrong time. They make it a point to feed back to each other their reactions and feelings about everyday events and about each other. By getting to know each other this way they are able to predict stresses to their relationship and adjust their plans accordingly. They reduce the chances of misunderstandings or arguments, of unhappiness or depression, or abrupt breakup.

For an intimate relationship to last, the participants need to feel safe to say what's on their mind, air both fear and fantasy. Caring intimates help each other to overcome diffidence and shyness, actively listen to each other in an effort to avoid misunderstanding and the dissemination of false clues.

CLEAR COMMUNICATION CHANNELS

The effects of poor communication habits are devastating. The inability to assert oneself about which movie to go to escalates into the inability to voice one's preferences about where to live, how to raise the kids, and what turns one on in bed.

Withholding one's feelings about a seemingly negligent incident escalates to keeping silent when the hurt is great and the issue important. If your lover never knows your dream, its fulfillment will never be put on the agenda. If he's never been told that you hate it when he blows in your ear, you lose your right to resent him for it even as it undermines your care for him.

Small lapses in communication have a way of turning into gaping holes if the void isn't filled. The effects of faulty communication turn up unexpectedly in other areas. Dismay about your lover blowing in your ear gets diverted into your inability to become aroused, or your burning the breakfast toast.

Lack of faith in another's direct communication leads to a tendency to try to read the other's mind or to try to decode the other's message. First it's "I bet he really would prefer to eat home." Then it's "He's just pretending he's too tired for sex. He doesn't love me anymore."

TRUST

Fear of betrayal or ridicule, fear that what they say will be used against them makes lovers withhold information from each other. Often they have reason to behave this way: members of their family or perhaps former lovers have turned their confidences against them or twisted them out of shape.

It required three months of therapy before Dee confessed her never-before-revealed sexual secret: that she could only have an orgasm lying on her stomach in a certain position. She had been through numerous unsatisfying relationships with her secret intact, certain that to reveal it would be embarrassing beyond belief and that the knowledge of her oddity would mean the end of the relationship. Even though her instincts told her that her current lover, Paul, would be understanding and even helpful, she became paralyzed every time she worked up her nerve to tell him. She would allude to the problem and then get upset that Paul didn't guess. It was in a series of couple-therapy sessions that Dee was able to share her problem with Paul and defuse this sexual time bomb.

When lovers trust each other, their sense of engulfment and of loss of control can become the source of pleasure and power rather than a fearsome and vulnerable state. Total abandon is, after all, one of the most sought-after and hard-to-come-by of sexual highs. But there's no "letting go" without the safety net of trust. Performance anxiety—doubts about one's sexual competence, pressure to perform—disappears in an atmosphere of trust. Trusting intimates are slow to pass judgments, accepting (even encouraging) quirks, foibles, differences. They try to assuage nervousness, are unafraid of tenderness or outrageousness, or the most sentimental romantic gesture. As much as possible they are image-free. Inhibition and intimacy don't mix.

A Time for Caring

CONCERN FOR THE CONTEXT

Another curious paradox of intimacy is that isolation kills it. In the thrall of the All-Electric Trip, couples tend to shut themselves off in their bed, in their home, protecting themselves from the hue and cry of the outside world. They put off the moment when the phone rings, or when it's time to go to work, or when the new lover must be introduced to friends. They want their lover all to themselves. They don't make the connection between their lover and the PTA meeting, or getting the laundry done. They don't realize that being with others *stimulates* the desire to be alone.

"Jim's insistence that our perfect love didn't need anyone else eventually destroyed it," says Emma. "For a long time I didn't mind that we spent all our time alone. Actually, I was flattered that Jim was totally uninterested in anyone else, and we were completely wrapped up in each other. We'd meet at a restaurant after work, or maybe at a movie. We'd be talking and touching all through dinner or the show. Jim would get me very turned on with his talk about how he was going to make love to me, and he liked me to be seductive too. We'd be sitting there in the restaurant and all I could think of was the minute when we'd get home and could fall into bed. Then we got in the habit of just meeting at Jim's apartment. He'd pick up food and I'd always have a special record or a new perfume. For a while it was great. But the predictable problems set in. We started running out of things to say. Remember, neither of us knew anything much about the other's work, we had no mutual friends to talk about. When I started hinting to Jim that I'd like to meet his friends, he got insulted, as though I wasn't satisfied with his company. When I suggested that we invite some of my friends over, he made excuses or put off the dates we'd make; he even started making remarks about how he didn't think he'd like my friends.

"I was crazy about Jim. I wanted my friends to meet him and wanted to show him off. Of course, all this time I was neglecting my friends, not finding time for my family, even letting up on my job—which is important to me. Jim would get very miffed if I tried to steal time for myself.

"It got to the point where I was so crazy from our aloneness that I even missed the excitement of other people around us in the restaurant. I was losing interest in our nightly sexual gymnastics, and I couldn't figure out why. I really wanted it to work out. I'd tell myself that he was as attractive as ever, that he was great in bed, and then my pussy would be dry as a bone, no matter how much I *wanted* to be aroused.

"Of course, I didn't tell Jim my problem. I thought it was just a passing thing. And Jim got worse about introducing his friends. I did manage to meet a few acquaintances casually, but no one important to him—though he kept promising. I thought maybe he was embarrassed to introduce me to his friends, though I didn't know why. Perhaps he had some secret past, or I was one of a long string. Now I know that he was afraid of the competition, afraid one of his friends would win out over him and steal me away. It would have been better to take the chance. Our great romance lasted all of four months and at the end, neither of us had much to say to the other."

There's no better testimony to the ill effects of isolation than the morguelike silence that fills the dining room at a Niagara Falls honeymoon hotel. The honeymoon is a horrible institution, a misguided example of the doubtful benefits of being far from the madding crowd. Newlyweds whose coupledom is not yet solid need the social context of friends and family far more than the old folks who think it's not important anymore to get away by themselves.

Couples whose main attraction to each other is sexual and whose professed interest in each other is sexual exploration and gratification are surprised when the thrill wears off so quickly. They think it's because they've tried everything, that the once great sex is becoming boring. More likely it's because there's no new input to enhance their context-poor sexual liaison. Sexual competence, so highly valued, means little without a larger context in which to express it. And bad sex, especially when there is no context to support it, is an acute misery.

The idea of pure isolated sex is a fantasy. There are detached, mechanical lovers who enjoy segregated sex. They can't have it otherwise, for care inhibits their pleasure. At the extreme, it is depersonalized, context-free sex that leads to hostility, exploitation, and rape. But for most people, sex in a vacuum soon palls. They need their intimacy to extend to other areas of their lives—to family, friends, community, shared interests, quiet conversations, joint problems. It is this lack of context that makes secret, illicit, or adulterous love affairs hard to sustain. The secrecy that is at first exciting loses its savor, and nothing new can be infused to enrich it.

"They say men are supposed to like unencumbered sex and get upset when women try to entangle them more deeply," says Russell. "Well, I've tried it and it doesn't work for me. I have several single buddies that I spend a lot of time with; we're often in a situation where it's easy to pick up a couple of women for an evening of fun and games. They're really into this—they're in the bars every night, they're attractive and articulate, and they have a great time. I feel like a freak sometimes because even when I think I'd like an erotic adventure, a jazzy one-nighter, even when I see a woman who turns me on, it's never much fun for me. At least, it's not as exciting as my fantasies of adventure and romance. I've been with women who are real chatty and charming at a party and have no hesitation about coming home with me. Then when I get there they don't want to talk, they don't want to be undressed or caressed, they just want to screw. They don't want to know about me, they don't want any tenderness. Some are pretty experienced, and the sex isn't bad. But then they want to get up and go home. Is it crazy that sometimes I can't get it up for the next big adventure? Who's crazy, them or me?"

The concept of context also applies to lovemaking itself. Some lovers have a tendency to define narrowly the components of lovemaking. The availability of information about sex notwithstanding, it's amazing how many people limit their erogenous zones to their genitals and measure the breadth of their sexual experiences by the number of positions they've tried. The contextualizers of the sex act—pillow talk, visual stimulus, sensitivity to touch and smell—broaden and intensify the base of sexual pleasure. The preoccupation with genital satisfaction is a most limiting approach to sexual pleasure. After all, the entire body is involved in the whole lovemaking process. The fixation on the genitals can cause problems—like premature ejaculation. Also, it's no fun.

It is natural that during the course of lovemaking there are times when all other thoughts and concerns are abandoned to the impulse for sexual fulfillment. Certainly oversolicitousness or concern for one's partner can intrude on one's own pleasure. At the wrong moments caring is out of context and can dampen sexual satisfaction. Sometimes sex needs to stand alone. But it is the context beyond the bedroom door that enriches and enhances the pleasure between the sheets.

MAINTAINING THE MAGIC

As we have said, when people fall in love the atmosphere is filled with tension and excitement; there's more than enough to do the job. The lovers take the suspense, the vibrations, the sultry air, for granted, as though it's an intrinsic part of their miraculous coupling, and pay little attention to it. Weeks or months later they awaken to the fact that their sizzling affair is settling into a dull routine. The sex is becoming ritualized, the conversation predictable. There are no surprises.

The routinization of relationships is the beginning of the end, one of the most pinpointable factors in the loss of sexual interest. Loss of passion *follows* the ritualization of sex. And then the lovers get fat!

The word tension has a bad press. People often think that the goal of a lasting relationship is to have it be smooth and stress-free. This is a false goal: the object is not to be stress-free but to direct the stress toward constructive use in the relationship. Tension is part and parcel of sexual arousal, a normal and desirable component of sexual pleasure.

The magic that keeps a love relationship exciting is not created by a wave of a magic wand but by the efforts and attention of caring lovers. They are careful to nurture the innovative and suspenseful qualities of their relationship; they guard against sameness, routine, predictability, lack of new stimuli. Caring lovers know that a certain amount of routine, of mundane detail, of day-to-day drudgery, is an inevitable part of life. But they refuse to fall into step with it.

Estelle is speaking:

"Gary and I lead very busy lives and our kids pretty much regulate our schedules, but we're lucky enough to have caught on early to the trap of routine and predictability. We don't have much free time these days to ourselves, and we're not big on heavy-handed programs to 'improve our relationship' (Yuck!), but we have learned a few things. One is that the kind of ten-minute quickie sex that we'd have when we were both tired at the end of the day was more depressing than satisfying. For one thing, it was always the same. Now we rarely have intercourse during the week. We're more likely to make out in the car for ten minutes in the driveway when we come home late from a town meeting. Or we'll neck on the porch swing while the kids are watching TV. Or I'll give Gary a massage and undress him while he's making phone calls. Or we'll share our morning shower. No pressure to be 'up' for sex, and by the time we're alone on the weekends we're very ready.

"Other things: I think Gary feels that I always have something interesting to say about what's going on—in the world or around the house—and he can't count on predicting my opinion. Also, I make it a point to bring new things into our life in small ways—a new magazine, a new paperweight for his desk, a new friend I think he'll enjoy. He's good at this too. And a master of the off-the-wall romantic gesture—a singing phone call on Groundhog Day, a new ribbon for my typewriter, breakfast, not in bed but in the bathtub."

PLAYFULNESS

Nothing quite takes the fun out of sex as taking it too seriously. The atmosphere of trust between lovers makes it the ideal situation in which to let one's hair down, to act silly or foolish. An element of playful, childlike regression is another ingredient in the recipe for sexual pleasure. A sense of humor allows lovers to laugh at their foibles and at their mistakes, helps overcome embarrassment and relieves pressure. Couples who play together stay together.

"Tess and I have several silly sex games that have become part of our repertoire, games inspired by movies we've seen, or friends or whatever. Games like 'Patty-cake' and 'Fingerlickin' Good,' and 'What's a Nice Girl Like You Doing in a Place Like This?' You have to be there to appreciate them—they're both too silly and too embarrassing to describe. Suffice it to say that the first involves a lot of talcum powder, the second is a dirty-talk parody of a TV commercial, and the third the silliest of takeoffs on a failed seduction. But Tess and I play them shamelessly and end up laughing so hard we cry."

PLANNING FOR PLEASURE

Although most people are aware that all work and no play is poor policy, they do very little to make sure their time doesn't get eaten up by duty or drudgery or just plain dullness.

Caring couples recognize the importance of fun and games and make sure they get their share by Planning for Pleasure. This means putting pleasure on the agenda and not leaving it to chance. Planning for Pleasure might entail two minutes for a snuggle when the couple returns from work, an hour of gin rummy, ten minutes for a cozy cup of coffee before the kids start clamoring for breakfast, a foot massage for a weary lover. The advantage of such planning is that pleasure is not left to chance. As nice as spontaneity is, one can't hold one's breath on the chance that a free hour for love will materialize out of a busy day. When lovers plan for pleasure, they show they care for the health of the relationship.

"Victor and I used to be very much of the one-of-these-days school of leisure activity. 'One of these days we'll see that play.' 'One of these days we'll have more time for tennis.' 'One of these days I'll tell you about that crazy encounter with Jake.' We were pretty miserable by the time we found out that one of these days never comes. Now whenever we start to leave things to chance, we stop and figure out how we can schedule our fun. Somehow in the last six months we've managed to find time for tennis, time to talk about things we'd usually put off or forget about, time to do twenty minutes of exercise together each morning, time for an occasional *douche à deux*—we're fond of gang showers. Sometimes we talk about our next lovemaking session in great detail. It doesn't always work out as planned, but the planning is great foreplay."

THE FIGHT FOR LOVE

Nowhere does the notion that caring means being nice do more damage than in the sexual arena. The romantic notion of aggression-free love has soured many a romance.

Research at the Bach Institute has for twenty years centered around the *constructive* use of aggression—not its denial or repression. For it doesn't really go away; it gets channeled into passive, indirect expression.

Caring lovers fight in and out of bed. They argue over chores, they assert their rights, they struggle for power or importance, they confront each other about behavior that upsets them, they needle each other about their politics, they tease each other about their shortcomings, they fight for more sex, or better sex.

To "sensitive, gentle" lovers this is horrifying. They don't want to hurt each other or make each other feel bad. She is "understanding" when he comes home late every night. He never complains about her dowdy clothes because it's "not important." She builds up his confidence in his tennis game even though she beats him and he's boring to play with. He always lets her choose the movie because he "doesn't care." They feel they accept each other as they really are.

Most people have been brought up to be "nice," never to hurt anyone. They feel guilty when they get angry, upset when they're around assertive people. But the fight for love is a natural one. It is feelings of love that bring out feelings of anger and hurt. It is feelings of vulnerability that make one fight for power and independence. Lovers get angry at themselves for their dependence, or at their lover for making them dependent. At themselves for giving in on an important issue, at their lover for not caring enough, at their lover for being flirtatious, at themselves for being jealous, at the hostility between men and women.

Caring lovers give each other the opportunity for the safe release of tensions and aggressions—they have love fights and they fight for love. At the Bach Institute we call this Fusion Sex: the fusion of sexual and aggressive energy in joyful erotic fulfillment. It is the fusion of love and aggression, of hostility and passion and positive feelings.

Many people who are upset by the idea of aggression and sex think that it implies sadomasochistic behavior, chauvinistic dominance, or destructive, hurtful manipulation. It is this thinking that has resulted in the passive, gentle lovemaking that soon drains erotic interest. Lovers who care for each other separate out the destructive, hurtful aspects of their anger and aggression from aspects that are playful, stimulating, and informative. Like any fair fight, love fights have mutually understood rules, rituals, time limits, and boundaries in a basis of equality. They're not free-for-alls.

No one is more vulnerable than a naked, trusting lover. The potential for inflicting pain and hurt, both emotional and physical, is very high. It is the basis of goodwill, the care and concern for the lover, that make love fights exciting and pleasurable (and safe) erotic adventures.

The essence of sexual aggression lies more in overpowering the partner and wresting control than in inflicting pain. Wrestling, pillow fighting, teasing, playful slapping and hitting, or tickling are used to overpower, subdue, or render helpless a lover at whom one is angry, a lover one wants to retaliate against or repay for indifference or bad behavior. At times love fights are playful expressions of minor upsets, at times the acting out of fear and hate. Lovers who accept and understand the role of love fights in their life have a safe outlet for the expression of aggression. It doesn't build up or get shunted aside, and it comes out in an exhilarating expression of erotic energy that enhances rather than tears down their love.

Fran and Ned are typical in many ways of the couples who come to the Bach Institute. They are nice, polite, solicitous. They never argue or fight. They love each other. They care about each other. They say they enjoy sex, but it hasn't been very good for the last year or so. They don't understand why they rarely feel turned on, why it takes them so long to get aroused, why Fran is always dry. As therapy progresses several things are revealed: Ned makes his approaches to Fran at times when she's very unlikely to feel turned on—while the kids are still up, when she has to leave the house in an hour. When they're in bed, he's full of questions about how she feels, solicitous of her pleasure. She acts quite passive and doesn't even make suggestions or take a dominant role.

As therapy progresses farther it turns out that Fran would like to be aggressive but she's afraid that she would shock Ned, whom she has decided "from little things he said" doesn't like aggressive women. As a matter of fact, her fantasies are of being superstrong and overpowering Ned, straddling him, tickling him, and licking him all over. She is afraid he'd be shocked and disappointed in her. And she gets turned off by all his concern for her; it makes her feel like it's a command performance, and she wonders why Ned never is interested in his own pleasure. Ned, it turns out, has become fixated on the idea that Fran is a pure, fragile woman who is sensual but who would be offended by unorthodox sex. He feels it his duty to be sure that she is satisfied before he worries about himself. When he masturbated, which was frequently, he fantasized about women (usually women he knew casually) who would make demands of him and taunt him with their sexuality. He would go along until he couldn't stand it anymore and they would battle for the right to satisfaction. The therapist's directive that they go home and have a pillow fight was the first step in Fran and Ned's love-fight training and the giving up of their old definition of "nice."

Sexual fulfillment can be hampered by misguided caring and niceness. The struggle for good sex can enhance care and love. People who say they are lovers and not fighters are making a big mistake. The price of being nice is very high.

CONCERN FOR SEXUAL SATISFACTION

For every couple, what constitutes sexual satisfaction is different. Yet many persist in thinking that there are certain things that constitute "good sex" or "bad sex," that there's an appropriate amount of sex, a set standard or priority for sex in one's life, or that there are certain things one should and shouldn't do in bed. Questions of how and how much dominate the search for satisfaction. It is the rare couple who recognizes that it is possible to make overmuch of sex, especially of *how* much sex. It is almost heresy to consider that for some couples sex need not have much importance in the broader context of a full and loving life.

While sexual knowledge is essential to satisfying sex, it often comes from the wrong sources. Looking for guidance from movies, myths, magazines, and Masters and Johnson, some couples overlook the very best source of information about their sexual satisfaction: each other. Inundated with ideas and images about the best sex or the right kind of sex, they forget that what's *really* great, *really* right, is nothing more than what *really* pleases them most. This is, after all, supposed to be an age of do-your-own-thing liberation. What better context is there for personal and private expression than between caring lovers in the sexual arena?

In addition to being sensitive and observant about what goes on when they make love, couples should discuss the composition of good sex. Each should know what constitutes sexual satisfaction for the other, what gives the lover pleasure, and exactly what turns the lover on and off. Caring lovers want to know and to accept the other's needs, desires, feelings, and quirks. Caring lovers try to instill confidence in the other's sexuality and are careful not to undermine or demoralize. Although they try to find safe areas for teasing, they are careful not to provoke jealousy, to dwell on past exploits, or to make hurtful comparisons. They become attuned to the rhythms and temperament of the other, sensitive to signals and modes of communicating. When there are problems, they work them out; they don't fall into the trap of accommodation or collusion. They pay attention to the language of their bodies, of their genitals, and learn to coordinate what they say and do with what they feel. Most of all they avoid the deadly, anti-intimate trap of faked passions, the lying and cover-up of faked orgasms. They join in the search and in the struggle for good sex.

Sexual confidence is the result of sexual experience, of accepting one's sexuality (and having it accepted by others), and of nurturing it through growth-producing channels—loving and learning liaisons. It is not a matter of sexual athleticism, of being a slick, accomplished Lothario or devastating femme fatale: such postures often cover a wealth of insecurity or exploitative intent. But couples who do not know each other well or do not accept each other are plagued with worries about "What should I do now?" "What does she mean by that?" "She probably expects me to come

A Time for Caring

again." "How can I tell him it turns me on if he talks dirty?" "I'm sure she thinks my penis is too small." "He'll think I'm weird if I ask him to lick my feet." "Is she trying to tell me she's too tired?" "Is he trying to tell me he's still hot to make love?" "When she laughs, am I doing the wrong thing?" "Does he like it when I grab hard on his balls?" "She won't love me if I say that." "He's probably used to women who are more docile." The couple builds up a stash of assumed rules and preferences that undermine their assurance and security.

AVOIDING SEXUAL BOOBY TRAPS

Avoiding sexual booby traps in the quest for mutual satisfaction and understanding is not easy. The effects of sexual ignorance combined with indirect or unclear channels of communication can be pretty awful.

Couples often try to compensate for their incomplete communication by constantly trying to "decode" the other's actions and signals. As a result, they're watchfully paying attention instead of enjoying their lovemaking. Besides, unless they are very knowledgeable and very observant, they are likely to misread the situation. Love tests based on overt sexual behavior are very hazardous.

Then what happens? The woman is on the lookout for the ease of arousal, the hardness and duration of the erection. She watches for his premature ejaculation, the length of his foreplay, his assertiveness. Does he seem interested? Does he fall asleep as soon as he's through? What does it mean that he doesn't get an erection when she sucks him?

The man listens for sounds of passion, tunes into signs of orgasm. Is her pussy wet? Are her nipples erect? Is her face flushed? Is she too uninhibited, promiscuous? Is she too clinging? What do all those orgasms mean?

Searching for textbook clues, insecure lovers draw conclusions about their own adequacy, about whether they're "good in bed," about who loves whom and how much. They ignore, for one thing, the differences in sexuality and in genitality. The genitals, it is true, express passion; they are a barometer of the unconscious feeling side of one's nature. But there are great extremes of individual differences in how quickly and strongly the genitals respond, and what they respond to. There is a tremendous inborn physiological factor. Some people's genitals are like human dildos; they respond to everything easily and indiscriminately. Others are sensitive to distraction or conflict, slaves to context. Genital fluidity may or may not conform to other aspects of one's sexuality, and yet people look to genital signals as to an oracle of truth.

In fact, genital proficiency compares with blushing—some people blush more easily and more often than others; it's their particular mode of expression. And others blush once in a blue moon (blue movie?), if at all.

A patient who had formerly come with an impotence problem returned to therapy, now afraid of losing his fiancée over what he termed the new deterioration of his sexual functioning. When questioned, he could only report one incident: he and his fiancée had made love, then awhile later they had started to fool around again, she licking and sucking his cock. He remembered feeling aroused and getting an erection, but the next thing he knew he had fallen asleep and his fiancée was in tears, insulted that he'd fallen asleep, sure that he couldn't love her. The next session they both came to therapy and she told the story, complete with all her interpretations of what had happened and how he had reacted and what it must mean. In the course of the session he was able to figure out that what actually had happened (aside from the fact that they *had* already made love) was that for the first time he really felt secure and safe in this sexual situation. He felt soothed—"I had the fantasy of a dog licking her puppy"—comfortable, and relaxed enough in this sexual context to fall asleep. After it was explained this way, his fiancée was able to feel good and positive about their solid sexual base.

Lisa tells a story about how good communication saved a touchy situation and aborted her lover's tendency to "decode" her sexual behavior.

"Greg and I had pretty good communication habits from the beginning. We'd talk about sex, make jokes, and either say or signal what we wanted. It seemed to flow pretty smoothly, and we had some quite fantastic lovemaking sessions. Then one day after we'd been dating a couple of months, we were making love, having a good time, teasing, fooling around. As I got very close to coming I began to laugh uncontrollably—kind of bubbly, mirthful, giggly laughter. And the more I came, the more I laughed. I wasn't paying much attention to Greg at first, just enjoying the sensations—it's not my usual response to a good orgasm, but it felt great.

"Then I noticed that though Greg was continuing to make love and trying to stay *with* me, he was upset and angry. After we were through he was very silent, and there I was with this big grin on my face. Right then I explained to Greg what had happened and how I felt and reassured him that I was laughing from the pure pleasure he'd provided, not in any way at him. Once his doubt was assuaged, he asked me more questions and we talked about it—it was good, because I really didn't understand it either. That was years ago and the Big Laugh as we call it has only happened about half a dozen times since. But now I feel free to enjoy it without worrying about whether Greg feels left out or hurt or puzzled, and he joins in, teasing me and prolonging our lovemaking. 'Are you having a *good* time?' he says, 'Are you *amused*? Can I be of *service*?'"

Another trap that couples fall into is to think that liberated lovers should not only share their sexual fantasies, they should act them out. They forget that sexual satisfaction is pair-specific and reality-based. It has to do with what makes both parties feel good; it is not helped by servicing each other's fantasies, which in any case destroys rather than fulfills the dream. Even the solo indulgence of fantasies has its limits. Lovers who spend too much time alone with their vibrators and their rape fantasies endanger their ability for love in the bedroom, in the here and now.

CARE-FUL ENDINGS

Every relationship is entitled to a good ending. Severing connections is always painful, no matter who is initiating the breakup, no matter what the cause. The parting is even more painful if it ends in acrimonious name-calling in pointless arguments, and regret. Yet with attention and concern for careful and caring leave-taking, it is possible to minimize the anger and bad feelings, to have an ending that doesn't leave a bad taste in the mouth.

A brief sexual interlude can be terminated with gestures of affection or tenderness, appreciation or good humor, that take the edge off the parting, calming fears of rejection. The difficult partings are those of long-term relationships, those in which much hope and care has been invested. Separation goes against the grain of human nature, so no matter how destructive the relationship and how desired the parting, very few people handle it easily or gracefully.

Even when lovers part for a few hours or a few days, they go through elaborate rituals of leave-taking: hugs and kisses, declarations of love, waving as the train leaves the station. The fear and pain of ending a relationship is so severe and so mixed with an unwillingness to give up, or to admit defeat, that lovers often do strange things to ease the pain. Suddenly they find fault with their beloved where none was before. His once endearing cuddliness now seems pathetic. His eccentric style of dress now seems just weird. Lovers lash out in anger, saying things they don't mean in order to obliterate the good things and take the sting out of parting. Others deny the problem, postponing the inevitable split by pretending that everything is fine, that nothing terrible is happening, hoping against hope that things will miraculously get back to normal. They drive each other crazy with mixed messages; their actions belie their words and feelings.

There are lots of endings to a relationship. Some end swiftly in anger, perhaps without explanation: one quick burst and it's over. Some fade away like autumn leaves . . . they've outlived their usefulness: seasons change, they die of boredom or routine, or of slow erosion. Some love affairs metamorphose into something else—the once intense lovers see each other only occasionally, or drop their sexual relationship for a platonic friendship. At the extreme, lovers will shout their way out of an intolerable situation in which they feel trapped, or they'll shoot their beloved in order to prevent the loved one from running away.[21]

It is painful to remember a relationship that didn't work out. But it is even worse to feel that it was all a waste, to have the good memories destroyed in a finale of needless bitterness, regret, and loathing. Good memories are the foundations of good futures.

A Time for Caring

Lovers should be able to leave a relationship intact and with enough confidence left to go on to the next.

Here are some of the ingredients of proper exits:

1. Acknowledge the end. Admit defeat instead of letting indirect aggression and mixed messages and bad memories pile up.
2. If possible, get the arguing and vindictiveness out of the way before the breakup. It *is* possible to put aside blame and bitterness. Ideally both partners should leave the relationship with an understanding of what happened and with the bitterness behind them. Once the decision to separate is made, try to be supportive of each other during this difficult time. Especially when there are issues of children, property, money, where there are likely to be future dealings between the lovers, a basis for ongoing discussion must be established.
3. Make an escape plan. Once the impending exit becomes apparent, plan ahead how to cope with the changes in one's life: financial adjustments, meeting new people, relocations, whatever is necessary.
4. Observe the breakup with a suitable ceremony. It may be a drink with friends or, as we have seen, a divorce party, an unwedding ceremony. It *is* helpful to take note of the occasion in the company of supportive friends and family.[22]
5. Allow a period of mourning. Sadness and depression are to be expected. Don't expect to bounce back immediately. It's hard to have a good time and be the life of the party while your heart is aching. Although it's good to try to distract oneself and find new pleasure and new ways to spend time, it's also important to go through and not around the period of sadness.
6. Rely on support systems. This is the time to call on family and friends for their understanding and help. They can help stem the trauma and aftereffects and can provide sympathy, a shoulder to lean on, as well as help reorder one's life and introduce new people.

19

The Intimate Care Plan

While it is possible to propose some guidelines for caring intimacy and to identify some common denominators of all sexual relationships, the fact still remains that what works best for each individual or each pairing is a matter of personal choice. Each person and each couple must cast about among all the possibilities, pick and choose from the information available what is suitable and satisfying for them.

It is also true that the sexual arena in which one's meeting and mating takes place exerts a powerful influence and that these days much of that influence isn't conducive to satisfying intimate connections. Nevertheless, the path to caring connections isn't blocked; it's merely obscured by the baffling three-ring circus of tantalizing images and misinformation.

One of your first tasks if you hope to improve the quality of your intimacies is to take a close analytical look at that environment: Who do you know and socialize with? What are the mores and morals of your friends and family? Your community? What kinds of intimacy do you see? What are the attitudes about sex? What's in the books you read, the movies you see? What is your social life like?

As you turn up any of the many contemporary saboteurs of caring intimacy, the most important thing you can do is put aside—without regret or second guessing, without worrying about what you're missing or what others will think—those influences that are care-less and devoid of intimacy. This means rejecting the propaganda about what constitutes sex appeal or popularity or sexual

A Time for Caring

enjoyment. It means taking a stand for the caring content of intimate relationships, whether they are one-night stands or long-term commitments. It means weeding from your life the anti-intimate influences, not listening to what friends and society say about your love life.

The Intimate Care Plan will help you as an individual or as a couple examine your environment and avoid the pitfalls of a careless relationship.

You may want to devise a plan for a life-style of short-term relationships or of casual sportsex encounters. You may want to give your attention to making the crucial transition from the All-Electric, Love Crazy stage to the serious grounding necessary for an ongoing relationship. Or you may need to revitalize a lagging marriage. Or reorder a relationship that is proving unsatisfactory to one or both parties.

Even if you do not have a sexual intimate, you can devise an Intimate Care Plan that will help you choose a sexual partner or partners and that will result in caring intimacy.

STEP ONE: DRAW AN INTIMATE CARE CIRCLE

Using the same principles outlined in Chapter 15, draw a picture of your Intimate Care Circle. For most people this is pretty simple: they are sexually intimate with their mate or current lover. On a sheet of paper draw a circle and place within the circle at the appropriate distance and the appropriate size those people with whom you have intimate relationships.

Your circle may look something like the ones shown on pages 200–201.

STEP TWO: MONITOR YOUR INTIMATE CARE HABITS

Many people think about their intimate relationships only when they are in the throes of a new romance or when problems arise. If a sexual encounter is unsatisfying or a spouse suddenly behaves unpredictably, alarms go off and the relationship becomes the focus of attention. But most people would have a hard time describing in detail what goes on in their intimate relationships. They find it hard to articulate how they communicate their sexual

A *Time for Caring*

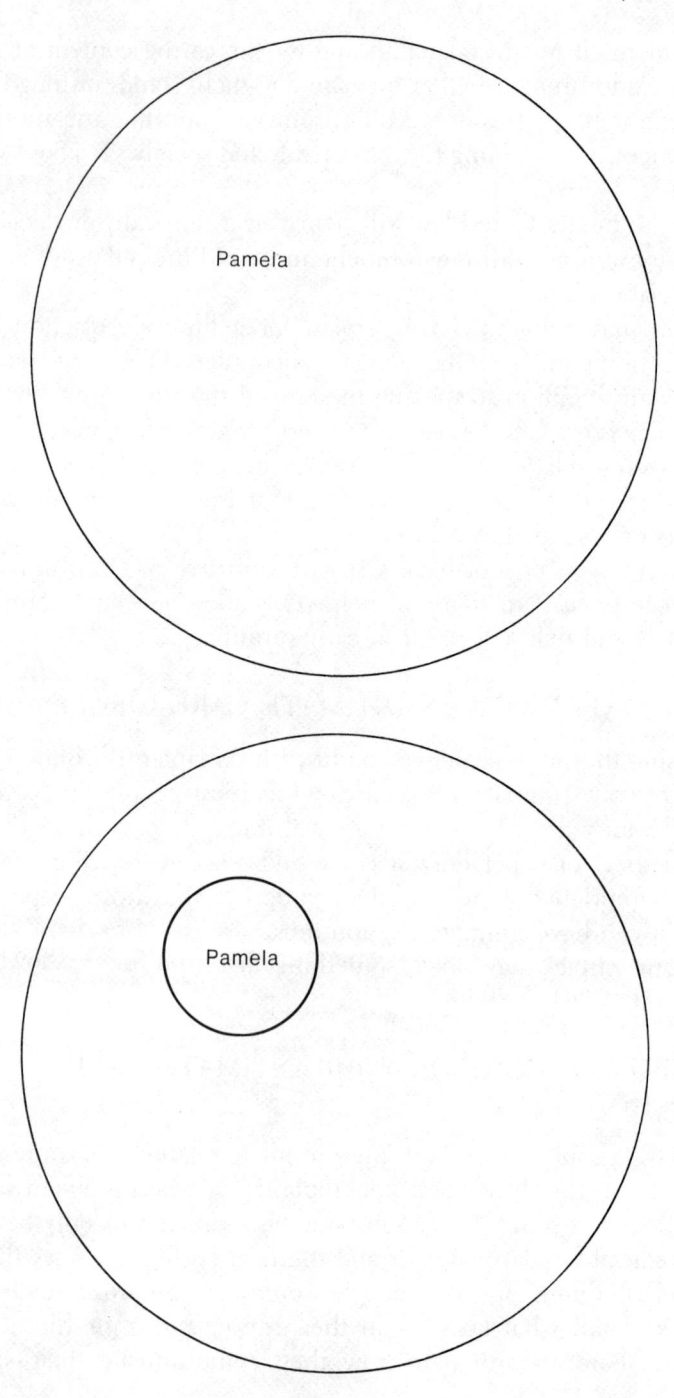

Pamela

Pamela

A Time for Caring

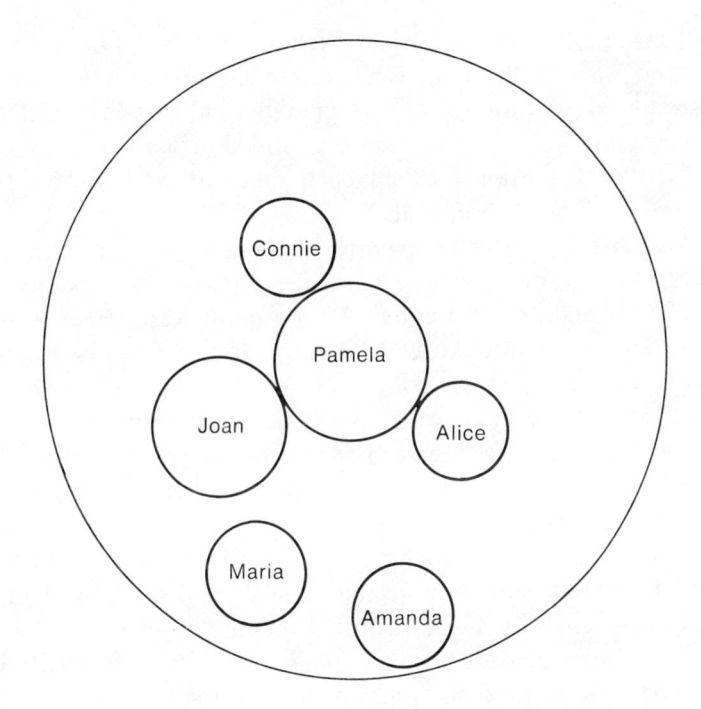

[Diagram: a large circle containing smaller labeled circles — Connie, Pamela, Joan, Alice, Maria, Amanda]

moods and desires, in what way they show concern for their relationship, what they do to keep their love alive.

But awareness of day-to-day habits of intimate care is a necessary step to improving that care. For a week or so before setting your intimate care goals, tune in and take notice of what goes on between you and your partner(s)—what you say and do, what feelings are exchanged, what problems come up. Be a reporter assigned to cover your relationship. Sniff out the facts. Get the story. Just the facts—don't try and draw conclusions now. Each day take a few minutes to note down actions or exchanges that give you clues to your habits of intimate care.

For example: Gail and Jack have been seeing each other for just under a year, and for the past two months they have been living together in Gail's apartment. *The examples used throughout this plan are from Jack's records.*

- Gail and I made time to have coffee together this morning instead of getting a late start and rushing off without talking.

- I made a lame excuse when I left and got out of clearing the table and walking the dog. I made it seem like I couldn't do it *because* of taking time for coffee, though I enjoyed the quiet few minutes with Gail and was in a better mood to start the day.
- Neither Gail nor I called each other at work today—that habit seems to be all but dead.
- Gail spent part of the evening clearing out piles of her junk from the "extra" room so that we can set up a small work area for my coin collection and library. At one point while I was sitting and reading, she came out with her arms loaded and did a comic pratfall—stumbling, then "falling" again when she tried to get up. I joined in and we made a big production out of getting the stuff to the garbage. She has a way of getting me laughing. I also think this was partly a message to point out that she was working her ass off while I sat on mine.
- I shopped for the dinner groceries as we'd agreed. I got everything at different stores—vegetables, meat, cheese. I liked it, in spite of my fight with Gail about it. I didn't tell her.
- I still managed to avoid stopping over at my old apartment and picking up more clothes and books to bring here.
- When we made love tonight, Gail made a big point a couple of times of moving my hand to caress her face.
- I was engrossed in my book this evening and didn't feel like making love. But it was okay, it doesn't take me long to turn on to Gail.

After you've made your notes for the day, go back over your list and see if you can get a sense of the balance of care in your intimate relationship(s). Ask yourself a few questions: "Is this what I wanted to do? Or what my partner wanted to do? Did I do it out of a sense of duty? Or desire? Was most of the care provided? Or consumed?"

STEP THREE: EXAMINE YOUR INTIMATE CARE PATTERNS

The purpose of the following questionnaire is to help you articulate the nature of your intimacies and find out how they might be changed or improved. But many of the questions that follow

A Time for Caring

will not pertain to you or to your pairings: it's impossible to standardize questions on such a personal matter. So answer those that make sense for you and let those that don't pertain go, or adapt them to your situation. Don't hesitate to draft your own questions.

1. Who is (are) the person(s) in your Intimate Care Circle? How long have you been together? Did you care for each other immediately? How long was it before you became intimate? How often do you see each other? Are you as close as you'd like to be? Too close? Do you choose to be with this (these) person(s)?
2. How did you meet this (these) person(s)? Where do you usually meet people? What do you do together? Do you have mutual friends? Do you socialize with each other's friends? Do you have mutual interests in sports, the arts, games, hobbies? What do you do in your leisure time?
3. How much time do you spend together? Apart? Would you prefer that it be different? Are there ever long separations? How do you feel about them? Are you comfortable with each other? Or reserved, embarrassed, uneasy? Why is this?
4. How has your relationship changed over time? Has it improved? Deepened? Worsened? Has it become routine, or more interesting? Do you tend to take each other for granted? Is it characterized by liking? Respect? Discomfort? Fear? Boredom? Do you expect the relationship to last? Do you want it to? Are you both involved in the relationship? Are you both concerned about it? Is it a difficult relationship, or easygoing? Are you both involved equally, or is it more important to one partner? Is the other partner detached, unconcerned? Do you both want the same things from the relationship? Do you know what they are? Are there areas in which your goals differ? How do you handle this situation? Do you ever fantasize about a more perfect love? Do you get upset about the day-to-day details of your life, the routine of your relationship? Is it changeable, or is it a necessary routine? Do you work at keeping the relationship out of the doldrums, do anything to make it more exciting?
5. How much talking do you do? Is one partner more communicative than the other? What do you talk about: work, the

news, your relationship, your moods? Are you able to make small talk? Are you both articulate, verbal? Are you interested in what the other has to say? Do you listen pretty carefully to each other? Are you likely to respond to each other? Do you keep each other up to date on the time you spend apart—at work, at home with the kids, with other friends? Do you ever find yourself with nothing to say? Do you think what you have to say isn't interesting to the other?

6. Are you both able to talk about problems or irritations? Does this lead to fights? Do you feel accused? Are you sympathetic to each other? Sensitive to the other's moods and feelings? Do you say directly what's on your mind? Do you trust each other to play fair with what you say? Are you suspicious of each other? Do you feel secure when you express yourselves openly? Are you likely to withhold your feelings? Why? Do you or your partner have roundabout ways of expressing yourselves? What do you do? Sulk? Be silent? Yell and scream about something unrelated? Do you know what makes the other angry? Do you avoid provoking the anger? Do you have any private signals or catchphrases that are your personal communication? Do you have any system for working out compromises, for settling fights? In other words, do you have a system for negotiating the negative aspects of your relationship? Do you resolve your fights, or are you likely to be angry for days? Do you ever go through periods of not speaking to each other, or walk out on each other? Does your fighting ever carry over to your lovemaking? Do love fights help? Or are they hostile and destructive?

7. Are you and your partner concerned about each other's wellbeing? How do you show it? Are you observant and sensitive to the other's moods? Do you trust each other with sensitive feelings? Do you go to each other for help? Advice? Sympathy? Cheering up? Are you interested in each other's goals, dreams, successes? What do you do to help? Give moral support? Advice? Your time? Do you respect the other's interests, ideas, goals? Are they at odds with yours? Is anything lacking in your concern for each other?

8. Is there a fair distribution of give and take in the relationship? Does your partner get a larger share of the attention, or care?

Does your partner do more of the work, take more responsibility, show more concern? Is one partner more dominating, the other more passive? Are there big gaps in any areas—intelligence, friends, independence, skills, wit, money, charm, sociability, kindness, status—between the two of you? Do the strengths and weaknesses balance out, or does one of you have an overwhelming share of the assets? Does one partner use this advantage to get out of a fair share of the responsibility in the relationship? Is there an ongoing battle for equity? Or do you both accept the doctrine of fairness? Are there rules about traditional duties and roles that hamper fair play? Or are there role reversals and flexibility of duties and concerns? Does the balance of power shift back and forth? Do both of you feel you're being treated fairly? Are you able to stand up for your rights? Is the providing and consuming of care shared?

9. How important is sex to you both? Do you both agree on its place in the context of your relationship? Would one of you like it to be more or less important a factor? How often do you make love? When? Where? Do you find enough time for lovemaking? Do you often find you're too busy? Or tired? Is lovemaking ever boring? Why? Do you ever have a hard time getting turned on? Do you usually have an orgasm? Do you ever fake orgasm? Or excitement? Lie about your feelings? Are you both satisfied with your lovemaking? In what way would you improve it? Has your lovemaking become ritualized? Are there rules or roles that govern your sex life? Are they traditional ideas about the role of male and female? Are you both in agreement about them? Are you able to talk about sex with your partner? Is it embarrassing? Informative? Fun? A turn-on? Do you fight for better sex? Do you each know how the other likes to make love? What arouses your partner? What satisfies your partner? What turns your partner off? Inhibits or frightens your partner? Are you attuned to each other's rhythms and sensitivities? Is there anything that puts you off or disturbs you about your lover's sex preferences? Do you feel free to experiment and explore sexually? Is there anything you'd like to do sexually that you haven't done? Are you afraid to share it with your lover? Do you fantasize often about sex? Do you ever share your fantasies with your lover? Do you try

hard to please each other? Too hard? Are you likely to worry about what the other is thinking and whether the other is enjoying the lovemaking or is satisfied? Do you read messages into each other's behavior without checking them out? Do you feel secure with your lover, trusting? Is your lovemaking ever as exciting as you've hoped it would be? Fantastic? Do you ever let go completely? Are you afraid of being out of control? Like it? Are your expectations for sex realistic? Do you always expect fireworks? Never expect them?

What is the mood of your lovemaking? Solemn? Joyous? Raucous or ribald? Gentle? Wild? Affectionate? Hostile? Loving? Loveless? Silly? Passive? Aggressive? Routine and ritualized? Adventurous? Does the mood differ each time you make love? What are your preferences? Are you both aggressive in bed at times? Do you have love fights? Or do you feel aggression has no place in bed? What starts your love fights? Are you angry when you start to make love? Do you fight fairly? Do you handicap each other so the power is equal? Are your fights usually a test of strength or power? Do you avoid hostile punishment or the inflicting of hurtful pain? Are these fights fun? Do they enhance your lovemaking? Make you feel more turned on?

10. How are your intimacy skills? Do both you and your partner(s) know how to be intimate—how to talk, make love, fight, share, be involved, trusting, playful, attentive, observant, concerned, loving? Or are there areas in which those skills need improvement?

STEP FOUR: EVALUATE YOUR INTIMATE CARE ⎯⎯⎯

Using the information gathered in steps one through three, make an assessment of the strong and weak areas of your intimate care habits. As you try to draw conclusions about your intimate behavior, look for repetitions, problems, trouble-free areas. Look for patterns. Divide a sheet of paper into two vertical columns labeled "Good Intimate Care/Strengths" and "Poor Intimate Care/Weaknesses" and in each column list statements that describe your evaluations of intimate care habits.

A *Time for Caring*

Here are some examples:

GOOD INTIMATE CARE/STRENGTHS

- I'm very affectionate; I like to cuddle and hug and kiss.
- I'm very good about birthdays and special occasions. I like planning surprises and thinking of special presents.
- I'm supportive of Gail's work. We talk about her job and she comes to me for advice. I'm proud of her successes.
- I feel less distracted by other women, less tempted to fool around than I did just a few months ago.
- We've been spending more time with friends. People think of us as a couple now, even Gail's family.
- We've stopped going to the big, depressing opening parties that Alan and Betsy were always dragging us to.
- We've started spending time by ourselves or with our own friends a couple of times a week.
- I make it a point to give Gail a more interesting and detailed report about my day, try to remember stories, news, gossip.
- I'm getting better about not withholding my anger when I'm upset about something. I try to force myself to say right away what's bugging me.
- Gail and I are both being more realistic about our relationship and not getting upset

POOR INTIMATE CARE/WEAKNESSES

- I get uncomfortable when problems come up. I tend to make jokes or try to be cheery, or give unwanted advice. It's hard for me just to be sympathetic.
- There's still a part of me that's holding out on our relationship—a little detached—like keeping my apartment. I don't admit this to Gail.
- I have a bad habit of needing too much of my friends' approval about Gail. When we're with her friends, I go overboard trying to impress them; then I get angry with Gail when she kids me about it.
- I get suspicious of Gail and find flimsy excuses to check up on her though I have no reason. I feel competitive with her old boyfriends.
- It's still hard for Gail and me to talk about problems or hurt feelings. She ends up angry as hell, and I sulk. We come out and say what's the matter at least, but then neither of us gives in.
- We both still have a bad habit of second-guessing each other's feelings, especially about each other, and of accusing each other of not caring as much as the other. Gail especially reads some meaning into every little thing.
- When I don't do my chores or do something wrong, Gail

GOOD INTIMATE CARE/STRENGTHS	POOR INTIMATE CARE/WEAKNESSES
and sulking when we have bad days or too much to do, or when we start worrying about whether we still love each other. • I still try to bully my way out sometimes, but I'm getting better about doing the shopping and the laundry. • I still find it embarrassing sometimes, but Gail and I are talking about sex more often. Also, I'm talking more while we make love and now that I'm more comfortable with it, it's been a real turn on for both of us. • I'm learning more and more about Gail and feel I understand her moods and needs better when we're making love. Sometimes I feel like I'm actually feeling her feelings with her.	accuses me of taking advantage of her, often brings things up in front of friends. • I have a feeling that Gail and I make love more often than either of us needs or wants to, but we don't want to hurt each other or be the one who suggests that we might be better off with a lighter schedule. • I haven't told Gail that she hurts me sometimes the way she grabs my balls. • Gail worries too much about whether I'm satisfied or about to come, and it turns me off.

STEP FIVE: SET INTIMATE CARE GOALS

Now it's time to set goals. The list of strengths and weaknesses you just made should help you. Make your goals realistic. They should be compatible with the amount of time and energy you can spend and should be things that are important to you now, and things that are possible to change. You may want to direct your efforts toward reinforcing existing strengths or toward building skills you feel you lack. Start by making a long list of all the things you'd like to change—no matter how difficult or trivial, then choose two or three that are manageable now and that reflect your priorities.

Here are some sample goals:

1. Stop hedging and make more of a commitment to our relationship.

2. Be a little more laid back when Gail and I socialize with her friends.
3. Make a pact with Gail to stick with our fights until we find a resolution and until we are back on terms of goodwill.
4. Make it a project to talk more with Gail about our sex life so that we're more honest with each other and get to understand each other better.
5. Stop calling Gail to check up on her when we're apart.

STEP SIX: MAKE A PLAN FOR IMPLEMENTING YOUR GOALS

Once you've established your goals, you need to figure out how to achieve them. You need a plan, a strategy, a schedule. Try to list as many possible alternatives and options for achieving them as you can think of. Go over all the possible sources and resources you have that might move you closer to your goals.

For example, take the first goal in step four: "Stop hedging and make more of a commitment to our relationship." Here are some possible ways to achieve that goal:

- Tell Gail that I've been keeping my exits open and that I'd like to stop being so wishy-washy. Be prepared for her to be angry or upset. Try to talk to her about it.
- Try to figure out why I find it so hard to make a commitment. Talk to Gail about it. Also to my therapist and to Fred. Even my mother might be helpful here. Read the book Fred was recommending last year.
- Give up my apartment. Do this in stages so I don't get cold feet. Move my stuff over to Gail's in the next week or so. Find someone to sublet the apartment. Fix up the extra room at Gail's so I have my own work area. Talk to Gail about moving some of her stuff to make room for some of my things that I'm attached to, so the apartment seems more like I'd choose it to be.
- Start introducing Gail as my girlfriend instead of my friend, or glossing over the introduction.
- Be less evasive with other women about my status. Be clear that I have a serious involvement.

Not every one of these options will be put into effect, but it helps to have a wide choice. The more specific you can be about how you'll meet your goals, the better.

STEP SEVEN: PAY ATTENTION

Once you've begun to put your plan into effect, pay attention to how you're doing. Be on the lookout for opportunities to advance your goals. Be watchful of forgetfulness. Note results of your actions. Is your plan working? What have been the reactions or results? Are you surprised? Displeased? Are you using the right tactics? Should you try something else? Are you being conscientious about your plan?

It's helpful to note in a diary or on a calendar at the end of each day those things that helped advance the cause. It also helps to make plans for the next day.

STEP EIGHT: BE SELF-SUPPORTING AND REWARDING

Every time you do something that brings you a little closer to your goal, congratulate yourself. Pat yourself on the back when you see signs of change. Be patient. Don't expect overnight changes. If you slip up occasionally, excuse yourself. Don't be self-punitive. Acknowledge small milestones. Reward yourself when you reach your goals.

When Jack talks to Gail about his problem, he should congratulate himself for his bravery. When he moves his things into her apartment, he should celebrate the occasion somehow. If he chokes up about introducing Gail as his girl, he shouldn't get upset, just be more resolved the next time.

STEP NINE: ENLIST THE HELP AND SUPPORT OF OTHERS

Don't carry the burden of change alone. Friends or family are always happy to help someone they love achieve something that's important to them. Share your goals with people you trust and who are willing to lend an ear, or give advice, or donate their time, or money, or energy. Ask for suggestions. Confess your difficulties. Be clear about what you need. Most of all, get your lover to be involved in your mutual goals—this is what intimacy is all about.

Jack might get his friend Fred to help him move his things over to his new apartment. He might work out a signal with Gail to remind him to introduce her properly.

STEP TEN: SIGN A CONTRACT AND SET A DATE TO REVISE YOUR PLAN _____

Make out an Intimate Care Plan form like the one below, fill it out, and sign it. Then keep it where you can refer to it easily. When it comes time to set new goals, refer to the earlier steps of your care plan for new ideas. (If you're with a new love, you may want to revise the whole plan!)

INTIMATE CARE CONTRACT

Name:_____

Goals:

1. _____
_____
_____
_____
_____

2. _____
_____
_____
_____
_____

3. _____
_____
_____

_____

_____

Strategy:
1. _____

_____

_____

_____

_____

2. _____

_____

_____

_____

3. _____

_____

_____

_____

_____

I will review this plan on _____

Date: _____

Signature: _____

20

The Family:
CRADLE OF CARING

The family, where caring begins, is under attack from all sides these days. Families are torn by divorce. They are separated and fragmented by job mobility and the ease of travel. They suffer the side effects of the emphasis on self-actualization, and of the changing roles of men and women. They are plagued by lack of skills and training in "familyhood."

The primacy of child raising as a family function has gone by the boards. Birth control and the population explosion have reduced the magic of having children. Today there are powerful antichild forces. Couples put off having children, feeling that their first responsibility is "to find themselves." Child rearing suffers in a society where the "self-actualization" of the parents is seen as a healthy priority and "sacrifice" as sick. Children are seen as a liability, as impediments to fulfillment and getting ahead. Women, many honorably trying to redefine their roles, are leery of being trapped in the traditional bonds of motherhood. Parenting is a low-status occupation in the modern hierarchy of values. Too, some couples who would like to have children are fearful of raising them in these difficult and careless times, so they opt for childlessness. The result is childless couples and a grandparent generation with nothing to grandparent.

Once a bastion against the outside world, the family is now besieged by the world on all fronts. The school, the neighborhood, the community, radio, television, movies, books: all have as much influence on the growing child as the parents—or even more. Parents have not only lost control over their children, they've lost confidence in their ability to raise them properly. They are constantly being told by the experts—doctors, teachers, psychologists, the government, big business—how to go about it, but the experts themselves have such widely divergent ideas that there is chaos in the child care field.

Convinced that others know better than they, parents are afraid to exercise their authority. They turn for help to books and away from their feelings and from what they know of themselves and their own children. They timidly and unquestionably relinquish their children's upbringing to school, TV, and unknown friends. They are poor models for children, who need to see those they love and respect make choices and changes in their lives if the children are eventually to do so themselves.

Many children today grow up in an environment in which their family plays a diminishing part. Raised with little sense of the potential strengths and supports, loyalties and responsibilities, of the family, they leave home without a backward look, leaving behind sad, sometimes bitter parents.

Today's parents, with so little power in the larger society, unable to provide much of the time or resources their children need, make a poor argument to the child for the primacy of the family.

REDEFINING THE FAMILY

One has but to try to picture a "typical" family to see one of its major problems: the definition is definitely up for grabs these days. The storybook nuclear family—breadwinning husband, homemaker wife, and 2.4 children—is a relic. The traditional extended family—the above nucleus closely surrounded by actively involved grandparents, cousins, aunts, uncles, and sundry others—is rarer still. A study by two Harvard University sociologists found that by 1990 two thirds of all households will be void of children under the age of fifteen, and that no one type of household will be typical. Yet many people cling to the archaic, perhaps romanticized view of the family unit—though few of them are part of such a configuration.

Families today come in myriad shapes and sizes. A third of today's children are raised by one parent. Fifteen million mothers work. Increasingly fathers stay home and take care of the kids while women bring home the bacon. Joint custody arrangements are more and more common. Single parents pool resources and live together for practical and financial reasons and for mutual support. Married couples forgo children; unmarried couples have them; single adults adopt them. Other couples don't marry. Groups of various configurations and life-styles live together communally and call themselves families.

These are not isolated cases or radical solutions: this *is* the modern family. So befuddling and nearly unrecognizable is the modern family with its myriad inscrutable faces that in 1980, attempts to hold a national conference on the family were stopped by the inability of the participants to agree on what constitutes a family and who should be allowed to participate.[23] So the beleaguered family, drastically in need of protection, eroding dangerously, hangs on for dear life while those who would come to its aid argue about the shape of the conference table.

The logical first step in supporting and strengthening the caring bonds of the family is to redefine it in terms that more accurately reflect its composition and dynamics. The new-fangled family deserves acceptance and respectability. It is important to stop feeling that any alternative to the traditional setup isn't a real family, important to stop comparing ourselves to an ideal difficult and unlikely in modern times, important that those of us who aren't part of a traditional nuclear family not feel like left-out orphans. After all, if our spouse or lover is not a "blood" relative, is it so important that our "children" or "brothers" be blood relatives?

Any assemblage of people defining itself as a mutual-support system, committed to caring for each other and sharing their resources over time, and to the nurture and growth of the children among them, has every right to call itself a family. Not a second-class family, or a marginal family, but the real thing, entitled to the same community and governmental support, the same day-care and tax deductions, the same protective legislation and maternity leave, accorded the traditional model.

Edith's story demonstrates the importance of overcoming our prejudices about what makes a "real" family:

"I've always considered myself somewhat unconventional, but it's surprising how old-fashioned ideas about 'family' have stuck with me. To me, my family has been my parents, whom I see twice a year, several brothers and sisters spread across the country, and a few long-lost cousins and uncles. Not exactly a close-knit group, and I must say I was very envious of friends with close families—even when their relatives seemed intrusive at times, overattentive, or uninteresting. The whole picture changed for me when I thought about whom I felt close to and committed to, whom I cared for and who cared for me. I turned up a surprisingly strong family of my own devising, one that pretty much fulfills my needs. My 'blood' family is part of this group, but it also includes the man I've lived with for many years, a few close friends, a former teacher, various children. In my new family I have several 'parents' closer and more supportive than my own, a little brother, an older sister, and several children in the form of nieces and nephews, friends' kids, and the little boy next door. I even have a couple of new grandparents. Quite a family!"

The family unit is the ideal care-nurturing unit; long-range hope for a more caring world lies with the family. The family is not dying; it is changing. We must continue to demand more recognition and support for the changes not only in family structure but in the roles of parents and the importance and status of children. Because it is being more realistically defined by ties of choice as well as duty or blood, because it is a better informed unit committed to caring goals, the new family unit has a good chance, if it is accepted and supported, of surviving the current wave of emphasis on self-involvement.

WHERE CARING BEGINS

"Before my baby was born, I had no sense of how I'd feel as a mother. I wanted the baby but had little interest in preparing for the event—fixing up a room, buying clothes and stuff. I had misgivings about leaving my job, which I loved. At times I wondered if I wasn't lacking in maternal instincts." The speaker is Dorothy, eight months after the birth of her daughter. "I still can't believe the feelings that came boiling out of me when Sarah was born. It was like a steamroller of joy and concern and love. I was overwhelmed and literally surprised at myself. It feels good; I realize that there was a big untapped well of loving and caring."

The best argument for the caring nature of the human species is the deep response of protectiveness evoked by the human infant. Untainted by concerns for reciprocity, or by fear of rejection or misunderstanding, feelings of concern and love bubble uninhibited to the surface. Everything about the way humanfolk raise their young offers testimony to their caring nature. The presence of care gets taken for granted; its absence is more dramatic. While the newborn of other species require care (if at all) for only short periods, the human infant needs to be cared for over a protracted period of time. If that care is absent or seriously flawed, the infant will die or suffer severe damage. If they survive, infants deprived of proper care grow up unable to care themselves; their trauma may manifest itself as psychosis or autism, or in various degrees of pathological antisocial behavior: disruptiveness, crime, and violence. The same neuron systems in the brain damaged by lack of touching and affections are associated with violence mechanisms.[24]

Humans learn to care by being cared for. People who reach maturity able to interact with others, to feel love, hate, care, sympathy—however imperfectly—do so because of the care surrounding them when they were very young. Whatever else comes along—people and circumstances, schools, the media—may enhance or inhibit that early modeling, but nothing can replace it. Fortunately, less-than-perfect childhoods notwithstanding, most of us reach maturity without major pathological symptoms.

One-sided arguments about man's basically evil or uncaring nature are preposterous in the face of the evidence: without highly developed caring tendencies he wouldn't be here to argue about what a bad boy he is. This is not to minimize or deny the human capacity for aggression, war, corruption, venality, or to overlook the pickle we've gotten ourselves into. But as time—aeons—go by, humans seem to evolve more protracted and complex patterns of caring for their young, involving decades of nurture, education, and support before said young are fully prepared to venture alone into the world. For the parent, it is a commitment of about a third of his lifetime. Man must need, and want, to care.

Ideas about early care-learning have suffered from our tendency to see ourselves as bad guys. It was long supposed that babies, because they get immediate response to their cries for food or comfort, because they quickly learn self-surviving ploys to assure their needs being met, develop a very one-sided and long-lasting sense of themselves as the center of the universe. And that these selfish creatures were disabused of their notions of sovereignty only through the difficult and painful process of socialization and with great shock and trauma to themselves.

In fact, the opposite seems to be true. The well-cared-for infant learns to give what it gets. Its innate caring tendencies come to the surface when they can be connected or recapitulated in the new world outside itself.[25]

The capacity for caring shows up at a very early age. Babies less than a year old will give a cry or look very sad when they perceive another person in trouble or pain. One- and two-year-olds will offer their bottle or a pat on the back to another child or a parent who seems upset. Or they may cry in sympathy. A young child will generously offer his own pillow or candy to a suffering sibling.

However, if the infant is not provided with examples of sympathy and help, if its own gestures are not supported and encouraged, the caring impulses atrophy. The message that others should be helped and not hurt has to be conveyed convincingly and strongly, not by punishment but with explanation and emotional force. Parents who teach their children not to be too generous, or who tell their children not to worry about others' suffering, destroy their caring impulses.

Children need to be shown care and to have safe outlets for showing it. Their desire to reciprocate and show appreciation needs encouragement. It's never too early to start.

The very best care-learning technique is of course the example of care and concern that a child can imitate.

Next comes feedback and reinforcement. Take notice of caring deeds. Smile or kiss or hug the child who's shown concern. "That was nice of you to help Daddy." "Sue was very sad until you shared your cookie." "I feel good when you hold my hand."

Look for opportunities to care, and pursue these opportunities. "Andy's upset about his fall. Let's see if we can cheer him up." "Why is Paul crying?"

A Time for Caring

Don't hesitate to ask for care: "Mommy's feeling tired. She could use a hug." "Would you please get me a glass of milk?" "It would feel so good if you would brush my hair."

Even lessons are in order: "When someone gets hurt, we should try to help them." "It feels good to share our things." "What would you do if Janie got sick?"

Teaching kids to share and take responsibility can be tedious and time-consuming. It takes patience when Amy wants to help do the dishes. It's messy when Tommy wants to feed his younger brother his cereal, or when Iris wants to stop and help the boy who fell down in the supermarket. But as with table manners or toilet training, patience and reinforcement are the key.

Kids discouraged from helping or responding to need get the idea that it's not important or expected of them. If they had the same idea about toilet training, adults would still be wearing diapers.

WHAT MAKES A CARING FAMILY?

Families provide the ideal setting for caring. Who else are we stuck with for a lifetime, many of those years at close quarters, in daily or minute-to-minute contact? Who else should we be able to rely on for support or understanding, to accept us and recognize our needs? Who else knows us so intimately—every quirk and irritating idiosyncrasy—and still accepts us? Families should provide a golden opportunity for knowing others and for being known, a chance of a lifetime.

Unfortunately the family setting is often abused for the very same reasons it might be productively used. Some families are torn by strife and bitterness. Each member goes his own way, taking the family's support for granted. Some members refuse to assume their share of responsibility, to live up to others' expectations for concern and participation. They don't acknowledge the needs of the individuals within the family and respect personal sensitivities or idiosyncrasies. The anger of many young people today is probably less racial and economic than it is an expression of fury and rage at the frustration of their needs for tenderness, intimacy, and care. The support, the encouragement, the example of caring they need is sadly lacking.

"Nice" families have equally serious problems. Plagued by quiet resentments, unmet expectations, and lack of communication, they fail to acknowledge the need for assertion, for accepting conflict, for making demands for care and concern.

Many families don't know how to *be* families. Family members become locked into fixed roles and let the roles define them. Fathers work all their lives at jobs they don't like to support families they don't know and come to resent. Mothers exhaust themselves on endlessly demanding husbands and children because they feel it's in their contract, and wonder why they end up not caring about them. Children grow up with little sense of family loyalty or responsibility and scant skills of caring or self-sufficiency. And these are families with all good intentions, trying hard to do their best by each other!

As we have said, children sorely need to see caring behavior modeled. They need to imitate people who hold themselves in high esteem. If today's parent cannot model job skills—how to make shoes or grow wheat or spin cloth—he can model psychological skills, can be an example of the search for a meaningful life and the fight for growth. If today's parent cannot model economic success, he can perhaps be an example of fairness and flexibility in the area of sex and gender expectations, so that his children will not have to choose between nurturing themselves or nurturing their children.

A good base for family care and maintenance consists of three things:

1. A forum for family communication, especially for the expression of anger and the resolution of conflict.

In order to know and understand each other well enough to care about each other, family members need to talk to each other in an atmosphere of trust and goodwill. They need a system for negotiating the negatives that bubble to the surface of family life. While this seems simple enough, most people, as we have noted, have poor habits of communication. They send mixed messages or expect to be understood without having to say what's on their mind. They air their anger in such indirect or hostile ways that it puts everyone else off and inhibits resolution of the conflict. Or they're so angerphobic that they walk around in stony silence. Families interested in improving their concern for each other must find time to talk to each other and work at undoing the crazymaking habits that impair communication. And they must learn to fight fair.[26]

2. Recognition of individual differences, needs, sensitivities, and the right to privacy.

One common mistake, even in well-meaning families, is to treat everyone the same. This is a misguided fairness-doctrine and often is rooted in lack of specific knowledge about each family member. Individual differences should enrich, not divide, families. "One for all, and all for one" is the motto of teams and armies, but only intermittently applies to families.

Each family member has certain rights and expectations of the group. These expectations should be outlined to everyone, and if fair and not in conflict with others, should be respected.

3. Establishment of the rights and responsibilities of each family member.

The family is an organism that requires energy and application if it is to live a healthy life. In order to support the whole, each family member must contribute his share, whether in time spent with the family, or chores, or money earned. Fairly allocated responsibilities come about not by accident but through a process of negotiation in an atmosphere of goodwill.

21

The Family Care Plan

You may be a father whose family consists of a wife and two kids; or a single adult whose family consists of parents in a far-off city and widely dispersed siblings; or a divorced mother who shares a house with three other single parents and your crew of children; a childless couple whose family is an assemblage of singles, couples, and children drawn together by a common ideology. Remember that it's not just blood that counts, it's commitment.

Whatever your case, the Family Care Plan will help you to examine your current state of family care and pinpoint strengths and weaknesses. You'll identify your family's ways and behavior, rules and rituals. You will be able to identify areas that could be improved and to make a plan for bringing about the change you desire. You may even realize that there are more people in your family than you imagined.

Ideally, the whole family should participate in formulating the plan—sharing observations about the way the family works, making suggestions for change, making a joint commitment to work for common goals.

(Because there are so many variables in the composition of modern families, all of the instructions and questions in the following plan will not apply to everyone. In some cases you will have to isolate the pertinent parts and adapt the questions and instructions to fit your situation.)

A *Time for Caring*   223

STEP ONE: DRAW A FAMILY CARE CIRCLE

Draw your circle on a large sheet of paper. Inside it place the members of your family at the appropriate distance from the center, according to how important they are in your life. For each make a brief notation of their relationship to you. Include all members who live with you, those who have moved away, the extended networks of older and younger generations of relations, and those close friends who have some influence over your kids or are part of your family dynamic—such as lovers (boyfriends or girl friends) who act as surrogate parents to your children, or friends of the children who are involved with the family.

Refer to the chart you made of your Caring Network in Chapter 14, to be sure you're not leaving anyone out. Don't worry about being precise, though. The object here is just to get a rough overview of your family layout.

Your Family Care Circle might look like this:

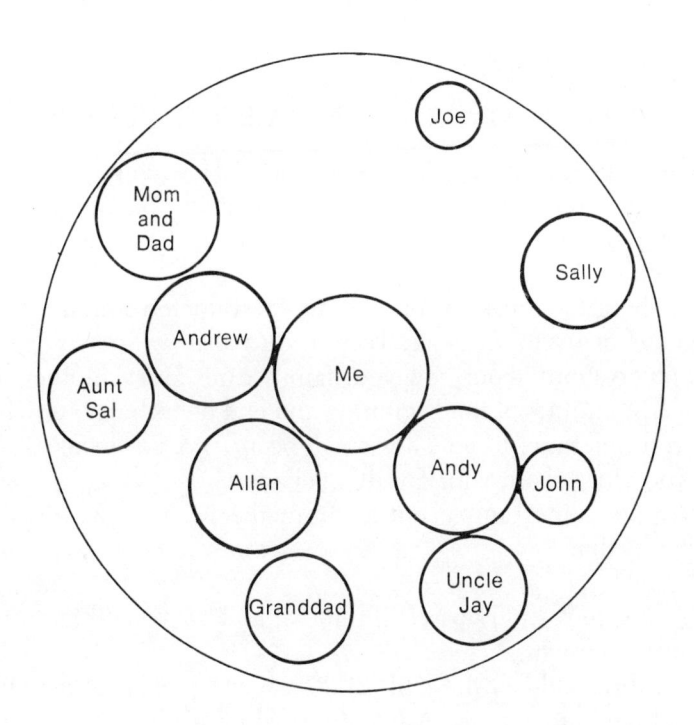

or like this:

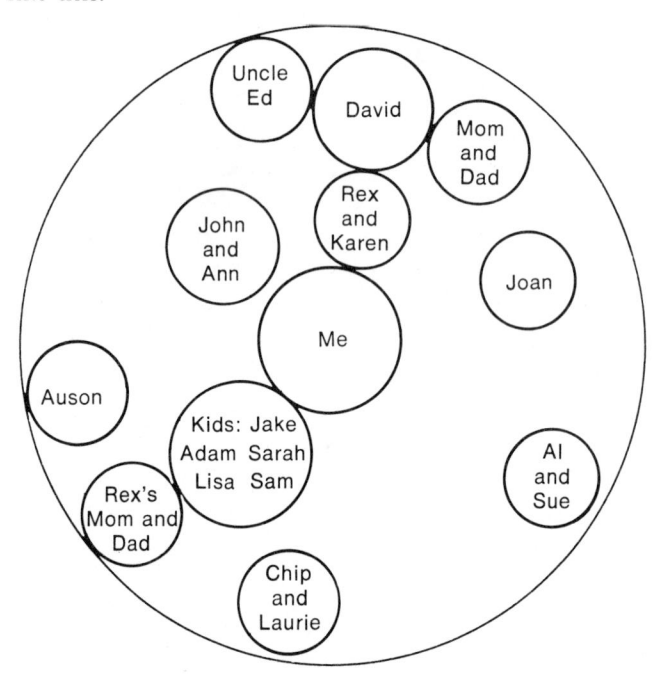

[Diagram: A large circle containing smaller overlapping circles labeled: Uncle Ed, David, Mom and Dad, John and Ann, Rex and Karen, Joan, Me, Auson, Kids: Jake Adam Sarah Lisa Sam, Al and Sue, Rex's Mom and Dad, Chip and Laurie]

STEP TWO: MONITOR YOUR FAMILY CARE HABITS

Who does the chores? Makes decisions? Has temper tantrums? Is never at home? Keeps their feelings bottled up? Comforts the unhappy family member? Acts as host? Tells the jokes? Weasels out of obligations?

For about two weeks before you try to evaluate your family-caring status or try to set goals, keep a journal in which you record your observations about how your family cares for each other. Use about five minutes at the beginning and end of each day, or whenever you find time, to note any small occurrences or incidents that give you clues about your family's behavior.

Here are some sample entries from the journal of a divorced mother of three:

1. Arlene took Brad's baseball mitt without asking and left it outside overnight.
2. All three kids set the table and cleaned up after dinner. Babs did her part sloppily; Arlene finished up for her.

A Time for Caring

3. I worked overtime to earn money for their summer vacation.
4. In the last twenty-four hours I've had to drive each of the kids somewhere.
5. The kids have all been pretty good about leaving me alone for an hour when I get home from work while I rest and take a bath and call my friends. Babs occasionally finds some flimsy excuse to bother me.
6. Brad's getting worse about picking fights with Arlene, and he never lets her join in on any of his activities.
7. When I was upset and tired after work today, Brad came and sat next to me and put his arm around my shoulder.
8. At dinner I had a hard time getting the kids to talk about their school day—as usual. Arlene gave a halfhearted report, but Babs sat and sulked and then went off to her room.
9. I spent the evening finishing up the curtains for the girls' bedroom.
10. I told the kids they'd all have to stay home on Friday night so that I could go out.

After you've made your notations for the day, go back over your list and see how the caring balances out. Is everyone doing their share? Is one person overloaded with responsibilities? Is someone shirking theirs? Or failing to show appreciation? In the case of the family in the example here, the mother of necessity bears a tremendous share of the responsibility. But her questions should be: Is there any way I can give the kids more responsibility? Are they being helpful? Are they appreciative? Who is goofing off? What can I do to help the kids get along better? Am I becoming too pressured and overloaded? What can I do?

STEP THREE: EXAMINE YOUR FAMILY CARE PATTERNS

The following questionnaire will help you investigate your family:

• Who is included in your family group? Do you all live together? Are you all related? Are there outside neighbors and friends you think of as family? Are there faraway family members?

How do you keep in touch with them? How often do you see them? How much time does each family member spend at home?

- Physical care: Is everyone in the family healthy? Are your home and neighborhood safe? Who gets sick in the family? Who takes care of them? Do you have a family doctor and dentist? Do you see them regularly?

How are the family's cleanliness and grooming habits? Does everyone manage to brush teeth and bathe and wash hair and wear clean clothes? Is it a hassle?

How many meals does the family eat together? Are you careful about diet? Fond of junk food? Is anyone overweight? Do the kids get to eat whatever they want? Or are there rules about food?

Are you a physically active family? How? Who is interested in sports? Or exercise? Or dancing?

Describe your home. Is it pleasant? Neat? Is there enough room? Is there room for privacy? Who shares a bedroom? Who helps clean and maintain the house? Does it cause problems? Does everyone agree on the desirable level of neatness and cleanliness?

- Family activities: How much time does the family spend together? Does everyone participate? Who seems to enjoy family activities most? Least?

What kinds of things do you do: share meals together? Do you talk a great deal at meals? About what? Who dominates the conversation? Is anyone left out? Do the children spend time together? What do they do? How much television does the family watch? Is there anything the whole family does together? Does the family have any shared interests such as sports, or swimming, or square dancing, or crossword puzzles, or chess, or Scrabble? Does the family vacation together or take daytrips or picnics? Go to the zoo or to a museum or amusement park? Do family members tend to have their own activities and go their own ways?

- Family responsibilities: Who earns money in the family? Do any children in the family work? Who makes decisions about money? Pays the bills? Is the household run on a budget?

How is money distributed in the family? Do children get an allowance? Do they have to work for it?

What is the family's attitude toward money? Do they take it for granted? Are they miserly? Generous? Unconcerned?

A Time for Caring

How are responsibilities divided up? What does each person do? Are responsibilities determined by traditional roles or are they flexible and negotiable? Do you feel everyone does a fair share? Or is one person overloaded? Does anyone try to get out of duties or make a big fuss about them?

Would you say your family is lenient or strict? Are there many rules? Do they often get broken? Who enforces the rules? What form of discipline is used: scolding? withdrawal of allowance or privileges? spanking?

- Emotional Care: Do family members talk to each other? How much? When? What about? Do children and adults talk to each other? Are there many secrets? Is it easy to talk about how you're feeling? Do other family members ask how you're feeling? Or do you all keep pretty much to yourselves? Do you have to pry information out of some members of the family?

How well do members of the family know each other? Are they sensitive to each other's temperaments and idiosyncrasies? Do they respect them? Is there any one family member you feel is favored, or who has special privileges? Is there a black sheep or scapegoat?

Is there much fighting in the family? Yelling and screaming? Who fights with whom? Are they fair fights? Evenly matched? How do they end? Are the conflicts resolved? Is good feeling restored? Do both parties end up getting what they want?

How is anger expressed by each member of the family? How does each person react when someone gets angry at that person? Are there members of the family who never yell or get mad? Is anyone sulky or withdrawn? Likely to go to their room when they're upset?

How is affection and love expressed in the family? Are hugs and kisses common? Do you express your care for each other verbally? Who do you go to for comfort? Who comes to you? Who keeps everyone laughing? Who's the pessimist?

STEP FOUR: EVALUATE YOUR FAMILY CARE PATTERNS _____

The next step in setting up a Family Care Plan is to assess the information that you gathered through drawing a Family Care Circle, keeping a journal, and going over the questionnaire. Look for repeated patterns. Draw conclusions. Try to be precise in your evaluations. Ask yourself bluntly: What is good? What is missing? Divide your findings into columns—"Good Family Care/Strengths" and "Poor Family Care/Weaknesses." Here are some examples from the evaluation of the divorced mother of three:

GOOD FAMILY CARE/STRENGTHS	POOR FAMILY CARE/WEAKNESSES
• The grandparents on both sides of the family spend a good deal of time with the kids. • The kids make friends easily and bring their friends home. • We have friends whom we consider family. • Everyone at home is healthy. • The kids are all active somehow. Brad plays basketball, Babs is a dancer, Arlene is just always on the move. • Their grooming habits aren't perfect, but they're good enough. • I work hard and save enough money to support my family modestly. We don't lack necessities. • Brad works after school. Arlene had a summer job last year. • All the kids have quite a few chores (compared to their friends). • They all get an allowance. • We discuss our expenditures for extras like clothes, movies, sports equipment, vacations. • Arlene is generous with her money. She buys gifts and surprises, makes loans. • Even though I'm gone all	• Both my mother and my mother-in-law have different ideas about how I should raise the kids, and try to interfere. • The children rarely see their father and haven't enough contact with male adults. • I don't like several of Brad's friends. • I don't have enough time for my own social life. • The kids eat too much junk when I'm not around. • The house always seems to be a mess, no matter how much time I spend cleaning. • There's not enough room in the house. Brad sleeps on the couch and the girls share a small room. Privacy is a problem. • I don't get any child support from my ex-husband. • The kids feel deprived and grumble when they can't do all the things their friends can. • Babs has to be monitored constantly to do her chores. She does them halfheartedly, sulking all the while. • Brad is very tight with his money. He won't pay for anything

A Time for Caring

GOOD FAMILY CARE/STRENGTHS	POOR FAMILY CARE/WEAKNESSES
day, we spend every evening together and do something together every weekend. • Brad is very emotionally supportive of me. • We're all pretty talkative; sometimes it's hard to get a word in edgewise. • There are things we all like to do—go to the movies, play cards, have lunch at the park. • Affection comes easy for us. We all hug and kiss, and we come to the rescue when there's a problem or crisis. • I think we know each other pretty well.	he thinks I should be expected to buy for him. • Brad and Arlene seem to fight all the time. • Brad is getting so involved with his friends he never has time to do anything with the family. He pooh-poohs my ideas about "togetherness." • It's hard for us to talk about intimate things, especially for Brad and Babs. Brad acts mean when he's upset; Babs goes to her room. • We don't handle conflict very well. Often fights end up with tears and angry words, and it's too intense for us to work out a solution to the problem. And it sometimes takes a while to reestablish good feelings. • I feel the kids aren't appreciative enough of how hard I work, and how tired and irritable it makes me.

STEP FIVE: SET GOALS

You have done all the groundwork, gone through the difficult process of self-examination and evaluation. Now it's time to take action.

Based on your feelings about what is good but could be better, and what is weak and should be eliminated, select your goals. Don't tackle all your problems at once. Pick what you feel is most important and what you have the time and resources for. You might start out by making a long list of possible goals, no matter how ambitious or outlandish, then choosing the two or three that appeal to you most.

Here are some sample goals:

1. Maintain better contact with the distant members of the family.

2. Develop a long list of activities the family is interested in, so we can vary our weekend outings.
3. Find a system for resolving family fights without so much hostility and tears.
4. Renegotiate the family responsibilities so that I don't end up exhausted all the time.
5. Get on a more regular meal schedule and a more balanced diet.

STEP SIX: MAKE A PLAN FOR IMPLEMENTING THOSE GOALS

The process of implementing goals begins with a search for options. Every problem has several possible solutions. It's up to you to decide how much time, energy, and money you want to spend to achieve your goals, where you can get help, what your alternatives are. Use your strengths to shore up your weak points. Enlist the help of the rest of the family or friends, community organizations, books. The more different approaches you can think of, the better your chances of hitting on a good solution.

Here's an example of a plan for implementing a goal from step three: Find a system for resolving family fights without so much hostility and tears.

(a) Read the book on family conflict recommended by my friend Allan.
(b) At dinner sometime next week, discuss with the family our problems about anger and fighting. Go around the table and ask everyone:
   How do you feel when you get angry? What do you do?
   How do you feel when someone gets angry at you? What do you do?
Ask them if they are interested in trying to solve the problem. If they are, ask for suggestions on how to go about it. Schedule another discussion.
(c) At the next discussion, talk about the following:
   What upsets you about things that go on in the family? About each member of the family?

Do you feel that the rest of the family know and understand you?

Do you feel your rights and expectations in the family are being met?

Are there special sensitivities that family members use against you?

STEP SEVEN: PAY ATTENTION

As you go through the process of implementing your goal, keep a watchful eye on your family's behavior and on the results the new plan has on the family. Note whether the changes have been beneficial, if you see the rewards. If you feel yourself backsliding, stop and figure out what is going on. Look for ways to modify and improve your plan. Be tuned in to the problems and successes.

As your family becomes more comfortable discussing their needs and conflicts at family meetings, you can introduce new problem-solving techniques. The "fair fight" tactic explained below enables family members to negotiate for specific things they want.

Ask each family member to make a list of the three things they would like to change most in the family and bring it to the next meeting.

At this meeting give each person a chance to fight for one thing he or she wants. The fight is with one other person—a parent or sibling directly involved. The others act as witnesses, and coaches, to see that the fight is fair, that information isn't distorted, that a spirit of goodwill is maintained and that both parties have equal opportunities to express themselves, that requests are reasonable and unreasonable promises aren't made. Continue the meeting until each person has had a fair fight. Write down the negotiated agreements and post them where everyone will see and remember them. Here's some examples:

Bill gets to choose the TV shows between 6:00 and 7:30.

No one can tease Elizabeth about her freckles.

Mom's room and the telephone are off limits between 4:00 and 5:00.

Dad expects the kids to help him around the house between 9:30 and 12:00 on Saturday mornings.

Have monthly meetings at which the family reviews the past month's agreements to see whether they're fair, whether they've been respected, and at which each family member gets to fight for one new right or change.

STEP EIGHT: BE SELF-SUPPORTING AND REWARDING

When you do something that brings you closer to your goal, pat yourself on the back. Be proud that you have actually been able to take responsibility and act. Reward yourself with a present, buy the family a special treat. Acknowledge your progress. Offer yourself feedback and support.

STEP NINE: ENLIST THE HELP AND SUPPORT OF OTHERS

No one can go it entirely alone. Tell your friends about what you are doing. Don't shy away from seeking the counsel of teachers, therapists, government welfare agencies, and clergy. Consider what kind of active participation in your goal you might get from your friends. Whom can you turn to for professional guidance? Explore these areas and you won't feel so isolated or burdened by your tasks. Finding out that your problems are not unique, that others can sympathize, is very important. You can often come up with unexpected insights or suggested options by talking to people outside the family circle.

STEP TEN: SIGN A CONTRACT AND SET A DATE TO REVIEW YOUR PLAN

Fill in the Family Care Plan contract below and set a date for reevaluating and reviewing the plan. When you come around to renewing your plan, redraw the Family Care Circle. See who has moved closer to you in the circle. See how the give-and-take between those in the circle has improved. When you choose new goals, see if new strengths and weaknesses have become apparent, if there are new issues to deal with. Ask your family to join in and make suggestions about goals. Then select new goals. Redefine the

A *Time for Caring*

options and begin again. You are well on the road to making your family circle a tightly woven network of care and growth.

FAMILY CARE CONTRACT

Name: _____

Goals:

1. _____
_____
_____
_____
_____

2. _____
_____
_____
_____
_____

3. _____
_____
_____
_____
_____

Plan for Implementing Goals:

1. _____
_____
_____
_____
_____

2. _____

_____
_____
_____
_____

3. _____
_____
_____
_____
_____

I will review the contract on _____

Date: _____

Signature: _____

22
Caring Friends

Friendship is probably the least examined of all human relationships. It is a difficult subject for scrutiny, for it covers a vast, hard-to-define territory. Yet friendships are a significant part of our social interaction—to some the most important part of the caring support system. In a recent magazine survey of friendship, 51 percent of the respondents said that they would turn to friends ahead of family in time of crisis.[27]

The nature of friendship is hard to pin down because it is the one human bond in which we have completely free choice, of both the person involved and the nature of the relationship. We are not born into friendships, as we are into families. There are no contractual ties such as define marriages or even business relationships. No laws govern friendships. We choose our friends and our friends choose us; it is an association actively (and mutually) arrived at and actively pursued. Though accessibility, proximity, convenience, or coincidence may at the onset appear to be the basis of friendship, the continuance and deepening of the bond depends on a complex set of criteria and determinants.

The breakdown of many traditional social supports—the family, community, church—and the tremendously complex and overwhelming nature of the world we deal with make friendship more important than ever. Companionship, connectedness, continuity, goodwill, perspective on our lives; these seem just the right prescription for what ails us.

Sadly, many people do not have adequate or satisfying friendships. They feel alone or rejected, alienated, unsupported, unconnected. They don't know how to go about making friends or keeping them, or they choose the wrong candidates. Today's social climate works in some ways against friendships, demanding increasingly that people fulfill public roles, that they take their place in the bureaucracy, compete in the marketplace, segmentalize themselves in order to fulfill the various roles society needs them to play. Status or profit, the criteria of the marketplace, creep in to influence their choice of friends. They are urged simultaneously to develop and perfect individual capabilities and to internalize their needs and drives. During adolescence and even as young adults many people form close, deep friendships that often endure through the years, the kind of friendships that are seldom replicated later in life. As people get older it's harder to let friendship in, so self-actualized are people on the one hand, and so socialized and politicized on the other. They become too much of a *self* to let others in, too preoccupied with things that preclude, or at the least inhibit, friendship. Surrounded by fellow humans in our far-reaching, free-choice, leisured lives, 67 percent of people in American society say they are lonely from time to time, and more than a quarter admit to periods of painful loneliness.[28] They are starved for caring connections.

ACQUAINTANCESHIP, PALSHIP, BUDDYSHIP

We usually make first contact with the people who become our casual friends through the ordinary circumstances of our day-to-day lives, and the dynamic of the acquaintanceship is usually defined by those circumstances. Proximity and accessibility play primary roles. We say hello to the neighbors, perhaps chat about local gossip, the kids, or household concerns. With other parents from the school organization we chat about our children's education, perhaps share car-pool chores. We talk business with our coworkers, complain about our jobs, go to lunch together, pass the time of day. At the health club we talk about fitness and sports and hash over our love life and current events in the steam room.

Sometimes these acquaintances become "palships." Pals are people we find we like to hang around with, usually for a specific reason. We find that we enjoy the company of a particular neighbor or coworker or discover common interests or temperaments:

A Time for Caring

we find that they fill a certain niche in our support system. We might have a friend who is fun to go to the movies with, and another we regularly play tennis with or go out partying with. We play the role of "tagalong" with one friend, going along on the fishing trips he enjoys, because we enjoy letting our friend lead the way, enjoy his discourses on trout flies and his enthusiasm, and like being out on the water. We have a friend with whom we like to take walks because she's good, quiet company, because we like to show off our knowledge of plants and flowers and we appreciate her interest. We have a certain person we call if we want to laugh, another for advice, perhaps yet another for sympathy.

"Buddyships"—close, intimate friendships—are something else again. While they may have originated due to sheer proximity or common circumstances or convenience, they escalate for entirely different reasons. An intimate relationship may develop in a neighbor, a coworker, an employer, a casual date, but intimate friendships have a very different dynamic from acquaintances and palships. The basic requirements of a buddyship are loyalty and trust in an atmosphere of intimacy. In fact, the kinds of things that make for more casual friendships—compatible age, occupation, social status, interests—are very far down the list of requirements for intimate friendships. Close friends do many things together that casual friends do—go to the movies, share a meal, attend a party, play tennis—but do these things *primarily in order to be together*. What intimate friends do for each other can be put very succinctly: *they care for each other*.

Good friends count on each other; they expect to do favors for each other, expect to come to the rescue when it counts. They share their resources generously. With close friends we escape from the burden of privacy and isolation, we can let down the defenses of our public image and behavior. We can forget about conformity and know that our idiosyncrasies, our secrets, our bad habits and weak spots, can be exposed without fear of censure or ridicule. We learn that we can be loved as we are, perhaps even because of our seemingly unacceptable traits. Close friends take an interest in what we have to say and in the things we do, and make us feel understood and *known*. We feel that our lives are important to our buddies. When our friends confide in us, or ask our advice or a favor, we are reassured that we have impact and that we have something valuable to contribute. Close friends support and encourage each other, contributing to each other's growth and well-being. In close friends we have the comfort of knowing that someone knows and understands us so well that we do not have to go into long explanations about our thoughts and actions. And close friends are uniquely able to do the tough things—caution us when we're about to do something rash, yell at us when we do something mean or self-destructive, chide us into doing things we've let go, stop us when we've gone too far. Only a good friend can be direct without doing damage, without embarrassing us and threatening the relationship, and only them would we trust to make the judgments in these difficult instances. In sum, friendships are by definition active caring relationships and make the same demands as other caring actions: be there, be aware, share, be fair.

WHAT ARE FRIENDS FOR?

Since we are at liberty to choose our friends and to determine the nature of the friendship, it follows that everyone ends up with a somewhat different "mix" of friends. One person has "dozens of close friends" but just one close pal; another has several trusted confidants and few casual acquaintances; yet another knows everyone in town, or on campus, but has no one to confide in. While one person likes to party with groups of friends, another prefers quiet dinners with just the closest buddy. Most people have different friends to fulfill various roles: intimate, trustworthy friends whom they can talk to and let down their hair with, friends who are good for a good time, friends they share a hobby with, friends they like to work with. Left to our own devices each of us tends to strike up a mix of relationships that suits our own needs and temperament.

One of the common mistakes of friendship is that we sometimes expect one friend—especially if that friend is also our spouse or lover or family member—to be able to meet all our needs. We hope they'll be both comforting and critical, our muse and protégé, our golf partner and intellectual companion.

Knowing which roles each of your friends play is important if you are not to have false expectations or to make unreasonable demands. You should be aware that your drinking buddy is not the person to turn to when a serious problem arises. Take note of the fact that a dear friend is the greatest sorrow-sharer imaginable but gets jealous when you have something to celebrate. Don't get too upset with your spouse and confidant who has no interest in your stamp collection.

One of the ways to have our caring needs met is to have a complement of friends who, among them, meet all our needs. Usually friends fulfill several functions, or their function changes according to the situation. Our tennis partner may also be our closest confidant, our harshest critic, and favored drinking buddy. Our problem-solving pal and chess buddy may also be our spouse or our daughter. Too, roles shift. Today you may lean on your friend; tomorrow he or she will need your concern and care and cheer. Today your friend takes you to the natural history museum and explains the intricacies of carbon dating; tomorrow he or she is in your workshop for an explanation of mortised joints.

It is worthwhile to examine your Caring Circle to see where there are gaps, where support is needed. It often happens that our friends dictate how we spend our time. Sometimes it's more to the point to have our own interests influence our choice of friends. Perhaps you never work in the garden because none of your friends has the slightest interest in gardening. The answer may be to introduce a friend to the pleasure of gardening, or to find a friend interested in gardening. If you don't have a single friend who'll level with you when you're on the wrong track, perhaps you need to find someone who will.

Following is a list of friendship roles, from the sublime to the ridiculous, to help you examine your Friendship Circle. In going over this list you'll probably come up with yet other roles that friends play, or you'll find that only certain aspects of these characters apply to your friends. Remember, too, that many of the functions listed describe roles that *you* play for your friends; you are the provider as well as the recipient of many kinds of friendship care. By comparing the kind of care you provide with the roles described, you'll get an idea of where your caring strengths lie and what kinds of caring you do best. And you may see areas where you're missing out. Or discover that you play some caring roles for yourself. At times you may be your own best adviser, or spirit lifter, or companion.

CONFIDANT

This is the friend to whom you can tell all, with whom you can discuss anything, a nonjudgmental confessor. Everything from the risqué to the ridiculous is safe here. A confidant listens to your marital problems, your trespasses, your most frightening or scandalous or shameful thoughts. Confidants know each other so well that they can practically speak in shorthand. Background information is already in place. Their buddy-talk is a predominant factor in the relationship. Rarely (though there are exceptions) is the relationship one-sided. Usually two friends play the role of confidant for each other.

COMFORTER

When we're blue, or hurt, or sick, or afraid, when the divorce becomes final or the bank forecloses, when trouble strikes, what we may need more than anything is a little tender loving care. Affection, protection, solace, a shoulder to lean on. Not advice, or criticism, or first aid. Even good cheer may be the wrong medicine, though our comforter may be our best spirit-lifter and cheerer-upper. It's good to have a friend who will make us a cup of tea or stroke our fur, or cuddle us in their arms and listen to our tale of woe. This friend is a safe harbor of calm ministrations and soothing words.

THERAPY BUDDY

A friend needn't be a psychiatrist to be therapeutic. This friend listens to your thoughts and dreams and problems and helps you to know and understand yourself. He's available in times of stress or trouble and may offer advice or diagnosis; he helps you interpret yourself and see who you are. An ally and liberator in your struggle with the Inner Enemy, he helps you act out your inner struggles.

ADVISER

Should you wear the navy dress or the black pantsuit? Will John be upset if you ask him to dinner? Should you sleep with him? Do you think you should spend your savings on a trip to Greece? How should you approach your boss for a raise? Should you have a curfew for your sixteen-year-old? It's good to have a friend to hash over such questions—a friend who knows you well, who listens carefully, and who likes to give counsel.

PROBLEM SOLVER

Some advisors go a step further and know just how to solve your problem. They come to the rescue in deed as well as word. They know the store that sells discontinued auto parts. They know just how to fix up that spare room and will pitch in and help you do it. They'll help you make a list of things to say when you ask for a raise and rehearse the confrontation with you.

GOOD NEWS AND BAD NEWS BUDDIES

The bad news buddy is the friend whom you turn to in times of trouble. When there's a crisis, he comes through, spending time, lending a sympathetic ear, helping out as best he can. He feels comfortable and competent when the chips are down. Another friend, the good-news guy, may be completely hopeless when problems arise. He stumbles over words of condolence, tries to make lame jokes to cheer you up. But when the news is good, he's the first to join the celebration, to congratulate you, to make you feel like a hero.

REALITY AND FANTASY BUDDIES

Your reality buddy is the friend who brings you back down to earth when your high-flying ideas get so wild and crazy or impractical that they threaten to cause problems or fail. This is the friend who gently reminds you that it's dangerous to try to get a suntan all in one day, or that you don't really have the money to buy that sports car. That Mary won't be very happy if you spend your whole vacation visiting battle sites, that you're taking a big risk buying a new house before you sell the one you're in. This friend isn't a spoiler: he's a voice of reason and stability trying to save you from being carried away by potentially harmful plans.

A fantasy buddy takes the opposite position. She's the one who says, "Oh, go ahead," who encourages you to fly when you're stuck in the mud of detail and doubt and "What if?" Your fantasy buddy supports your ideas and dreams and helps you aspire to new things. She encourages you to take tap-dancing lessons, to submit the poetry you've been writing on the sly. She believes you'll succeed if you start your own business, or try to make a soufflé. She encourages you to stop being a stick-in-the-mud, to buy a lottery ticket, to believe in your potential.

SPECIAL INTEREST BUDDIES

This is a big category. These are the pals with whom you share a common interest. Sometimes the shared interest is the only cement in the friendship: You don't even see this pal unless you're playing chess or going fishing. You may like to go to the movies with one friend because he or she always has interesting observations and insights, or because you both like to analyze movies. With another friend you go to art galleries, or shopping for clothes, or play pinball. Your common interest may be food or fashion, population control or current events, organic gardening, butterfly collecting, fly-tying, folk art, or bowling.

A special interest friend may be a "good time" buddy. This is the friend we lunch with at work most days, or gossip with at coffee-break time, or go drinking with, or to the beach with, or play poker with, or exchange jokes, or try to pick up dates with.

Another kind of special interest friend is the person we look to for mental stimulation. The one who has the inside track on local politics, or who recommends interesting books, or who likes to discuss moral issues, or play word games.

FRIENDLY ENEMY

This is the friend with whom you love to fight. Every time you get together you end up arguing about sports or politics. If your friend takes one position, you take the other. Or perhaps you are supercompetitive with each other on the racquetball court, or in your field of work; perhaps you're trying to outdo each other's coin collections. Or you're poker adversaries, chess rivals. Your rela-

A Time for Caring

tionship may be one of constant teasing, friendly faultfinding, of trying to outdo each other in an exchange of insults. These relationships, while seemingly antagonistic on the surface, are a wonderful release. Because they allow such a healthy and unthreatening release of hostility or anger, they often make for great closeness between the "enemies."

PLATONIC PILLOW TALK BUDDY

In these times of troubled misunderstanding between men and women, a close friend of the opposite sex is a caring and positive link to the other side. This buddy may be someone with whom you've had a sexual relationship that has evolved into friendship; perhaps you still make love occasionally, especially in times of stress and need. Often one's platonic buddy is seriously involved with someone else; there may or may not be a sexual attraction between you. An increasingly common contemporary version of this arrangement is the close and loving liaisons between gay men and straight women. But the predominant characteristics of this friendship are the confidences, often about each other's love life and sexual activities. This is the person who helps us understand the opposite sex, who advises and informs us how the other half lives, free from jealousy or competitiveness or threatening conflict. It is an alliance that may include casual dates, especially during periods when you're not involved, it may include rooming together, or daily talks on the phone. In its resonance and dynamics, it is worlds apart from a close friendship with someone of the same sex.

MENTOR AND PROTÉGÉ

A mentor is the friend who sees your potentials and helps you to achieve them. Your mentor may be a teacher or parent, a boss or older coworker, or just an interested and encouraging friend. He or she teaches you, answers questions and gives you advice, uses his or her influence and knowledge to smooth the way for you—usually on a path the mentor has already traveled. Your mentor is your champion and supporter, devoted to seeing you grow and prosper and get ahead. He or she wants to see you progress and expand your horizons. Your mentor is someone you respect, whose example you aspire to. The example may be one of character or morals, of athletic prowess, of how to have a good time or get ahead in business. It may encompass a whole life-style or belief system. A mentor may also fill the role of muse, inspiring by example or by love. This is the person in whose name we write a poem, the Gipper for whom we win the ball game.

There is a darker side to this kind of Pygmalion caring. Sometimes the tendency is to develop the protégé along lines that fit the mentor's image or map, rather than to develop the protégé's natural potential. This missionary approach to caring can produce resentful rather than grateful protégés. Eventually the natives rise up against masters who want them to change in ways the master dictates—no matter how glorious or beneficent their visions.

A protégé is someone we take under our wing, for whom we act as mentor. This is a person whose character or ability we believe in, or are attracted to; perhaps he or she reminds us of ourselves at an earlier stage of life. In this relationship we get to be the caretaker and to pass on our knowledge. Such a friendship is a way of repaying our own mentor; the responsibility often helps us to maintain our own high levels of caring and character. We see ourselves and our abilities through new and affirming eyes.

NOSTALGIA BUDDY

This is the friend who grew up in the old neighborhood, or went to school with you, or worked at your first job, or got married at the same time you did. He is your mirror to the past, your living scrapbook of memories. He remembers you as you were then; he reminds you of yourself as you were and gives you a valuable reference point. He's the one with whom you can reminisce about the good old days, with whom you can go over and over the same stories that are talismans of your past.

TRAVEL COMPANION

Even our closest confidant may be impossible to travel with; it's a very specialized knack. A good travel companion is someone you know well and with whom you're able to pass the time unstress-

A Time for Caring

fully; who does his share of the talking, who shares your interests, who can take turns leading and following, can handle the unexpected, whose natural pace is compatible with yours. It's a complicated relationship that covers many different kinds of activities, requiring a complementary sort of give-and-take.

ALLY AND CRITIC

Everyone needs a cheering section, someone who's behind them all the way. Your ally is the person you can count on to believe in you, to take your side, even when the whole world seems against you. Right or wrong, this friend's primary concern is you and your well-being, and in standing with you when the chips are down.

A critic is every bit as important as an ally. When we've insulted someone, when we're tempted to do something dishonest, when we're gaining too much weight, our critic will take on the tough and unwelcome task of pointing out our folly. The critic is willing to yell back, to take our disdain and abuse. It is one of the hardest tasks of friendship. It takes someone we know well, someone who can accept us with our worst traits.

ADVENTURER AND SHELTERER

Adventurous friends are ones who are game to try something new, willing to test your limits and encourage you to overcome trepidation and timorousness. They're sure that if you stand up to the boss, he'll back down. They think you should take chances at switching careers. Climbing mountains or walking home in the dark doesn't scare them, and in their company you cast off your dread and gain confidence. They help you enjoy rather than recoil from life's excitement.

When life's excitement becomes too much, however, it's nice to have a sheltering friend, a calm soothing oasis of quiet and reason. Especially if you tend to be high-strung and hyperactive, shelterers give you a vacation from yourself. They are like the calm in the eye of the storm—the storm being you and your hectic life. When you enter their circle, you relax and shed your burden of worry and fear.

LEADER AND TAGALONG

Sometimes it's fun to be the leader in a friendship, to be the one to show your buddy a new skill, introduce a friend to a new idea or sensation or restaurant or person. Your own interest in art, for example, is enhanced by being able to guide a friend on a museum tour, pointing out the nuances of printmaking, awakening in your friend an area of appreciation heretofore foreign.

At other times you play the role of "tagalong." It may be the same friend who is your art appreciation apprentice whose footsteps you follow when it comes to cooking. It's this friend who has you chopping onions and peeling potatoes, who teaches you to make a perfect omelet, who introduces you to the pleasures of kneading bread. You become the trusting sidekick, the able-bodied assistant, the student.

CHOOSING AND MAKING FRIENDS

It is not as though there is a magic formula for friendship. The chemistry is different in each case, the catalyst often a mystery. Some combinations are stable, others volatile.

We all start out as strangers to each other. Unless we are interested in people, open, curious, anxious to explore, we'll remain strangers. A desire to sniff around, find out what makes people tick, to learn and to be amused, is the first order of friend-making. If there is any secret to making friends, it is that interest and desire are powerful aphrodisiacs.

Take a look at your own attitudes about meeting new people and how you go about it. What is your response to new faces? Are you usually curious about others? Do you show your curiosity? How? Are you likely to sniff around a bit before you decide if you're interested? Do you consider yourself observant? A good judge of people? Do you convey a feeling of openness or receptivity? Or do you seem aloof? What signals do you send out? Do you display yourself or withhold? Are you easily rebuffed? How much do you rely on first impressions? Are you usually right? Is your first impression likely to change? Do you get easily involved with others? End up caring about them?

The second requirement for making friends is the wherewithal

A Time for Caring

or skills to do so. Shyness, aloofness, fear of rejection, or difficulty in carrying on a conversation limit our chances of getting to know people.

Sometimes our problem with making new friends is merely one of social skills. Sincere interest in others is not always enough to overcome the inability to "say the right thing." But if the interest is there, social skills can be built up slowly, and self-confidence tends to grow along with them. It is helpful to remember that *most* people are somewhat shy, and that few people can resist someone who shows an interest in them. In fact, one of the nearly surefire ways to make a friend is to understand the difficulties of first meetings and take responsibility for putting the other person at ease. It's also a sure way to forget, at least momentarily, one's own shyness.

Many "tricks" of meeting people really boil down to caring concern:

- Do not base your interest in making a new friend on any outside consideration such as money, or status, or power. Self-interest precludes other-interest: it's an impossible situation. Be clear about your interest in the other. The famous or powerful often become peoplephobic or abusive of others because they don't trust others to be free of self-interest; they have no faith in their personal worth free of their image.

- Display yourself. Don't launch into an interview or twenty questions. Say something about yourself: an observation, your reaction to meeting the other. "I've got a bet on Fillip in the next race, but I'm not a very good handicapper. I just pick a name that sounds like a winner."

- Show others that they have made an impact on you. "You really seemed excited during the last race. I hope your horse won."

- Don't waste time on aloof or uninterested people. It's not worth the effort or the discouragement. People who are interested are also more interesting.

- Develop your own tricks to help you over the shyness of first meetings. An opening "line" that works for you. A conversation-starting piece of jewelry or clothing. A well-rehearsed joke. A news item. Props and crutches are permissible in the interest of improving friendship skills.

- One of the best ways to make friends is to have your present friends introduce you to new people, and for you to look for ways to have your friends meet each other. Don't jealously hoard friends for yourself. Introduce friends who have a mutual interest in hiking or who each have preschool children. Ask a friend if he or she know anyone who would enjoy going to craft fairs with you. A large network with lots of crossing ties is stronger and makes for an expanded caring environment.

Understanding what kinds of friends you want, the qualities of friendship most important to you, and the kind of friend you *are* is necessary for chosing the right friends. It is possible to be inundated with acquaintances and pals who fail to satisfy our needs or are even destructive of our own best interests.

First of all, do you have room for friends? How many friends do you need? There is always the danger of becoming oversaturated with people, spread too thin with friendships we don't want to be bothered with. It is important to know how to resist the friendships others proffer when they impose on an already overloaded network. People-collecting is a modern hobby that entails always being with others, making contacts, going to parties, cruising, collecting phone numbers. It's a hedge against loneliness, an image support system that can easily get in the way of true friendship.

Another alluring but dangerous kind of friend is the sycophant, the person who indulges your not-so-nice traits, who makes excuses for you, who goes along with your every whim and never makes demands. Often this same person isn't very nice to other people but buys your friendship with his insidious form of total acceptance.

Ask yourself what interests you in others. Brains? Sexuality? Curiosity? Energy? Ethical principles? Do you like people who ask for advice or help with problems, or with ideas? Are you attracted to erratic, enthusiastic people, or to sober, level-headed types? People who are like you or different? Serious or devil-may-care? Quiet or talkative? People with lots of interests, or people who take an interest in your pursuits?

Are there openings in your Caring Circle that might be filled, where you feel something is missing? Do you need a friend to share your enthusiasm about your favorite hobbies? Who likes to go along on shopping trips? Who introduces you to new things? Who's good for advice? Who comes to you for advice? Who will

A Time for Caring

tell you when you're out of line? Who will listen to your jokes? Who can make you laugh? Who inspires you?

Can you describe how you are as a friend? How much time do you have for friends? What do you do with friends? Are you a leader or a follower? Listener? Adviser? Cheerer-upper? Full of compliments or criticism? Like to play ball or chess? A crisis solver? A good-time pal?

SABOTEURS OF FRIENDSHIP

Friendships are delicate. They need nurturing, proper care, and maintenance. Governed by no rules or conventions, they can, if they are abused or pulled too far out of shape, be interrupted or terminated at will.

A sound friendship can withstand a goodly amount of stress, or shift, or neglect. But if one or both parties too often undermines the foundation of trust and goodwill on which it rests, all is lost. Probably few things are more irreparably damaging than a friend's betrayal.

Change and carelessness are behind the demise of most friendships. Change is inevitable, and the shift of focus or balance in life will try a friendship's mettle. A friendship can be taken for granted only so long as both parties understand and live up to the rules and care about its continuance.

How do friendships change?

THE CONTEXT CHANGES

One party gets married and is no longer available for gin rummy and long discussions. One couple of a foursome has a child: that couple's interests shift to family and home building. A friend moves to another job, another city: proximity and availability are the problems.

Still, if the emotional content of the friendship and not just the activities involved is paramount, it is often possible to realign the friendship, to find a new and satisfying framework for it. Sometimes, though, the change in circumstances is the beginning of a slow and inevitable growing apart.

Sarah recounts her experience:

"I swore that our having a baby wouldn't affect any of our friendships, but it is amazing how our friends have shifted around in the scheme of things. Though I didn't think I'd be too easily domesticated—home and hearth never had overwhelming appeal for me—I guess it was inevitable that I'd get involved with other mothers like myself, other young couples concerned with growing infants. Many of our old friends—especially those who we would go out with to movies, restaurants, parties—we see much less often now. Some of them aren't much interested in coming here for dinner, are plainly bored if we talk about our new 'family.' And I find I've lost interest in some of the things that used to concern me—new restaurants, the office shoptalk. Even some of my good girl friends and I don't seem to have much in common anymore. But my friend Diana and I have stayed close, even though we don't *do* the things we used to—drinks after work, shopping, movies. Occasionally we get out together, but usually she comes by and we polish off a bottle of wine and talk about the same old thing we always talked about. We still visit on the phone and seek each other's advice. The content of our relationship was evidently more important than the circumstances."

THE STATUS CHANGES

A shift in the balance of power or influence, in success or failure, can throw an established friendship for a loop. If one party shoots ahead while another stays behind, if one party becomes dependent so there's no longer a taking of turns, if the basis for give and take becomes too out of balance, the friendship is on a shaky base.

Bart and Anne have been friends for years, lovers at one time. Now in their fifties, both writers and scientists, both divorced, they share many interests, keep each other up to date on the details of their love lives, feel free to call each other about anything anytime. Each has a fair share of concerns and problems. In the past few years, however, the balance has shifted. One of Bart's books has become a popular best seller and he is becoming widely known and respected even outside his field. He is invited to lecture for a fat fee, asked to sit on prominent panels. His love life is fine; lots of interesting women all but throw themselves at him. His son is successfully following in his field.

Anne, on the other hand, has been trying to get published a book she worked on for several years, but which publishers felt hadn't much potential for commercial success. Attractive as she is, there aren't many men her age available, and those that are date younger women. She is tired of loveless liaisons. Her very bright daughter has dropped out of school and is drifting.

Their relationship has changed without their knowing it. Bart is often out of town or too busy to spend as much time as usual with Anne. Anne, jealous of Bart's success, finds it hard to commiserate with his problems. They seem frivolous next to hers; she feels that he is teasing her, flaunting his success. How can she listen to his lament about his new girl's nail-biting habit when *she* can't even find a date? Is she supposed to get upset about the Dutch publisher's low-royalty contract when she can't even sell her book? "Not a dry eye in the house," she says sarcastically when he spills his latest tale of woe.

Bart counters by trying to be tactful, not bringing up his lightweight complaints, sometimes withholding news of his successes and accomplishments. He even tries drumming up envies of his own—his covetousness of Anne's house, his wish that he could play the piano as well as she.

In this stressful situation it took a great deal of care and attention to get the friendship back on a new and even keel: a couple of long, sometimes loud and acrimonious, discussions, an exchange of long and detailed letters in which each aired concern about the friendship and reaffirmed the love and care they both hope will hold it together.

LOSS OF FAITH OR RESPECT

Close friends often share similar beliefs and principles; at the least they are not offended by the other's beliefs or behavior, even if they disagree. But when a friend does something we can't abide, or persists in destructive behavior that we are helpless to stop, it tests the limits of friendship.

A friend's increasingly intransigent religious fanaticism or racial slurs can completely destroy our care for them. A friendship with someone whose drinking is becoming more and more serious and who becomes surly when we try to help cannot be sustained.

Andy and Aaron have been friends since medical school and practice in adjacent communities; both are heart specialists. Aaron feels that Andy has been getting increasingly knife-happy, performing surgery at every opportunity. Andy defends his actions, saying he believes in the surgery. Aaron feels that it's the easiest—and most profitable—course for Andy. Also, he disagrees in principle with less-than-vital surgery and feels he's standing helplessly by as Andy becomes, as he calls it, "corrupted." Andy and Aaron have discussed and argued this issue several times, and it has stretched their friendship to the breaking point. Aaron feels that the rift is too deep, and their integrity and pride too sensitive, to withstand the strain. Their friendship will not survive.

BETRAYAL

This is the toughest one of all, for it goes to the very foundation of goodwill and loyalty on which friendship is based. Because of the element of trust inherent in friendships, they are vulnerable to betrayal—even if that betrayal is merely thoughtlessness or expediency.

At a party Irv tells a story that's embarrassing to his friend Glenn, an amusing story that gets lots of laughs, but a story that Glenn feels violates their confidence. Irv excuses his behavior: "I didn't think you'd mind."

Sally and Beatrice have been friends for years, even as Beatrice has made a very successful marriage and become a respected hostess and community leader. But Beatrice has become increasingly upset as she finds that Sally has been dropping Beatrice's name in shops, using it to get jobs or just to impress people. Sally has also taken to inviting her own friends over to drop in on her good friend Beatrice. After all, she says, "What are friends for?" Beatrice feels used; she feels Sally has become more interested in her status than in her.

There is a big element of mentor and protégé in Grant and Larry's relationship. Larry is in his first year of a quite prominent

A Time for Caring

teaching appointment, an appointment that Grant was influential in helping him secure. Toward the end of the term Larry organized a symposium in which he asked Grant to participate. Grant's acceptance has greatly impressed the school and the other participants. However, on the day of the symposium Grant—in a foul mood, distracted by other things, and perhaps becoming jealous of his protégé's rise—shows up late, behaves in a boisterous and argumentative manner, and monopolizes the entire symposium. Larry is crushed and angry and feels set up by Grant. Grant feels Larry was getting too big for his breeches, though he secretly admits he's behaved badly. It will take a long cooling-off period followed by a careful and apologetic rapprochement to restore their friendship.

23

The Friendship Care Plan

Few people have the "mix" of friendships they would like. Perhaps they have lots of pals and not one close confidant. Or no one to share their interest in basketball with. Or to take long walks with. Or they haven't developed the qualities needed for keeping friends. Or aren't willing to devote the time, energy, and concern necessary for friendship.

The Friendship Care Plan is designed to help you evaluate both your current friendships and your current friendship caring abilities. It will steer you toward ways of improving the friendships you have and encourage you to open up new possibilities where there are gaps in your Friendship Circle.

Remember that your requirements for friendship differ from everyone else's. There's no correct mix or balance: your Friendship Care goals should be responsive to your own desires.

STEP ONE: DRAW A FRIENDSHIP CARE CIRCLE

This is a two-step process: first, make a list of your friends—from acquaintances and pals to close buddies. Your Network chart will help you. Remember, this list may include some or all or none of those who are also your lovers or coworkers or family. Second, draw a circle on a large sheet of paper and place your friends inside at the appropriate distance from the center of the circle. If you wish, connect these individuals to you with arrows indicating how the friendship flows—from you to them, from them to you, or both directions. Your circle may look like this:

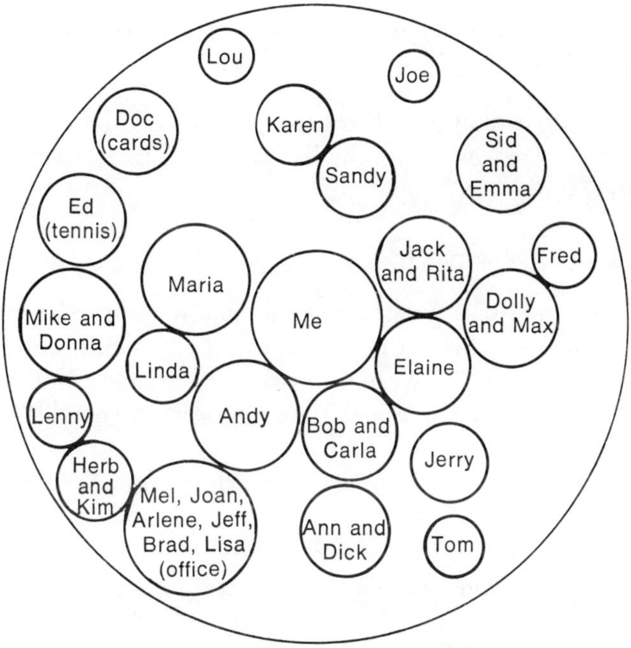
Lou
Joe
Doc (cards)
Karen
Sandy
Sid and Emma
Ed (tennis)
Jack and Rita
Fred
Maria
Me
Dolly and Max
Mike and Donna
Linda
Elaine
Lenny
Andy
Bob and Carla
Jerry
Herb and Kim
Mel, Joan, Arlene, Jeff, Brad, Lisa (office)
Ann and Dick
Tom

or more like this:

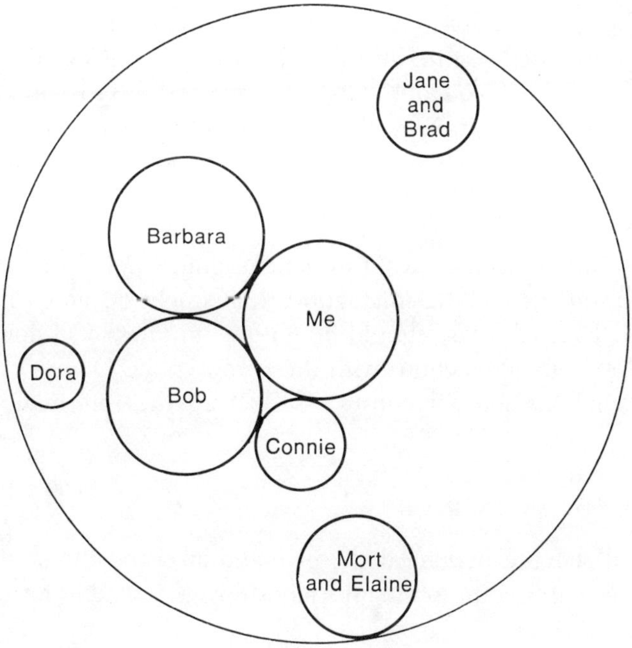
Jane and Brad
Barbara
Me
Dora
Bob
Connie
Mort and Elaine

STEP TWO: MONITOR YOUR FRIENDSHIP CARE HABITS

We are often unaware of exactly how we act and interact with our friends. Two exercises can help us get an overview of our friendship styles.

FRIENDSHIP CARE JOURNAL

Over a period of a week or two take a few minutes each day to jot down in your calendar or on a sheet of paper your observations about what goes on between you and your friends. Note the following things as they appear (or don't appear) in your life:

- Who have you spent time with? How much? Alone? In a group?
- What activities were involved?
- What subjects did you talk about when you were together?
- What gestures of friendship have you made? Gifts? Phone calls? Time? Attention? Compliments? Favors? Advice?
- Who have you *not* seen or spoken to? Why?
- What did you want to do or say that you held back from? Why?
- Who extended gestures of friendship toward you? Called? Came to visit? Asked you out? Cheered you up? Fixed you dinner? Were there any surprises? Did you expect to hear from someone that you didn't? Whose company did you enjoy? Who was boring? Demanding? Depressing?

These questions are meant as general guidelines. There are literally hundreds of little interactions that might be noted in your journal. Every day you should find a few minutes to sit down and reflect on your interactions with those you know. Do not evaluate or censor your journal entries. Collect all the information you can.

THE ME/NOT ME EXERCISE

We all have experienced the give-and-take and the shifting of direction that is common to all friendships. We tend to form some

A Time for Caring

friendships in which we are the strong or supportive partner, others in which we're the dependent or tagalong member. Within even the most balanced friendship the balance sometimes tips to one extreme or the other. We may have a bad time and suddenly need a lot of support and understanding that our friends may or may not be able to handle. Conversely, we may have a friend who is going through a crisis and placing heavy demands on our time and energy. This kind of fluctuation is normal, healthy, and to be expected. However, sometimes we find that we are stuck in the role of giver or of taker. This might be the case in one specific relationship; perhaps it's true across the board. It is helpful to identify the give-and-take ingredients of our friendships, and see what we do willingly and what we consider unwanted burden or duty.

The Me/Not Me exercise is designed to let you see how well-balanced your friendships are and how well your friendships fulfill your needs. At various points during the day, when you are involved in activities with friends, ask yourself whether what you are doing represents you fairly or not. "Is this me? or not me? Is this something I choose to do? Or not?" Also note whether you are providing or consuming the care.

For example:

I called Jane today. (She is sick.) Me/Provide

Carl took me to lunch. Me/Consume

I baby-sat for Frieda's kids while she went to the doctor. Not Me/Provide

I spent most of the time making cutouts with Amy. Me/Provide

I spoke to Fred about the trouble I'm having with Steven. Me/Consume

Linda and I went shopping for furniture after work. Not Me/Provide-Consume

I called my sister. Me/Provide

I called Aunt Alice. Not Me/Provide

I wrote a letter to Susan asking her to return my camera. Me/Consume

Gwen called to thank me for dinner. Me/Consume

I helped Jessie at work finish a project. Me/Provide

STEP THREE: EXAMINE YOUR FRIENDSHIP CARE PATTERNS

This step is designed to help you take a close look at your friendship care attitudes and habits. Don't evaluate your responses to the following questions; that comes later. Just look at the dynamics of your relationships and identify the component parts.

1. What kinds of friends do I have? How many people do I count as acquaintances, as casual pals, as close friends? Is any category overburdened? Underfilled? Does that mixture feel right?
2. How do I meet people? Am I shy? What do I say to people? Am I observant? How do people react to me? Is it easy for me to make new friends?
3. What attracts me about people I meet? What makes me want to continue a friendship? What turns me off?
4. What do I do with my casual friends and acquaintances? What kinds of friendships do I have with people in the office? In groups and clubs I belong to? People I meet at parties or on the street?
5. Whom do I go to for advice? On my personal life? On my career? About family matters? About sex? My love life?
6. Whom do I share my interests with? Go to the movies, play tennis, take classes with? Discuss the news, take walks, go partying with? Would I like to find friends to share other interests with?
7. Whom would I call on in a crisis? If I needed comforting? Or cheering up? Who entertains me? Makes me laugh? Inspires me? Whom can I sit around quietly with, just passing time?
8. Whom do I go to for intellectual conversation, comment, opinion? Whom do I admire and look up to? Whom do I set an example or take the lead for?
9. Who calls on me for emotional advice? Intellectual conversation? Companionship? Activities?
10. What is the physical and/or sexual nature of my friendships? What gestures of friendship such as hugging, kissing, sexual overtones, or touching are involved?
11. When am I lonely? In a crowd? At home alone? Occasionally? Chronically? What do I do about it? Whom do I turn to? Do I enjoy being alone? How much time do I spend?

What difference do I feel between being alone and being lonely? Would I like to have more time to myself? Am I overloaded with people?
12. Do I have friends I deeply care for? Who care for me? Which friends do I enjoy most? Why?
13. How am I at maintaining friendships? How long do my friendships last? What usually breaks them up? (Fights? Separation? Boredom? Negligence?) Do I work at maintaining my friendships? At keeping in touch and up-to-date? Am I able to fight with my friends, to disagree and argue? How do I resolve conflict with friends? Do we have a system for negotiating our differences?

STEP FOUR: EVALUATE YOUR FRIENDSHIP CARE PATTERNS

Assess the information gathered in steps one through three. Try to look at your responses with a sharp eye. What kind of friends do you have? What is it you like and dislike about them? What is missing? What is strong? Divide your responses into two columns: "Good Friendship Care/Strengths" and "Poor Friendship Care/Weaknesses." To get some idea of the way your list might look, study the examples below.

GOOD FRIENDSHIP CARE/STRENGTHS	POOR FRIENDSHIP CARE/WEAKNESSES
• I'm involved in lots of group activities, so I meet many people. • I like to joke; I'm good at cheering people up; I'm usually happy when a friend has good news. • My friends and I share the same interests: Anne and I play gin together; Artie comes over to play basketball; Ed argues politics and current events with me when we get together.	• I almost never have time to myself; I end up spending time with people I hardly know or care about; I can't say no. • When a friend is having serious trouble and worries, I get very uncomfortable; I don't know how to behave and end up making dumb jokes. • I seem always to be the leader; I haven't anyone that I go to for advice, or that is a particular inspiration to me.

GOOD FRIENDSHIP CARE/STRENGTHS	POOR FRIENDSHIP CARE/WEAKNESSES
• I'm quick to side with my friends when they need me. • I'm a very good listener; lots of people ask me for advice, especially about getting jobs. • I have two college friends that I've known for more than ten years.	• Sometimes I lose friends because I'm afraid to confront them when I'm upset about them or about something they've done to me. • Now that John has moved away, I don't have anyone I can call up anytime to tell my troubles to. • I never write letters.

STEPS FIVE AND SIX: SET FRIENDSHIP CARE GOALS AND MAKE A PLAN FOR IMPLEMENTING THEM

Now that you have pinpointed some of your friendship strengths and weaknesses, it is time to select those that you want to emphasize or improve. Remember to keep your goals realistic.

Don't tackle too much, and put your efforts where they'll produce the greatest benefits. Start with simple, easy-to-accomplish changes so you'll gain confidence from seeing quick results before tackling major issues. Once you determine your goals, figure out exactly how to go about achieving them. Consider all your resources and options. Use your strengths to help you.

Here are a few examples of the kind of goals you might establish:

1. Try to develop a closer friendship with Barbara. Accept her invitation to teach me to play tennis. She likes word games; I'll show her how to do those English crosswords. Try and get over my shyness and tell her how much I enjoy her company and her serenity and sense of humor. Tell her about myself, especially about my breaking up with Allan last month. Ask her about her husband and about the house they rent in the country. Invite her over for dinner next week.

A Time for Caring

2. I will try to stop being the listener all the time with Mary and get her to listen to me, too. How? By bringing up my feelings more often. By not rushing in to give advice to her so much. By telling her that there are times when I can't really deal with her problems. By asking her to hear me out when I have something on my mind.
3. I will make myself write letters to friends out of town so that I take a more active role in maintaining these friendships. I'll make a list of those I want to write and set a quota of two letters a week, which I'll write on Sunday afternoons when I do my accounts. When my friends write, I'll make it a rule to answer on Sunday of the same week. When I go to the lake this summer, I'll take a batch of stamped, addressed postcards.

STEP SEVEN: PAY ATTENTION

Once you decide how to implement your goals you must be on your alert to notice how you handle these tasks. Make them part of your daily agenda. Look for opportunities to further your objectives. See how often you slip from your goals. Notice the results of your actions. Notice when you get closer to your goals. What are the results then? Don't shy away from the crucial task of self-examination.

STEP EIGHT: BE SELF-SUPPORTING AND REWARDING

When you are successful, even in small ways, pat yourself on the back. If, for example, you find you are now slipping into the role of listener and not just offering advice or counsel, congratulate yourself. But if you let too much time go by before you answer letters from your friends, don't chastise yourself or feel guilty. Just drop a card. And then congratulate yourself for *that*. You're entitled to an occasional lapse. After all, you're only human. Encourage yourself with a reward when you feel you've made real progress. Keep a list of possible rewards to choose from; let the upcoming reward encourage you along the way.

STEP NINE: ENLIST THE HELP AND SUPPORT OF OTHERS _____

This is a particularly vital step in the Friendship Care Plan: since your goal is to improve your friendship skills, asking friends for help is part of the deal. Ask your friends to introduce you to new people. Strengthen and reinforce your existing network of friends. Suggest that you and a friend include another mutual acquaintance in your activities occasionally, or ask a friend to help you find a fishing buddy. If you are uncomfortable in groups, enlist the support of a friend. Tell him that you are trying to overcome your shyness and need his help. Ask him for suggestions. Don't be afraid to ask if he'd stick with you for the first half hour at a party, or help you meet others, or take care of introductions for you. You may want to tell a coworker that you are trying to improve your relationship with someone in the office and suggest that the two of you make a point of going out to lunch with her soon. Tell your friend you'd like to meet someone interested in folk dancing. Whatever you do, don't turn away from those who can be the greatest source of support and understanding.

STEP TEN: SIGN A CONTRACT AND SET A DATE TO REVISE YOUR PLAN _____

On page 263 is a form to fill out that details your Friendship Care Plan. Your signature on that form is a commitment from you to improve friendship caring.

After you have implemented your first set of goals and worked to change your friendship patterns, you may want to redraw the Friendship Care Circle from step one and set two new goals for yourself. You may be surprised at how your friendships have altered. Some people likely are now closer to you than before, some reciprocate more. Others have become less close because upon examination the relationships did not hold up. Therefore it is vital, as with all other care plans, to keep in touch with how your friendships are changing.

FRIENDSHIP CARE CONTRACT

Name: _____

Goals:

1. _____
_____
_____
_____

2. _____
_____
_____
_____

3. _____
_____
_____
_____

Plan for implementing goals:

1. _____
_____
_____
_____

2. _____
_____
_____
_____

3. _____
_____
_____

I will review this plan on _____
Date: _____

Signature: _____

24
Caring in the Community

The concept of community has also changed drastically in recent times. Once, "the community" encompassed the neighbors, the church, the school, perhaps the town or village, and only peripherally the state, the nation, and the world. Today we speak of a world community, for everyone's day-to-day horizons—expanded by lightning-quick communications, international trade and travel—take in the entire globe and, of late, the whole universe. It's a rather staggering task to function confidently as an individual in such a large, unwieldy, and unknowable context.

Everyone handles this modern dilemma differently. Some broad thinkers are able to see the big picture and deal with the world on a global level. Often, however, they lose sight of the individual and those close to home—like friends and family. Most people break down the world into manageable pieces—the family, the neighbors, the local community, the professional world, the country, and so on—and deal with each level as best they can, as needed.

It is very tempting to shy away from the big, cruel world, to build defenses against its intrusions. For their own self-preservation people often feel that they must choose not to care, since they feel powerless to have an effect on events or situations, are sickened and discouraged by the evil and catastrophe in the world. The withdrawal into autonomy and "self-improvement," the move to isolated, "self-sufficient" communes, are ways to keep at bay a world that is too much with us.

Perhaps this retreat has been a necessary defense for the punch-drunk individual, has offered a time to recuperate and regain strength. But it is not an answer, for the world must finally be dealt with on community terms, in league with and not at odds with the rest of the species. The world community needs the support and participation of its individual members if it is to survive and grow; so, too, does the individual need the participation and support of the community. Rather than retreat, we must step up our involvement with others, put ourselves out there in the world. The individual can only liberate himself through caring for the others in his life: participation, not defensive isolation, relieves the individual from feelings of loneliness and powerlessness in a hostile world. The larger community needs all the help it can get to address the huge problems of mankind and the more manageable problems of the local neighborhood.

The feelings of people today about the world are often reflected in their attitudes toward strangers. It is the nature of modern life that every day we see (or pass on the street, or rub shoulders with, or drive by on the highway, or talk to in stores or buses) hundreds, perhaps thousands, of people who are total strangers to us. A far cry from just decades ago when everyone knew everyone else in the small town and the arrival of a stranger was rare and novel. Nowadays we are often out in the world alone, away from our families, surrounded by strangers. In a trip to the supermarket we come across more strangers than the average person a century ago ran into in the course of a year, even a lifetime! Our fear and defensiveness is perhaps understandable, as is our desire not to be overwhelmed by the crowd or constantly intruded upon, but it is certainly a hindrance to our own well-being and to that of the community. As long as everyone is seen as a threat—the new neighbor, the new coworker, the new girl in class, the foreigner, the woman in front of us at the check-out counter—we are on our guard against intrusion and closed to the positive benefits of friendship, community, mutual support, fearlessness, security, and the like.

Frank's story illustrates how the sense of community protects those within it but sets the outsiders apart from its protection, even making it possible to exploit them:

"Last year when I was in upstate New York, I borrowed the car of friends I was staying with and drove to visit another old friend who lived about two hours' distance across the Hudson River and into the mountains. About two thirds of the way there my car heated up, and it kept getting worse, so that about ten miles from my friend's house I realized I'd have to stop and do something about the car. I was very upset because it wasn't my car, so I wasn't familiar with its quirks and I didn't know how serious the problem was. As I looked for a place to get the car looked at, I was getting more and more anxious. I started worrying about worrying my friends, and about my health and how taxing all this stress was, and worrying whether I'd brought my medicines, and so on. Then I came over a hill and there in the valley below was a big, gleaming service station—which I drove into with mixed relief and trepidation. Relief, of course, that I'd found a source of help. Trepidation because I didn't know them, and didn't know the car so I couldn't judge the seriousness of the problem. I could see behind the station a huge junkheap of old cars, and I had sweaty palms just seeing my friend's car join the heap. Well, sure enough, as soon as the owner started to look at the car he was full of dire predictions: 'Two weeks, $400, looks pretty bad, tsk, tsk.' He got his coworkers to look at the car; they corroborated his opinion. At that point, near to panic, I gave up hope of solving the problem myself and called the friend I was on my way to visit. He said he'd come for me. You can imagine my surprise—and the surprise of the people in the gas station—when my friend walked in and it turned out he knew a couple of the people in the station. And they knew his local reputation and involvements. Suddenly the whole picture changed. The car might not be in such bad shape after all. They could probably even fix it by the next day, and so forth. I drove off with my friend and they called his house an hour later with still more good news. All that was needed was just a minor parts-replacement.

"I got the car back the next day for about $70. The point is that while I was a stranger they exploited me with no qualms whatsoever. But as soon as they were dealing with someone within their community, they bent over backward to be helpful and reasonable. My friend told me that in the local area, that station is considered highly technical and reasonable. Obviously, outsiders get different treatment; there's a different set of rules."

There are hopeful signs lately that more and more people are beginning to see the necessity and the desirability of strengthening their ties and concerns with the world at large. Scores of books have appeared in the last couple of years in the areas of community action, the environment, world politics and perspectives, books that address the evils of self-involvement or hedonism. Big corporations are initiating programs that give their employees time-off or bonuses to reward their social concerns or for time spent in volunteer community work. Activist groups no longer simply picket and wave signs: they are politically savvy, they know how to deal with the real world, with local politics and the community; they are better informed about the larger picture. Communal groups function smoothly within the world, not outside it, getting their economic support from jobs and sources within the system, working in league with the established community.

In big cities block associations have become the neighborhood unit. The residents of each block join forces to beautify the area, to fight crime, to support city legislation. They hold social events to get to know each other better, and organize street fairs to raise money for local improvements such as trees and flowers or litter baskets. In any large city nowadays there are concerned community groups to handle the kind of counseling problems that small towns are better equipped to deal with intimately—support groups for the widowed, for alcohol and drug users, for potential suicides, for victims and families of specific diseases, for bereaved parents, for people who are just plain lonely. Another community-building custom that seems to be coming back is barter. The doctor trades his services for his patient's plumbing expertise, or legal advice, or craftwork, or typing, or bookkeeping. The kind of cooperation and support once provided by the church or the farm co-op or the town council seems to be coming back in new forms.

Involvement in the community at a level that benefits the individual and the group is the best hedge against anxieties and fears of the big, cruel world, and the optimum way to expand the caring environment. People who become involved inevitably come to a more positive view of themselves and of human nature in general, for they are suddenly placing themselves in circles of more caring people. People who become involved are able to see outside themselves and feel liberated from the isolation and loneliness of self-involvement and from the fear and encroachment of exploiters. They have the reward of seeing positive things accomplished, things that they helped to bring about. They gain a sense of personal impact and power, a greater faith in the value of their contribution and of the potential for change in the world out there. With an understanding of how the world works comes a conviction that the world *can* work, given the proper attitude and application, and that there are many other people, *just like themselves*.

"It isn't hard to see why I've always had such a negative view of the world," says Carlo. "My father always came home full of stories about people he'd cheated out of insurance claims or about a fast buck he'd made cheating a 'sucker' who had joined his buddies' poker game. He was full of bad news and was always enjoying a laugh at someone else's expense. He made fun of my mother for believing in her 'religious nonsense,' of my sister for wanting to be a nurse and 'save the world.' I of course became one of those kids who cut school and cheated on tests and made fun of anyone who carried books home from school. When I met Evelyn—she was a waitress at a restaurant where I was peddling restaurant supplies at the time—she struck me as the most simpleminded do-gooder. I used to put her on all the time and laugh about her to my friends—but I kept coming back. As I got to know her better, meet her friends, and become involved in her life, I finally became convinced that she was for real. It was a revelation to me that you could get by by playing it straight, that there was a whole world of people who weren't out to con you, whom you didn't always have to be watchful of. Sometimes I still catch myself being cynical, but I find I'm much less afraid of new situations and find much more to like in the people I meet, and even turn up good news when I read the newspaper."

The way in which each person allocates his concerns for the world beyond his doorstep will tend to be defined by that person's particular interests, vision, and temperament. One person's involvement might center around a cause or idea that he believes in—the environment, amnesty, or the right to abortion. An avid environmentalist might lead a clean-up drive in the local community, support the national candidate who promised environmental aid and reform, subscribe to all publications regarding the environment, and donate money to the cause of international environmental concerns. Another person's involvement might be dictated by their concerns for their family and therefore center entirely around the local community. This person's activities might range from the local clean-up drive to voter registration to the school lunch program to the funding of the local theater group. A person who works well with people might put all energies into counseling; a person with power or expertise or political clout might focus on speechmaking or lobbying. Those with money often choose to fund those causes they believe in. Each person must find his place and learn to allocate his time, or money, or skills, or power where they will do the most good for themselves and the community. Making one's caring count is a responsibility.

"I'm the classic case of someone who professes to care about the community but never does anything about it," says Marie. "Every once in a while I'd think that I ought to get involved, but I was always 'too busy,' and besides, I didn't know what to do. It took doing a Community Care Plan to show me what interested me and what I could find the time to do and what I was capable of.

"When I started trying to pin down my interests, I found that I'm not at all political and I have little patience with committees or phone calling or letter writing. I also acknowledged that I had limited time to devote to community projects and that a sense of personal impact was important to me.

"There are two things I'm currently involved in that satisfy my criteria for community stuff. One is a group of advertising women I've organized that is working on an ad campaign to support the ERA: I get to use both my clout in the business and my copywriting experience. Also, I'm teaching a writing course this fall at the state prison under a state-funded program. I'm terrified about this, but Mel has been very supportive. In preparation I set aside one night a week to review my rusty English grammar and style books and prepare class projects.

"I'm still no Ralph Nader, but I've come a long way. I feel like a valuable member of society—part of the solution instead of part of the problem."

It is necessary to care about the world, not as a substitute for caring about friends and family, but as part of the balance. The world needs friends and must operate as if there were no strangers. Caring for those outside our immediate circle may seem time-consuming and fatiguing, it may seem hard to see the results, but caring people must share responsibility for what they find when they set foot outside their door.

25

The Community Care Plan

The Community Care Plan is aimed at making us feel a part of our community, country, planet. The object is not to become a full-time activist but to kindle our connections to the society around us, to overcome fear and shyness about participation and increase our sense of personal impact, to let us look at and consider the challenges of the world, to shore up our supports to and from the community and develop skills that contribute to the general good.

There are many ways to take part in community activities. Each person must find the kind and degree of involvement that satisfies him, that makes him feel comfortable, and that uses his particular skills and temperament to the greatest benefit of the group.

For some of us this might mean starting from scratch—reading a newspaper and watching the news on TV, opening ourselves up so we can find out what's going on. Interest in issues, participation in voting, reading magazines, talking about community matters—these activities can all help us build a bridge between ourselves and the outside world. Getting to know one's neighbors is a place to begin. This might mean simply taking the time to stop and chat, or going for a Walk/Talk (page 304). Finding others with whom to barter goods and services is another way to become involved.

For others, more direct action and participation may be appropriate: they may join the PTA or march against nuclear power, or write to their congressman, or join a food co-op, organize a medical self-help group, or volunteer at the hospital, or run for city

A Time for Caring

council. The object is to find a level of belonging to the community that is acceptable to you. But you will find that whatever degree of action is most appealing, the curiosity and interest required to find out or do something about what is going on in your world will make you feel a little more alive, a little more connected, a little more caring.

This care plan is less formally structured than the previous ones. The basic objectives are the same, however: to explore your current circle of community caring, to identify what you'd like to know more about or do more about, to figure out how to pursue your goals and to sign a contract committing yourself to new goals.

STEP ONE: EXAMINE CURRENT COMMUNITY INVOLVEMENT

DRAW A COMMUNITY CARE CIRCLE

If your circle represents the world community, break down the arena into concentric circles by the proximity of each area—the neighborhood, the village or city, the state and the nation, the world.

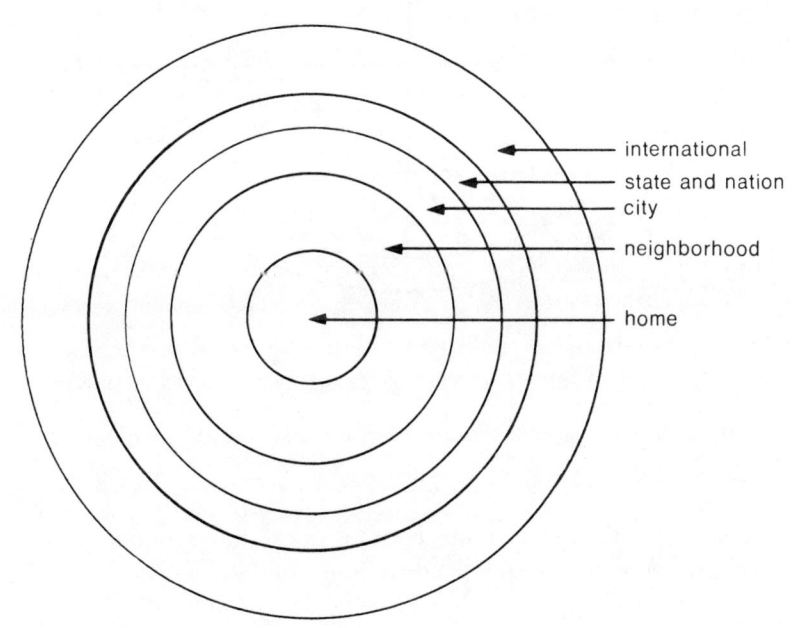

- international
- state and nation
- city
- neighborhood
- home

The above circle reflects the involvement of someone who's concerned about home and the local neighborhood and international concerns, but not so much about city, state, and national affairs.

Next, divide the circle up like a pie to show what topics are of greatest (and least) concern to you; and indicate the nature of your involvement(s) in each area:

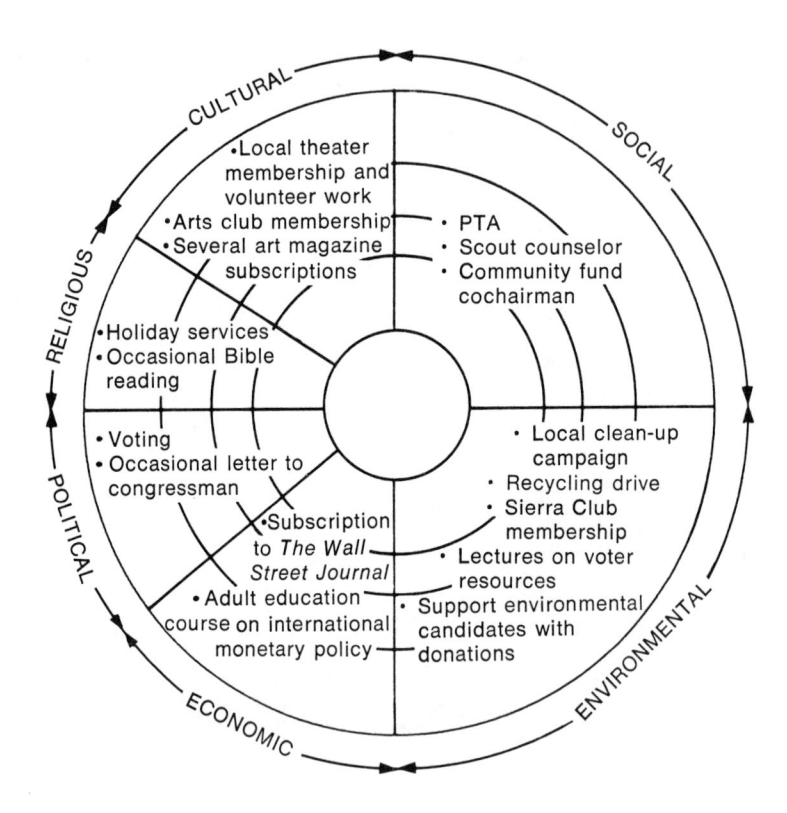

(Circle diagram divided into sectors labeled CULTURAL, SOCIAL, ENVIRONMENTAL, ECONOMIC, POLITICAL, RELIGIOUS:)

- **Cultural:** Local theater membership and volunteer work; Arts club membership; Several art magazine subscriptions
- **Social:** PTA; Scout counselor; Community fund cochairman
- **Environmental:** Local clean-up campaign; Recycling drive; Sierra Club membership; Lectures on voter resources; Support environmental candidates with donations
- **Economic:** Subscription to *The Wall Street Journal*; Adult education course on international monetary policy
- **Political:** Voting; Occasional letter to congressman
- **Religious:** Holiday services; Occasional Bible reading

IDENTIFY YOUR CURRENT STATE OF COMMUNITY INVOLVEMENT:

Do you read the papers, watch TV news, subscribe to specialized journals? Vote?

Do you talk with friends about issues of local and national importance? Are your friends involved in community affairs?

A Time for Caring

Do you attend community meetings, school meetings, political rallies? Do volunteer work? Belong to any clubs? Special interest groups? Professional associations?

Do you donate time or money to charities and volunteer organizations? How much time? Or money? To which ones?

Do you know who your state and national representatives are? Your city council representatives? Do you vote? Campaign for politicians or causes you support? Do you ever write letters to public officials? Publications?

Do you belong to any international organization? Speak a foreign language? Travel?

What issues, ideas, or causes interest you most? Least? How do you become involved in supporting them? Do you feel overinvolved? Would you like to do more? Is anything stopping you from greater participation? Do you have the skills you feel you need to be helpful? Are you more likely to be concerned at a local level, or are you more interested in global issues?

STEP TWO: DECIDE HOW TO BECOME MORE INVOLVED

Are you satisfied with your current participation in community affairs? How would you change your involvement? Would you like to put in more time? Would you switch your focus from church affairs to involvement in local politics? From watching the TV news to taking a political science course? From concern with world hunger to local job opportunities for women? From studying Spanish to volunteer work with the handicapped? What would you have to do to make the desired changes? Would you have to give up some leisure time, or a hobby you enjoy? Get baby-sitting help with the children? Organize the neighborhood parents? Study nursing? Face up to long-term fears, or inadequacies, or shyness? What stands in the way of actively pursuing your community concerns?

Sniff around at all the possible areas until you find what interests you, what makes use of your skills and connections, what channels are open for pursuing these interests. Try to think up as many options as possible; be creative in dreaming up new ways to get involved; whatever your unfulfilled wishes are, now is the time to identify them.

STEP THREE: SET GOALS AND FIGURE OUT HOW TO ACHIEVE THEM

MAKE A LIST OF COMMUNITY CARE GOALS

Be realistic about the amount of time, energy, and money you have to spend on community involvement at this point. You can always increase your activities later. Be specific in defining your goals.

If your interest lies in the area of the international community, determine clearly how you'd like to get involved. A pen pal? An exchange student to stay at your home during the summer? Subscriptions to international publications? A course in diplomacy or foreign policy? A lecture series? Volunteer work for an international relief fund?

If you're interested in improving the local community environment, how would you go about it? Join the PTA? Campaign for a local politician? Blitz the local papers with letters? Organize a street clean-up drive? Learn more about the community board's voting record? Donate money to the local organizations you feel are most effective? Use your influence in the business community to raise money for a youth center? Encourage your family and friends to join you in a picket line?

Here is a sample list of Community Care goals:

1. Get in the habit of reading a daily newspaper (not just the sports section and the financial news).
2. Be more careful about separating garbage, return bottles instead of throwing them away.
3. Attend my monthly Rotary meetings.
4. Brush up on my Spanish.
5. See about getting a kid from the Fresh Air Fund to stay with us this summer.

MAKE A PLAN TO IMPLEMENT YOUR GOALS

Be specific about how you can fulfill your new commitments. Figure out what it's going to cost and where the money will come from. Find out what skills are called for and how you can learn them. Enlist the advice and support of friends, family, and community organizations in achieving your goals. Schedule the necessary time into your day.

Here's how the list of Community Care goals above might be implemented.

1. Get home delivery of the newspaper and read it with breakfast. Call the subscription office today. Try to encourage Sandy to read it too so we can talk about it.
2. Buy a supply of plastic garbage bags and an extra garbage pail to put under the sink next time I go to the market. Clear a little extra space for bottles.
3. Have my assistant Joan keep my schedule clear for Rotary meetings and remind me a day ahead.
4. Ask Marcia where she studied last year. See if there's a place where I can take a course on Tuesday nights starting this summer when Sandy is bowling. Also check to see if there are tapes available at the library.
5. In February call the Fresh Air Fund to see what the procedure is and if there are any forms to fill out. Find out if there are any special requirements for the house, or the child's room, or activities. See if any of the neighbors would be willing to share in trips and special activities.

STEP FOUR: WRITE OUT AND SIGN THE COMMUNITY CARE CONTRACT _____

COMMUNITY CARE CONTRACT

Goals: 1. _____

_____

_____

2. _____

3. _____

4. _____

5. _____

Date for revising plan: _____

Signature: _____

Date: _____

Keep this contract where you can refer to it often to remind you of your commitments and help you plan your daily Caring Agenda.

26

The Purchase of Caring:
SOME THOUGHTS ON PROFESSIONAL CARE

Today so much of the caring that used to fall within the province of family and friends is bought in the marketplace. Paid professionals take care of us and our families; we purchase caring the way we purchase groceries and cars. The once humble caring profession has become big business.

Like so many other aspects of modern life, caring know-how and concern has slowly been usurped by bureaucracies and social institutions. Control over the caring aspects of our lives has slowly shifted to the experts. To a certain extent, of course, this makes sense: hospitals certainly provide expertise and facilities in excess of what the individual or the family has to offer. Schools are in many ways better geared to educate our children than are parents. The problem is that the take-over has been overwhelming. Bowing to the superior knowledge and power of the pros, the individual has abdicated, a little too willingly delegated his responsibilities, allowed the shift of power. The individual is loath to challenge the superior knowledge and sophistication of the professional or institution. The result is people who are afraid to question their doctor or the social services on which they depend for their support, afraid to give their children guidance or discipline different from that of their child's school. Worst of all, the caring skills of the individual atrophy from disuse, or they are never learned.

Today nursing homes care for the elderly, either because no one at home has had experience in tending to the needs of the sick or aged, or because no one at home can take enough time out from a busy life to tend to them. Death is far removed from everyday life; three quarters of the deaths in the United States take place in institutions, monitored by professionals and machines.

Christopher Lasch makes the point that death and infirmity are particularly frightening in a society that has no fond memories of the past, and thus no standard by which to value the future.[29] Death is a fearful and mysterious experience, even when we are surrounded by friends and family. How much worse if added to the normal anguish about dying is the knowledge of institutionalization far from home.

Psychotherapists and social workers rather than our families and friends are our emotional confidants. In addition to the mammoth health and welfare institutions, the huge university complexes, the proliferating nursing homes, care is provided by the personal secretary or assistant, the gardener, the chauffeur, the social secretary, the baby-sitter. Even the bartender, the stewardess, and the prostitute become part of the paid caring support system. We overuse easily available professional care; it's no wonder we've become incapable of taking care of ourselves.

The fact is that most people know they're not getting the real thing and know they're giving up a lot for both the convenience and the valued expertise of the professional carers. But their lives are too busy to permit them to take care of their own caring, and now they've gone and lost the knack. Their skills have become blunted, their abilities are untested. They're fearful of bungling or mishandling the situation, or they don't see how they could possibly find time or reorder their lives to do the things they now leave to the state or pay others to do.

They're all specialists: their knowledge tends to be substantial in one area and totally lacking in others. And they live in a society that little values the menial work associated with caring. They've become fearful of infirmity, of aging, of disease and death, in a world that so highly values youth, vitality, and beauty, and that little values experience or wisdom or duty or the past.

The hunger for caring leaves many people open to those who would exploit this need. Thus the stories about aging, senile Aunt Sarah who was bilked out of her small fortune in her last years. Or Uncle Bob who went gaga over the waitress in the local coffee shop and left his money to her in return for a phony show of affection. The irony of these stories is that they are often related by relatives angry over losing out on Aunt Sarah's remaining dollars or Uncle Ed's stock certificates, blind to the realization that their relatives turned to these apparent "swindlers" for the care they couldn't get from their families.

Caring exploitation too operates on a much larger, more institutionalized level today, even though the great majority of caring professionals bring to their work a high level of expertise combined with a sincere desire to help others—an often difficult and thankless task in the face of overwhelming care-lessness around them. Nursing homes advertise caring environments, employment services advertise home nurses or baby-sitters who "care." Care units are ready, for a fee, to rush to your home in your hour of need. These exploiters, attuned to the tremendous hunger for care, are ready and waiting to sell the *pretense* of care to the susceptible and uncared for. This commercialization and exploitation of caring is the ultimate travesty, perhaps a fitting punishment for people who are all too willing to let others do it.

We're paying dearly to be cared for, not only with our money but in terms of human need for authentic caring. Today the professional sector is bearing the brunt of health care, and as a consequence the quality of that care is slipping. What we have now is an unworkable mishmash of helpless, ignorant, unskilled health-care consumers and overworked, increasingly impersonal, burned out, sometimes exploitative health care professionals.[30] Health care professionals are overwhelmed by the sheer numbers of people they must care for on inadequate budgets, in overtaxed facilities with undertrained staffs. They are forced to spend far too much time on paperwork and simple, rote services that could be handled by the individual.

The "burned out" professional is becoming a common phenomenon. Teachers leave their field by the scores, unable to care about educating apathetic students toward whom they must also act as parent, disciplinarian, sex educator, and social director. Doctors who feel taxed by neurotic, hypochondriacal, and care-starved patients eventually cease to care about anything but their fees.

It's crucial that the balance between the professional and consumer sectors be restored. The care consumer must again take on the part of the caring concern that it can responsibly and competently shoulder, so that health care professionals can apply their knowledge where it's most needed, and so that health care facilities can be used more efficiently. A less helpless private sector will free the professional sector to increase the knowledge that has so much improved the quality of our lives.

WHAT CAN BE DONE?

What's most sorely needed to set things back on the track is a massive program of consumer education. The professional community must take the lead in helping to restore to the individual the confidence and ability to care. They can facilitate the teaching of the range of caring skills that can be handled by the individual. They can focus on preventive medicine and therapies. They can work to remove the mystery that surrounds health care, can encourage the formation of self-help groups, of health fairs, of consumer publications such as the successful *Medical Self Care*[31] and the latest guide book for patients, *Fight for Your Life*.[32]

Mental health care is a good example of a field where, with information and education, a good deal of responsibility could be restored to the consumer. Psychology is distinct from other sciences in that much of the body of knowledge in the field can be made available on a self-help basis. It is, in fact, a profession that ideally could become obsolete as far as private practice is concerned, where client take-over is inherent in the process. Many factors get in the way of this best of all possible scenarios, however: unlicensed, incompetent practitioners, techniques with little therapeutic basis, and added to this, the mystifying aura of mumbo jumbo that still envelops the profession.

There have been tremendous beneficial effects of the boom in mental health care. It is no longer restricted to the elite; it is available where needed. It is no longer a taboo subject; the general public is far better informed nowadays about the basics of mental health. It is no longer restricted to narrow medical models of psychiatry. There is a growing openness in the mental health field to new disciplines, new thought, new influences. Mental health practitioners combine individual and group therapy, gestalt and behaviorism, Zen and drug therapy. While there may be only one right way for a mechanic to fix a carburetor, there's more than one way to treat a phobia.

There are also serious problems in the mental health field. There is a bewildering variety of therapies available to the consumer, each one professing to be the answer to all ills. Everything from traditional analysis to behavior modification, to Rolfing, primal scream, est, and aroma therapy is touted as better than the others. The confused consumer, desperate to begin to find a way out of his or her problems, is additionally burdened with the responsibility of choosing the right course. It's probably safe to say that the more vehemently a practitioner claims that one narrow approach is right, the less sure the consumer can be that this is so.

Sometimes it seems that in our overpsychologized age everyone is in treatment. Therapy has in some cases become a substitute for personal responsibility for mental health care. Lacking in self-help skills, lacking a supportive Caring Network or even religious faith, the client looks to the therapist to fill the gap. The therapeutic community must share the blame for the client's lack of personal confidence and skill, because it has set itself up as an omnipotent oracle possessed of truth and wisdom unavailable to the client except through private treatment. Guru-itis is antithetical to the mental health mandate; the conscientious therapist (even the ideal guru) works to make himself obsolete.

Another fly in the therapeutic ointment is the setting of unreachable standards for the patient's mental health. Today's patient aspires to be happy, successful, strong, self-sufficient, stress-free, capable of coping with every situation. It is an unrealistic picture bound to disappoint and to leave the client feeling more inadequate than ever. It is no wonder that people enter therapy with excessive demands, unreasonable expectations, and a hunger that can't be satisfied.

WHAT CAN YOU DO TO LESSEN PROFESSIONAL DEPENDENCE?

LEARN ABOUT YOURSELF

Be responsible for knowing your needs and wants, likes and dislikes, your feelings, capabilities, aspirations, goals, fears, strengths, weaknesses, quirks.

BE REALISTIC

Don't aspire to unreachable goals or an unreachable level of success. Accept your own capabilities and work within them, not beyond them. Don't fall prey to a media-induced image of personal fulfillment. Accept that life is often difficult, stressful, and problem-ridden; don't expect it to be otherwise. No amount of professional help can change that.

RECOGNIZE YOUR RIGHT TO PROBLEMS AND HURTS

Don't expect to be able to cope with everything, or to be unaffected by problems. Be fair with yourself in times of difficulty; don't be self-punitive.

RECOGNIZE THE LIMITS OF SELF-MANAGEMENT

Avoid being too proud to seek help. Know when you can use support—that of friends and family or of experts.

TAKE CARE OF YOURSELF

Do what you can to stay healthy. Don't neglect self-care. Allow time for repose and reflection. Don't sabotage your health with poor eating, drinking, smoking, overwork, lack of exercise.

LEARN SKILLS AND ACQUIRE KNOWLEDGE

They will help you cope and give you confidence. If you can type, you won't be dependent on a secretary. If you can change a tire, you won't have to call a tow truck. If you can figure out by yourself why you're down in the dumps, you may not need a therapist. The more basic skills you know, the less you need to rely on others, the more confident you'll be of your ability to cope. And the more active a participant you can be when you must call on outside help. Read a few of the many medical and psychological self-help books now on the market. Learn how your mind and body work. Learn how hospitals function. Learn the symptoms of common diseases. Learn how to take your temperature, apply a splint. Know how to probe your feelings when you're feeling down, how to cheer yourself up, how to get relief when you're overstressed. Acquire a book on emergency medical care; stock the medicine cabinet. Maintain a relationship with a doctor, a psychologist, a dentist. Do your part to relieve the burden on the professional community. Ignorance is stressful and inexcusable.

MAINTAIN AND MAKE USE OF YOUR CARING NETWORK

The more you can rely on family and friends to help you through normal day-to-day problems and stresses, the less you'll need professional care. A strong caring environment is the best antidote to stress, the best preventive mental health measure.

TAKE PART IN CARE-PROMOTING COMMUNITY ACTIVITIES

Health fairs and medical self-help groups are becoming increasingly popular as growing numbers of people are making the effort to assume more responsibility for their health and well-being.

WHAT ARE THE PROFESSIONAL/CLIENT RESPONSIBILITIES IN A THERAPEUTIC CONTEXT?

Inherent in the professional/client relationship is an important paradox: whatever the caring content of the relationship, it is by definition contractual care. And it is paid for in hard currency. Yet in almost all cases, if the relationship is to be effective and therapeutic, especially in the mental health field, a measure of real concern for the client is vital. It can also be maintained that intrinsic concern for the patient is vital to the professional if he or she is not to become apathetic, burned out, ineffectual. Another complicating factor of the relationship is its temporary nature: intense and intimate as it may be, it lasts only so long as the need exists or the care is paid for. One of the first tasks of the professional and client is to understand and accept the nature of their caring contract and to determine the optimal emotional tenor—how much personal concern and attachment is correct, needed, and beneficial.

The responsibility of the professional is quite clear-cut. It can basically be summarized as follows:
- attention to, and concern for, the client
- detect, reinforce, and maximize the self-help and self-care potential of the client
- provide tools of doing, thinking, feeling that will effect improvement and cure, and maintenance
- keep up with advances, changes in field; be open to new ideas, enrichment
- work to improve broad social environment, community growth, consumerism, and so on

But it is the client's responsibility that concerns us in this book: the individual's responsibility to know when professional help is needed, to choose the therapist, and to get optimum benefit from that therapy.

SOME GUIDELINES FOR CHOOSING A THERAPIST

1. Have an idea of the kind of therapy or therapist you feel would be effective for you and for your problems. Find out what kinds of therapy are available. Read about various psychiatric theories and treatments. Talk to friends who have been in therapy about the process or about their therapies. Get the names of people they recommend.
2. When you call or see a therapist for the first time, don't be afraid to ask questions of him or her. Find out how often they like to see patients, how much they charge, how long therapy usually lasts, what techniques and processes they use. Decide whether you feel this therapist will be effective for you—whether you'll get along (or whether it's necessary to get along), whether you feel comfortable with the therapeutic process outlined. Don't hesitate to "interview" other therapists before making your decision.
3. Ask yourself a lot of questions:
- Is your therapist isolated from his professional community? Does he keep up with what's new in the field, attend lectures or conferences, confer with his peers? Is he open to new ideas and techniques?
- Does your therapist try to isolate you? Does he try to be your

A Time for Caring

friend and tend to discourage your connections with friends and family? He should be helping you to expand, improve, and solidify your network. He should not be intimating that his love and concern for you goes beyond the limitations of the hour, the fee, and the strictures of the professional/client relationship.
- Does your therapist give you self-help tools? Does he answer questions about your treatment and teach you ways to know and handle your feelings, ways to improve your ability to manage your own mental health? Does he overmystify the process of therapy and make you feel that it's beyond your ability to understand? Does he allude to "deep-seated" problems that are never clearly explained?
- Is your therapist willing to mix it up with you? That is, does he give you critique, indicate openly when he's feeling bored or irritated, share his frustrations, and invite you to do likewise?
- Is your therapist always loving, kind, accepting, and gentle, and does he treat you with kid gloves? If the answer is basically yes, ask him what he does with his aggressive feelings. Ask him whether you're so perfect that he never gets angry, bored, or frustrated with you.
- Does your therapist play a godlike role by remaining aloof and detached and never revealing his own personal feelings? Ask him why he's afraid to allow himself to be a real person in the room. Beware of the old-fashioned naive answer that you as a patient are there for an hour, which is to be spent exclusively discussing your feelings. There is another person in the room who is interacting and experiencing feelings. Why is he afraid to reveal them? Therapy at its best is a relationship between two people reaching for a mutual emotional reality.
- Are you comfortable getting angry at your therapist? What happens when you do? Does it make you feel guilty or "sick"? Does your therapist suggest that these feelings are exclusively a part of *your* problem, or does he share his own negative feelings honestly and give you encouragement to share yours?

27
A Professional Care Plan

The objectives of a Professional Care Plan are: to assess the professional care you're now getting; to make a determination about the quality of that care; to evaluate what's needed and what can be discarded. The plan also focuses on improving the quality of the care you receive; it will help you to determine how you might reclaim some of your caring duties now handled by institutions and care professionals.

STEP ONE: EXAMINE YOUR PRESENT CONSUMPTION OF PROFESSIONAL CARE

WHAT KINDS OF PROFESSIONAL HELP DO YOU USE?

Whom do you consult for medical problems? General practitioner? Internist? Dentist? Gynecologist? Psychiatrist? Chiropractor? Home nurses? Other specialists?

What governmental agencies do you deal with? Social Security? Medicare? Welfare? Clinics?

Do you have children in school? Day care?

Do you have religious affiliations? Seek counsel from clergy?

Which of the following services do you use: lawyer? accountant? chauffeur? carpenter? plumber? electrician? other?

DETERMINE WHAT SERVICES ARE ACTUALLY PERFORMED

Go over the list of professional helpers in your life and answer the following questions for each:

A *Time for Caring*

How often do you seek their service?

What services have they actually performed for you in the last year or so?

How much have you paid for that service?

How good do you feel this professional is in his or her field?

How do you feel about the caring concern of this person?

Are you able to talk openly with this person?

Does he or she answer your questions and keep you informed?

Are you receiving the quality of service you feel is correct? (If not, would you consider replacing this person? How would you go about it?)

Are you assuming your responsibility in this relationship?

Are you providing information and following the professional's advice?

Are you asking for services you should be handling yourself?

STEP TWO: MAKE AN EVALUATION OF THE PROFESSIONAL CARE YOU'RE GETTING

To determine what changes would be most effective in your professional caring arena, make a chart to assess the strengths and weaknesses of the professional care you're now getting. Consult the information you assembled in step 1 of the care plan. Evaluate the need for the service, the quality of the service, and your own responsibility.

GOOD PROFESSIONAL CARE/STRENGTHS	POOR PROFESSIONAL CARE/WEAKNESSES
• My gynecologist is extremely competent and makes it a point to keep up with the latest research and developments in her field. • She's very good about explaining her treatment.	• It takes months to get an appointment with her. I feel she's too quick to prescribe drug treatments. • I'm often sloppy about following doctor's orders. Sometimes I neglect to take pills, etc.
• The therapist I see is one of the most caring people I know.	• My therapist has a tendency to give advice too readily rather

GOOD PROFESSIONAL CARE/STRENGTHS	POOR PROFESSIONAL CARE/WEAKNESSES
He is very intuitive and has what is for me a sensible and multifaceted approach. • I'm very good about presenting my problems to the therapist and not leaving out important details.	than helping me to find my own solutions. • I tend to forget about my therapy between sessions. I should be more careful about making notes, writing down dreams, going over the previous session. • I dump on my therapist a lot of useless garbage and trivia that I could discuss with a friend.
• The school that Josh attends is very well equipped, and they use the latest teaching techniques. There are many school activities, good sports teams, and classes in lots of exotic things I never studied—computers, ethics, Russian.	• There's too much pressure on getting into college at the school. The teachers only take a personal interest in the supersmart kids. • I have a tendency to let the school take care of everything. They teach sex education, but I know that I should also talk with Josh about sex and tell him what I feel and believe, and what I expect of him. • I should be more involved in Josh's courses—know something about what he's studying, who his teachers are.
• The home-nursing service that comes in to take care of my mother is reliable as far as being there. The nurses seem qualified.	• The nurses are often curt and sour and rarely show any warmth. • I could cut the nursing service down by half if I wanted. But I'd have to learn how to give Mother her shots, and the kids would have to help too. And I don't relish the thought of bedpans. • Also, I'm spending too much money on this service.

Write down as many pluses and minuses of your current professional caring picture as you can think of, even the most trivial.

STEP THREE: SET GOALS

The information you gathered in step 2 will help you to establish your professional caring goals. Choose goals that are manageable and that have maximum effect. Try to achieve optimum service from the caring professionals you use and maximize the areas in which you assume responsibility for your own care. When determining your goals, think of all the possible ways you might approach the problem.

For example, if you feel your doctor does not show enough real concern for you, you may decide to confront him and request that he explain his treatment more to you and take a more active interest in your well-being. Or you may try to find another doctor, or else join a medical self-help group to augment the doctor's care. If, for example, you are plagued by skin trouble, you may be able to do some research yourself, read books, talk to people, study nutritional information, and come up with your own program of skin care. By making that a self-care project, you may well end up with a more personalized course of treatment and feel confident about your ability to help yourself. If you are having trouble with the courts, the best solution may be to learn the basis of law on your own, with the aid of your lawyer friends. When you have some information about the process and about your rights, you'll be in a far better position to demand proper care and to prevent neglect or misguided care.

Here are some sample goals:

1. Establish a better relationship with my doctor.
2. Find a new dentist.
3. Learn emergency first aid.
4. Keep records of what's going on between therapy sessions.
5. Have a talk with Josh about sex.
6. Join single-parents' group.

STEP FOUR: MAKE A PLAN FOR IMPLEMENTING THESE GOALS

Be specific about what you hope to achieve and how you will go about it.

Here, for example, is a plan for implementing goal 1: "Next Thursday when I see Dr. Geller, I'm going to tell her that I'd like her to give me more complete details on this course of treatment she has me on. I'll also tell her that I feel she is somewhat defensive when I question her treatment, and that I still question the amount of pills she has me taking. I should also tell her that I have no doubt of her competence and of her knowledge, and that I'm for the most part happy with her services. When I go I'll bring a list of questions. I especially want to find out if there's anything more I can do in the way of exercise or diet that would improve my condition or prevent further deterioration. Perhaps she can recommend a book. Also, I'll ask her what reservations she has about my part in our relationship. Sometime this week I'll talk about this whole situation with my friend Carmen and sort of 'rehearse' it with her. Meanwhile I can call the community service office and see if they're planning any services or health care fairs where I might learn more about bone diseases or meet others with the same problems."

STEP FIVE: WRITE OUT AND SIGN A CONTRACT

PROFESSIONAL CARE CONTRACT

Goals: 1. _____
_____
_____
_____

2. _____
_____
_____
_____

3. _____
_____
_____
_____

Reevaluation and Revision Date: _____

Signature: _____

Date: _____

Keep this contract where you can refer to it often. It will help you in preparing your daily Caring Agenda.

Part IV
Learning to Care

28

Learning to Care:
GOING INTO ACTION

Everyone has the capacity to care, but as the old adage about sexual prowess goes: "If you don't use it, you lose it." Skeptics will argue that the ability to care is something one either has or doesn't have, and that it's not possible to learn to be caring. Not so. As with most other things, learning to care is mostly a matter of time, energy, application, and nerve. If people learned caring from their families at an early age, and continued to be acknowledged for that caring through their lives, it would be all to the good; they wouldn't be victims of stifled impulses and insufficient know-how. If people grew up in a world that called for caring skills, that rewarded altruistic life-styles, they wouldn't fear the consequences of baring their sentiments and would be possessed of the latest equipment to do so. Most of all, caring talents wouldn't be so hidden; there would be no need to strengthen these atrophied muscles.

Learning to care is not difficult; no special courses or paraphernalia are required. You choose your own course of learning and go at your own speed. As you increase caring skills and confidence you become more interested in people and things that were far less fascinating before. Life seems to offer more possibilities and fewer threats. The process itself—the games, exercises, and rituals we suggest—is fun to experiment with. At first, you may feel strained or uncomfortable trying out these exercises. Techniques may seem to inhibit spontaneity; you may feel that mechanized learning sabotages content. This ambivalence is understandable. But just as with learning a foreign language or table manners (even toilet training), what at first seems forced and artificial soon becomes perfectly natural. It becomes a part of you; you no longer think about.

The first task is to get over the fears and inhibitions that block caring action. An elderly man on the street looks like he might need help with his packages. But we pass him by—with many excuses. "He didn't really need help; he walks here every day." "He'll think I'm a busybody." "He'll think I want to rob him." "He'll expect me to take him all the way home and help him unpack his groceries, and I don't have time." Any one of these things may be true. He may not need help, in which case he will likely say so, politely. He may think that you're a busybody, but that's *his* problem. Isn't that exactly what's wrong with the world, what you're trying to do something about? The same goes for "Maybe he'll think I want something." It's also possible that when you put him at ease, he'll quickly see that you don't in fact "want" anything. Maybe he will expect too much, but it's up to you to state any limitations or to put yourself out for the extra effort. The point is that your impulse was to help the man carry his packages, and what you want to do is get over the fear of offering the help. Chances are he'll be delighted at your offer and you'll feel true to your feelings and stronger because you acted on them.

You hear that someone you've recently met just won a coveted fellowship. Your impulse is to call and congratulate her. But you stifle the impulse: "She'll think I'm angling for a job on her staff." "She won't even remember me." "I don't want to intrude." All pretty flimsy excuses. Chances are she'll be surprised and happy to hear from you, she'll feel good that she's supported in her hour of triumph, and of course she remembers you. If she misinterprets your message, that's too bad, and no loss for you. If your kindness someday turns into a favor returned, so much to the good. You don't have to second-guess the motives of sincere impulses.

The biggest enemies of caring are fear and incompetence. Fear of having one's actions misinterpreted or misunderstood. Fear of being rejected or of being used. Fear of being thought silly, naive, or gullible. Fear of seeming uncool or unaristocratic in a world that reveres detachment and is uncomfortable with warm feelings. Incompetence in literally not knowing quite how to express caring feelings or carry out caring actions.

A Time for Caring

Fred's case is a good example of how lack of basic skills inhibits care for others.

"A couple of months ago one of the women in my office remarked to me that she and some of the other office people were put off by my superior attitude. I was surprised and ashamed, because I recognized my own defenses. For some reason I'm almost incapable of just chatting with someone without having to have some important point to make, or some issue to discuss. Somehow I don't have the nerve just to start a conversation about the weather or the weekend coming up; I'm afraid I won't know what to say next, so I usually have a whole speech worked out. It's no wonder that people think I'm a stuffed shirt. In the last month or so I've been making a conscious effort to talk to people without a plan in mind, to let the conversation go where it may. At first I was full of fear of embarrassing, tongue-tied moments. I chose the most sympathetic people to talk to, or the most talkative. I've learned that most people like to talk casually, and that several people specifically wanted to get to know me but were put off because they thought I demanded serious conversation. I was wrapped up in my own shyness and not much aware of what others might want from me. The first dozen times I started up a chatty conversation, I was scared stiff. But I'm getting pretty comfortable at it, and now that I'm more observant of the people I'm chatting with and their interests, I find I have lots of things to say. Sometimes I'm even aware of putting *them* at ease."

In a world that often trivializes caring emotions, many people try to hide their feelings. They pretend that the heartrending movie didn't affect them; they quickly dry their eyes when the lights go up. They deny that love need be intertwined with their sexual lives. They train themselves to suppress their feelings.

What the world needs now is people who will admit to their feelings. This is the first step, and an important one, to realigning one's caring priorities. Taking a stand about caring is not as silly as it may sound. It accomplishes several things. It helps us to see ourselves in a new light, to take ourselves and our feelings seriously. It implies a commitment to acting in a positive and growth-enhancing manner. It gives credence to the fact that caring is healthy, nonneurotic, stimulating, rewarding, and attractive.

To care takes guts. It's not for the camp follower or the conformist, the yes-man or the up-to-the-minute faddist. It means making a break from old models and habits, admitting that the old rules of modern life don't work and aren't really fulfilling.

To care or not to care is a choice. It is not necessary to place an announcement in the newspaper or to wear a T-shirt bearing your intentions. But it means taking what can easily seem like the hard road, for living up to the commitment to care requires getting into caring shape and staying in shape through daily routine.

Gerry reports:

"Not too long ago, as I walked a familiar route in my neighborhood, I passed an elderly woman whom I'd often seen standing under the awning of her apartment building or walking along the street with other neighborhood regulars. She seemed to be intently looking at the passersby questioningly, as I'd noticed before. On impulse I stopped and said, 'Hello, how are you?' To which she replied, 'Well, I'm fine, except that I don't seem to be able to walk around the corner to my sister's these days without a bit of help. Could you give me a hand around the corner?' Which of course I did. Gladys, as her name turned out to be, has some 'regulars' who help her on her rounds, but when one of her friends isn't available, she usually looks for a sympathetic face and asks assistance. 'Most people are more than happy to help me out,' she said, 'but they're also a bit shy to ask, so I just do the asking for them.' "

It turned out that ailing Gladys was making her daily trip to spend the night at the apartment of her ailing older sister (Gladys claimed to be eighty-two), who no longer can care for herself.

Most people don't have a very clear picture of how they express their caring, of the ways in which caring is a part of their lives.

A father might say, "Oh, you know, I work pretty hard to keep my kids in food and clothes. I try to do something special with them on the weekends. My wife and I make it a point to get out by ourselves once a week, and she likes that." Or, "Well, I do the usual things, and I don't believe in spanking the kids, and I'm always there if they need me." Or, "I haven't the faintest idea, but everyone seems to be pretty happy."

If you ask the same person what kind of caring he needs and wants, or what kind of caring he gets from his friends and family, he will very likely have just as hard a time coming up with an explanation. "Oh, I can't complain, Jane never bothers me about the money I make and never forgets my birthday." Or "Oh, well, you can't expect much attention from teen-age kids these days." Or "I have a very loving wife, I feel cared for in many ways." Or "I don't need much attention."

When asked to put these things into words, most people are pretty much in the dark; it's just not something that they've given a lot of thought to. But knowing ourselves in our caring contexts is very important if we're going to function efficiently and productively as caring people, and if we're going to be able to ask for and get the caring we need from our loved ones—families, friends— and from the community.

Chris reports:
"I was cringing inside when I started to do my caring inventory. I was sure it would prove I was really a selfish bastard. Well, it's true that there are some major gaps in my caring abilities—I seem to be helpless at many things that other people end up doing for me. But I uncovered several things that I hadn't really thought of as part of my caring skills, and which I actually enjoy. I've taught many people to juggle—it's especially fun to teach someone who has no confidence in their athletic ability. I seem to be the person in our office who gets lunch groups together and introduces the new employees. At home it's our house where our kids' friends congregate after school, and I think it's partly because my wife and I are people these kids can talk to. And I'm a very diligent gardener—I go around watering and talking to other people's plants."

Taking a caring inventory is the way to go about getting a picture of our individual caring ways and abilities. A happy by-product of this inventory is that we are often surprised by how many potential caring connections we have, how much our caring ability is there working for us, how much caring ability we possess, and how many caring acts we do in fact perform. It is ironic that most of us tend to think we are more selfish and self-involved than we actually are.

Armed with our inventory of caring, we are able to evaluate our needs, our potentials, our level of interest, our style. Then we can decide what kind of action (if any) we want to take in building strengths, redefining certain arenas or caring roles, pulling back or reaching out. We have the information we need to practice Quality Caring.

Exuberant Carla is one of those people who's afraid of no one, who leaves smiles in her wake. Her problem isn't lack of skill or nerve, but time.

"Until recently my approach to caring was pretty haphazard. I went on the assumption that everything would get done. When you lead a busy life, sometimes that's the only comfort. But a series of things made me realize that maybe I needed a caring agenda: my youngest son came home with a terrible grade in math, and I'd been promising to help him. Two friends called within a week and bawled me out for not writing. A visit to the dentist I'd been postponing became an emergency visit requiring root-canal work. I realized I hadn't spent a morning reading in months. Wherever I looked, things weren't being cared for properly. I just hadn't been paying attention, for they were all things I *meant* to take care of. Finally I've learned to keep a caring list, just as I do for the groceries, and give priority to those things that are important—for myself, or the kids, or my friends. It's become a way of life for me. I'm much more aware of what needs care; before, I was neglectful, even if it was unintentional."

It's up to you to decide how many of the lessons of caring you wish to put into practice. All we can tell you is that the rewards tend to parallel the level of caring practice.

GETTING INTO SHAPE FOR CARING: ACTION EXERCISES

Caring fitness involves reconditioning the caring apparatus by exercising long-dormant caring feelings and skills. Inhibitions and fears about expressing caring concern must be slowly overcome through a process of carefully stretching the taut, unused muscles.

A Time for Caring

All the exercises in this and the next two chapters are geared to limbering up those caring muscles. They are all simple exercises, designed to work on different feelings or to improve specific skills. By doing these exercises, through their repetition and progressive nature, you will strengthen and stretch your Caring Capacity, enlarge your network of caring connections, and expand the caring context of your everyday life.

Many people are resistant to the kind of drill drudgery implied in doing repetitive exercises. But some are more resistant to the change that success would imply than to the exercise itself! Some become so fixated on the goal that they are blinded to any enjoyment inherent in the process. And some, paradoxically, feel that they are being selfish by spending so much time on self-improvement.

If you are reluctant or skeptical about the amount of work or drudgery you foresee in the exercises that follow, take heart: the process of doing the exercises is quite enjoyable, the payoff in caring confidence is great, and what may seem self-indulgent is very much in the interest of those in your Caring Circle.

It's useful to think of each exercise as strengthening a specific muscle group, as improving a specific skill, or as curing a specific ailment. The exercises in this chapter are geared toward improving communications skills. Chapter 29 is about raising caring consciousness by doing exercises that make us more aware of our own and others' caring ways and needs. The exercises in Chapter 30 are all partnered exercises to be done with lovers, spouses, friends, and family members.

As you practice these caring exercises you may be surprised to notice changes in yourself—in your responses and reactions to things. You may find that just your new awareness of the caring context of common situations, just the tentative gestures you first make toward caring actions, will give you added confidence and a heightened sense of what's going on around you. You may find yourself doing things differently, even switching friends or making new friends, spending your time differently. You may well feel a marked increase in your sense of self-worth, or have a feeling of increased impact.

The people around you may also notice the difference and may be surprised or thrown off-balance. Caring people are interesting to others because they are lively and observant. Others gravitate toward the energy and emanations of caring people.

There are thirty-three exercises in all. Glance over them and select those that are interesting to you or seem particularly germane to your problems. Don't force yourself to try exercises that do not appeal to you or are too difficult at this stage. The key is to be comfortable with your new efforts. You want to be able to stick with them. Once you choose the exercises needed to build your caring skills, be sure and schedule them into your day. It is important that you repeat them over and over until they become habit and are integrated into your daily-life pattern. A hit-or-miss approach to the exercises won't produce any lasting benefit.

Be on the lookout for ways to improve your caring skills. As a problem comes up, seek out the new exercise that will help you cope with it. Once you decide to use a particular exercise, read over the information about it a couple of times until you understand how it works and what to look for when you practice it. Once you've gotten all you can from a particular exercise, discard it, at least temporarily, and try something else.

Be flexible in your use of the exercises. Don't be afraid to adapt them to your particular needs or problems or to personalize them so they're more suitable to your way of doing things. .

You may want to stick to the guidelines exactly as they're presented, or you may prefer to loosen up the structure of the game. Most of all, you should enjoy the games and exercises. They're meant to be fun.

❂ WALK/TALK

The Walk/Talk provides a setting in which to exchange our thoughts and feelings with someone in a nonpressured, pleasant context. A Walk/Talk takes the conversation into the fresh air, where ideas and feelings can be exchanged at an ambling pace, in a nonconfrontational style. Observations and comments on the passing scene can break tension, fill in the pauses, and provide a shared experience.

We can have a Walk/Talk with a friend, lover, child, or spouse . . . in short, with anyone we want to spend time with, to feel closer to, or to discuss a special problem with as informally as possible.

A Time for Caring

HOW TO GO ABOUT IT

1. Decide whom you'd like to have a Walk/Talk with.
2. If there's a specific subject you want to discuss, think about what's on your mind and what you'd like to say. If it will help you, make some notes.
3. Invite your friend to join you for an open-ended stroll or a specific errand. Set up time and place.
4. Remember that you want the conversation to have a relaxed, unforced tone. Don't blurt out your thoughts as you take your first step! Let the conversation grow. Ask after your companion. Update each other on what's going on in your lives.
5. When you are ready to discuss your special topic, don't be coy. Be direct. Make clear that you have chosen your companion for a special confidence. For example: "John, I'm really glad we have this time to stroll together because it gives me the chance to ask your opinion about a problem I'm facing at work." Or, "Mary, I've been thinking a lot about that picnic we went on last week. One reason I wanted to take this walk with you is so I could talk to you about how much you upset me. I'm hoping you'll tell me why you said what you did, so we can get it cleared up."
6. Share the pleasures of the walk. Stop and look in shop windows, gaze at flowers, watch kids skating. Break up the talk, keep it low-key, a natural part of everyday life, as natural as putting one foot in front of another.

WHAT IS ACCOMPLISHED?

1. It is a way to integrate serious conversations and exchanges of feelings into everyday life.
2. We can test our ability to take personal risks in a "safe" environment. Even if we do not manage to say all that we wanted, the walk can still be a pleasant shared experience and we have lost nothing.
3. The process of pinpointing whom we want to Walk/Talk with and what we want to say to them helps us to clarify our thoughts and feelings and to find good outlets for our caring impulses.
4. It's a way to learn to be at ease spending time with others.

❀ SHARING THE INNER DIALOGUE

The caring process, as we have said, involves the open and attentive exchange of personal information. Those of us who have trouble making connections with others, opening up, asking for advice, revealing thoughts, are shutting ourselves off from the care others can give. Our emotional isolation inhibits the balance of give-and-take necessary to caring relationships. This exercise will help achieve that balance.

HOW TO GO ABOUT IT

1. There's nothing more to this exercise than letting others in on some of the thoughts and feelings spinning around in your head. But it's easier said than done. Many people feel that others will not be very interested in their thoughts—the nonsense, odd bits of information, and idle observations. They wait for something important to say. To share the inner dialogue one has to feel free to chat about simple things and to trust others with small confidences.
2. One consideration in this exercise is the appropriateness of the person you share your thoughts with, and of the situation. Don't try to amuse the boss with your stream-of-consciousness revelations in the middle of the workday. Don't be insulting or mean in the guise of opening up your thoughts to others. Don't sabotage your care-learning by confiding in someone you know is hostile or angry.
3. Be aware of opportunities for talking intimately with others, and don't let them pass. If you're going to visit a friend, make it a point to be aware of, and to share, some of your thoughts. When you get together with your mate or date, share your thoughts of the moment.
4. Practice this exercise until it becomes a habit. It's a basic tool of Quality Caring.

WHAT IS ACCOMPLISHED?

1. We learn not to be afraid to share our feelings with others. In fact, it gives us a sense of connectedness and communication.
2. We learn to deal with others' responses to our feelings. We learn about their sensitivities, about how others care for us, and what caring difficulties they may have.
3. We learn to trust, and thereby strengthen the Caring Network.
4. By sharing our thoughts with others we relieve our overtaxed minds of a good deal of excess baggage.
5. From others' responses we get a sense of ourselves; it expands our horizons.
6. We learn not to censor our thoughts and feelings, and to feel at home even with simple confidences.

❁ IN CONFIDENCE

Many people have a hard time letting their hair down, admitting to others that they are feeling blue, that something is wrong. We are sometimes too conscious of our image and put on a good face to keep it intact. We may be reluctant to burden others with our troubles, fearing rejection or thinking that we have no right to ask for help or sympathy. Even when we are pretty good at chitchat or sharing the inner dialogue (page 305), we keep serious stuff to ourselves. This exercise helps us recognize the subjects that we usually bottle up inside, and gives us practice in expressing those feelings to intimates and even acquaintances in a natural, matter-of-fact fashion.

HOW TO GO ABOUT IT

1. Make a mental list of the feelings and problems you are currently having. Ask yourself: "Have I told anyone about this?" Select one topic that you want to try confiding in someone else.
2. Pick the person to whom you would like to express that feeling.
3. Think of what you are going to say. Rehearse it. Get comfortable with the idea of talking about it.
4. When you have tackled one "confidence," make plans for expressing the next.
5. As a variation, try the Tea and Sympathy exercise (page 338) about your fears and hidden feelings. The dynamics of the exchange would be the same as in a regular Tea and Sympathy, but your concentration would cover any confidences you'd like to air, not necessarily connected to the events of your day.
6. There are a lot of different kinds of "secrets" you might want to share, some small and trivial, some large and serious. It is important to express them both. For example, you might come up with a list like this:
I miss Frank when he is out of town.
I am afraid of flying.
My spouse and I are having trouble getting along.
I'm really having a hard time paying for my fancy new car.
I had a fight with my best friend.
I don't feel good about the way I look.

WHAT IS ACCOMPLISHED?

1. You learn what topics and feelings you are reluctant to share with others.

2. You learn that people do not react badly when you express your feelings as a matter of course. In fact, shared confidences create stronger bonds.
3. You learn to trust others with "pieces" of yourself, a vital step in forming a caring relationship.

❋ A PENNY FOR YOUR THOUGHTS

Being interested in others, inviting their confidence, and learning to listen to *another*'s inner dialogue is just as important as listening to our own. In this exercise we ask others to share their thoughts with us. To achieve their trust we must make an effort to make them comfortable, to share our own thoughts and feelings, to listen undefensively and, most of all, to care!

HOW TO GO ABOUT IT

1. In situations where the other person is shy, or where the relationship hasn't thus far included confidences, it's up to you to set the stage. For one thing, you must be genuinely interested in those whose confidence you encourage. And you must set an example by being free with your own thoughts. Be observant of the things that might draw the other out. It doesn't have to be a particularly profound or interesting subject; the object is just to open up a bit.

    By saying, "Whenever I get nervous about a work deadline, I suddenly find myself thinking of mindless errands to do, or making phone calls I've put off for days," you invite the other to share the idiosyncrasies of their procrastination.

    When you tell another what you observed on your way to work, you invite their telling of like information, or you trigger their desire to open up to you.

    If you sense that your potential confidant has something in particular on his or her mind, you can ease onto the subject with a confidence of your own. For example: Mary asked Allen over for dinner. She suspected that he was having a hard time at work. As she was setting the table she said, "You know, Allen, I've been thinking a lot about my job lately. Trying to figure out where it is headed, afraid I'm not keeping up, wondering if I should switch fields. Do you ever wonder about your job? Is it making you happy?"
2. When you are with people you care about, make it a habit to check out their thoughts.
3. Actively listening to what the other has to say is as important as gain-

A Time for Caring

ing their confidence. It's a unique opportunity to break through to the soap opera of another's mind and to know them well, to be able to see their uniqueness and to use your observations and knowledge to improve your relationship and to make your caring more specific.

WHAT IS ACCOMPLISHED?

1. Inviting others to confide in us makes them feel comfortable and closer to us. It shows that we care. It reinforces the bonds between us and strengthens the Caring Network.
2. We learn more about the others we care about, we become more aware of similarities and differences, and we can be more specific and sensitive in our actions with them.
3. Usually we learn that others have many of the same thoughts and feelings as ourselves; we feel less isolated.

❁ PERFECT STRANGERS

Many people, as we have seen, are wary of getting involved with strangers—passersby, shopkeepers, bus or plane passengers, even neighbors—and even in the simplest situations. We fear that we will be snubbed or ridiculed if we try to express a friendly greeting. We are reluctant to intrude on others even when we sense that a stranger may need help, directions, or support. When approached by a stranger asking for advice or help, there is often the fear that by complying we may open ourselves up to exploitation or danger, to scheming or manipulation. Often we feel we don't have time or need for making connections with "outsiders." But we all are "outsiders" to someone. And it is by expanding the scope of people we can call "insiders" that we expand the safe caring environment.

The object of this exercise is to learn how to have at least minimal contact every day with some of the many strangers with whom we cross paths.

HOW TO GO ABOUT IT

1. Your job is to make at least one contact daily with a stranger: a passerby on the street, a shopkeeper, a person sitting next to you on the bus, someone sitting in a waiting room, a lost-looking tourist, the person next to you in the check-out line at the grocery, and so on.

   The "content" of the encounter isn't important—it can be simply a greeting or a chat about the weather, or the news, or business, or an offer of help or a request for some.

2. During the day be on the lookout for suitable opportunities. For example: Next time you go into a neighborhood store, strike up a conversation with the shopkeeper. Inquire about the merchandise, ask for information, ask how he or she is. Any simple, friendly question will do; intellectual repartee is not required.
3. If you are shy or reluctant to break the silence barrier, plan your encounter. Review the situations you expect to be in during the day. Say to yourself, "I'm going to the cleaners, so when I get there I'll try striking up a conversation with the lady behind the counter." Or "When I park my car in the garage, I'll ask the parking attendant the directions to the restaurant."
4. Look for situations where you can respond to someone else who is reaching out to strangers for help. If you notice someone standing on a corner fumbling with a street map, ask if you may help with directions. If you hear anyone ask, "Does anyone have the time?" be the one who volunteers the answer. And when *you're* the one who's forgotten your watch, ask the time.

WHAT IS ACCOMPLISHED?

1. By increasing our feeling of community and overcoming our fears of strangers we can overcome feelings of isolation and get a more positive view of the world. By bringing out the best in others we enlarge the safe caring environment.
2. We develop a greater interest in our day-to-day life and make ordinary events special.
3. Every contact we make with a stranger builds our self-confidence in our ability to deal with the complex demands of the world. We learn that we can be flexible and cope with unfamiliar situations.

❁ HONEY, I'M HOME

It is important to keep current about the big and small events of our day with those we love if we are not to become isolated and out of touch. Yet for many of us, keeping the members of our Caring Circle posted is a habit that must be learned. This exercise helps us prevent the slow drift apart that can result if we don't take the time to keep those we love informed every day about what we do and how we feel. The simple exchange of information that we initiate in this exercise should be a part of our daily practice.

HOW TO GO ABOUT IT

1. Set aside a specific time each day—five minutes will do fine—to recount your day to those you're closest to. It might be when you first come home from work, at the dinner table, driving the kids to school, or over the phone. Share some of your thoughts and experiences of the day. It doesn't have to be earthshaking information; just a report, simple chitchat, anecdotes, news tidbits, or observations will do. But no generalizations. And enthusiasm counts.
2. Ask questions of the person you're speaking with about their experience of the day.
3. Choose a good quiet time. This is your responsibility. If your wife is fixing dinner, bathing the kids, and chasing the dog, don't expect her to appreciate your attention, or your demand for hers. If it's your husband's habit to watch the news when he comes home, hold off on the discussion until the program is over.
4. Collect information for your report: make mental notes of whom you saw and what transpired, of the funny incident at the office, the interesting statistic in the paper, the intense pressure you felt at the office meeting, the flowers you saw in the neighbor's yard. Soon the habit of reporting this information will become more automatic.
5. In the classic comedy situation the man comes home from work announcing, "Honey, I'm home."
"How was your day?" says dutiful wife.
"Oh, fine. And yours?"
"Okay. Anything happen at the office?"
"No, the usual. You?"
"Nothing special."
It's not really such a funny scenario. For this exercise, "Honey, I'm home" is just a beginning. Follow it up with a question about the other's day. "Did you have a good day? What did you do? Did you get over to the exhibit? How was the ball game?" If your partner responds with details, all the better. Encourage more. But this is *your* exercise. If they say, "Same ol' stuff," at least you asked. It is then clearly your turn to talk. Don't be put off by the other's reticence. Set an example.

Remember to be specific. Give details. "This morning I talked to Mr. Stone. He sends his regards to you. And that's unusual for him. You know how forgetful he is about names. I think he's in better spirits now he's got that new assistant. We got together to discuss the new magazine project. He's full of statistics and charts, but I think he is still a little reluctant. That makes me confused." If you relate events and your feelings about them, you give your partner something to respond to. Wait for comments and input before going on.

WHAT IS ACCOMPLISHED?

1. You cement your Caring Network by making your family and friends part of the daily events of your life. The give-and-take that develops gives both parties the needed information to care more specifically and personally.
2. You learn to ask for and accept support and understanding from others and learn that formerly unimportant everyday events can indeed be of interest. You become more observant.
3. You keep cobwebs from forming on the lines of your Caring Network.

❂ ASKING FOR CARING

Being able to ask for and accept caring help from others is as important as providing it, but people are often reluctant to ask directly. We fear that we will appear weak or flawed or that we will open ourselves to rejection, ridicule, or obligation. Sometimes we think that we should not have to ask for care, that others should be able to read our minds and do just what we want without being given any clues or encouragement. This exercise teaches us how to express our caring needs, to pinpoint them and set about having them fulfilled.

But hand in hand with asking for care goes the responsibility of making it possible for others to respond. For one thing, our requests should be— except in emergencies—reasonable within the context of the relationship, and they should be appropriate to the person asked. The friend who's got all the time in the world to listen to your troubles on the phone may not be the right person to ask to help build bookshelves. And if we ask someone to baby-sit for the kids, we should find ways of facilitating that favor. We might offer to pick them up and take them home, to make dinner for the kids beforehand, or to baby-sit for their kids in return.

HOW TO GO ABOUT IT

1. Write out a list of caring acts or behavior you feel you don't get from your Caring Network. For example:
    - I wish the children would care more about helping around the house.
    - I wish I could get more of a reaction from the kids when I take them someplace.

A Time for Caring

- I wish my friend Mary would take the time to call me more often.
- An occasional backrub would be wonderful.
- I wish my wife would take care of the finances sometimes.
- I wish my assistant would take more care with my phone messages.
- I wish Jessie would bring me a cup of coffee while I'm watching TV.
- I wish I had someone I could talk with about my frustrations at work.

2. When you have identified situations where you want to ask for care, plan the situation ahead—the person, the place, what you'll say. Express your feelings clearly and specifically. Don't say, "Gee, I wish somebody around here would do the dishes once in a while." Say, "Jessie, I would appreciate it if you would take care of washing the dishes tonight." Don't forget to state your responsibility, if any, in connection with your request. "I'll clean the table and stack the dishes as soon as we're through dinner. And Jane will dry them and put them away."
3. Also be on the lookout for spontaneous occasions for asking for caring. Identify your feelings "on the spot." Look for chances to express your desire for care from others. "Could you help me a minute with this package?" Or "Do you have time to talk about a problem with me now?"
4. Don't overload one person with your requests and make sure you express your thanks. Let the person know you realize that they are making an effort, and tell them how it makes you feel. "Mary, thanks for calling today. I love to hear from you and know that you are thinking of me. I'll try and call you more often too."

WHAT IS ACCOMPLISHED?

1. You learn to identify the kind of caring you want from your friends.
2. You learn to express caring wishes without worrying about how they will be received, because you are committed to finding ways of helping others implement them.
3. You give your friends a chance to show care for you.
4. You become less isolated, less defensively self-sufficient, and feel the support and affection of those around you. The caring balance is maintained, and you guard against exhaustion.

❀ STRAIGHT FROM THE HORSE'S MOUTH

One of the most important communications skills of caring is the ability to express our feelings—both positive and negative—directly to the person they concern.

There are many things that inhibit direct communication, however. Fear of rejection, fear of hurting the other's feelings, the desire to be "nice," all interfere. Habits of indirect communication are often ingrained and difficult to break. In this exercise the object is to learn to communicate one small bit of information in a straightforward way so that others learn what's on our mind straight from the horse's mouth.

HOW TO GO ABOUT IT

1. Identify your feelings and the person at whom they're directed.
2. Plan what you will say. Be very specific. "I'm calling to say that I laughed harder with you last night than I have in years. I'm looking forward to getting together again soon." "Your coming to work late so often puts me in a bad position. It makes me nervous to cover up for you." "It would mean a lot to me if you would read over what I've written so far."
3. Rehearse. Practice saying out loud what you want to say. Think of the setting. Will you make a phone call? Will it be at the dinner table? When your child comes home? If possible, get a friend to run through the situation with you.
4. Make your communication at the earliest opportunity. Don't let time pass or you will lose your nerve and what you have to say will lose its impact.
5. Don't judge the results. The object of the game is to gain confidence about expressing yourself. The reward is in reassuring yourself that you can take risks and say what's on your mind and accept the consequences. You may very well get action with your direct approach, but that's all a bonus.
6. Even if it is just a small issue, get in the habit of making a direct statement about something every day. "I won't have time to drive you to school today." "You're the person I want most to talk with."
7. Beware of generalities. If your impulse is to say "You look pretty today," make the comment more specific. "The way you did your hair today makes you look particularly pretty." Or, in a more serious vein, don't say, "You made me angry last night." Say, "Your attitude toward my date was very cold. I thought you could have been more hospitable and have directed some of your conversation toward him."

A Time for Caring

In order to be specific you must be observant and tuned in to your feelings, but by doing this you can be sure that you have made yourself clearly understood.

The direct, specific approach is important when dealing with strangers, service personnel, and the like. If you have trouble getting a glass of water from your waitress, telling your taxi driver how to take the most direct route to your destination, or dealing with strangers in a crowd, try expressing yourself more directly. Say, "Driver, I want you to take Twelfth Street across town," or suggest, "Say, do you think Twelfth Street would be the good route?" instead of just wondering why you're taking a different route, and getting upset about it. "Sir, we all are tired of waiting in this line, but if you would stop pushing me it would be a lot more pleasant" is better than groaning silently and cursing the man under your breath.

WHAT IS ACCOMPLISHED?

1. You learn to identify your feelings with precision.
2. You take responsibility for expressing them directly.
3. You learn to overcome inhibitions about saying what's on your mind, and you gain confidence in your ability to take a risk.
4. You open the way for others to be direct with you.

❀ OUT ON A LIMB

Sometimes it's dangerous to care. We have feelings we fear will threaten our relationships to others, have opinions that might offend, have controversial topics we tend to sidestep or cover up. As a result we end up making accommodations we later regret. Or we collude in behavior that we disdain. Or allow a small hurt to mushroom as a result of our silence. Or mislead others about our true feelings. Each person has a different definition of a "tough" situation. For one, it's asking the boss for a raise. For another, it's merely standing up to our spouse's criticism. For another, it's confronting a close friend about his overweight. Or it's talking about sex. It is in facing up to these difficult situations that caring is put to the test. Out on a Limb is designed to help us through our fainthearted moments.

HOW TO GO ABOUT IT

Out on a Limb assumes that you've worked on some of the basic caring skills: listening, sharing the inner dialogue, asking for the caring you need. The object here is to pick a person or situation or subject that so far has seemed fearful or fraught with risk, but that you're ready to tackle with a bit of encouragement.

1. Define the situation clearly, and your feelings about it as well. "I'm going to tell Sally that I am upset by her borrowing money and acting as if she isn't expected to pay it back." "I'm going to tell Jim that I wish he would talk to me more when we're making love, that it makes me feel he's aloof when he never says a word."

    Start with something small. Don't sabotage your caring confidence by tackling the most fearsome problem first.

2. Acknowledge your fears. List all the things you think might happen, the reasons you've shied away from this confrontation.

    "Sally will think I'm accusing her of stealing. She'll make me feel stingy for wanting the money. It will break up our friendship."

    "Jim will think I'm making fun of his lovemaking. He'll think I'm too forward about sex. He'll think I'm fishing for more involvement. He'll feel threatened and leave."

3. Identify what might be gained by facing up to the situation.

    "Sally will respect me for standing up to her; she has the attitude that I'm a soft touch. She'll pay the money back. She's not comfortable keeping the money; she'll feel closer to me once we have it out. I'll feel better about myself for being direct with Sally. As it is, I'm angry with myself as much as with her for not being direct with her."

    "The important thing is to let Jim know how I feel without worrying too much about his reaction. If he changes, fine, but that's secondary. He may even be just shy, and he'll be pleased that I want to be closer to him."

4. Identify the risks of *not* facing up to the situation.

    "I'll get more and more upset with Sally and it will ruin our otherwise good friendship unless things change."

    "I like Jim very much, but if we go on like this, he'll never get to know what I'm really like and it will be harder to change things. It will just lead to more accommodations."

5. Plan the confrontation carefully. Think of just what you want to say. Keep in mind what you hope to gain. Try to anticipate the arguments or reactions of the others. Think of possible options or solutions to possible conflict. Set the stage by planning to have this confrontation at a time and place where both parties will be comfortable and as relaxed as possible. Write down what you need to remember, even make verbatim notes of what you're going to say. If you're hoping to solve a problem, think of as many possible solutions as you can, even if some seem impractical or farfetched. Be prepared to negotiate and

A Time for Caring

be prepared, at least initially, for a negative response to your forthrightness. Be prepared to persist.
6. Rehearse. Go over what you're going to say out loud until you know it by heart, until you're as calm as you can expect to be under the circumstances.
7. Do it: Go Out on a Limb!

WHAT IS ACCOMPLISHED?

1. You learn to be brave with your caring concern. This is very reassuring to you and to those around you.
2. You share your deepest feelings with those around you, at the same time deepening your caring connections.
3. You avoid the accommodation or collusion that sabotages honest relationships.

❀ "THIS IS FOR YOU BECAUSE . . ."

It is as hard for some people to show thanks or affection as it is for others to criticize. We are afraid of seeming silly, or soft, afraid the gesture will be rejected or misunderstood.

This exercise is designed to help overcome fears and embarrassment about making overtures to others or giving gifts or tokens of esteem. A kiss, a hug, special food, a gift bought or made, is offered as a special gesture of our feelings.

HOW TO GO ABOUT IT

1. Pinpoint why you want to show your thanks or appreciation, and to whom.
2. Select an appropriate gesture or gift—appropriate for you and for the occasion.
3. Deliver it clearly with a message about why it is given.
4. Rehearse. Plan what you are going to say and when you are going to present your gift.
5. For example: Your office workers have all pitched in to help you finish up a big project. You are grateful but don't know quite how to tell them—your group hadn't been close before. Consider baking cookies and dispensing them during a coffee break. When you hand them out, make a point of saying, "These are just a token to let you know how much I appreciated all of your help in making our deadline last week."

6. Get into the habit of showing your appreciation with simple gestures. "You deserve a big kiss for doing such a good job on your homework." "You've been working hard all day. Why don't I fix you some lunch?"

WHAT IS ACCOMPLISHED?

1. You learn to enjoy the pleasant feelings that come with expressing your affection and feelings to family or friends.
2. Your friends enjoy the feelings of being appreciated and recognized. And that in turn makes them more outgoing toward you. It's a magic cycle.
3. You overcome feelings of shyness or awkwardness and become proficient at expressing thanks appropriately.

❧ THE TRULY PERSONAL GREETING CARD

Sentiment is often suspect these days, and many people are out of practice at expressing it. When the occasion calls for it—a birthday, a wedding, a death in the family—we rely on the greeting card writers to put words in our mouths. In this exercise you'll try your hand at forging your own messages of care or concern.

HOW TO GO ABOUT IT

1. Make your own greeting card. It doesn't have to be fancy—no clever drawings or cartoons required. Just a message on a piece of notepaper or a blank card.
2. Plan what you are going to say on a piece of scrap paper. Correct and rewrite until you say exactly what you'd like. Try to be as personal and as specific as possible. Don't take the easy way out with clichéd phrases. Show your feelings:

    "I'm very happy about your engagement to Chris. I remember when you'd first met her, and you and I sat up all night talking about your unhappy relationship with Dolores and how afraid you were that things wouldn't work out with Chris. She's a lovely woman, and I wish you both the best."

    "When we were in high school, your father was my favorite of all my friends' parents; I used to come by after school as much to play catch with your Dad as to see you. I know you are devastated by his sudden death and send you every sympathy. I hope your happy memories of him will help soothe his passing."

WHAT IS ACCOMPLISHED?

1. You learn to identify exactly what your feelings are on a given occasion.
2. You overcome fear of sentiment and strike a blow against detachment and "cool" behavior.
3. You let your friends know they are special, and that you see their unique qualities.
4. You establish a personal caring ritual.

❊ TODAY I'M GOING TO . . .

This exercise provides good practice for writing out a daily Caring Agenda (page 368) and makes caring actions a part of daily life. When caring plans are made for each day, chances for expressing care do not slip by. Rehearsing potential caring activities lets us think them through, get comfortable with them, and find the best time to carry them out. By creating a daily list of caring goals we see what kinds of caring skills we have, what we like to do, and what opportunities come up over and over in our life.

HOW TO GO ABOUT IT

1. Each morning, sit down and write out a list of possible caring actions for that day. Consider your schedule, the amount of time you have, how you are feeling, whom you would like to see or talk to, and whom you don't want to deal with. Be realistic and don't overschedule yourself. You may "owe" twenty letters, but don't try to take care of them all at once. Haven't you ever heard of writer's cramp?

    For example: "Today I want to call Betty in the hospital and see how she is feeling."

    "Today I want to write Grandmother a birthday note."

    "Today I want to spend a couple of quiet hours in the evening with Fred."

    "Today I want to buy that vase for myself at Cormer's."

2. Think through each caring action. Don't get caught unprepared. Ask yourself:

    "What will I say to Betty? How shall I express my concern without sounding too worried?"

    "When will I have time to write Grandmother? What do I want to tell her?"

"Will Fred want to, or have time to, spend a couple of hours with me? When should I ask him? What will I say if he tells me no?"

"Have I the extra money for the vase this week? Will they be open on the way to work?"

3. Refer to your list during the day as a reminder of your plans. Check off completed items. Take a minute to reflect on the results.
4. Watch for overload. If you seem to be overtaxing yourself, review the previous day's list to see if you have the tendency to overprogram. Don't discourage yourself by tackling too much; that's poor self-care.

WHAT IS ACCOMPLISHED?

1. You learn to increase your Caring Capacity gradually by setting daily goals, meeting them, and reinforcing your caring self-image.
2. You learn to be aware of the caring you do for others and for yourself in any given day, as well as of the care you request. The balance between the two will help you be aware of your strengths and weaknesses.

❈ A LITTLE BIT AT A TIME

In the process of learning caring skills, occasionally we come up against a situation that seems too difficult—or too hot—to handle. It may be a matter of confronting a long-standing fear, of dealing with someone who intimidates us, of handling a tough job or a particularly scary confrontation. Rather than backing off completely, the answer is to tackle the situation step by step. In A Little Bit at a Time the situation is broken down into manageable, bite-size pieces.

HOW TO GO ABOUT IT

1. Identify the situation that seems so difficult. Go over your fears and apprehensions. Arlene's ten-year-old daughter, Enid, had a problem:
    "Now that Grandmom is sick, I'll have to go visit her in the hospital. I love Grandmom, but I've never been to a hospital. I don't know how to care for sick people. I'm afraid she'll be very weak and old and I'll be afraid to look at her."
2. Arlene was able to help Enid break the situation down into a series of steps that allowed her to approach the situation slowly and to overcome her reservations. here's the plan she worked out with her daughter:
    (a) Send a note to Grandmom.

(b) Call her on the telephone and talk to her about what it's like in the hospital.

(c) Talk to my friend Lisa who had her tonsils out in the hospital and ask her what it's like.

(d) Go with Mom to the hospital and bring Grandmom one of my drawings. Stay only a few minutes.

(e) If I can, go back again and ask Grandmom if there's anything I can do to help her.

By going step by step you can reduce your fears and surmount the barriers you feel to wading into an unpleasant, demanding situation. If you master the first step, it will give you strength to move on to the second.

WHAT IS ACCOMPLISHED?

1. Accurately gauging your threshold of caring is an effective way of making sure that you do not demand more of yourself than you are capable of giving at your present level of skills. It would be nice if we all were supermen and women, but we aren't. If we feel pressed or threatened, we tend to retreat for self-protection, then end up doing even less than we're capable of. And we foil our chances for learning how to do more and more.
2. We gain confidence in our caring abilities and guard against being overwhelmed when we build caring skills a little bit at a time. And confidence is the foundation for taking caring risks and stretching our Caring Capacity.

29

Getting into Shape for Caring:
EXERCISES FOR BUILDING CARING CONSCIOUSNESS

One way to build caring skills is just to become more aware of how we care, of what we need, and to have at our disposal the same information about the others in our Caring Circle. The exercises in this chapter are all designed to increase our sensitivity to the needs and behavior of ourselves and others, and to gather information that will be useful in practicing Quality Caring. Many are guided imagery exercises that allow us to tune in to our hopes, fears, and dreams, or to speculate about those of others.

❀ TUNING IN TO THE INNER DIALOGUE

In order to open up to others we must first become tuned in to what we think and feel ourselves. Caring requires a sharp awareness of our own inner dialogue. We are all thinking about many things all the time. While we wash the car we ponder our mortgage payments, wonder how our kid is doing in camp, notice the color of the sky and the chipping paint on the porch, reminisce about some special romance, and feel angry at our mother-in-law—all at once. This inner dialogue is endless, though often we neglect to pay it enough attention. If we repeatedly fail to stop and tune in to our inner thoughts, we lose touch with what's going on within and can be overwhelmed by feelings we can't understand or identify. When that happens, it's a sign that we're out of touch with ourselves and failing in self-care.

HOW TO GO ABOUT IT

1. Set aside time in every day to sit with your thoughts: five minutes after lunch, ten before bedtime, a minute between phone calls.

A Time for Caring

2. Let your mind drift. Relax, but at the same time try to be aware of what you're thinking about right now. Without disturbing their flow, try to catch and notice the thoughts that pass through your mind. Don't get so anxious to trap them that your mind shuts down.
3. At first when you try this, your mind may go blank. To get your thoughts going, ask yourself questions: Was I angry any time today? Did anything unusual happen today? Did I speak with anyone new today? Which of my friends did I talk with? What did we talk about? Did I want to talk to someone I didn't get to? Was I nervous today? Did I laugh?
4. To help make the thoughts more conscious, try saying them aloud as they occur. "This pencil needs sharpening . . . Have to call Marion . . . Cats are a bore . . . Why are pencils yellow . . . My tan is fading . . . Marion's car is yellow . . . Sun's out today . . . Is it lunchtime . . . Tomatoes in season soon . . . Water plants . . ."
5. Don't make any attempt to analyze your thoughts at this point and don't make judgments about them. Our inner thoughts contain a lot of nonsense, trivia, useless garbage, seemingly meaningless connections, and if we're lucky, some useful information, perhaps a gem here and there.
6. Eventually your goal is to learn how to tune in to your thoughts throughout the day. Once you learn the art of tuning in to your thoughts, get into the habit of stopping for just thirty seconds several times a day to ask yourself: What am I thinking about *now*?

WHAT IS ACCOMPLISHED?

1. The first thing you find is that there's a lot more on your mind than you may have thought.
2. Paying attention to your thoughts is a way of knowing who you are—what you like and dislike, what you need and want, what you hate, what amuses you, how you think, where your imagination roams. It's crucial to self-care.
3. Once aware of and able to articulate your feelings and thoughts, you can begin to share them with others. That is an important first step toward becoming a more open, accessible person.
4. You will learn firsthand that everyone's mind courses with thoughts, worries, problems, solutions, nonsense, dreams, bits and pieces of ideas and emotions. You can learn to draw others out, to be responsive to their needs, once you understand your own.

🌸 CARING CAMERA

The ability to observe people and situations keenly is an integral part of effective caring. Many of us are shy or reluctant or even lazy about fully using our observational powers. In this exercise we use a camera to help us develop this skill. The scrutiny of faces, of the scenes and objects in our environment, is necessary in order to take a good picture. It often happens that we see in a photograph what we missed with our eyes. But in this age of instant photography shutterbugs many people still take hastily composed, out-of-focus pictures. And sometimes the camera actually impairs observation, for we count on the camera to do our seeing for us. Nevertheless, when we take a photo, we capture a fleeting moment and hold it in our hands. This gives us a unique opportunity to examine and reflect, as well as to compare what we noticed at the time with what was actually going on.

HOW TO GO ABOUT IT

1. Pick a person to photograph; tell them about this exercise.
2. Spend some time observing them through the camera without taking pictures. Use this time to concentrate your attention and thoughts on the subject.
3. Put film in the camera. Plan to use the whole roll to take many different pictures of the person, from different angles, in subtly different moods, situations, and activities. But take the whole roll of film in just one session or even in just an hour.
4. Set goals. For example, decide to take a flattering picture of your subject. Make a judgment about when you think they look good. Then snap. Learn to read faces. Try to "capture" moods or attitudes. Act on your observations. See how different one person can look from various angles and with different expressions. Try to capture happy, sad, comic, bemused, stern, and soft expressions.
5. When the pictures are developed, sit down and study them. Are you seeing things in the pictures you missed in real life? Were your photos of people flattering, warm, distant, critical? Varied, carefully composed, thoughtful, judgmental?
6. Note the effect of your picture taking. Is your subject camera shy? Are you shy about taking the pictures, about intruding or getting so close? Camera shyness, on either side of the camera, is often an indication of low self-esteem. Be aware of the power you have in taking the picture—to be caring and flattering, or unflattering and misrepresenting the others, to be a creator or destroyer of self-esteem and understanding.

A Time for Caring

WHAT IS ACCOMPLISHED?

1. By examining the photos you learn to see how you see others.
2. Unexpected things in the picture alert you to areas where you should increase your powers of observation.
3. The ability to capture what you see—happiness, sadness, anger, and so on, gives you confidence in your perceptions.
4. If you have omitted or missed what you wanted to photograph, work on paying attention to what's going on around you more carefully.
5. If you find you were shy about taking pictures of others, ask yourself, "Why was I reluctant? What was I worried about?" Discover your own reluctance to explore your Caring Network.
6. If you found your subject was uncomfortable or shy about having pictures taken, try to discover why. Learn about your subject's insecurities and discover ways you can help the subject become more comfortable in front of the camera.

❀ HOW AM I DOING?

This exercise takes its name from a personal ritual of Ed Koch, the mayor of New York, who opens his press conferences by asking the assembled reporters, "Well, how am I doing?" Periodically we need to set a specific time aside to reflect on our caring skills. The purpose of the exercise is to assess our new caring skills, note what progress we've made, decide what areas we want to work on. It's easy to be so busy that we lose sight of our progress—or lack of it. The result is an imbalance in our caring: caring needs not being met, gains going unrecognized. It is important to pat ourselves on the back for our progress and to learn to be comfortable with our emerging feelings of care—for ourselves and for others.

HOW TO GO ABOUT IT

1. Set aside a fifteen-minute period once a week (or at least every other week) for reflection.
2. Go over your caring thoughts, feelings, and actions during the past week. Jot down any new feelings, skills, and problems that have come up. Review any new exercises you've tried, contacts you've had in your Caring Networks.
3. Focus on your new strengths so that you are consciously aware of new abilities.
4. If there are noticeable gaps in your caring activities, or a particular

problem that must be coped with, decide on an exercise that might help.

WHAT IS ACCOMPLISHED?

1. You learn to appreciate your efforts and to see that there is progress.
2. You learn to take time for yourself, time to savor the good feelings that caring can give you.
3. With periodic reflection it's possible to catch problems and imbalances before they become acute.

❋ IF I HAD TO CHOOSE

We cannot get the care we need if we don't have a firm idea of what we want *and* of how to ask for it. This exercise lets us identify what we want from a situation by helping us learn to recognize our personal preferences. We learn to overcome our fear of "rocking the boat" if we have to disagree with someone to make our wants understood. We gain confidence in our ability first to know our preferences and then to express them clearly.

HOW TO GO ABOUT IT

1. Adopt the habit of examining your daily activities to see whether you're choosing them or vice versa. For a start, look at the basic, simple situations in which you make decisions: you choose to wear your jeans or a dress, to drive or take the bus to work, to eat dessert or to pass it up. It may help you to write down at the end of each day a list of the simple choices you have made.
2. Ask yourself if these choices were really what *you* wanted, or were they made to please or appease others, or were they made without much thought.
3. Once you become aware of the decisions you make and what influences them, move on to a more active position. Take a minute in the morning to predict the possibilities of the day's decision making, and think through your choices. Plan how you'd like to respond to each choice. Anticipation of upcoming situations will inhibit the "I don't know" or "I don't care one way or the other" or "I'd rather leave it to someone else and not make waves" reaction.

Start with small things:

"I've had a craving for seafood. I'm going to make sure I have a meal at the Cauldron this week."

A Time for Caring

It gets tougher when the decision involves other people and their wishes, especially if we've heretofore adopted a more passive role.

"I'm going to pick the movie when the family goes out this weekend."

"When Mel calls, I'll tell him that I'd rather watch the game on TV than go fishing with him."

"I'll help Sally with her sewing project, but I'll tell her this is the last time."

4. If you are having trouble getting started, the If I Had to Choose game will help make you aware of your needs or preferences. Write out your responses to the following kinds of questions if it helps you crystallize your thoughts:

If I could have anything for dinner tonight, I'd choose _____.

If I were going to paint my bedroom, I'd choose the color _____.

If I could pick three books to read on my vacation, they'd be _____, _____, and _____.

Pose a question in this form to yourself whenever you are going to make a decision, especially when you are deciding about big issues in your own life, your job, your friends, your home: "If I could choose to do any job, what would it be?" "If I could live anywhere, where would it be?" "If I could be closer to any of my friends, who would it be?" Find out how you really feel about the big issues in your life. See how you can best take care of yourself.

WHAT IS ACCOMPLISHED?

1. By recognizing and expressing your wants you gain confidence in your self, get a greater feeling of self-worth.
2. Sticking up for your wants makes you take responsibility for what you do and what happens to you.
3. Learning to make value judgments about what is good or bad for you sharpens your self-perception.
4. Articulating exactly what you want lets your family and friends know you better, opens new routes for communication and understanding, even takes responsibility *off* their shoulders. *Always* having to choose the movie can become a chore.

❈ THE ONLY PERSON I KNOW

Everyone in our Caring Network is unique. Often, however, untrained powers of observation and lack of time and interest get in the way of our seeing what is special in each person. When we learn to recognize each person's complexities, we are better able to cherish and care for our friends, mates, and family members and for those special qualities they bring to our relationships. By focusing on individual quirks in this exercise, we hone our powers of observation and abort our tendency to pin labels on people. If the boss is slightly intimidating, it is hard to find a way to develop a good relationship with her if we sum her up by saying, "She's a hard-nosed business woman." But if we look behind that label to pinpoint the qualities that make us characterize her so patly, it's not too easy to write her off in one clichéd phrase. We are forced to discover the characteristics of her personality that make her unique, and make her human. "She's quick-witted, works long hours, is intolerant of laziness, somewhat shy, very observant, and not afraid to make decisions." This tells us something about her beyond a social stereotype and helps us to personalize and intensify our relationship with her.

HOW TO GO ABOUT IT

1. Each day select one person in your Caring Network to concentrate on.
2. Visualize the person in your mind's eye. Remember what they wear, how they look, what their voice sounds like, their gestures, where they live, their hobbies, their job, their family.
3. Look for the idiosyncrasies, the things that don't fall into patterns, the unusual. Search for nuances, telling details.
4. Think about that person until you can come up with at least five traits that separate that person from others. Write down the five unique qualities. For example:
    John is the only person I know who can fall asleep at a busy party.
    John is the only man I know who blushes.
    John always cuts everything on his plate into small pieces before he starts eating.
    John is the only person I know who ties his own trout flies.
    John is one of the few people I know who makes it a point to ask me about myself.

WHAT IS ACCOMPLISHED?

1. We sharpen our powers of observation.
2. We discover new and pleasant things to appreciate in those around us and take new interest in our surroundings.
3. We see that those who seem imposing are more approachable than we imagined, and that those who seem withdrawn or unknowable are, on closer inspection, as full of complex qualities as anyone else.

A Time for Caring

4. We gather the information we need to be specific and appropriate when we deal with each person.

❋ WHAT IF . . . ?

Have you ever asked yourself, "What if . . . ?" Usually we are frightened of this question, evoking as it does images of possible disaster without solutions. Through guided imagery this exercise shows us how to use our imaginations to help us find solutions to potentially difficult situations. It is a form of realistic caring to be prepared for possible occurrences so that we can act responsibly and appropriately, considering what is best for ourselves and others. Unless we plan for crises and know there are contingency plans or escape hatches available, we can be too overwhelmed to act sensibly when something comes up suddenly. By imagining ourselves in tough or unforeseen situations we can rehearse our responses, find ways to lessen our inhibitions and fears, and take the time to consider how others are going to react and feel in the same situation.

HOW TO GO ABOUT IT

1. Think about a person, problem, or situation that would be difficult for you to handle. Try to imagine what your reaction might be and the feelings involved.
2. How would you like to modify your basic response? What seems good about it? What seems bad?
3. Come up with as many options for dealing with it as possible.
4. Come up with a solid idea of a contingency plan.

The kinds of situations you might consider are:
What if . . . Jerry suddenly called me for a date?
  . . . Fred became ill?
  . . . A stranger came up to me on the street and asked for directions?
  . . . I told Alice she needs to lose weight?
  . . . I won $10,000 in the lottery?
  . . . I were fired from my job?

As you examine your responses and look for options, consider your actions, thoughts, feelings, and others' responses. For example: What if I lost my job?

(a) What would my financial situation be? How long could I get by before I got another job? Would I get unemployment? What are the job openings that I could qualify for?

(b) Would I be willing to move?

(c) How would I tell my wife?
(d) What could my wife do to help?
(e) How would losing my job affect my self-image? Is my reaction realistic?
(f) Do I feel prepared to look for a new job?

Once you have asked yourself all the pertinent questions, look for optional solutions.

(a) I could get unemployment.
(b) My wife could get a job.
(c) I could get a part-time job and go to school to train for a new job.
(d) I could ask my friends to help me find out about job openings.
(e) We could set up a baby-sitting exchange with friends so my wife and I could both work.
(f) We could sell the second car, or even the house if we had to.
(g) I could look into working in another city.
(h) The kids could get jobs after school.

As you find time, do this exercise for all likely contingencies in your life and for when you are faced with particular situations.

WHAT IS ACCOMPLISHED?

1. By examining our preparedness for handling crises we can see where we have neglected to take care of ourselves. We may be able to change what we are doing—or not doing—to improve our ability to contend with an emergency.
2. We lessen the chances that we will panic in a crisis if we have a firm idea of our options before it strikes.
3. We grapple with tough caring situations in our imagination, building our caring powers and confidence so we are able to handle stresses without abandoning a caring stance.

❀ SURVEYING THE CARING LANDSCAPE

This is another guided imagery exercise in which we think about a specific friend, family member, lover, and so forth, to bring to mind all the various ways they show and accept care. Keep your definition of caring behavior very broad: the habits and methods of caring vary enormously from one person to another. One friend may rarely say thank you or hand out compliments but is always there when we need advice and support. Another friend may be full of caring gestures, gifts, small words of endearment, but uncomfortable with intense personal conversations. Each person has his or her own system of care based on personal abilities

A Time for Caring

and sensibilities. There just isn't any one proper way of showing care. Don't judge others' caring habits during this exercise. The point is to learn to see each member of our Caring Network as an individual with special needs and ways of contributing to our caring environment.

HOW TO GO ABOUT IT

1. Sit in a quiet spot and focus on an important person in your Caring Network.
2. Review your recent dealings with your friend, where you went, what you did, what you talked about, how the relationship felt.
3. Think about your general impression of the person: Generous? Talkative? Quiet? Shy? Gregarious? Inquisitive?
4. Ask yourself, "How does my friend show care for me?" Does he call often? Remember my birthday? Stop by spontaneously for a visit? Make an effort to introduce me to his friends? Ask me about my work, family, mate? Notice when I'm feeling good, or bad, before I mention it? Tell me how he feels about me? Tell me jokes? Tell me about good books he's read? Tell me about good movies? Ask me for my opinion about politics? What specific things has he done lately?
5. Ask yourself, "How does he let me know how to care for him?" Does he like to be hugged or kissed? Is he comfortable when I compliment him? Does he solicit and listen to my opinion? Does he let me fix him dinner? Get him things to make him comfortable? Give him a backrub?
6. Make a list of the responses that come to mind. For example: Steve is lavish with birthday and Christmas presents.
He often calls just to say hello.
He is not embarrassed if I kiss him in public.
He often asks my advice on problems at the office.
He asks me to rub his back when he is tense.
He likes me to ask him about his feelings.
He cooks dinner for his friends on Sunday.
7. Note any caring actions that you discover the other person doesn't do or can't accept from you.
He can't take a compliment.
He can't accept help when he's sick.
He has a hard time being serious when I have a problem he doesn't identify with.
8. As you find time, do this exercise for each important person in your Caring Circle.

WHAT IS ACCOMPLISHED?

1. You become aware of the caring ways of those you are close to.
2. You identify and appreciate what is done for you and learn how to care most appropriately for those close to you.
3. You identify your own caring behavior in each of your relationships and give yourself credit.

❇ WHAT CAN I DO FOR YOU?

This is a guided imagery exercise that lets us expand the kinds of caring options we have when dealing with our friends, family, mates, and so on. By taking the time to imagine different kinds of caring actions appropriate to a specific person, we gain practice in observing individual needs and expand the definition of caring acts. Learning to identify a wide variety of caring possibilities gives us more confidence in our caring abilities. Many of us want to show we care but don't know what we have to offer. By writing out a long list of possibilities, by trying to come up with a long list of small gestures, seemingly trivial, or frivolous or impractical actions, we discover that there are many simple ways to mobilize our caring impulses.

HOW TO GO ABOUT IT

1. Select one person in your Caring Network: your mate, child, best friend, a family member.
2. Begin by thinking about that person and what you might do for them in the most general way. If you have selected your husband, for example, start with the role definition: i.e., what can one do for a husband, a lover, a male?
3. Then be more specific and ask: What can *I* do for *my* husband?
4. Think about as many things as possible. Don't judge whether they're practical or whether you actually want to do them or whether they would be appreciated. The idea is to be imaginative and prolific, to broaden the narrow definition of caring in specific relationships.

   Let's look at some of the possible actions you could put on your list.
   Call him at work.
   Give him a massage.
   Learn to play golf.
   Get a picture of us framed.
   Try and get him to talk more about his preferences in bed.

A Time for Caring

Wear the blue blouse that he likes.
Plan a vacation for us.
Assume responsibility for some of the financial planning.
Remember his birthday.
Be nicer to his friend Bob.
Try to get home before he does sometimes.
Help him diet.
Sing him a song.
Tell him more about the details of what happened at work.
Tell him I love him more often.
Tell him a joke or funny story every day.
Tell him about his bad breath.
Cut his hair.
Order the part for the lawn mower.
Make him breakfast.
Teach him how to cook.
Go shopping with him.
Keep the kids out of his desk drawers.
Give him more notice about our weekend plans.
Let him have a night a week to himself.
Help him take care of his sick mother.
Teach him how to play tennis.
Spend an hour talking to him each night after the kids go to bed.
Make his favorite dinner once in a while.

What can I do for my child, Susan?
  Read her a bedtime story more often.
  Let her stay up late once in a while.
  Spend time with her alone.
  Tell her about my schooldays.
  Raise her allowance.
  Let her help me with the household chores.
  Plan a special birthday party.
  Buy her some new books.
  Ask her about school every day.
  Help with her homework.
  Play catch with her.
  Make a dentist appointment.
  Answer her questions about sex.
  Tell her more about our family history.
  Buy those cookies she likes.
  Help her get into Little League.

Have a conference with her teacher.
Help with the scout troop.
Let her take more responsibility for preparing dinner sometimes.
Have her friends sleep over.
Buy her a new pair of shoes.
Let her spend the weekend with her grandmother.
Keep her room neat.
Take her to the library.
Make sure someone is in the house when she comes home from school.
Listen to her gripes about Dad and me.
Don't force her to wear clothes she hates.
Don't force her to eat food she hates.
Sew a new skirt for her school play.
Help her fix her hair.

WHAT IS ACCOMPLISHED?

1. You discover how simple it is to think of ways to show that you care, and how many possibilities there are.
2. You unlock your caring feelings and build confidence in your ability to care.
3. You focus on the needs and desires of others and increase your sensitivity to their caring needs.

❊ IMAGE CONSCIOUS

This exercise helps us become aware of how we present an image to the world in day-to-day situations and interactions and how we are influenced by others' images. We dress a certain way to go to the bank, another to go to a cocktail party. We present ourselves in ways dictated by situations and feelings outside ourselves. Rarely do we ask ourselves, "Is this really me? Is this how I feel the most comfortable?" When someone asks us what we do for a living we feel pressured to glamorize, overstate our position, to build ourselves up, to elicit appreciation and respect via our negotiable assets.

No one can be image-free, nor is it particularly desirable. Our images give clues to others about who we are, background information that paves the way to further intimacy.

It is necessary to fulfill others' expectations in some situations, to be aggressive in presenting ourselves: when we are at a job interview, we play a specific role. If the image we present publicly is a fair representa-

A Time for Caring

tion of our private self, there's no conflict. But imaging can become dangerous if we feel constant pressure to present a façade, especially if it's far from the truth. Imaging should serve us, not trap us, and shouldn't blind us and others to what's behind it. The purpose of this exercise is to become aware of the manifestations of imaging and, especially if you feel you're overdoing it (or are oversusceptible to others' images), to try and cut down before you get too addicted.

HOW TO GO ABOUT IT

1. The next time you go to a party or find yourself in a social situation, try not to ask people, "What do you do?" Don't force them to rely on their image to communicate with you.

   Try to avoid giving out loaded information or talking about self-aggrandizing subjects. Find common interests like personal observations or feelings about the situation, politics, art, or cooking to talk about.

   Take note of what attracts you about others: the way they dress, certain looks, their status or celebrity. Tune in to how others present themselves.

2. As you go through your daily activities observe the ways in which you "present your image." Notice the difference between how you feel on the inside and the way you present yourself to the rest of the world. Try in small ways, and when it feels comfortable, to close that gap. Look for situations where and for people with whom you can drop your mask.

WHAT IS ACCOMPLISHED?

1. By removing unnecessary imaging you let others see you more clearly, and you feel more sincere and truer to yourself. You pave the way for others to develop care for *you*. You feel more secure as you gain confidence that others like you for yourself, not for your image.
2. By looking behind others' images, by learning to recognize image-free behavior and freeing yourself of your addiction to symbols and images, you can get to know people whom you might have ignored before. Your Caring Circle expands.
3. You remove the anxiety and pressure from yourself that you may have felt when you worried about meeting image requirements and about the gap between you and your image.

30

Getting into Shape for Caring:
EXERCISES FOR TWO

Caring doesn't take place in a vacuum. We can learn caring skills on our own to some extent, but it always helps to bring others in to share the care-learning process. The exercises in this chapter all involve two people. Some of these exercises deal with handling grievances and disagreements, others with giving and asking for caring, or with keeping up-to-date with each other. Some cultivate our Caring Capacity, others deal with recognizing our limits. In each case we discover our caring feelings and check them out. We share the agonies and ecstasies of our relationships in a safe context. With our partner we affirm the commitment to improving our caring relationships and get the added bonus of giving and getting immediate feedback on caring actions. The last three exercises in this chapter are sexual games, specifically designed to improve caring concern in intimate relationships, and to have fun in the process. Each of the partnered exercises is designed to become more natural and spontaneous as we get used to doing it. The structures are flexible. In each instance we should look for ways to integrate the methods and intent of the exercises into our daily lives.

❀ ATTRACTION/RESERVATION

We all like some qualities and dislike others in those we care for. We also make assumptions about what others like and don't like about us. This exercise gives us a chance to tell those we care for what we like and dislike about them *and* to find out how they feel about us. By writing out

A Time for Caring

lists of attractions and reservations and then sharing them in a "safe" situation, we can break down the barriers that often keep us from the most active kind of caring give-and-take. Once we have become comfortable with this orderly exchange of Attraction/Reservation, we should try to make the exchange of such caring feelings a natural part of our friendships. It is a good way to learn to say what we like and dislike without fear of argument. It also provides a chance to check out our perceptions of ourselves and others, and we learn to be direct, to take risks, as well as to increase our caring honesty.

HOW TO GO ABOUT IT

1. Ask your partner to join you in a brief Attraction/Reservation exchange. If your partner is unfamiliar with this book, explain how the exercise will help your caring relationship.
2. Each partner writes out a list of three qualities that the partner likes and three qualities that the partner doesn't like about the other person.
3. When you have finished that list, write out a second one in which you try to guess what your partner has written about you.
4. Each person reads his or her three likes and three dislikes without interruption.
5. Don't interrupt, disagree, comment, or censure the reader. If you feel compelled to say something, limit it to, "I didn't know you felt that way!"
6. When you have both read your first list, read your lists of assumptions. See where they agree or disagree with what your partner actually wrote down.

NOTES

A typical exchange might go like this:

Mary's list of likes:
1. I like the way you always remember my birthday and our anniversaries.
2. I like the way you make a point of introducing me to your friends so they know I'm someone special to you.
3. I like the way you react to social and political issues. You really do care about what happens in the world around you.

Mary's list of dislikes:
1. I don't like the fact that you never let me know if you are going to be working late. It hangs me up and keeps me from making plans for myself.
2. I don't like the fact that you resent it if I am too aggressive sexually.

3. I don't like the fact that you cannot get along with my family.

Steve then reads his lists:
1. I like the way you always ask me about my day and are sincerely interested in my work.
2. I like the way you show affection, with a gentle touch on my shoulder, a kiss on the cheek, by holding my hand.
3. I like the way you take care of yourself, you are always learning new things, and you keep yourself in good shape.

Steve's list of dislikes:
1. I don't like the fact that you talk on the phone a lot when I'm home.
2. I don't like it that you spend so much time and thought worrying about your mother and brother.
3. I don't like it that you don't understand when I tell you I don't feel like making love.

When you are done with the exchange, compare what was said to you with what you *thought* would be said. What were the surprises? What did you correctly predict? Ask yourself, "How did I feel about the likes and dislikes? What made me happy? What hurt my feelings? What seemed fair? Unfair? Did I discover something I'd like to change? Or a criticism I'm extremely sensitive to?"

WHAT IS ACCOMPLISHED

1. You learn—often unexpectedly—what others like about you. This builds caring confidence and gives you a better perception of how you're perceived.
2. You learn what others dislike about you—but you learn it in a caring context, well balanced with reaffirmation. This lets you understand that caring can be given and received even in difficult situations. You don't have to be perfect to get or give care.
3. Your partner learns that you see him or her more than superficially, that you think about them as an individual personality and don't label them. Trust is built on both sides.

TEA AND SYMPATHY

We all need someone to talk to, to tell our troubles to. But sometimes we don't want to get into a long, involved conversation about our feelings; we just want to get them off our chest. Other times we are nervous about telling our family or friends how we feel because we don't know how they'll react. Tea and Sympathy lets us have a one-way conversation

A Time for Caring

with someone who agrees to act as a sounding board for our feelings and to offer sympathy but no comments or advice. This is a pattern we should try to adopt in our daily exchanges with friends. Sometimes, and we have to be able to gauge the right times, we should lend support without making a big deal of it, without offering advice, and find ways of letting our friends in on how we are feeling without drawing them into a long, complicated discussion.

HOW TO GO ABOUT IT

1. Explain the premise of Tea and Sympathy to a friend. Ask your friend to join you. (Ideally, you can each take a turn at Tea and Sympathy.)
2. Start with general information—what went wrong at the office, how the traffic was terrible, what you think about the elections. Let yourself ramble a bit, clearing out petty irritations.
3. Bring in more personal or serious matters. Express the anger you are feeling with friends or family, or even with the person listening to you.
4. Keep it brief, no more than five minutes or so:
   Talker: I'm feeling pretty bad. May I have a Tea and Sympathy with you?
   Listener: Right now? Sure. Do you want to go for a walk?
   Talker: I'm falling so far behind in my work. Every time I think I'm getting ahead, something else comes up. I don't know what to do. I'm afraid it will look as if I'm doing a bad job. That's really not the case. So many little distracting things come across my desk. I should have an assistant to do them, but I don't. And if that weren't bad enough, I'm afraid that my best friend is angry at me. I think it's because I told him I would pick him up on Saturday, and then when I didn't go, I forgot to tell him I wasn't coming. I tried to tell him it was a mistake. I had a lot on my mind. But it really made him angry. I don't know what to do about it.
5. Remember, the listener can't interject comments or opinions, other than a brief word of acknowledgment or sympathy.

WHAT IS ACCOMPLISHED?

1. You are able to blow off steam without getting into an argument or remaining so irritable that you pick on others unnecessarily.
2. You learn to trust others to listen to your troubles without being critical or judgmental.
3. You build your caring relationship by sharing negative feelings in an understanding, accepting environment.

4. You initiate a process of mutual give-and-take with friends that can carry over into day-to-day interactions.

❋ BLINDWALK

Blindwalk is a game in which each party takes a turn leading the blindfolded other on a short walk. It is fun and teaches several important things about caring. It is, first of all, a game about trust, or mistrust. We find out how we handle responsibility for another's well-being. We explore how we feel about giving up control of our well-being to another. This exercise reveals how we act as a leader and react as a follower. It points up obstacles that stand in the way of our asking for care and clues us in to whether or not we or our partner is in fact trustworthy.

HOW TO GO ABOUT IT

1. With your partner establish physical guidelines for the blindwalk: on the first floor of the house, in the backyard, only in the living room. Note any special caveats, especially when doing this exercise with children: "Don't forget I'm much taller than you, so I may not be able to go everywhere you can. Be sure to warn me when to duck." (See also Handicapping, page 342.)
2. Set a time limit of two or three minutes.
3. Cover your eyes with a blindfold or keep your eyes tightly closed.
4. The leader takes your hand and/or gives you directions. "Walk three steps ahead, then turn left and stop. Put your hand out until you feel the tree trunk," and so on. The leader can give as much instruction (or as little) as he or she wishes. The same goes for body contact or physical assistance. The leader can add interest to the trip by making it a "tactile tour," encouraging the blindfolded partner to touch flowers, water, and the like.
5. When the time limit is reached, change roles. Repeat.
6. When you both have taken turns, discuss the walk. Talk about how you felt being the leader. Did you think your partner was cooperative? resistant? nervous? Talk about how you felt being led. Did you trust the leader? Did the leader act responsibly? Were you trusting? Compare your feelings with your partner's.

WHAT IS ACCOMPLISHED?

1. We confront our feelings about being a leader. We see how fairly and responsibly we accept the role, and how caringly we fulfill it.
2. We discover how we feel about being led. If we are nervous or un-

A Time for Caring

trusting, we can discover whether it is justified or not, and whether this defensiveness interferes with our ability to accept care.
3. We have the chance to build trust between our partner and ourselves, an essential part of a caring relationship.

❁ PERSISTENCE/RESISTANCE

Persistence/Resistance is an exercise that lets us turn disagreements and deadlocks into dialogues and solutions. One of the toughest times to maintain a caring attitude is when we are asking for something or explaining something that is important to us and are meeting with misunderstanding or hostility. But this is precisely the time when we should strive to be more open and undefensive, for if we lose sight of our caring feelings, if we forget that we want to resolve our differences, it gets difficult to find options and solutions. Persistence/Resistance teaches us to speak our minds forcefully, and to listen to our partner's disagreements without losing sight of our ultimate goal: to resolve our differences to both parties' satisfaction; to keep our relationship healthy; to find realistic, workable solutions.

HOW TO GO ABOUT IT

1. When a disagreement comes up, call a time-out for five minutes while each of you formulates a clear way of expressing your opinions.
2. Begin the discussion with a simple statement of the problem. "I am angry because you won't agree to go on a vacation this year."
3. Tell your partner how you feel about it. "I feel like you don't want to spend that much time with the family, and it hurts my feelings."
4. At this point your partner should feed back to you, as close to verbatim as possible, what was just said: "You're angry because I won't agree to a vacation. You feel that I don't want to spend time with the family, and that hurts you."

    This feedback step should be followed by both parties after each exchange. Repeating what was said prevents one of the major problems of clear, direct exchange: the tendency to misinterpret, to distort, or to dismiss what's been said.
5. Let your partner respond in a simple way. "I don't want to go on a vacation because we can't afford to go where I want to."
6. You then each take turns expressing your opinions in one simple sentence. "Why can't we come up with an alternative? I would like to go to the lake."

7. As each person expresses an opinion, both should look for options. "The lake's no good, it doesn't have a golf course. Find a lake with a golf course and we'll talk about it."
8. Take time to develop as many options as possible. Persist with what you want while listening to what the other has to say—not just what you want to hear—and seeking areas of mutual agreement. Remember to feed back verbatim after each exchange. Consider different locations for your vacation. Look for things to do on day trips from home. Consider taking separate vacations. Find out if you can arrange to get away without the kids for a couple of days.
9. If both parties are committed to finding a resolution, some compromise will be reached.
10. An all-or-nothing attitude is very destructive. Accept the fact that you can't always get everything you want.

WHAT IS ACCOMPLISHED?

1. You learn how to express your opinions and make yourself heard without getting embroiled in an insoluble fight.
2. You and your partner have a chance to express anger and disagreement within a context of goodwill.
3. Developing options takes two-way caretaking. Your caring abilities are expanded and you see your partner's active care for you.
4. Overcoming fear of confrontation lets you develop caring honesty and allows your caring needs to be met.

❀ HANDICAPPING

Handicapping is a process of establishing physical or intellectual equality between people who care for each other. It shows us how to even up the balance of power in our relationships and to come to terms with the notion of equity. Particularly when dealing with children or subordinates, it is crucial to maintain an atmosphere in which both parties are free to express feelings and opinions. It is possible to be burdened with the pressures and responsibilities of power as well as with inferior physical or verbal skills that can't compete. Since caring is a give-and-take, a process of sharing and giving support, power imbalances can stymie open exchange.

Often Handicapping comes naturally. We change our pace when walking with a child. We adjust our speech to make it easier for the foreigner in the group. He, on the other hand, has to trust the goodwill of the group, not expect to be the leader, and enjoy being a tagalong.

A Time for Caring

Handicapping is done by mutual consent. It's no different from a handicap in a golf or chess game; it makes the competition both more equal and more fun. For example, if you and your child are going to do a Blindwalk (page 340), you both should agree to make your physical relationship more equal. You may agree to take child-size steps. If you and your spouse are going to deal with a disagreement by acting out a Persistence/Resistance and one of you is louder or more glib, you may set verbal handicaps. If you are forceful and articulate while your spouse becomes tongue-tied or slow to speak, remove that imbalance by agreeing to limit your responses to two sentences, to speak in a quiet voice, or to allow your partner more time. This may free your spouse to be more aggressive, to assert ideas without fear that he or she will be stepping on your territory.

As you can see, both parties must agree to recognize and redress the power differences. If both people are committed to the idea of increasing caring and communication, it can be worked out easily. Keep these goals firmly in mind.

HOW TO GO ABOUT IT

1. Whenever you notice a power imbalance in a given situation—no matter whether you are the more powerful or the weaker person—comment on it. "I think we are having trouble getting along because one of us feels like the underdog."
2. Find out what your partner thinks about it. Discuss your different perspectives.
3. When you have both agreed that some change needs to be made, work together to come up with the longest list of options possible. Look for as many solutions as possible. Don't rule out anything. You should each ask yourselves: "What can I do to change this?" and "What would I like to do to change this?"
4. When you have considered your options, select one or two and test them out. Be flexible. If they don't work, try something else.
5. Remember, though, that if you handicap the "stronger" person too much, they then become the "weaker" and you have to adjust the balance again.

WHAT IS ACCOMPLISHED?

1. You become aware of power imbalances and prevent them from wearing away at your relationships.
2. The burden of always being in control is removed. The frustration of powerlessness is removed.
3. The very act of accepting a handicap is an act of caring. It sets the

stage for improving your overall caring abilities and cements your Caring Network.

🌸 MINDREADING

Mindreading is an exercise that uncovers the difference between what we *think* others think and what they *actually* think. We often do not have an accurate picture of others' thoughts and feelings, likes and dislikes. We make assumptions that may or may not be true. If we don't check out our assumptions, we're likely to act on wrong information. Then we wonder why others aren't exactly thrilled with our behavior. We may, for example, assume that a friend is too busy to spend time with us because he rarely calls. Perhaps he is just too shy. We may assume that a friend loves modern furniture because his apartment is full of glass and chrome. It may, in fact, be a legacy from a former tenant. We may for years avoid mentioning a friend's scar, only to find it's not a bit embarrassing to him. The mindreading exercise shows us how easy it is to get off on the wrong track, and teaches us how to check out our information before we act upon it.

HOW TO GO ABOUT IT

1. Choose a subject about which you and your partner will read each other's mind. It could be just about anything: what you like to eat, what your favorite movies are, your favorite activities, your most detested activities, your sexual preferences, your dream vacations.
2. As an example, say that you've chosen as your topic Favorite Leisure Activities. You and your partner each write out two lists. On the first list note down your three favorite leisure activities. On the second list note down the three activities you think your partner will list as *his* three favorite activities.
Here is a sample list:
My three favorite leisure activities
   (a) Hiking
   (b) Tennis
   (c) Sketching
My friend's three favorite leisure activities
   (a) Baking
   (b) Reading
   (c) Folk dancing

A *Time for Caring*

3. Each partner now reads the list of activities he thinks the other has on his list.
4. As your partner reads his list, see how it compares with your assumption of what he would say; then see how well he did in figuring you out. Note the difference between your assumption and the reality. See what you can learn both about the tendency to read others' minds and about the necessity to check out your assumptions.

WHAT IS ACCOMPLISHED?

1. You learn about others in your Caring Circle directly, so you don't have to guess. They in turn learn about you. You increase your chances of being appreciated and understood. Often you learn something new about how others see you.
2. You learn how important it is to check out your assumptions about people. You improve your power of observation.
3. You avoid the trap of acting on misinformation and of having others misunderstand you. You lessen the chance of hidden resentments and increase the probability of appropriate actions.

❃ THE MENU GAME

The Menu Game is an amusing variation of Mindreading and Persistence/Resistance. It helps us to check out our assumptions about what our partner likes, to see if they are true or false, and tests our ability to resist pressure and stick to our guns. By trying to guess what our partner wants to order in a restaurant and trying to get him or her to go along with our assumptions, we can stage this symbolic confrontation in a lighthearted context. We see how we might act and react in such situations without getting into a real disagreement.

Caring is often blocked when people do not really see each other for who they are. If we can accept differences of opinion, take the time to check in with our friends to see what they feel, we can learn to like them for who they are and be more considerate and sensitive about individual preferences.

HOW TO GO ABOUT IT

1. Play the game next time you go to a restaurant with one other person. Each of you choose three items—such as the entrée, dessert, and beverage—you think your partner will order.
2. Compare your assumptions with your partner's actual choices.

3. Then, if you want to continue the game a step further, try to convince your partner that your assumptions are what he or she really wants—i.e., that you know better than your partner does. "But you love soft-shell crabs. I know you'd like to have them. Why don't you order them?" Keep it up, even after your partner sticks up for his or her choice. "But they have such a short season. You won't be able to have them next week." Or "They're really much better for you than pasta." "You're just being stubborn. I bet you didn't see them on the menu." Think of every ridiculous argument you can conjure up. Learn to tolerate and enjoy this kind of nonharmful teasing.
4. See if your partner (or you) can stick up for what is really wanted. See how you both handle the conflict.

WHAT IS ACCOMPLISHED?

1. You see how people easily acquiesce, or stick up for themselves and try to get what they want.
2. You become aware of whether you and your partner pay attention to each other's desires and feelings.
3. You check out assumptions about each other and learn that you can't have a good, open relationship unless you both are given the chance to express your opinions and act with self-care.

❁ BELTLINES

Part of caring about our friends and families is to be aware of their vulnerabilities and sensitivities and to respect them. We try to avoid "hitting below the belt." But some people deny that they have beltlines. They feel it's immature or petty to have off-limit vulnerabilities, so they deny their fragility. Some people are afraid that if they reveal their sore spots, others will take advantage of that knowledge and look for opportunities to aggravate those sores. Fearful of exploitation, they don't trust others with their secrets, and so they deny that there is any way to hurt or tease them.

Sometimes a denial of any vulnerability gives people an excuse to be insensitive to others. Conversely, a refusal to tease at all or to be the least bit risqué often marks a lack of interest or involvement. As beltlines are valuable in helping us avoid unnecessary hurt, they're also a way of identifying areas in which we're open to teasing.

It is easy to hit below the belt unwittingly because we are oblivious to our partner's feelings or because we have not been given enough information to know where that beltline is. Yet this kind of carelessness can

A Time for Caring

destroy trust and create conflict. It is important to share our sensitivities and articulate what areas we feel are out of bounds, and to identify as well the areas in which we are open to teasing, those things we are not especially bothered by.

Beltlines cover many areas: how we feel about our personal appearance, our jobs, our friends, our ability at sports. In short, they are anything about which we feel extremely sensitive or unsure of ourselves. Once beltlines are established we agree with our partner, friend, mate, or relative to consider that subject off limits.

HOW TO GO ABOUT IT

1. Each person should write a list of five beltlines.
   For example:
   > I don't like it when you tease me about being overweight.
   > It makes me feel bad when you criticize my friend Steve.
   > I think it's unfair when you bring up my past love affairs.
   > I don't like being teased when I cry at the movies.
   > I don't like it when you make negative comments about me in front of others.

   It will help you to clarify your beltlines if you try to go back over the times in your life when you felt hurt and remember what it was that was so upsetting—put yourself on a tour of your Hurt Museum.

2. Discuss the beltlines with your partner or family until you agree on those you feel are fair. Try to establish three beltlines for each party. Be aware if either of you is being oversensitive; it's no fun if there's nothing you can tease each other about. Try to come up with areas where you don't mind being teased: "I don't mind if you tease me about being bald, or about my bowling game, or the way I dress."

3. Once you have established beltlines it is the responsibility of each person to observe them. If your partner forgets or ignores a beltline, stick up for yourself and insist on its maintenance. In day-to-day situations, if someone inadvertently hits you below the beltline, take the opportunity to communicate your feelings. "It makes me feel very bad when you tease me about my curly hair. I know it doesn't seem like a big thing, but it bothers me. Would you please not do it anymore?" If we are unsure of another's beltlines, take the time to say, "Hey, does it bother you when I mention how short you are? If it does, just let me know and I'll cut it out."

4. Remember, it's necessary to tease or joust lightheartedly. It provides a safe anger-release and cultivates playful intimacy, *but* only when it doesn't hurt another's feelings. Once beltlines are known, safe teasing can continue.

WHAT IS ACCOMPLISHED?

1. By communicating our sensitivities we alert those who care for us to possible areas of conflict. Many of our inner hurt feelings are very personal, and we cannot expect others to know what they are unless we announce them.
2. By learning others' beltlines we can take care to avoid hurting their feelings. Caring grows when trust exists. The shared knowledge between friends that they won't hurt each other's feelings lets that caring trust flourish.

We all have rough spots in our intimate affairs—times when sexual communication or fun seems to fade, when sex becomes routine. Rather than feel desperate, bored, angry, or rejected, caring intimates do something about it. Caring sexual games are an amusing and unthreatening way for intimate partners to get over rough spots and learn more about each other. The games outlined here are aimed at increasing sensual, sexual, and emotional understanding between caring intimates.

❇ LOVE ARREST

Lovers are often so busy with work, children, television, and life in general that they often don't find time when they're not preoccupied or upset or exhausted to spend with their mate. In Love Arrest a couple agrees to spend a minimum of eight hours (it could be two days!) in their own bedroom in total isolation: no phones, no television, no reading—except out loud to each other.

HOW TO GO ABOUT IT

1. Make plans carefully and in detail: it's half the fun. Have everything you need on hand so that you don't have to leave the room. Prepare any food. Gather any games or books, toys, clothes, towels, bath oils that you need. You may want to plan an agenda for conversation, especially if there's a special problem to work out or an issue you've been putting off discussing.

   Remember, anything goes. This is a chance to do things you haven't had time for, or have felt inhibited about. You may want to spend the whole time talking, or making love; you may want to

A Time for Caring

have a pillow fight, or give each other a massage, or play chess, tell dirty jokes, read poetry to each other, or entertain each other with song and dance.
2. Set the date well in advance. Tell those who need to know that you'll be incommunicado.
3. Even if you and your lover can't find time to play Love Arrest, discuss what you would do *if* you could find the time. This is fun and often opens up discussion about hopes and wishes for the relationship.

WHAT IS ACCOMPLISHED?
1. You and your mate renew your commitment to intimacy.
2. You are able to instill new enthusiasm, closeness, and fun into your sexual relationship and escape your usual routine. By spending eight hours or more concentrating just on yourselves, you push worries and distractions from your minds and get back to the kind of simple, loving intimacy and pleasure you shared when you first met. There will be—temporarily—no kids, no bills, no meetings. Just the two of you.
3. You learn more about each other and perhaps work out problems that have been simmering for a long time.

❀ PILLOW FIGHTS

Many well-intentioned couples make the mistake of thinking that anger and aggression have no place in their sexual relationship, and so they're always "nice" and loving. They're making a big mistake. Often these people end up turned off to each other and resentful; they don't understand why they're having problems when they really care about each other. They need to understand that anger and just plain assertiveness are acceptable ingredients of a sexual relationship and can even enhance it. The pillow fight, that old childhood favorite, when regulated by Handicapping is a playful and safe avenue for sexual partners to express anger and aggression.

There are many times when we want to bop the one we love. But we aren't really deeply furious, just frustrated, irked, generally grumpy. There can be a shared intimacy when two partners can laugh, fight, and love at once. A pillow fight is the perfect release in the perfect context.

HOW TO GO ABOUT IT
1. Begin by establishing equalizing handicaps. (See page 342.) Strength must be equalized if it's to be a fair fight.

2. Set a time limit and allow for time-outs if one partner becomes overwhelmed or exhausted.
3. Let it all out!

WHAT IS ACCOMPLISHED?

1. You and your intimate partner can release anger while acting out sexual/aggressive feelings in a context of fun. You overcome fear of assertive behavior and of taboos against aggression. A partner who is usually weaker or passive learns to assert him- or herself.
2. Establishing handicaps makes both partners aware of basic power imbalances and makes it possible to fight as equals.

❊ SLEEPING PRINCE/SS

Routine kills sexual excitement. Adherence to strict roles or to rigid ideas of lovemaking kills sexual excitement. Unfortunately many couples get trapped into thinking that there are rules about sexual intimacy, roles they must play. One common pattern is that the male feels he must be dominant/assertive/active, the woman retiring and passive. Or both parties feel that they must always be equally active. Sleeping Prince/ss helps couples with stifling rules or ingrained routines to explore new roles and to experience new feelings. It gives sexual intimates a way to show their partners what they enjoy, what makes them feel good. It is a way to overcome shyness and to become comfortable with fantasy and playfulness and to expand the sexual context.

HOW TO GO ABOUT IT

1. One partner lies face down on the bed. If one partner in the relationship is usually the more active or dominant, that person should be the Sleeping Prince/ss.
2. The other partner then does whatever he or she wishes that will provide pleasure and sexual/sensual enjoyment.
3. The Sleeping Prince/ss must remain totally passive—no talking, making suggestions, using one's hands, or trying to take an active part.

The active partner can do anything that is pleasurable that he or she desires: talking, giving the partner a backrub or a bath, entertaining them with song or dance, making love.

A Time for Caring

WHAT IS ACCOMPLISHED?

1. By turning around the traditional roles in the sexual relationship, both partners have the chance to see how the other half feels and to see the benefits of being more flexible. The active partner learns that being submissive is enjoyable and doesn't threaten sexuality—that it can be a pleasure and a relief to give up some of the burden of being the dominant force. The active partner will also realize the disadvantage of always being the submissive partner. The submissive partner by becoming the aggressor unleashes feelings long stifled, can choose and direct the sexual activity. But the submissive partner also learns the drawbacks of being the aggressor all the time. Both parties, then, learn firsthand that flexibility of roles allows for the greatest pleasure and mutual satisfaction.
2. Release from any role—or image—frees up our inner caring feelings and lets others see us for who we really are. By relaxing the rules we learn to understand our own and our partner's sexual feelings and needs. We escape from routine. We try new things and overcome our shyness about communicating our desires or fantasies to our partner. We experience new feelings and learn the importance of exploration and experimentation.
3. Partners learn how to let go, shed their inhibitions, and become playful. They learn that there's no need to feel bashful when this kind of fun exhibitionism is sanctioned in a safe caring context. They learn the value of "being silly."

31

Research and Development:
DISCOVERING YOUR OWN CARING STYLE

If you've tried some of the exercises in chapters 29 and 30, chances are you're becoming aware of new things about yourself and those around you. Likely these are things you'd not noticed before: certain things you say, certain ways of doing things, surprising reactions to events in your life. The purpose of this chapter is to develop further that awareness, to get a clear picture of how you are as a caring person.

An awareness of our caring ways enables us to pinpoint our strengths and weaknesses, to shore up areas of poor caring, and to build on the strong points. With a clear understanding of our peculiar idiosyncrasies, of what we're receptive to or what turns us off, of our needs and predilections, we have in hand the information needed to deploy our caring energies efficiently without exhausting ourselves, so that we are able to maintain a balanced caring diet.

STEP ONE: REVIEW

If you've done some of the exercises in chapters 29 and 30 and have devised any of the caring plans called for in chapters 15 through 28, you have already accumulated a good deal of information about your caring ways and needs, your goals and accomplishments. The object now is to review this information to see what it reveals about how you go about giving and getting care.

A Time for Caring

Don't try to draw conclusions at this stage. Just be an investigator searching out clues and patterns. There are no right or wrong answers to the questions below. They're meant as prods to the search for clues to your caring ways.

HOW TO GO ABOUT IT

1. Check over your caring plans. Have you met your goals? Do you feel more comfortable with those specific arenas of caring? Have you run into new problems? Was there a common factor in the problems you experienced or in the goals you set out? What strategies have been most successful for you?
2. Look at the Me/Not Me exercise in each of these chapters. Has the balance of Me/Not Me activities shifted? Are you stuck in one or the other? Is it more balanced in some arenas than in others?
3. Review the Caring Journals that you kept in connection with your caring plans. Use these journal entries to help you see where you are today. Try to get a sense of the evolution of your caring abilities; pinpoint your current strengths and weaknesses. For example: How are you at taking risks? At trying out new caring skills? At asking for care? At sticking up for yourself? At paying attention to the Caring Balance in your life? What are the major obstacles to your caring progress? Have you felt the rewards of your caring?
4. Look again at the diagrams you made of the Caring Network (Chapter 14) and of your Caring Circles in each arena. What can you learn from them about how you care? Is there a balance of give-and-take? Are there noticeable gaps or overabundances? Is the network in good repair? Are you keeping in touch with those who are important to you? Are you alert for weak spots? If the diagram were redrawn to your ideal specifications, how would it differ?
5. What can you learn from the exercises you've tried? Which ones were easy and enjoyable? Which difficult? Were there some that put you off completely? Which were the most rewarding? Which of your caring skills needed the most work?

STEP TWO: QUESTIONNAIRE

The following questionnaire will aid in getting a clear picture of your caring ways by calling on you to think about your past, your childhood, old loves, friends, and family. You'll get a better idea of how you learned about caring and build a picture of the development of your caring nature through remembering the large and small caring events and habits in your life. Try to tune in to your inner self and give yourself leisure to let your mind drift over each question. Be sensitive to remembered details and be tough about seeing the bad as well as the good. And always try to think of instances or situations that verify your answers.

> Note: Not all questions will pertain to your own life; others will seem very general. When responding try to determine what is true *most of the time*; there are no clear-cut answers. It's not necessary to write down answers to each question, but try to mull over each a bit to see what memories or information it triggers. Make notes to help you in the next step of evaluation and planning.

SELF-CARE QUESTIONS

- Think about your image of yourself as a child. Were you confident? Independent? Can you remember things you were able to do for yourself? Certain skills you had—could you ride a bike, read well, make yourself lunch, walk to school alone, cheer yourself up when you were sad, introduce yourself to new friends?

- Did your family encourage you to learn new things? To do things for yourself? Were you able to ask them for help if you ran into trouble? Did you stick up for the things you wanted? Were your wishes respected? Or did you more often end up going along with others? Did your family do everything for you? Were you spoiled? Were they afraid of your trying new things? Afraid you'd get hurt? Did they reward your progress in learning?

- What things can you remember doing for yourself—taking a walk, buying something special with your allowance, learning about a subject that interested you, starting a program of muscle-building or a diet, teaching yourself to swim, reading a book that seemed important, thinking out a solution to a problem or thinking about nothing in particular, making a new friend, confronting a teacher? What things did you have trouble with? What were the results? Can you remember what things gave you the most pleasure? Which were the most painful?

LOVE RELATIONSHIP QUESTIONS

- Think about your first romance. Do you remember how you felt? Were you in love? Were you happy? Nervous? Was the feeling mutual? How did you first get together? What did you do on your first date? What did you do together? How often did you see each other? What did your friends and family think about the romance? How long did the relationship last? How did your feelings change toward each other? Did you fight? Grow apart? Move away? Change in your interests or needs? How did the romance end? How did you feel afterward?

- Think about your first sexual relationship. Do you remember how you felt? Were you in love? Were you happy? Nervous? How old were you? How long had you known the other person? Where did this first sexual encounter take place? Were you excited? Did you want the sexual consummation? Were you comfortable being with your partner? Did you enjoy the lovemaking? Was it disappointing? Did it change the relationship between the two of you? Did you feel loved? Sexy? Exploited? How long did the sexual relationship continue? Did it grow and change? Become routine? How did it end? How did you feel after it was over?

- How many times have you been in love? Do you fall in love easily? Or hardly ever? Do you walk around starry-eyed? Do you usually think it will last forever? Are you fond of romantic gestures? Is the love returned? How long do your relationships usually last? What happens when the first intensity wears off? Are you able to adjust? What do you think goes wrong? How long has your longest relationship lasted? How do your relationships usually end? Do you leave, or does your partner? Do you exit in anger, suddenly? Or does the romance die slowly until you drift apart? Do you usually want out first? How do you feel when it's over? Do you get involved again right away?

• What about the sexual content of your relationships? Is it of primary importance? Are you interested in sexual variety? Do you jump from partner to partner, or do you feel that sexual relationships improve with time and practice? Do you think that you're sexy? Do you worry about what your partner thinks? Are you usually satisfied sexually? Can you talk with your sexual partner about what pleases you? Do you know what arouses and satisfies you? Your partner? Are you always excited by sex? Ever feel it's boring or routine? Does sex for you have to be part of an intimate relationship, or are you more comfortable with more casual sportsex? Are you content with your sex life? Do you have fantasies of the ideal sexual relationship?

FAMILY QUESTIONS

• Describe the "layout" of your family. Were there lots of relatives close by? Did you see them often? What kind of relationships did you have with your grandparents? Is there divorce in the family? Are you one of many children? An only child? A city or country kid? Poor? Well-to-do?

• Was your family talkative or quiet? Strict or permissive? Did you have a favorite sister or brother? Parent? Why? Did the family do things together? What? Were there any special activities or trips in which everyone participated? What did you do to celebrate birthdays? Christmas? Do you remember a special birthday or gift? How did you fit in? What do you remember most vividly about your homelife? What were your favorite family activities? What did you like to do together most? Read? Play board games? Be read to? Have company? Play catch? Could you usually find someone to do these things with? What are your saddest memories? Do you remember any family crises—an illness or death, loss of a job? How did the family solve the problem?

• How did things work in your family? Who went out to work? Who was home when you got home from school? Who doled out the punishment? What was it? Who did you go to with a problem? Were you confident of getting help? Or sympathy? What kinds of help did you ask for? Did anyone ask you for help or favors? Who took care of you if you were sick? Who helped with homework? Or if you had a fight with a friend? Did you have many responsibilities? Or was everything taken care of? What were your special chores? Did you do them willingly? Were they too difficult or time-consuming? Did they interfere with your fun? Were you rewarded for them? With an allowance? Did you get enough attention? Did you ever get special treatment? Were you ever disappointed in your family? Did you remember feeling neglected or misunderstood about something?

- Was yours an affectionate or demonstrative family? Did both parents hug and kiss you? Until what age? Were you embarrassed by affection? Did your parents or brothers and sisters show affection to each other? Did you know your parents loved you? Did they say so?

- How was anger expressed in your family? Was it ignored? Did it come out in circuitous ways? Was there yelling and screaming? Did your parents or brothers and sisters fight? Did their fighting bother you? Are you afraid of fights? Do you enjoy them? How was punishment meted out? By spanking? Having privileges taken away? Allowance cut? Do you remember why you were punished in specific instances? How did you feel?

(Now go over the same family questions and answer them for your *current* situation.)

SOCIAL QUESTIONS

- Do you remember your best childhood friend? How did you meet that friend? Why do you think you became so close? What did you do together? What did you talk about? What made that person special? What happened to this friend? Are you still in touch?

(Answer the same questions for your best friend as a teen-ager, and in college or early adulthood.)

- Did you make friends easily as a child? Or were you shy? Did you ever want to be friends with someone you were too shy to approach? Were you afraid of strangers? Or did you prefer being alone? Did you have many friends or just a few close friends? Was there a crowd or a neighborhood group you palled around with? How did you fit in? What did you do together? Play games? Watch TV? Tell jokes? Did you think of yourself as popular? Were you considered attractive? Describe how you looked. Were you uncomfortable socially? Did you participate in all the school social activities? Plays? Dances? Did you want to? Were you chosen for sports teams? For class offices? What things did you do by yourself?

- Do you remember doing anything for a friend or having a friend do something special for you? Was helping each other out part of the friendship? Or sharing secrets? Or giving advice? Or cheering each other up? How did you feel about asking a favor? Or being asked? Or did the friendship center around shared activities or hobbies? Were you affectionate toward any of your friends? Did you exchange gifts or birthday cards? Invite them for lunch? Were you ever hurt or betrayed by a friend? How did you cope with the situation? What caused the problem? Did you resolve it?

(Now answer these same questions for your current friendships).

- How do you keep in touch with your friends nowadays? Are you on the telephone often? Do you write to friends who are far away? Send postcards while on vacation? Do you have friends you don't hear from for years at a time? Friends you've regretfully lost touch with?

- What is your current mix of friends like? Many pals? A few close ones? Are you satisfied with your friendships? Do you spend enough time alone? What do you do with your friends? When you're by yourself? Are there friends you can ask for help? Who come to you for help? Do you often ask favors of friends? Or are you likely to take care of things yourself? Do you do different things with different friends? Do you wish you had friends to share certain thoughts or certain interests with? Do you take the initia-

A Time for Caring

tive in your friendships? Or are you a follower? If you meet someone you like, will you make the move to further the friendship? Are you an entertainer? A party giver? Are you comfortable meeting new people? How do you do at cocktail parties? Do you prefer to spend time with just one friend? Or a group? Do you feel that people like you? Do you talk about yourself easily? What do you say? Or are you likely to ask about the other person? Do you reveal personal information, or are you more likely to talk about the weather or news events, or tell jokes? How are you as a host? As a guest?

WORK QUESTIONS

- Did you like to go to school? Did you enjoy the schoolwork and the studying? What were your favorite subjects? Was there a teacher you especially liked? Why? Was there much homework? Did you do it willingly? How were your grades? Was there much pressure on academic achievement? How did you feel about getting good grades? Was it important to you? Did you have to work very hard at your studies? Did you ever cut classes? Cut up in class? What other school activities were you involved in? Were your friends involved in the same things? Did your family participate in any way?

- Do you remember your first job? Was it a summer job? Working for your family? Was it enjoyable? Difficult? An interesting experience? Did you resent having to work? How did you feel about earning money? What did you do with the money you earned?

- How were the chores distributed in your house? Did everyone have specific chores? Try to remember what each person (parents included) did. How did you feel about doing your chores? Were you cooperative? Were you asked to do too much? Did you get an allowance? Was it fair? How did you spend it?

- What kind of work do you do now? Is it what you like to do? Do you take pleasure in going to work? Are you fairly paid for your work? Is there a different kind of career or work you'd choose?

If so, are you pursuing what you want? Are you happy with the amount of time you put in at your work? Do you "work" on your home or your hobbies in your free time?

• How do you get on at work? Is there a great deal of pressure and competition? Do you like this? Would you be inclined to pitch in and help coworkers on a project? Are you a better follower or leader? More comfortable with those above or below your job level? Is there a sense of teamwork in your work? Or do you pretty much work alone?

• Are you sociable with the people you work with? What do you do socially with coworkers? Chat? Have lunch? Participate in office parties or other activities? How? Are many of your friends work-related? Do you socialize outside the office? Are any of your close friends also your coworkers?

COMMUNITY QUESTIONS

• What kind of community do you live in—a small town, a big city, a rural area? Is there a sense of neighborliness on your block? In the community? Or does everyone go their own way? What organization or charities or causes are popular in your community?

• Do you socialize with your neighbors? Participate in community causes? Are you too busy? Not interested? Have you ever done volunteer work? Do you feel it's your duty to do your part? How do you feel about public assistance? Welfare? Community job-programs? Are you involved with things that directly concern your family—PTA, church groups, city council, block associations, social clubs? Or do certain issues interest you—the environment, voting rights? How much time do you give to community interests? Are you a leader in these situations, or do you pitch in with whatever needs to be done? Do you donate money to certain causes? Use your influence or power to get action? Do you belong to many clubs? What kind?

- Do you have a sense of personal effectiveness? Or a sense that what your group is doing will have impact? Do you believe your participation is important no matter what? Would you like to get more involved in community action? Are you shy about participating? Are you afraid you haven't the right skills?

- Do you read the newspapers each day? Watch the news on television? What interests you? Do you feel there's too much bad news? Do you get the feeling that the world is hostile, or doomed? Or do you feel hopeful for the future, for improving the quality of life? Do you vote? Do you feel it's important? Do you feel a part of the larger community?

- How do you feel about strangers? Do you talk to people on the bus, or passersby on the street? Do you know the shopkeepers you deal with? Do you ever offer help to a stranger who looks lost, or ill? Would you go up and introduce yourself to a new neighbor? Do you ever pass the time chatting to someone standing in line with you? Do strangers ever try to talk to you? Have you ever had a bad or frightening experience with a stranger?

STEP THREE: DEFINING YOUR CARING STYLE

Now the task is to evaluate the information you've gathered in steps one and two, and see what you can learn about the way you care.

Take several sheets of paper and divide them into two columns headed as follows:

I do . . .	I don't . . .

Make a separate sheet for self-care, sexual care, family, social, work, community.

Using the information you've gathered from the review in step one and the questionnaire in step two, try to pull out the hard facts about your caring style and enter them in the appropriate column. Look for patterns and repetitions, both caring and careless. Things that you did once or twice aren't indicative of anything. And be fair with yourself. Don't exaggerate either your care or your carelessness.

One exercise you can use to help yourself ferret out your caring habits is to ask, "What did I do when . . . ."
>   . . . I was sick?
>   . . . my mate criticized me?
>   . . . my friends asked a favor?
>   . . . I didn't feel like making dinner?
>   . . . guests stayed with me?
>   . . . strangers asked for directions?
>   . . . I felt like making love?
>   . . . my kids got in trouble at school?
>   . . . I was overtired?
>   . . . my friend needed to talk and I was busy?

Here are some sample entries:

SELF

I do . . .	I don't . . .
• I make it a point to go to the dentist once a year. • I treat myself to gifts when I've worked hard or am feeling blue. • When I'm all wound up, I take a hot bath. • I don't hesitate to call Sandy or Mike when I need advice or a sympathetic ear. • I've been sticking to my exercise program. • I take a little time each day	• I never manage to find a doctor I like or get regular checkups. • I'm careless about spending money. Often I buy too many frivolous things I don't need and that I tire of easily. • I stay up too late on work nights. • My apartment is always a mess, and I feel uncomfortable when I spend much time at home.

to assess how I'm feeling and what's happening during the day.

- I waste a lot of time reading junk magazines and then end up having to work instead of getting a good night's rest.
- Unless I'm with friends or at work, I never eat properly—just soda and candy bars.

SEXUAL

I do . . .

- After a long time I'm finally involved with a man I really care about.
- He's very affectionate when we make love.
- He gives a great backrub.
- I feel very confident in bed with him.
- I feel I'm more sensitive to his needs as I know him better.
- Sometimes I like to kid around in bed; it's fun making love and laughing.

I don't . . .

- I can't tell him when I object to something. I'm afraid of hurting him.
- He doesn't seem to care whether I reach a climax or not.
- He doesn't enjoy oral sex as much as I do.
- He still feels a little defensive if I'm too aggressive.

FAMILY

I do . . .

- I'm pretty good about keeping in touch with Mom and Dad and my sister.
- We always make it a point to spend the holidays together.
- I feel good about having helped Mom and Dad more last year. I think they know they can count on me.

I don't . . .

- I'm terrible about keeping up contact with more distant relatives, especially Aunt Kit and Uncle Ed.
- I wish my sister Adele and I were closer. We always avoid personal subjects when we see each other. It would never occur to me to call her just to chat.

• I enjoy my nephews and feel I give them something special.

• My family is very separate from my everyday life and my friends. I could include them in more of my doings.

SOCIAL

I do . . .	I don't . . .
• I'm comfortable at big parties. I can put people at ease. • I have lots of friends. • I like to give parties. • People at work like me. • I've enjoyed introducing Janice to photography. • I go out of my way to meet new people. • I like to show people around my town.	• I'm terrible about writing letters or keeping in touch with old friends and relatives. • I always forget birthdays. • Since Allen moved away I don't have a good male friend to confide in. • Often I'm too busy to spend much time alone with my close friends. • I don't have much patience with people's problems. • I don't take criticism well. • I make snap judgments about people on first impression.

WORK

I do . . .	I don't . . .
• I'm very diligent and conscientious about my job. • I enjoy the competition among the people in my company. • I keep up with the news in my field. • I generate enthusiasm for our work at the office.	• I tend to let my work become routine and then I feel bored. • I procrastinate during the day and often end up working on weekends. • I don't feel strongly about the work I do anymore. • I don't have the guts to start over in a profession I'd like more.

A Time for Caring

COMMUNITY

I do . . .	I don't . . .
• I keep up with the news. • I often chat with strangers and make it a point to get to know new people in the neighborhood. • I do my part in our neighborhood association. • I set aside part of my earnings for charitable donations.	• I'm careless about voting; it seems a waste of time. • I have no patience with committees and groups; I get bored. • I'd like to do something to help the environmental clean-up drive, but I don't know how to go about it.

In each category try to think of as many things as possible, no matter how trivial. Often it is in small things that we uncover our idiosyncrasies.

When you've completed this stage of your analyzing, summarize what you've learned. Write out a brief statement that clarifies for you the important facts about how you go about caring. Try to articulate the essential facts about your caring habits. Pay particular attention to whether your Caring Network is in good order, whether you're an active carer and have established any caring rituals.

Your goal is to learn what kind of carer you are. The summary should tell you whether you like people with ideas or enthusiasm, people who need help or need to provide it, whether you're stimulated by art or artifice. You should also learn what turns you off, what kind of caring you can't provide, what kind of people you can't abide.

Here's an example: "I take good care of myself physically. However, I overindulge myself with meaningless possessions and drive myself crazy by being overcritical of myself. I have many sexual encounters. It's not hard for me to meet new people and sometimes I have fun, but I can't seem to sustain a sexual relationship. I seem to concentrate a good bit of caring on my friends. I like to entertain them and help everyone have a good time. I'm good at giving advice and love to introduce people to new things and encourage them. However, when a crisis arises, I'm not very good at handling things or being supportive. I love my family and am usually the one to initiate discussions and activities. But I don't spend much time with them on a day-to-day basis. In fact, I get bored if there's not something special going on. And often I'm not very observant about their moods. I'm very much up on the news and I vote, but I'm a total disaster when it comes to community activities. I don't belong to any clubs or organizations, and I never volunteer my time to charity. I would say my caring is reasonably balanced between giving and getting. However, I probably get more than I give from my family, and with my friends it's the other way around. If I have any personal caring rituals, they would be: the hot bath I take after work; the big first-day-of-spring party I 'throw' each year; the three newspapers I carry in every day for my office group to share; the special restaurant I take my parents to every year on their anniversary."

STEP FOUR: SET CARING GOALS

Just seeing how you go about caring will enhance your ability to do so. Perhaps you are content with your present level of caring and with your present skills. It's not necessary to be good at every aspect of caring. It is important to make use of the skills you have and apply them more frequently and appropriately, important to solidify through frequent use the caring rituals you've established, and to keep paying attention to opportunities for caring.

If there are gaps in your caring skills or needs that you'd like to remedy, now is the time to set goals for improving your caring ways.

In enumerating your goals, be specific about what you hope to achieve. Is it a certain skill that's missing? An existing strength you want to build up? A potential ritual you'd like to reinforce? An area of caring that's been neglected—family or friends or in the community? A need for care that's been neglected? And be realistic; don't tackle too many things at once.

Here are some examples of caring goals:
- "Since I enjoy introducing people to new things, I'm going to be on the lookout for ways to do more of this."
- "I'm not happy about the way I avoid getting involved in others' problems. I'm going to look into this further and find out

A Time for Caring 367

what I can do to overcome it. Maybe it's just a matter of skills. I don't know how to handle these situations, so I feel helpless and useless."

- "I get such pleasure when Sally and I spend a Sunday afternoon together alone having brunch and reading the paper. But we hardly ever find the time to do it. I think we should make it a ritual to spend a solo Sunday afternoon every other week."

As you did in the case of your caring plans, you must make a plan for achieving your goals, decide what's needed in the way of time, practice, money, help from friends or family.

32

Becoming a Caring Activist

Caring Activists are people whose caring activities are integrated into their daily lives. They don't just go around feeling sympathetic or caring, they act. And they work at improving and monitoring their caring consciousness and skills so that their acts are effective. Caring Activism doesn't come naturally. It's a result of attentiveness and planning.

STEP ONE: PLAN A DAILY CARING AGENDA

The Caring Agenda is the basic care-planning tool, a checklist of planned caring actions that you schedule into each day. It serves as a constant reminder of caring goals, duties, and aspirations. The Caring Agenda helps monitor the balance of caring, prods you to practice caring rituals, hounds you if you're postponing caring tasks, keeps you from getting caught off guard. The few minutes a day spent planning the agenda pays off handsomely in the efficient deployment of caring energies.

HOW TO GO ABOUT IT

1. Set aside five or ten minutes each day to prepare the next day's agenda. In the first minute or so, just relax and think about what needs to be done, what current caring problems need to be taken care of. Ask yourself questions to help you plan, for example: What's going on at the office? Who in the family most urgently needs attention? I'm feeling so tired from work-

ing on the clean-up drive. What can I do to perk myself up? I wonder if there's anything I can do to help Sid while he's recovering? Whom do I owe letters to? Whom have I lost touch with? What care-learning exercises am I working on now?

   Note: It's helpful to keep a running list of people you want to call, visit or write to and a reminder list of birthdays and special occasions. You can consult this list when preparing your daily agenda.
2. Make a list of caring activities for the coming day. Be realistic; don't bite off more than you can chew. The quality of your caring is important; overloading yourself is likely to sacrifice quality. You want to feel good about yourself at the end of the day, not irritated by what you haven't accomplished.
3. Figure out when, where, and how you're going to accomplish these things. You don't need to go into elaborate detail. Still, it's helpful to earmark a certain time for a particular task or to note down any particular information you want to convey in a phone call. It's also helpful to prerehearse a potentially difficult caring task. The more carefully you plan, the more likely you will be to fulfill your agenda efficiently and with the least possible anxiety.
4. Pay attention to the Caring Balance. After you make your list, label each item on your agenda with a P, C, or S to indicate if the action is one of care providing, care consuming, or self-care. This will give you an idea of the balance (or lack of balance) in your caring routine. Every day will not reflect a perfectly balanced schedule, but over a period of weeks you can see if you consistently do more care-consuming than providing or are lacking in self-care, and so on. You'll also see if certain caring arenas are overstressed at the neglect of others: if your family's being ignored while you spend too much time on community activities, for example. Or if you're neglecting your health while tending to your family's demands. This will help you see which kinds of caring actions you need to stress and which you need to ease up on.

   Note: You'll notice that few of the things on these agendas are specifically care-consuming. Most of the care you consume is instigated by others, unless there's something special you ask for. But in evaluating the Caring

Balance in your life, review the day to see who called you, or wrote, or did a favor, or stopped to chat, or gave advice, or brought a gift, or did your laundry, or cooked your dinner.

5. Your agenda should include as a matter of routine a few minutes to make an entry in your Caring Journal and to reflect on your Inner Dialogue so that you stay tuned to your feelings and actions. Any caring exercises or rituals you're working on should also be included on the agenda.

Here are a couple of sample agendas:

Wednesday, May 14

- Ⓟ • Call Patty.
- Ⓟ • Call Gigi to give her the information about the party.
- Ⓒ • Ask Frank to come over after tennis and help me put up the new blinds.
- Ⓟ • Go pick up Grandma's laundry after work and take it over to her.
- Ⓢ • Play tennis (6:30).
- Ⓢ • Take vitamins (with lunch).
- Ⓟ • Write to Eddie to tell him how upset I am that he dropped out of school.
- Ⓟ/Ⓢ • If Judy calls, tell her I can't take care of her dog anymore unless she gives me money for food.
- Ⓟ • Take Jenny to lunch and ask her how the job is going. Offer to help with writing the prospectus.
- Ⓢ • Do my nails (before work).
- Ⓟ • "Perfect Strangers" exercise. Talk to that redheaded lady who's always at the Laundromat.
- • Caring Journal entry—tomorrow's agenda.

Thursday, May 15

- Ⓟ/Ⓢ • Talk to Judy about the dog since I didn't get to it yesterday.
- Ⓟ • Bring in food for the coffee break at work. (Pick up food at deli on way to work.)
- Ⓢ • Take my suit to the tailor (on way to work).
- Ⓢ • Clean the kitchen (after breakfast).
- Ⓟ • Help Annie move to her new apartment this evening.
- Ⓟ • Take flowers to Annie.
- Ⓟ • Call Frances to see how her broken arm feels.

A Time for Caring

- Ⓟ • Write to my folks (lunch hour).
- Ⓟ • Call my sister, make plans for getting together.
- Ⓒ • Go to the Carlsons' for dinner.
- Ⓟ • "Perfect Strangers" exercise. Woman at flower shop, perhaps someone waiting to be served at deli.
- • Caring Journal entry—tomorrow's agenda.

STEP TWO: KEEP A CARING JOURNAL

A Caring Activist uses the Caring Journal as an ongoing record of all aspects of self-care, care consuming and care providing. It is a personal diary of caring obstacles, accomplishments, goals, rewards, successes, failures, and insights. Depending on your time and interest, you may make each day's entry as brief or lengthy as you wish. However, it's important to make an entry each day. Use the questions that follow to help you recall and evaluate your caring day. Each day's entry should include the following items:

1. Review the day's Caring Agenda. What did you accomplish? What were the results of your actions? (Appreciation? Silence? Criticism? Self-confidence?) How did you feel about your actions? How did you feel about the responses to your actions? What was most rewarding?
2. Examine those items from your agenda that you did not accomplish. What were the problems you faced? Were you hesitant to follow through? Why? How can you handle caring tasks that are hard to tackle? Are you overloaded?
3. Look at your Caring Network. Are you keeping in touch with people who are important to you? Did you spend much time with family? friends? lovers? coworkers? What did you do? Did you meet anyone new? Have an intimate conversation? Did you have an opportunity to share your thoughts, ideas, feelings, home, possessions? Is your caring environment safe? Did you encounter any unpleasant or careless situations? Are there people in your life you'd rather see less of? Can you do something about ridding yourself of toxic people?
4. Check out the Caring Balance. What did you do for yourself today? (Read? Take a walk? Buy a new tie? Get a good night's sleep? Repair the towel rack?) What kind of caring did you

provide? (Give advice? Do a favor? Keep a friend company? Help with a chore? Do the usual household duties? Share your lunch? Tell the kids some new jokes? Write a letter? Compliment your spouse's sense of humor?) How did you do at consuming care? (Who called you? Did you ask a favor? Did anyone help you get your work done? Did you get a compliment? Were you able to accept whatever care was offered you? Or criticism?) Are you doing your share of caring? Receiving your share?

5. Monitor your care-learning progress. Are you becoming more observant? More sensitive to others' needs and feelings? To your own? Can you usually figure out how to handle a given situation appropriately and efficiently? Are your skills adequate to your caring challenges? In what areas do you feel you've improved? What still needs work? Are you becoming more confident of your caring abilities? More able to take risks? Are you aware of your own caring strengths? Do you make use of them? Do you have personal caring rituals? Are you working on any particular caring exercises? Do you feel more self-confident? Are you seeing the rewards of your caring actions? What are they? Are you aware of new feelings?

Using the above questions as guidelines, fill in the daily Caring Journal form. Rate each area good, fair, or poor. At the bottom of the page write a few lines that summarize the day's caring or that point up special factors that help you understand and evaluate the current caring status.

For example: "Today I spent a lot of time caring for myself. I'm still recovering from the two weeks of round-the-clock caring for Gary. I didn't have the time or strength to do caring things for others, except to do my usual household chores. I think that it will take me a few days of focusing on self-care to build up a reserve of energy so I can extend myself again. At the moment I feel drained, but I want to keep tabs on that so I don't get too self-absorbed. But I feel good about being able to tell when I need to recoup. And I feel good about having been able to help Gary."

CARING JOURNAL

Date _____

Caring Agenda Completion	Good	Fair	Poor
Caring Network Intimate Care			
Family			
Friends			
Community			
Caring Balance Self-Care			
Care Providing			
Care Consuming			
Care-Learning Progress			

Summary and Evaluation: _____

_____

_____

_____

_____

_____

_____

_____

STEP THREE: RECOGNIZE AND DEVELOP PERSONAL CARING RITUALS

In addition to the common social rituals we all depend on, most of us have a whole slew of personal rituals. Some we use to communicate special feelings of love and affection to our closest friends and family. Favorite songs, special ways of celebrating birthdays and holidays, personal words of endearment, family traditions, routines repeated between two or more people, are all rituals that touch our lives with personalized gestures and feelings. It may be our custom always to bring flowers when we visit a special friend, or to call our lover by some silly name when we want to communicate a deep feeling of affection. We may make it a habit to fix our spouse a cup of tea each night before we go to bed.

Other rituals convey messages of anger or hurt. Fighting rituals are as important as loving ones in supporting relationships. As football games and boxing matches can be viewed as ritualized hostility releases, so too do individuals need safe and mutually understood rituals for expressing anger. Pillow fights, sexual slapping or pinching, a time of day set aside for gripes, teasing . . . all can be ritualized forms of anger-release.

Still other rituals we use to care for ourselves. They may be the day-to-day routines that give a pattern to our lives, or they may be special things that we do on specific occasions—for instance, when we're hurt or lonely or celebrating or deserving of a reward.

Part of the task of being a Caring Activist is to become aware of the caring rituals of your daily life and be on the alert for actions and habits with ritual potential. Once recognized, they should be used at every opportunity and refined and reinforced until they become second nature.

SOME HINTS FOR IDENTIFYING YOUR CARING RITUALS

1. Review agendas, journal, the questionnaire in Chapter 32. Look for repeated gestures such as gift giving, frequent visits to a special restaurant, playing a favorite song, having the same thing for breakfast each day, an annual outing with the family. Don't feel that a gesture is too trivial or eccentric to mention. It is the small and very personal habits that form a large part of our ritualized caring actions.
2. Consider your relationship with those closest to you. Jot down those things that you tend to do over and over again with and for each person.
3. Think about what things others say or do for you that make you happy or reinforce your feeling of being cared for. Think

about the things you do for yourself under various circumstances.

Here are some examples of others' caring rituals that will give you an idea of the kinds of things that qualify.

1. "Andrew and I always start off with the same record—one of our favorites—when we sit down to dinner with friends. People now know that we do this and look forward to it because it symbolizes the beginning of a gathering of friends. It reinforces our Caring Network."
2. "Every Christmas our family plays charades. This is part of our celebration in the way that stuffed turkey or caroling or hanging stockings is for other families. We all look forward to playing together and prepare especially elaborate and tricky charades. Our other family custom is that those who can keep their eyes open stay up for the movie *A Christmas Carol*, a particular version with Alastair Sim that always is shown very late Christmas Eve. We've all seen it twenty times, but it's a ritual."
3. "Once a month a different person is put in charge of bringing a special treat to the office. Sometimes it's sweets, sometimes exotic food. Everyone takes half an hour to hang out together, bosses and secretaries alike. It has built group spirit and camaraderie."
4. "I remember vividly that when I was a child my mom would make a special Sunday 'Toothpick Picnic' for us kids that we would eat in front of the fireplace or in the attic, depending on the weather. It would just be simple cold cuts and cheese, fruit, and vegetables cut into squares and served on toothpicks, but it seemed grand to us and very adventurous. It's a custom I've now passed along to my own kids, with equal success."
5. "When I need some reassurance and attention from my spouse I just have to say, 'Hug Alert!' That is our personal distress signal: whatever is going on, wherever we are, he knows to take the time to give me some comfort. This comes in handy when we're in public or when we've been too busy and preoccupied to keep each other up-to-date. We've even used it when we're fighting, to reassure each other of our underlying feelings of concern and love."

6. "Before we go to bed at night my spouse and I always sit down and have a cup of tea together, no matter how busy or tired we are. This gives us time to talk quietly and decompress from the day's busy activities, and keeps us from drifting apart."
7. "I have noticed that I've developed the habit of calling my friends by their initials, like LT (for Lew Thomas) or GG (for Grace Goodman), as a form of affectionate nickname."
8. "Whenever I want to look really spiffy—if a big occasion is coming up or if I want to feel confident about myself, I take the time to do my nails: a real manicure. I use this as a personal ritual to tell myself, 'You're ready to go out and get them!'"
9. "I'm the family archivist. I'm always taking photos of our travels, our activities, our friends. Then, at the end of each year, I make an album. A few years ago I started sending 'leftover' pictures to friends and family. Well, most everyone loved getting the pictures so much that it's become a habit with me to take extra pictures and do an annual 'picture mailing.' It's something I feel proud of and something that's unique to me."

Once you've identified your caring rituals or certain behavior with potential as caring ritual, the next step is to incorporate and reinforce it into your everyday life. Here are some guidelines:

1. Give it a name, like "Hug Alert" or "Toothpick Picnic" in the examples above. This gives your action a more concrete status as a ritual.
2. Clarify its form. Don't just say, "I take a hot bath at night" or "I send pictures to my friends." The more you can pinpoint the specifics, the more solid and personal the ritual becomes. List the specifics of your ritual. "As often as possible I take a hot bath as soon as I get home from work. First I turn off the telephone. I pour a glass of wine and take my mail and set it on the table by the tub. I pour a little bath oil in the tub, and while the bath is running I undress and brush my hair vigorously. Then I soak in the tub for about ten to fifteen minutes, sip my wine, and read the mail. I leave my thick terry robe on the hook by the door so that I can wrap up when I get out of the tub."

3. Schedule it into your Caring Agenda. Whether it's your daily bath or your annual photo mailing, remind yourself and make time to do it.
4. Look for opportunities to use it. If you and your spouse have a secret distress signal like "Hug Alert," call on it to smooth over the difficult times where possible. The more you use a ritual, the easier it becomes.
5. Where appropriate, share it. Let your family and friends in on your rituals. Don't keep them a secret. Say, "This is one of our favorite songs. We like to play it when friends come to dinner." Or "Here's a copy of an article about fishing that was in yesterday's paper. I like to clip articles about things my friends are involved in."

STEP FOUR: MAINTAIN AND STRENGTHEN THE CARING NETWORK

Keeping the Caring Network in good shape is essential to Caring Activism. It's an ongoing commitment that takes work and careful attention. As a fisherman checks his nets daily, we must be alert to snags and weak spots in our network, to small holes which, if neglected, will become so big that our valued relationships will slip through.

Maintenance of the Caring Network is a matter of keeping in touch with the members of your network, keeping current with each person's activities, making a special effort to stay in contact with those who are out of town or who move away.

Strengthening the network requires upgrading the quality of care and deepening existing bonds.

There are several ways of tending to the Caring Network:

1. Have a clear understanding of your Caring Network: who your family and friends are, what ideas and issues you're involved in, who provides you with care and vice versa. Keep updated lists of people you want to call, or write, or visit, so you can schedule them into your daily agenda. An up-to-date address book and birthday record is another useful network-maintenance tool.
2. Let others know how important they are to you. Be clear about

how they fit into your life. Tell them you value the contributions they make to your network and solicit their goodwill and participation. "Mary, I hope you know how much it meant to me when you stopped by to help with the kids. I hope we can always do such things for each other. It gave me a great feeling to know I could ask for your help."
3. Don't let geographical distance inhibit the caring connection between you and your friends. When someone in your network moves away, or if you go on an extended trip out of town, it will take extra effort to keep current and to offer support and care. But it can be done. Clip local news stories, save bits of news or gossip, forward mail and messages, let your friends know they're missed.
4. Encourage the expansion and overlapping of networks. Be the sponsor of get-togethers at which you can introduce your friends to each other. Have your friends bring in new people to the group. Give some thought to people you know who share like interests and concerns and be the catalyst for getting them together. For example: If you have two friends who love to play Scrabble, invite them over to play. It will give them common ground to form a friendship, in addition to their connection with you. Or if an out-of-town friend tells you she knows someone who is going to be in your area on business, offer to have her friend to dinner. Be the liaison between your sister who's buying a puppy and your friend who's selling them, between your coworker who's unhappy in her job and your neighbor who's hiring new staff. Build your interconnecting network.
5. Be alert to chances for deepening existing relationships. Schedule Walk/Talks: page 304), take time to think about your friends' needs and interests and suggest activities you know they will like. Find common interests, encourage and support their goals and dreams, solicit their confidences.
6. Find the time. This most important of all qualities is the only way to be sure your network will thrive. Don't get too caught up in your day-to-day struggles to find time for those you care about. Your daily agenda will help you do this.
7. Be open to new people and experiences. Don't cut off possible opportunities for expanding the Caring Network by being fearful of strangers, threatened by competition from others, too

smugly satisfied with the status quo, or by too narrowly defining or imaging others.
8. Don't be afraid to make judgments. Evaluation of your network is important. People who try to be friends with everybody end up neglecting those who should get more specialized attention. It's part of Caring Activism to establish criteria of careworthiness and not to overload the Caring Network with unrewarding people and things that use up precious caring energy that would be better spent elsewhere. A well-maintained Caring Network also maintains a reasonable balance of give-and-take and doesn't neglect a whole arena of caring—the family or self-care—while being overbalanced in another.

STEP FIVE: BE PREPARED TO HANDLE TOUGH CARING SITUATIONS

The greatest test of our caring commitment and skill is our caring response "under fire," that is, in situations where there are problems, a crisis, confrontation. Handling the touchy situations is an inevitable part of Caring Activism. You cannot get away with doing just the easy tasks, with being the "nice guy," with the fun side of care, with giving compliments or gifts. Sooner or later a situation will arise that requires your strength to see your way through the demands of love and the responsibilities of care. You may not be entirely comfortable with the demands made on you, but dealing with them head on is part of the caring contract. Family illness, death, personal problems come to us all at one time or another. Paradoxically, these difficult and stressful situations often prove the most rewarding in terms of bringing people together and provide an increased sense of self-worth from coping with them. And although today you may be called on to offer care and support to someone in trouble, if your network is strong you will receive the same when you are in need.

CARING IN CRISIS

When illness strikes a family member and you are called on to provide daily care, when someone is going through a divorce or the death of a loved one and needs endless support and comfort, when continued demands for care, perhaps from an unlovable but dependent relative, seem to threaten your ability to care or make you feel resentful or afraid, there are some things you can do to ease your task.

1. Face the job ahead. Don't kid yourself. Make a list of the time and kind of care you imagine you will be called to give. Work your regular schedule around the caring demands. Make an agenda that provides time for yourself and for friends, even if it is in shorter supply than usual.
2. Educate yourself about the crisis at hand. If you're suddenly called upon to care for someone who's ill, read about the illness you're dealing with. Learn the symptoms and treatment and expected course of the illness. Get someone to teach you how to give shots or change bedpans or give a massage or change sheets while the patient's in bed.

    If you're suddenly responsible for others' care after a death or crisis in the family, learn what you need to know about wills and probate, mortgage payments and insurance claims, and car tune-ups and budgeting.

    Don't hesitate to ask for help. Call on your friends and your friends' friends. Make use of community groups and services. Don't let ignorance or shyness hamper your ability to provide care and add to your own stress.
3. Whenever possible tell those you are caring for about your schedule. Let them know when you plan to be available and why you are not *always* going to be around. Let them know what other things in your life you have to attend to. Try to get their input and suggestions to tell you how and at what times they'd like to be able to depend on you for care.
4. Set up a support network for *yourself*. Enlist friends and family. Ask some people to step in for you for short periods of time to free up your time. Ask others to do errands and favors for you so you do not have so many outside tasks to attend to. Have an escape hatch . . . a place you can go to let off steam, a friend you can vent anger and frustration on or who will cheer you up. Avoid becoming overly exhausted by the demands on you.
5. Face your own fears. For example, if you are caring for someone who is ill, you may find that just going to the hospital

A Time for Caring

takes all your strength. Devise a system to ease you into your tasks. Get a friend to accompany you the first few times you go. Speak to the doctor to get explanations of problems that the sick person is experiencing. Time your visits so you can see the patient when he or she is not being given tests or resting.
6. Give yourself credit. Don't be a martyr. Recognize what a positive and caring thing you're doing. Give yourself a pat on the back.

CARING CONFRONTATIONS

We all have found ourselves in the middle of a discussion that has disintegrated into exchanges of opinions such as: "You don't know what you're talking about." "That will never work." "I'm right and you're wrong!" "That's not fair." To resolve the disagreement and reach some kind of mutual understanding, we have to muster all our caring reserves. There are also situations where mistrust pollutes our relationship, when we need desperately to overcome bad feelings and find ways of explaining our point of view. How sympathetic can we be to a friend's marital crisis if we think divorce is the logical answer, not reconciliation? How can you help your son apply to out-of-state colleges if you don't really want him to leave home? Each of these situations threatens our ability to care because we feel angry or frustrated or in opposition to the other person. But there are some simple steps we can take to assure our ability to act caringly:

1. Be clear about your position. Tell the other person "where you're coming from." Explain your bias or reasons for a conflicting point of view. Let the other see that there are two sides to the story. And remember that yourself!
2. Persist with goodwill. Remember that you want a solution, not an argument. At times like these it's crucial to be aware of the other's Beltlines (see page 346) and special sensitivities. Fair fighting is essential.

    If your son is serious about going to college on the opposite coast, present all your arguments, both practical and emotional, about why you'd like him to be closer. "It will be an added financial burden if you're far away." "We'll miss you terribly." "You're not very good about writing letters." Avoid name-calling and guiltmaking. If he's sensitive about being shy, don't make remarks about the possible difficulty making friends.

3. Be prepared to negotiate. Think of as many possible solutions to your conflict as you can. List all options. Find areas where compromise is in order.

"If you go away to school, you must promise to write at least every two weeks." Or "We'll expect you to get a part-time job so that you can pay your fares home on vacations." Or, "If you go to school nearby, I'll see what I can do to help you find a job out west next summer."

4. Accept responsibilities. If someone is asking you to do something you don't want to do, ask yourself, Is this a caring duty? Am I being fair? Oversensitive? Exploited? If your husband wants to ask people for dinner whom you dislike, can you see his side of it? Does he fulfill similar obligations for you?

5. Look for ways of making your compliance easier. In the situation cited above could you get your husband to help prepare the dinner so you did not have to do the work all by yourself? Find ways of exchanging caring responsibilities.

6. Be part of the solution. If you've mustered your courage to tell your friend about his bad breath, or to challenge your spouse about his drinking, or to tell your friend you think her boyfriend is a disaster, be prepared to offer advice and suggestions for correcting the problem and to be available for support.

Think the situation through. Plan what you will say, and when. Be sure to reassure the other of your love and concern, no matter how angry you are or how seemingly intractable the problem. Let the other know that you're interceding *because* of your friendship, not to sabotage it.

When you tell your friend that you dislike her boyfriend and feel he's no good for her, give your reasons. Be reassuring about your concern for her well-being. If and when your friend decides to leave her boyfriend, don't let your concern stop there. Make suggestions about how the situation can be changed and how you might help. "Barbara, I know it's not a good time now, but when you move to your new apartment in September, it will be easier for you to break up with Allan.

You'll be very involved with your new home, and I'll be living close by. I won't be started on my new project yet, so I'll be available to help you move and give you a shoulder to lean on. Besides, you have so many friends who would love to be able to help *you* out for a change. Also, we'll be going to the concert series in September. We're bound to meet some new people."

7. Be prepared for failure. There will be times when a friendship, or even family ties, will not survive a difficult confrontation. A friend will feel hurt and criticized when you try to get him to lose weight; nothing you say will salvage the friendship.

Your daughter is angry when you won't let her stay out as late as the other kids; your explanations don't satisfy her that you're not just trying to spoil her fun.

It's always a risk to face up to a serious problem. You have to weigh the relationship and the seriousness of your feelings on the issue. You must decide if the relationship can withstand the confrontation and whether or not you're willing to take the risk of testing it. And you must weigh the consequences for the relationship and for your own self-esteem if you *don't* face the problem.

Sometimes a temporary respite or cooling-down period is all that's needed before the friendship can be resumed. But there is always the chance of doing irreparable damage, even with the best intentions. The Caring Activist must be prepared when necessary to take the chance.

PLANNING AHEAD FOR DIFFICULT CARING SITUATIONS

There is no way to be completely prepared for disaster or crisis. However, you can diminish your fear of the unknown and minimize possible trauma by becoming aware of what you would do if such situations arise.

Use the "What If . . . ?" exercise on page 329 to help you prepare for potentially difficult or troubling situations. By thinking through such situations calmly you become familiar with your fears and strengths, you plan what you would do, whom you would turn to, what can be done now as a preventive measure.

STEP SIX: BE PREPARED TO COPE WITH CARING BURNOUT

Caring fatigue sets in when our lives get out of balance—when we've overdone it in the care providing department with too little care consuming or attending to self-care.

Sometimes this is unavoidable: we've been nursing a sick spouse or trying to care for several small children, or we're working day and night on an important project with a deadline coming up. But sometimes it is avoidable. We're involved with people who want too much—a mate oblivious to our needs, children with incessant demands for attention, friends who pour their hearts out to us constantly but never have time to listen to our thoughts. Sometimes we are worn down simply because we do not have sufficient caring skills to handle even a normal load of caring. Or we don't know how to ask for care, or reject that which is offered. Sometimes people misguidedly use caring as a way to make others dependent or to present themselves as unselfish or martyred.

Whatever the cause, all of us suffer the Caring Blues sometimes. We feel fatigued, apathetic. We just *don't care*. At such times we need to restore the Caring Balance, to consume caring and attend to our self-care. This is not always easy, because often the cause of our caring burnout is still present: our spouse is still ill, the kids are still young and need constant attention, we still have only care-demanding friends. Of course we should try to get help with the source of the problem. We might get friends, relatives, or a nurse to take over some of the bedside care for our spouse, or we might form a mothers' baby-sitting co-op to provide free time for ourselves in exchange for helping other mothers in similar situations. But even if we can't come up with this sort of assistance or make any basic changes in our lives, we can still act to treat the Caring Blues.

1. Attend to self-care. Set aside some time to do things for yourself. Make a list of the kinds of simple activities that give you pleasure: taking a bath, reading a book, sitting quietly for fifteen minutes, talking with a friend, buying flowers, baking bread, jogging. Do not be afraid of indulgence. Pick at least one self-care activity a day and make a point to fit it into your

schedule. This is especially important if you're one of those people who are always doing things for others.
2. Trade off or let go certain other duties. If you feel pressed for time because you need to provide care for someone every day, let other duties slide. Let the house get messy, don't attend meetings that are not absolutely necessary, tell your friends you would love to hear from them but that they will have to understand if you don't contact them regularly.
3. Find a sympathetic ear. Find someone to complain to, to vent your frustration to, to ask for advice, to express your fears to.
4. Ask for help. Learn to be more of a caring consumer. Request care. Tell your kids to make dinner, tell your spouse to go to the grocery store, ask your friend to run an errand.
5. In cases of major crisis, see if there are community organizations and social services that can come to your aid. Volunteers are often available to tend the sick, federal funding may pay for day care, psychological counseling may help a troubled friend more than you can and will help remove the total burden of understanding from your shoulders.
6. Find time to review your journal and agendas to see how badly your caring routine is out of balance. Confront the problems, acknowledge the weak spots. Set new goals.
7. When you have time, try and get to the root of the problem. If caring fatigue is chronic—the result of a stressful relationship or an inability to consume care or to be self-caring—the solution lies in making changes. It's up to you to know when it's time to stop doing everything and get the kids to do their share. It's up to you to figure out why you have such a hard time being good to yourself and try to change your ways.

STEP SEVEN: PERIODICALLY EVALUATE YOUR CARING STATUS

It is a good idea to look back over your agendas and journal once a month or so to see what trends are developing, what problems remain, and what goals have been met. By reviewing the daily balance of care consuming and providing, and by rereading your journal to see how your feelings of accomplishment have evolved, you will get a sense of how far you've come and will be able to restructure your goals for the future. Ask yourself the following questions:

1. How has my Caring Network changed? Have there been any changes in my intimate relationships? In my family relationships? In my community relationships? Have I met any new people? To whom am I closer now? With whom have I been able to share my feelings? Who has been more open with me? With whom am I spending more time? Whom have I weeded out from my network? To whom would I like to become closer? Am I learning to spot opportunities for caring? Becoming more observant?
2. Am I taking better care of myself? What kinds of changes have been made? Am I in better physical shape? Do I stick up for myself more? Have I learned to say no? Do I tune into my inner dialogue and keep in touch with my feelings? Have I learned to share my feelings with others? Have I learned to listen to others' feelings? Can I ask for things I need?
3. How am I doing at keeping my agenda and journal? What caring goals have I had trouble meeting? What items on my daily agenda have I had trouble carrying out? Am I trying to do too much? Too little? Have I spotted any habits that might become personal caring rituals? Am I working on improving my caring skills? What exercises am I doing? Am I doing them regularly? Should I try new exercises? Have I achieved any of my caring goals?
4. What would I like to set as new goals for the future?

    (a) Get closer to Mary. Talk to her more, share my feelings with her more.

    (b) Make it a habit to spend one evening a week by and for myself doing whatever I want.

    (c) Set a schedule for writing letters to friends and relatives so I keep in touch.
5. What rewards am I seeing for my efforts at being a Caring Activist? Disappointments?

33
Future Care

It could be argued that it's necessary to care in order to *have* a future. Having devastated the environment through carelessness, it will require care to save it. Having screwed up the economy trying to buy happiness the old way, it may be necessary to try something new. A caring stance will be necessary to combat crime, to inhibit war, to promote cooperation in the face of coming scarcity.

Caring has tremendous power to change the individual and society. At a time when many people (even communities and nations) are floundering, the choice to care is a worthwhile cause to which to dedicate ourselves. We need dedication, order, and purpose at a time when we feel that we have little control over our lives. We need a vision, a dream to aspire to. In choosing to care we *make* a purpose for ourselves; we give ourselves reason to believe in our own potential and capabilities. It is human nature to feel good when we help someone, human nature to feel bad when we do not, or when we hurt someone. A caring stance gives us a framework within which to feel good about ourselves.

The 1960s and 1970s were consciousness-raising decades in many areas of human endeavor—ecology, race, sex, nutrition, art, music. In every case the movement started in some small pocket of society and grew, not without resistance, to make an impact on the community at large. Our culture, and our times, have unique capabilities for grass-roots growth. Change in our society is more likely to push up and proliferate from below than to be imposed by law from above. Every individual who becomes caring-conscious and who takes action to expand his caring environment is a seedling for grass-roots change. The change will not occur overnight, for carelessness, corruption, crime, cynicism, and fear are deep-rooted and tenacious obstacles to overcome. But caring can become social policy.

Caring, like everything else, is dependent on the cultural attitude toward it. As long as caring is seen as foolhardy or naive or unprofitable, it will be hard to convince people to take up its challenge. To win converts to caring on a broad scale, caring must be shown to have high status and value—the social equivalent of a string of pearls or a Cuisinart.

What's needed is an imaginative approach to caring promotion. There's no reason why courses in ethics or caring cannot join the school curriculum along with sex education, nutrition, or French. As ethical values change, caring will permeate policy and legislation. Caring rituals and festivals can be encouraged to offset those that are non-caring in nature. By finding room for good news we'll leave less space for bad news. Good advertising will make people want to care, want to jump on the caring bandwagon.

Group membership is essential to broadening the base of caring commitment: in a caring society, we *are* our brother's keepers.

The Caring Utopia is a long way off, and there are many obstacles en route. But it is crucial that the decision to seek this utopia be made soon, for we are fast approaching a point beyond which it will be hard to change direction. It is vital to shift our energies to caring *now*. If our society develops along lines of caring and cooperation, there will be tremendous potential for growth, for joy, for interest and involvement in everyday life. The route to caring is paved with self-esteem and respect for others. Along the way are many of the rewards we've been seeking on other roads. The route to caring does indeed lead to the We Decade.

Notes

1. Lionel Tiger, "My Turn: A Very Old Animal Called Man," *Newsweek* (September 4, 1978), p. 13.
2. Lewis Thomas, *The Medusa and the Snail: More Notes of a Biology Watcher* (New York: Viking Press, 1979).
3. Frank Robertson, "The No Generation," *New West* (January 14, 1980), pp. 34–39.
4. Philip Slater, *Wealth Addiction* (New York: E. P. Dutton, 1980).
5. Thomas, *Medusa and Snail*, pp. 8 and 9.
6. Kenneth L. Woodward, with Scott Sullivan, "Ideas: Jean-Paul Sartre, 1905–1980," *Newsweek* (April 28, 1980), p. 77.
7. Georgia Dullea, "Style: Why Do We Buy? The Answer is Symbol," *The New York Times* (May 20, 1980), p. B14.
8. Quentin Crisp, *How to Have a Lifestyle* (New York: Methuen, 1980).
9. Philip Hallie, *Lest Innocent Blood Be Shed* (New York: Harper & Row, 1979).
10. Kenneth L. Woodward, with Carol Honsa and R. Ramanujam, "Nobel Laureates: Peace: Mother of the Poor," *Newsweek* (October 29, 1979), p. 60.
11. Barbara Myerhoff, *Number Our Days* (New York: E. P. Dutton, 1979).
12. Herbert Gold, "The Rise of the People People," *Atlantic Monthly* (March 1979), pp. 127–129.
13. Richard Boeth, "The Phony Photographer," *Newsweek* (September 19, 1977), p. 43.

14. A full description of crazymaking behaviors and how to cope with them can be found in *Stop! You're Driving Me Crazy* by George R. Bach and Ronald M. Deutsch (New York: G. P. Putnam's Sons, 1979).

15. George Bach and Yetta Bernhard, *Aggression Lab: The Fair Fight Training Manual* (Dubuque, Iowa: Kendall/Hunt Publishing Company, 1971), p. 174.

All the games, exercises, and rituals used at the Bach Institute are described, with full instructions.

16. Norman Cousins, *Anatomy of an Illness* (New York: W. W. Norton, 1979).

17. See also Bach and Deutsch, *Stop! You're Driving Me Crazy*, pp. 280–86.

18. George R. Bach, "Spouse Killing: The Final Abuse," *Journal of Contemporary Psychotherapy* (November/December, 1980).

19. Tom Robbins, *Still Life with Woodpecker* (New York: Bantam Books, 1980), p. 108.

20. *Ibid.*, p. 4.

21. Bach, "Spouse Killing: The Final Abuse."

22. Bach and Bernhard, *Aggression Lab*, p. 174.

23. Lynn Langway, with Lucy Howard and Donna M. Foote, "Life/Style: Family Politics: White House Conference on Families," *Newsweek* (January 28, 1980), pp. 78 and 79.

24. James W. Prescott, "The Brain: Alienation of Affection," *Psychology Today* (December 1979), p. 124.

25. Maya Pines, "Good Samaritans at Age Two?" *Psychology Today* (June 1979), pp. 66–67.

26. A full treatment of family conflict and communications skills can be found in *How to Fight Fair With Your Kids . . . and Win!* by Luree Nicholson and Laura Torbet (New York: Harcourt Brace Jovanovich, 1980).

27. Mary Brown Parlee and the editors of *Psychology Today*, "The Friendship Bond," *Psychology Today* (October 1979), pp. 43–54, 113.

28. Zick Rubin, "Seeking a Cure for Loneliness," *Psychology Today* (October 1979), pp. 82–90.

29. Christopher Lasch, *The Culture of Narcissism: American Life in an Age of Diminishing Expectations* (New York: W. W. Norton, 1978), p. 41.

30. George Bach, "The George Bach Self-Recognition Inventory for Burned-Out Therapists," *Voices*, 15, No. 2 (Summer 1979), pp. 72–76.

31. The quarterly *Medical Self-Care, Access to Health Tools*, is published by Medical Self-Care. Subscriptions are available for $10 per year U.S.A., $12 per year Canada, and $15 per year other foreign countries by writing to P.O. Box 717, Inverness, California 94937.

32. George Bach, Ph.D., and Cedric B. Emery, M.D., *Fight for Your Life: How to Get the Most Out of Your Doctor* (Chicago: Playboy Press, 1982).

Bibliography

Adams, Virginia. "Sex Therapies in Perspective." *Psychology Today* (August 1980), pp. 35 and 36.

Adler, Jerry, with John Carey. "The Science of Love." *Newsweek* (February 25, 1980), pp. 89 and 90.

Ashby, Neal. "Kind Kids are Nice to Know." *Parade* (October 21, 1979), pp. 16 and 19.

Bach, George R. "The George Bach Self-Recognition Inventory for Burned-Out Therapists." *Voices* 15, No. 2 (Summer 1979), pp. 73–76.

———. "Spouse Killing: The Final Abuse." *Journal of Contemporary Psychotherapy* (November/December, 1980).

———, and Bernhard, Yetta. *Aggression Lab: The Fair Fight Training Manual.* Dubuque, Iowa: Kendall/Hunt Publishing Company, 1971.

———, and Deutsch, Ronald M. *Pairing.* New York: Avon Books, 1971.

———, and ———. *Stop! You're Driving Me Crazy.* New York: G. P. Putnam's Sons, 1979.

———, and Goldberg, Herb. *Creative Aggression.* New York: Avon Books, 1974.

———, and Wyden, Peter. *The Intimate Enemy: How to Fight Fair in Love and Marriage.* New York: Avon Books, 1968.

———, and Emery, Cedric, M.D. *Fight for Your Life: How to Get the Most Out of Your Doctor* (Chicago: Playboy Press, 1982).

BAKER, RUSSELL. "Sunday Observer: Perceiving the Candidate." *The New York Times Magazine* (September 28, 1980), p. 32.

BEIER, ERNST, and VALENS, EVANS G. *People-Reading: How We Control Others, How They Control Us.* Briarcliff Manor, N.Y.: Stein & Day, 1975.

BOETH, RICHARD. "The Phony Photographer." *Newsweek* (September 19, 1977), p. 45.

BROCKMAN, JOHN, ed. *About Bateson: Essays on Gregory Bateson* by Mary Catherine Bateson, Ray Birdwhistell, John Brockman, David Lipset, Rollo May, Margaret Mead, Edwin Schlossberg. New York: E. P. Dutton, 1977.

BRONFENBRENNER, URIE. *The Ecology of Human Development.* Boston: Harvard University Press, 1979.

BROZAN, NADINE. "Style: New Marriage Roles Make Men Ambivalent About Fatherhood." *The New York Times* (May 30, 1980), p. B5.

———. "Style: Volunteerism: New Paths." *The New York Times* (June 3, 1979), p. 56.

BRYER, KATHLEEN B. "The Amish Way of Death: A Study of Family Support Systems." *American Psychologist*, 34:3 (March 1979), pp. 255–61.

CASTLEMAN, MICHAEL. "A Consumer's Guide to the Condom Comeback." *Medical Self-Care, Access to Health Tools*, No. 9 (Summer 1980), 35–37.

CLARK, MATT, with GOSNELL, MARIANA. "Medicine: Doctoring Yourself." *Newsweek* (April 2, 1979), p. 89.

CLECKLEY, HARVEY M. *The Mask of Sanity.* 5th ed. St. Louis: C. V. Mosby, 1975.

COPELAND, ROGER. "Theater in the 'Me Decade.'" *The New York Times* (June 3, 1979), pp. D1, D20, and D21.

COUSINS, NORMAN. *Anatomy of an Illness.* New York: W. W. Norton, 1979.

CRISP, QUENTIN. *How to Have a Lifestyle.* New York: Methuen, 1980.

DEGLER, CARL N. *At Odds: Women and the Family in America from the Revolution to the Present.* New York: Oxford University Press, 1980.

DULLEA, GEORGIA. "Is Joint Custody Good for Children?" *The New York Times Magazine* (February 3, 1980), pp. 32–41.

———. "Style: Why Do We Buy? The Answer is Symbol." *The New York Times* (May 20, 1980), p. B14.

DURDEN-SMITH, JO. "Male and Female—Why?" *Quest/80* (October 1980), pp. 15–19, 93–99.

ELLIOTT, GEORGE P. "The Enemies of Intimacy." *Harper's* (July 1980), pp. 50–56.

EMERY, CEDRIC, and BACH, GEORGE R. *Fight for Your Life: How to Get the Most Out of Your Doctor.* Playboy Press, 1982.

FARRELL, WARREN. *The Liberated Man.* New York: Random House, 1975.

FRANCKE, LINDA BIRD, with ABRAMSON, PAMELA, SIMONS, PAMELA ELLIS, COPELAND, JEFF, and WHITMAN, LISA. "Life/Style: Going it Alone." *Newsweek* (September 4, 1978), pp. 76–78.

———, with SHERMAN, DIANE, SIMONS, PAMELA ELLIS, ABRAMSON, PAMELA, ZABARSKY, MARSHA, HUCK, JANET, and WHITMAN, LISA. "Life/Style: The Children of Divorce." *Newsweek* (February 11, 1980), pp. 58–63.

FRIEDAN, BETTY. "Feminism Takes a New Turn." *The New York Times Magazine* (November 18, 1979), pp. 40, 92–102, 106.

GAYLIN, WILLARD. *Caring.* New York: Alfred A. Knopf, 1976.

———. *Feelings: Our Vital Signs.* New York: Harper & Row, 1979.

GOFFMAN, ERVING. *Encounters: Two Studies in the Sociology of Interaction.* Indianapolis: Bobbs-Merrill, 1961.

GOLD, HERBERT. "The Rise of the People People." *Atlantic Monthly* (March 1979), pp. 127–29.

GOLDBERG, HERB. *The Hazards of Being Male: Surviving the Myth of Masculine Privilege.* New York: New American Library, 1977.

———. *The New Male: From Self-Destruction to Self-Care.* New York: William Morrow, 1979.

GREENING, TOM, and HOBSON, DICK. *Instant Relief: The Encyclopedia of Psychological Self-Help.* New York: Seaview Books, 1979.

GWIRTZMAN, MILTON. "Restored Treasure." *Newsweek* (September 10, 1979), p. 15.

HALLIE, PHILIP. *Lest Innocent Blood Be Shed*. New York: Harper & Row, 1979.

HARLOW, HARRY F., and MEARS, CLARA. *The Human Model: Primate Perspectives*. Silver Spring, Md.. V. H. Winston & Sons/John Wiley & Sons, 1979.

HARRISON, BARBARA GRIZZUTI. *Off Center*. New York: Dial Press, 1980.

HASKELL, MARTIN R., and YABLONSKY, LEWIS. *Criminology: Crime and Criminality*. New York: Rand McNally, 1977.

HEIIJTS, JOSEPH HUBERTUS. *Geurssensbildung*. Cologne: J. P. Bachem, 1969.

HODGSON, SUSAN A.; HORNSTEIN, HARVEY A. and LaKIND, ELIZABETH. "Socially Medicated Zeigarnik Effects as a Function of Sentiment, Valence, and Desire for Goal Attainment." *Journal of Experimental Social Psychology*, 8:5 (September 1972), 446–56.

HOLT, PATRICIA. "The View from the West: The End of 'Me-ism' in (Western) America." *Publishers Weekly* (November 26, 1979), p. 18.

"How Men are Changing." *Newsweek* (January 16, 1978), pp. 52–61.

ISEN, ALICE M. "Success, Failure, Attention, and Reaction to Others: The Warm Glow of Success." *Journal of Personality and Social Psychology*, 15:4 (1970), 294–301.

JAILER, MILDRED. "Business: Time Off for Good Behavior." *TWA Ambassador* (October 1979), pp. 38–40.

JANEWAY, ELIZABETH. *Powers of the Weak*. New York: Alfred A. Knopf, 1980.

JOHNSON, SHARON. "Single Parents Try Out the Shared Life." *The New York Times* (August 21, 1979).

LANGWAY, LYNN, with HOWARD, LUCY, and FOOTE, DONNA M. "Life/Style: Family Politics: White House Conference on Families." *Newsweek* (January 28, 1980), pp. 78 and 79.

LAPHAM, LEWIS H. *Fortune's Child.* New York: Doubleday, 1979.
LASCH, CHRISTOPHER. *The Culture of Narcissism: American Life in an Age of Diminishing Expectations.* New York: W. W. Norton, 1978.
LEAKEY, RICHARD E., and LEWIN, ROGER. *Origins: What New Discoveries Reveal About the Emergence of Our Species and Its Possible Future.* New York: E. P. Dutton, 1977.
———, and ———. *People of the Lake.* New York: Anchor/Doubleday, 1978.
LEE, MELVIN, ZIMBARDO, PHILIP G., and BERTHOLF, MINERVA. "Shy Murderers." *Psychology Today* (November 1977), pp. 68–70, 76, 148.
LEPPER, MARK R., and GREENE, DAVID, eds. *The Hidden Costs of Reward: New Perspectives on the Psychology of Human Motivation.* Hillsdale, N.J.: Lawrence Erlbaum Associates/John Wiley & Sons, 1978.
LeSHAN, EDA. "The Family Is *Not* Dead." *Woman's Day* (August 7, 1979), p. 26.
LOBSENZ, NORMAN M. "How to Give and Get More Emotional Support." *Woman's Day* (September 20, 1977), pp. 73, 148, 150.

MACCOBY, MICHAEL. "Corporate Character Types: The Gamesman vs. Narcissus." *Psychology Today* (October 1978), pp. 60 and 61, 113 and 114.
McEWAN, IAN. *In Between the Sheets and Other Stories.* New York: Simon & Schuster, 1979.
MARSHALL, BERNICE. *Experiences in Being.* Belmont, Calif.: Brooks/Cole Publishing Company, 1971.
MAY, ROBERT. *Sex and Fantasy: Patterns of Male and Female Development.* New York: W. W. Norton, 1980.
Medical Self-Care, Access to Health Tools. All issues.
MEHTA, GILA. *Karma Cola.* New York: Simon & Schuster, 1979.
MILLER, SHEROD, NUNNALLY, ELAM W., and WACKMAN, DANIEL B. *Alive and Aware: Improving Communications in Relationships.* Minneapolis, Minn.: Interpersonal Communication Programs, Inc., 1975.
MITCHELL, LISA. "Endowing the Future: Humanist Laura Huxley

Sees Our Children as the Ultimate Investment." *Westways* (April 1979), pp. 43–45, 65ff.

MOLTER, HAYA, and BACH, GEORGE. *Psychoboom.* Düsseldorf: Diederichs Verlag, 1977.

MORROW, LANCE. "Epitaph for a Decade: A Lost War, a Discovery of Limits—and Good Cause for Optimism." *Time* (January 7, 1980), pp. 38 and 39.

MYERHOFF, BARBARA. *Number Our Days.* New York: E. P. Dutton, 1979.

NICHOLSON, LUREE, and TORBET, LAURA. *How to Fight Fair with Your Kids . . . and Win!* New York: Harcourt Brace Jovanovich, 1980.

NIERENBERG, GERALD I., and CALERO, HENRY H. *How to Read a Person Like a Book.* New York: Hawthorn Books, 1971.

NORTON, MARY BETH. *Liberty's Daughters: The Revolutionary Experience of American Women, 1750—1800.* Boston: Little, Brown, 1980.

"One Parent Families Rose 79% in Decade, U.S. Report Indicates." *The New York Times* (August 17, 1980), p. 29.

PARLEE, MARY BROWN, and editors of *Psychology Today.* "The Friendship Bond." *Psychology Today* (October 1979), pp. 43–54, 113.

PILEGGI, NICHOLAS. "Who'll Save the Children?" *New York* (December 18, 1978), pp. 53 and 54.

PINES, MAYA. "Good Samitarians at Age Two?" *Psychology Today* (June 1979), pp. 66–77.

PRESCOTT, JAMES W. "The Brain: Alienation of Affection." *Psychology Today* (December 1979), p. 124.

RABOW, JEROME, MANOS, JORJA J., and ENGELBERG, LAURIE. "Separate Realities: A Comparative Study of Estians, Psychoanalysands, and the Untreated." *Small Group Behavior,* 10:4 (November 1974), 445–74.

RAINIE, HARRISON. "Survey Finds Us Still Ringed by Family Circle." *Daily News* (June 3, 1980), p. 4C.

RESENER, MADLYN. "4. Burnout: The New Stress Disease." *Harper's Bazaar* (August 1979), pp. 92 and 93, 36 and 37.

RINGER, ROBERT J. *Restoring the American Dream*. New York: QED/Harper & Row, 1979.

ROBERTSON, FRANK. "The No Generation." *New West* (January 14, 1980), pp. 34–39.

ROSS, HARVEY. *Fighting Depression*. New York: Larchmont Books, 1975.

ROTTER, JULIAN B. "Interpersonal Trust, Trustworthiness, and Gullibility." *American Psychologist*, 35:1 (January 1980), 1–7.

RUBIN, ZICK. "Seeking a Cure for Loneliness." *Psychology Today* (October 1979), pp. 82–90.

SALE, KIRKPATRICK. *Human Scale*. New York: Coward, McCann & Geoghegan, 1980.

SATOW, ROBERTA. "Up Front: Pop Narcissism." *Psychology Today* (October 1979), pp. 14 and 15.

SCHUR, EDWIN. *The Awareness Trap: Self-Absorption Instead of Social Change*. New York: McGraw-Hill, 1977.

SEABROOK, JEREMY. *Oedipus Wrecks: Mother & Son*. New York: Pantheon Books, 1980.

SLATER, PHILIP. *Wealth Addiction*. New York: E. P. Dutton, 1980.

SOLOMON, ROBERT C. "Our 'Sick' Society." *Newsweek* (September 17, 1979), pp. 24 and 25.

SPIELER, JOSEPH. "The Possible Crash of 1980 . . . and How to Make the Most of It: Part Two—Interview with Warren Johnson." *Quest/79* (October 1979), pp. 29–35, 86–88.

STEIN, HARRY. "Ethics: On Becoming Mr. Ethics: How to Lose Friends and Feel a Lot Better About Yourself." *Esquire* (June 1980), pp. 20 and 22.

———. "Ethics: Just Good Friends: Measuring the Unspoken Thoughts that Mark the Beginning or the End of Friendship." *Esquire* (August 1980), pp. 21–23.

STELLVERTRETUNG, THELMA. *Für Die Anderen Dasein*. Institut für Theologisch—Pastorale Aus (1979).

STERN, BARBARA LANG. "Courtesy: It's Good for You: Meeting Rampant Rudeness with Pleasant Social Contact Can Relieve Stress." *Vogue* (October 1979), p. 84.

STOLLER, ROBERT J. *Sexual Excitement: Dynamics of Erotic Life.* New York: Pantheon Books, 1979.

STRUPP, HANS H., and HADLEY, SUZANNE W. "A Tripartite Model of Mental Health and Therapeutic Outcomes, with Special Reference to Negative Effects in Psychotherapy." *American Psychologist* (March 1977), pp. 187–96.

SWARD, KEITH. "Self-Actualization and Women: Rank and Freud Contrasted." *Journal of Humanistic Psychology*, 20:2 (Spring 1980), pp. 5–26.

"The Talk of the Town: Notes and Comments." *The New Yorker* (April 28, 1980), pp. 33 and 34.

"Task Force Urges City to Improve its Efforts in Child Abuse Cases." *The New York Times* (May 25, 1980), p. 36.

THOMAS, LEWIS. *The Medusa and the Snail: More Notes of a Biology Watcher.* New York: Viking Press, 1979.

TIGER, LIONEL. "My Turn: A Very Old Animal Called Man." *Newsweek* (September 4, 1978), p. 13.

TUCHMAN, BARBARA W. "An Inquiry into the Persistence of Unwisdom in Government." *Esquire* (May 1980), pp. 25–31.

VANDENBERG, BRIAN. "Play and Development from an Ethological Perspective." *American Psychologist* (August 1978), pp. 724–38.

VITZ, PAUL C. *Psychology as Religion: The Cult of Self-Worship.* Grand Rapids, Mich.: William B. Eerdmans Publishing Company, 1977.

WHEELIS, ALLEN. *How People Change.* New York: Harper & Row, 1974.

WHITE, ART. "Arctophilia Runs Amuck: A Hug of Teddy Bears Gathers for a Convention in Britain." *Time* (June 11, 1979), p. 50.

WISPÉ, LAUREN. G., ed. *Altruism, Sympathy, and Helping: Psychological and Sociological Principles.* New York: Academic Press, 1978.

WOODWARD, KENNETH L., BEHR, EDWARD, and JENKINS, LOREN. "A Church in Decay." *Newsweek* (October 1, 1979), pp. 71 and 72.

WOODWARD, KENNETH L., with HONSA, CAROL, and RAMANUJAM, R. "Nobel Laureates: Peace: Mother of the Poor." *Newsweek* (October 29, 1979), p. 60.
———, with Scott Sullivan. "Ideas: Jean-Paul Sartre, 1905–1980." *Newsweek* (April 28, 1980), p. 77.
WOODY, ROBERT HENLEY. *The Use of Massage for Facilitating Holistic Health.* Springfield, Ill.: Charles C Thomas, 1980.

ZILBERGELD, BERNIE, and EVANS, MICHAEL. "The Inadequacy of Masters and Johnson." *Psychology Today* (August 1980), pp. 28–34, 37–43.